La Serenissima

In memory of

CAROLYN HILL

Director of the Oklahoma City Museum of Art
(1994-2008)

La Serenissima

Eighteenth-Century Venetian Art from North American Collections

Oklahoma City Museum of Art

Publication Notes
This catalogue has been published in conjunction with the September 9, 2010-January 2, 2011, exhibition *La Serenissima: Eighteenth-Century Venetian Art from North American Collections,* which was organized by the Oklahoma City Museum of Art.

Oklahoma City Museum of Art
President and Chief Executive Officer: Glen Gentele
Curator for Collections: Alison Amick
Editor and Curator: Hardy George
Associate Curator and Curatorial Coordinator: Jennifer Klos
Copy editor: Jo Ann Reece
Catalogue designer: Eric H. Anderson

Oklahoma City Museum of Art
Donald W. Reynolds Visual Arts Center
415 Couch Drive
Oklahoma City, OK 73102
Telephone: 405-236-3100
www.okcmoa.com

Library of Congress Control Number: 2010932398
ISBN: 978-0911919-12-7

Cover image:
Giovanni Battista Tiepolo (Italian, 1696-1770)
Juno Triumphant, as Queen of the Air, ca. 1735
Oil on canvas, 91½ x 86 in. (213 x 231 cm)
Sarah Campbell Blaffer Foundation, Houston, 1983.4
(cat. 20)

Back cover image:
Unidentified artist, formerly attibuted to Michele Marieschi (Italian, 1710-1743)
detail: *View of Venice: SS Giovanni e Paolo and the Scuola di San Marco,* ca. 1756-60
Oil on canvas
Fine Arts Museums of San Francisco,
Museum Purchase, M. H. de Young Memorial Museum, 48.1
(cat. 47)

La Serenissima

Eighteenth-Century Venetian Art from North American Collections

Contents

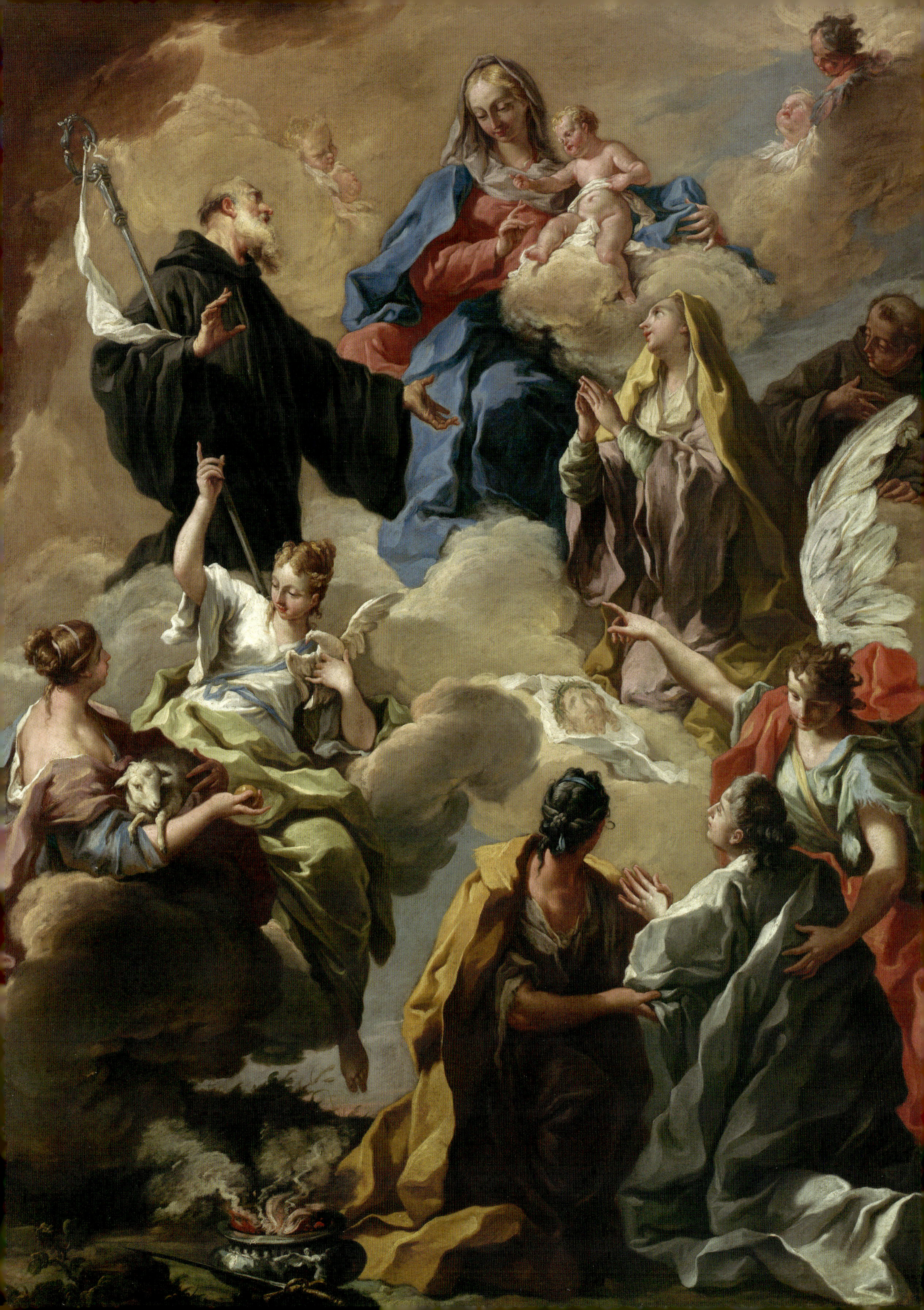

Preface and Acknowledgements

Glen Gentele

For over a millennium, the Italian coastal state of the Most Serene Republic of Venice, or La Serenissima, flourished as a center for sea trade and the arts. Here an important final phase of late Baroque mythological and biblical painting took place. Venice also became an important destination on the Grand Tour, where its aquatic setting and unique network of canals, palaces, and churches inspired a talented group of view painters, especially during the eighteenth century. Today, collections throughout North America hold many works from this prolific period.

La Serenissima explores anew mythological, biblical, historical, and genre works by artists such as Pietro Longhi, Sebastiano Ricci, Giovanni Battista Tiepolo, and his son, Giovanni Domenico Tiepolo. It also casts new light on the achievements of Venetian view painters, including master painters Antonio Canaletto, Bernardo Bellotto, Luca Carlevarijs, and Francesco Guardi. These artists created exquisite paintings of Venice's streets and waterways that had a broad appeal and influenced many artists living both in and outside of Venice.

This exhibition underscores the fact that the last flowering of religious Baroque painting and a high development of view painting took place in La Serenissima during a time of declining trade and at a critical point in the ongoing war with the Ottoman Turks over the dominance of seagoing trade routes. The decline of Venice's religious art was not a slow and painful process brought about by a lack of faith or declining moral values, but a sudden interruption caused by Napoleon's invasion of the traditionally impenetrable city in 1797. While the religious, symbolic, and mythological works commissioned by the church and aristocracy abruptly ceased, the influence of view painting, associated with the works of Canaletto, Bellotto, and Guardi, lived on and became connected with mainstream developments in English and French art of the early nineteenth century.

Giovanni Battista Pittoni (Italian, 1687–1767)
DETAIL: *Saints Presenting a Devout Woman to the Virgin and Child*, 1720s
(CAT. 14)

The *La Serenissima* exhibition brings together ninety works from thirty collections that cover important regional developments—not only in religious and topographical painting, but also in genre and portraiture. Altogether the art undoubtedly displays the inimitable aspects of Venetian taste and culture in the age of the Grand Tour and through the decline of the Republic, brought about by Napoleon's invasion of Italy in the last decade of the century.

I would like to extend my sincere thanks to Hardy George, Ph.D., for conceptualizing, developing, and realizing the *La Serenissima* exhibition and for setting a high standard for curatorial excellence with his intellectual rigor, humor, and enthusiasm. Dr. George's painstaking organization of the exhibition and catalogue was expertly supported by numerous individuals at the Oklahoma City Museum of Art, and for their assistance we both extend special thanks to Alison Amick, Ernesto Sanchez Villarreal, Christina Hicks, Jim Meeks, Jack Madden, Sarah Lytle, museum interns Laney Monsey, Jenny Elayne Cartmell, Sarah Grlicky, Sanger Clark, Cynthia Pacheco, volunteer Ann Bishop, and everyone on staff who provided support through their individual roles as part of the team.

The essays in this volume include new scholarship on works that have not received due public attention in recent years. The *La Serenissima* catalogue offers an opportunity to learn more about the extraordinary eighteenth-century Venetian paintings and prints from outstanding collections across North America that are included in the exhibit. For their entries in the exhibition catalogue and for their essays, I would like to extend special thanks to the contributors: George Knox, Ph.D., Professor Emeritus, University of British Columbia, for his entries and his essay on eighteenth-century Venetian art collected by the Vanderbilts, William Butterworth (president of the John Deere company), William Randolph Hearst, and other titans who built their great mansions at Newport, Moline, Illinois, San Simeon, California, and Blairsden, New Jersey; Allison Palmer, Ph.D., Associate Professor, Art History, University of Oklahoma, Norman, for her essay on the seventeenth-century Roman Baroque tradition's role in the development of large decorative works, ceiling paintings, and altarpieces in Venice; Jon L. Seydl, Paul J. and Edith Ingalls Vignos, Jr., Curator of European Painting and Sculpture, 1500–1800, Cleveland Museum of Art, for his entries and his essay on Francesco Guardi's biblical paintings and related works in the Cleveland Museum of Art; and Andria Derstine, Ph.D., Curator of Collections and Curator of European and American Art, Allen Memorial Art Museum, Oberlin College, for her entries and her essay on the Venice view paintings of Carlevarijs, Canaletto, and Guardi in North American museums. For their catalogue entries I wish to also acknowledge Edgar Peters Bowron, Ph.D., The Audrey Jones Beck Curator of European Art, Museum of Fine Arts, Houston; John Marciari, Ph.D., Curator of European Art and Head of Provenance Research, San Diego Museum of Art; Ana Dieglio, European Painting and Sculpture Intern, Cleveland Museum of Art; James P. Anno, M.A., Art

History, Class of 2010, University of Oklahoma, and Alexandra Libby, doctoral candidate in the Department of Art History and Archaeology at the University of Maryland. I gratefully acknowledge the many public and private collections and museums across North America who generously lent their extraordinary works of art to this exhibition. Catalogue copy editor Jo Ann Reece and Eric Anderson, catalogue designer and professor of art, University of Oklahoma, deserve special thanks for their work on this publication.

For its leadership role as the museum's Presenting Season Sponsor, I convey my deepest gratitude and sincere thanks to the Inasmuch Foundation. To our Leading Season Sponsors, Chesapeake Energy Corporation, Devon Energy Corporation, OGE Corporation, Allied Arts Foundation, and the Oklahoma Arts Council, I wish to express my sincere thanks and appreciation. To our Supporting Season Sponsors, Bank of America, Crawley Petroleum, E. L. and Thelma Gaylord Foundation, Kirkpatrick Foundation, MidFirst Bank, and SandRidge Energy Corporation, I extend very special thanks. To our generous Contributing Season Sponsors, Cox Oklahoma, GlobalHealth, and *The Oklahoman*, I extend gratitude and thanks. Exhibition Sponsorships from the Oklahoma Humanities Council, and James C. and Virginia W. Meade add significant recognition to the Museum's programs and are greatly appreciated. And we extend special thanks to the Sarkeys Foundation and to Sonic, America's Drive-In, for their generous support given through arts education endowments, and to the Thatcher Hoffman Smith Film Endowment for support of the Museum's film program.

I would like to express my sincere thanks and gratitude to the Board of Trustees of the Oklahoma City Museum of Art for their commitment, support, and leadership; their contributions of time, personal resources, and expertise truly make this institution great. To the docent corps, our many friends, members, and volunteers throughout the community, thank you for bringing such enthusiasm and critical support to the institution.

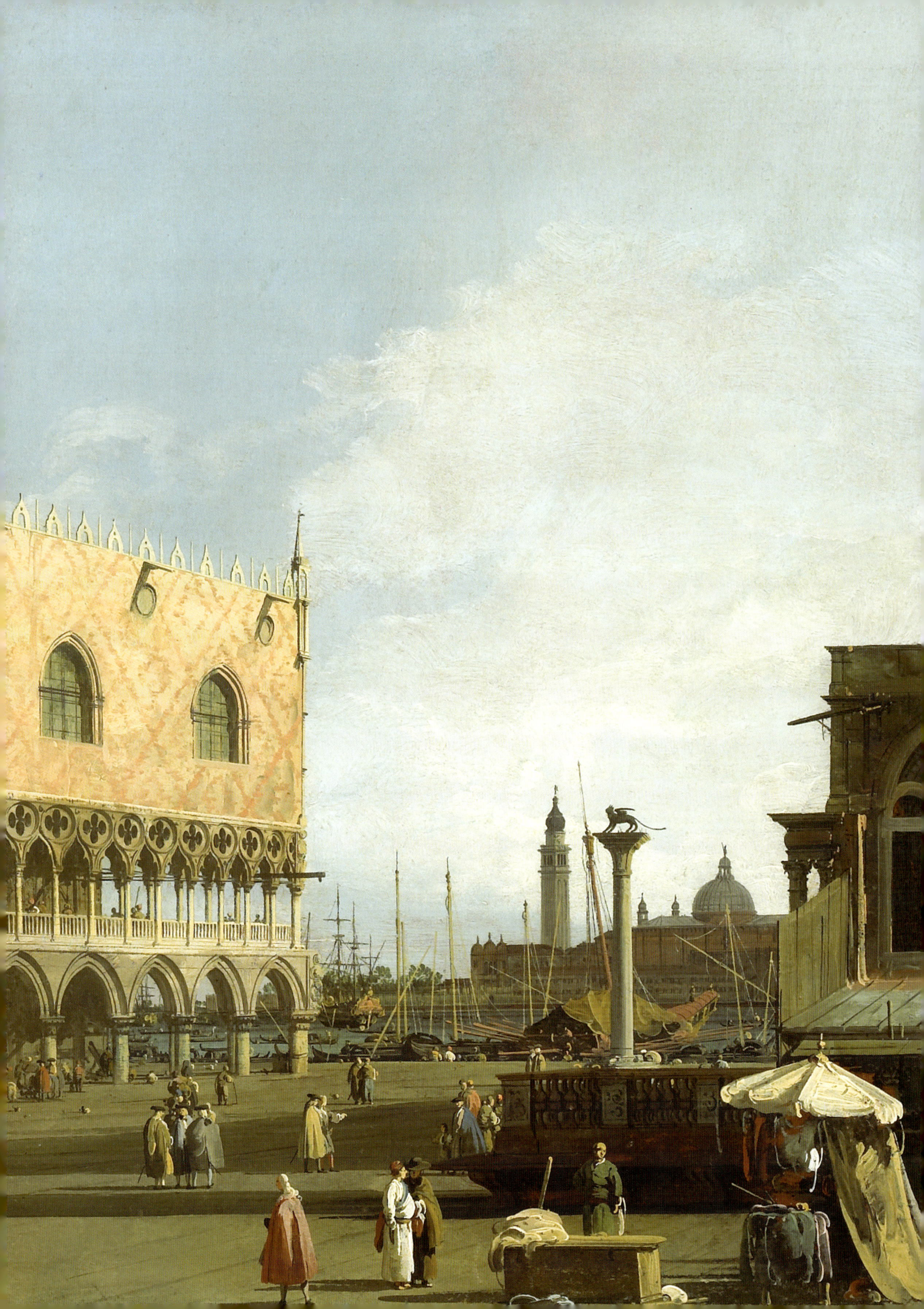

Introduction

HARDY GEORGE

Venice was born in the last years of the Roman Empire, and it became a great maritime power with strategic holdings in the eastern Mediterranean and ready access to the East-West trade routes. The proximity of Constantinople and the Eastern Byzantine Empire left its mark on the splendid design of Venice's architecture. The city of islands became the most remarkable and defiant of the Italian city states. On the Grand Tour route to Rome it came to be regarded by visitors from England and Northern Europe as a captivating city of pleasant diversions. Venice's sumptuous palace architecture on the Grand Canal could be enjoyed, as it still is today, while making one's way by gondola from the mouth of this serpentine waterway toward the Rialto Bridge and the geographical center of the city. But the city's political and social center is visible even before entering the Grand Canal. For early visitors who approached the city by boat from the mainland at Fusina, the distant architecture appeared to float upon the broad lagoon. As the visitor drew closer, the individual buildings became recognizable: the great baroque dome of Santa Maria della Salute, the Dogana del Mar (custom house) marking the entrance to the Grand Canal, and facing the broad lagoon, along the Riva degli Schiavoni, are Jacopo Sansovino's Zecca (the Mint) and Library of Saint Mark, with its colonnade of piers faced with Roman Doric and Ionic columns. On the opposite side of the Piazzetta can be seen the Gothic arcades and continuous tracery of the Doge's Palace, and the Bridge of Sighs, connecting the Palace and the Prison with its rusticated pilasters. This section of Venetian topography, with its mix of architectural styles, was a favorite subject of eighteenth-century view painters from Luca Carlevarijs (1663-1730) to Antonio Canaletto (1697-1768). The yet to be revealed visual treats that awaited visitors are the decorative wall and ceiling paintings of Titian (ca. 1487/90-1576), Tintoretto (1519-1594), and Veronese (ca. 1528-1588) in the Ducal Palace, the Frari church, and the Scuola di San Rocco. For

Canaletto (Giovanni Antonio Canal) (Italian, 1697-1768)
DETAIL: *The Piazzetta: Looking South*, ca. 1740-46
(CAT. 36)

those with an interest in more recent art Giovanni Battista Tiepolo's (1696-1770) work could be seen in churches, such as the Gesuati, and distinguished visitors, like the Comte de Caylus or Joshua Reynolds, could view Tiepolo's work in the Scuola del Carmine (the Carmelite Confraternity) and the Ca' Labia, where some of the very best monumental decorative paintings could be seen and experienced. Fortunately, today there are a number of collections in North America that hold examples of late Baroque Venetian works from this prolific period.

The art of eighteenth-century Venice, particularly the large-scale decorative paintings, came to be appreciated and collected in North America sometime after the art of Renaissance Florence, Rome, and Naples, and after Flemish, Dutch, and Spanish art of the sixteenth and seventeenth century. For Americans who visited Venice on the Grand Tour of Italy, the late Baroque art of the city's lavish palaces must have appeared overly refined, excessively ornate, and devoid of serious content. They were more accustomed to American history paintings of the late-eighteenth and early nineteenth century by John Trumbull, John Vanderlyn, and Rembrandt Peale, which are sometimes characterized by a heroic narrative realism or by all too carefully composed and arranged figures in classical dress, acting out a story of high moral consequence. Many times Washington was the heroic protagonist in scenes from the War of Independence. Murals depicting scenes from American history by Edwin Austin Abbey and others were commenced in the Capitol rotunda in 1878, and in 1905 George A. Reid painted murals in the Parliament Buildings in Ottawa. This represents a significant movement in North American decorative painting that could well have inspired a later appreciation of large-scale Venetian history painting, particularly in the United States.

The art of colonial and post-colonial America and that of the Canadian loyalists shared aesthetic values based on a common British heritage. Later, in the second half of the nineteenth century, both the United States and Canada experienced a period of growth and great prosperity that made it possible for wealthy industrialists and railroad magnates, in both countries, to imitate the manner in which the earlier European entrepreneurs, made wealthy by the early industrial revolution, had amassed large collections of Old Master art and helped establish the first public museums.

In the post-Civil War period, New York became an important financial and cultural center, and there were a growing number of art galleries that dealt in European Old Master paintings and there was increasing art patronage and related benefits for growing collections like the Metropolitan Museum of Art. During this period Montreal was experiencing a similar "golden era," during which time the city became the financial hub of the country and large private fortunes and art collections were formed. The results can be seen in the Montreal Museum of Fine Arts, which from the beginning, like museums in the United States, depended on the generosity of private individuals. Three very important eighteenth-century Venetian works in the museum's collection, Giovanni Battista Tiepolo's painting of *Apelles Painting the Portrait of Campaspe* (ca. 1725-26), Francesco Guardi's *Storm at Sea* (ca. 1770), and Canaletto's *Interior of San Marco, Venice* (ca. 1760), all came from the collection of the Canadian Pacific Railway mogul William Van Horne (1843-1915). This bequest from Van Horne's daughter, Adaline, also included El Greco's *Portrait of a Man of the House of Leiva* (ca. 1580-1585) and Jacob van Ruisdael's *The Bleaching Grounds at Haarlem* (ca. 1670).

The early collectors of Old Master works in the United States either established their own museums to house their collections, as did Isabella Stewart Gardner, Henry Walters, and J. Pierpont Morgan, or they helped establish and broaden the European art collections in early museums like the Metropolitan in New York, the Museum of Fine Arts in Boston, or the Philadelphia Museum of Art. Of these numerous post-Civil War collectors, however, few were as discerning as Isabella Stewart Gardner (1840-1924) in Boston; Henry Gurdon Marquand (1819-1902) in New York, who helped plan the Metropolitan Museum of Art in 1869; Benjamin Altman (1840-1913), a New York merchant and collector who gifted a large number of Old Master works to the Metropolitan; and J. Pierpont Morgan (1837-1913), also in New York, who continued his father's business as a merchant banker and began collecting, in 1890, mostly incunabula, rare books, manuscripts, and drawings. In Philadelphia one of the most important collectors of the period was John G. Johnson (1841-1917), a highly successful lawyer who represented the majority of the large trusts in the United States.

Isabella Gardner was advised in her collecting by the art historian Bernard Berenson, a former student of Charles Eliot Norton, the Harvard Professor of Fine Arts who introduced the first art history courses in the United States. She visited the London studios of James McNeill Whistler and John Singer Sargent, both of whom painted her portrait. In 1888, she bought her first Old Master painting, and that summer traveled to Venice where she became interested in its palatial architecture, but not necessarily the decorative works of Tiepolo or other eighteenth-century Venetian artists. Later she bought Titian's *Rape of Europa* (ca. 1560), as well as works by Raphael, Rubens, and, with the advice of Berenson, works by Giotto, Piero della Francesco, and Botticelli. Gardner's house, a Renaissance Revival palazzo, became a public museum in 1903.

John Singer Sargent (1856-1925) was patronized by Isabella Gardner, and his painting of *El Jaleo* (1882) occupies a prominent place in her Boston Palazzo.

Sargent's painting of *A Venetian Interior* (Royal Academy of Arts, London) shows the Curtis family from Boston in the sumptuous salon of the Ca'Barbaro in Venice, which they had acquired in 1885. Isabella Gardner, Henry James (1843-1916), and Sargent were all guests there. Before Mr. and Mrs. Curtis occupied Ca'Barbaro, Tiepolo's ceiling painting of *The Glorification of the Barbaro Family* (ca. 1772, The Metropolitan Museum of Art) and his four oval paintings, as well as his ceiling painting in another room, had been removed and sold. After being bought and sold by collectors in France *The Glorification* was purchased by Stanford White, the architect, who placed it in the Fifth Avenue home of his client Colonel Oliver H. Payne. After Payne's death it was given to the Metropolitan by Mrs. Henry Osborne Havermeyer in 1923.

Although the American collectors of the 1890s acquired Barbizon school and Impressionist works, they still acquired large numbers of Old Master works. Benjamin Altman first collected American and Barbizon works in the 1880s and 1890s, and it was not until 1905 that he started collecting Dutch and Flemish Old Master paintings and began building what was generally considered the foremost collection of that time. Although he consulted experts in his acquisitions, he ultimately depended on his own judgment. By the turn of the century his collection included a number of Rembrandts, works by Vermeer, Hals, Van Dyck, Velásquez, Holbein, Dürer, Mantegna, Botticelli, and a Titian (*Portrait of a Man*). Like Isabella Stewart Gardner and others, while Altman's collection of Renaissance Italian painting included a Titian, this hardly represented a nascent interest in the work of Tiepolo and the Venetian eighteenth-century artists.

John G. Johnson's trust clients included J. Pierpont Morgan and Henry Clay Frick. Johnson began to travel to Europe in the 1880s, and by 1892 he had collected 281 works of art, 27 of which were by Netherlandish and Italian Old Masters. This included five Botticellis and two large panels by Roger van der Weyden. The rest were on the whole nineteenth-century French works, many of which were Barbizon and Impressionist paintings. Like Gardner and Altman, Johnson's preference was for Italian Renaissance painting. He left his collection to the city of Philadelphia, and it is located in the Philadelphia Museum of Art.

William T. Walters (1819-1894), from Baltimore, made his fortune after the Civil War in investment banking and railroads. He first collected American landscape painting and then contemporary French painting. His son, Henry Walters (1848-1931), became an even more avid collector. The large number of art objects he collected could not be properly housed in his Baltimore residence, and he decided to build a museum in the same neighborhood. His collecting interests became even more far-reaching than his father's, and he began to collect works of all periods and civilizations. In 1902 he bought the collection of Don Marcello Massarenti (1817-1905), a high ranking Church official under Leo XIII (1810-1903).

The Massarenti collection of more than 1,540 works contained, perhaps by default, Giovanni Battista Tiepolo's large oil painting of *Scipio Africanus Freeing Massiva* (1719-1721), as well as a more modest-sized painting by the artist, which had formerly been attributed to Luca Giordiano, of the *Virgin and Child.* The *Scipio Africanus* painting; Gregorio Lazzarini's large-scale oil of *The Golden Age* (ca. 1700) (cat. 10), which had been given to the Boston Athenæum in 1861 by George Washington Wales as a work by Luca Giordano; Tiepolo's *The Investiture of Bishop Harold as Duke of Franconia* (ca. 1751-52), which entered the Metropolitan Museum of Art in 1872; and a *bozzetto* (oil sketch) of the *Apotheosis of a Poet* (n.d.) by Tiepolo, which had been given to the Museum of Fine Arts, Boston, by Denman Waldo Ross in 1906, were among the first important eighteenth-century Venetian history paintings to enter museums in the United States.

In the 1890s, the architect Richard Morris Hunt (1827-1895) built Marble House, at Newport, Rhode Island, for William Kissam Vanderbilt and Biltmore, at Asherville, North Carolina, for George Washington Vanderbilt (1862-1914), and the architect Horace Trumbauer (1868-1938) built The Elms, at Newport, Rhode Island, for Edward Julius Berwind (1848-1936). These showplaces and other great houses at Peapack-Gladstone, New Jersey, and the Butterworth home (now the Butterworth Center) at Moline, Illinois, were decorated with ceiling and wall paintings by Antonio Pellegrini (1675-1741), Giovanni Battista Tiepolo, and other eighteenth-century Venetian artists, marking an important turning point in the collection of Venetian art in the United States, as George Knox explains in his essay, "Tiepolo among the Titans," in this catalogue.

Works by Canaletto, the principal artist associated with Venetian view painting, were not favored during the first wave of American collecting of works by European Old Masters. In North America there were no imitators of Canaletto, as there were in eighteenth-century England, so his works were not as well known. William Van Horne bought a Canaletto of *The Ducal Palace: the Scala dei Giganti* in the 1890s. In 1910 the Metropolitan Museum of Art acquired Canaletto's *Entrance to the Grand Canal from the Piazzetta*, and in 1917 the Museum of Fine Arts, Boston, acquired the *Grand Canal: S. Geremia and the Entrance to the Cannaregio.* Nevertheless, landscape, topographical, and marine subjects were of primary importance in North American painting throughout the nineteenth-century. Also, Venice was one of the favorite subjects of artists like James McNeill Whistler (1834-1903), John Singer Sargent (1856-1925), William Merritt Chase (1849-1916) and Thomas Moran (1837-1926), and the Montreal artist James Wilson Morrice (1865-1924).

Some American travelers would have had the opportunity to see Canaletto's work while visiting England. The eighteenth-century English Grand Tourists were among his principal patrons. Some of these patrons built country houses in the Palladian manner and wanted Canaletto paintings to be part of the interior décor. His paintings were bought for the houses of the landed gentry, and Joseph Smith, the British Consul in Venice, sold his collection to George III, which became a significant part of the Royal Collections, where the largest concentration of Canaletto's work is found. With the establishment of the National Gallery, London, in 1824, a country house invitation or, even more unlikely, an invitation from the royal family, was no longer necessary in order to see Canaletto's views of Venice. By the second half of the nineteenth century, a selective representation of the artist's work could be seen by all visitors in this great public museum. Even though the artistic ties that existed between England and Colonial America in the eighteenth century became less pronounced in the nineteenth century, the cultural connections and shared taste in art collecting did not greatly diminish.

The *La Serenissima* exhibition is made up of history paintings (mythological, classical, and biblical); genre subjects and portraits; the graphic works of Giovanni Battista, his son Giovanni Domenico Tieopolo, and Canaletto; and topographical and view paintings. The first group includes large paintings of *The Golden Age* by Gregorio Lazzarini from the Boston Athenæum (cat. 10), *Juno Triumphant, as Queen of the Air* by Giovanni Battista Tiepolo from the Sarah Campbell Blaffer Foundation, Houston (cat. 20), and *The Building of the Trojan Horse* by Giovanni Domenico Tiepolo from the Wadsworth Atheneum Museum of Art (cat. 24). There are also biblical paintings, such as *The Entombment* by Giovanni Antonio Pellegrini from the John and Mable Ringling Museum of Art (cat. 12) and Giovanni Battisa Piazzetta's *The Madonna and Child Appearing to Saint Philip Neri* from the National Gallery of Art (cat. 13).

The genre and portrait paintings are smaller, more intimate paintings of the daily activities and interactions of the Venetian bourgeois, aristocratic, and proletariat classes, as shown in Pietro Longhi's painting *The Concert (The Mandolin Recital)* from the Fine Arts Museums of San Francisco (cat. 27), and his somewhat erotic and satirical painting of *The Temptation* from the Wadsworth Atheneum Museum of Art (cat. 26). There are also anonymous portraits of coquettish and beautifully attired young women by Giovanni Domenico Tiepolo from the Cleveland Museum of Art and another by Pietro Rotari from the Museum of Art and Archaeology University of Missouri-Columbia.

Prints by Canaletto, Giovanni Battista Tiepolo, and Giovanni Domenico Tiepolo will have a special place in the exhibition, emphasizing the unusual talents of these three artists as both painters and celebrated graphic artists. There are etchings from Antonio Canaletto's series of *Vedute (Views)*, from Giovanni Battista Tiepolo's series of etchings titled *Vari Capricci* as well as ones from his *Scherzi di Fantasia*, and works from Giovanni Domenico Tiepolo's *Flight into Egypt* series. Prints in the four series are from the Cleveland Museum of Art, the Fine Arts Museums of San Francisco (Legion of Honor), the National Gallery of Art, and the University of Toronto Art Centre. The prints included in the exhibition will give museum visitors an idea of the varied but related subject matter in each series.

The Venetian view paintings include works by Luca Carlevarijs, Antonio Canaletto, Michele Marieschi, and Francesco Guardi, and the exhibition concludes with early nineteenth-century artists, such as Ippolito Caffi and J. M. W. Turner, who were influenced by Canaletto's work and the romantic interpretation of Venice's mysterious and slightly derelict beauty.

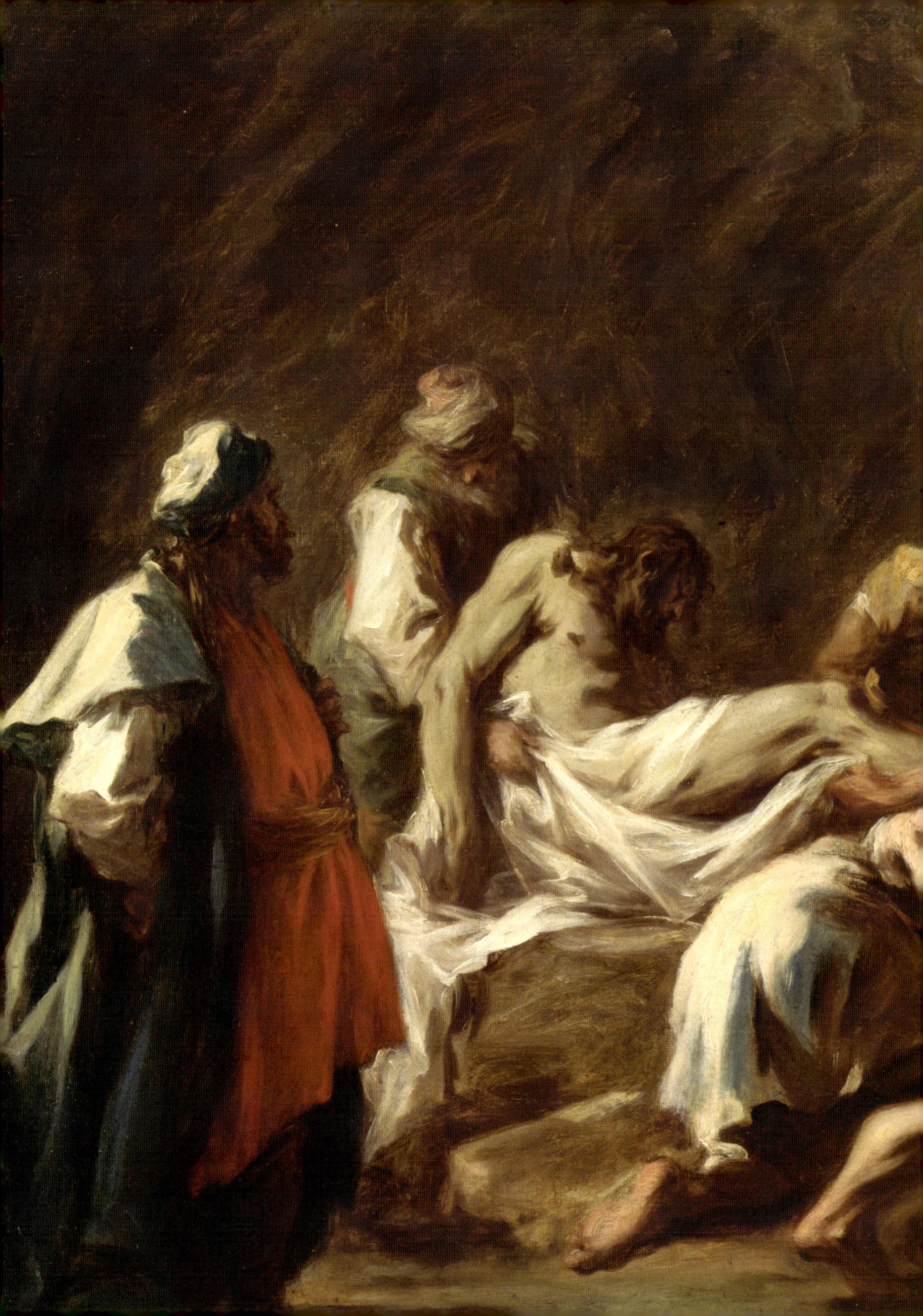

History Painting

Mythological, Classical, and Biblical Subjects

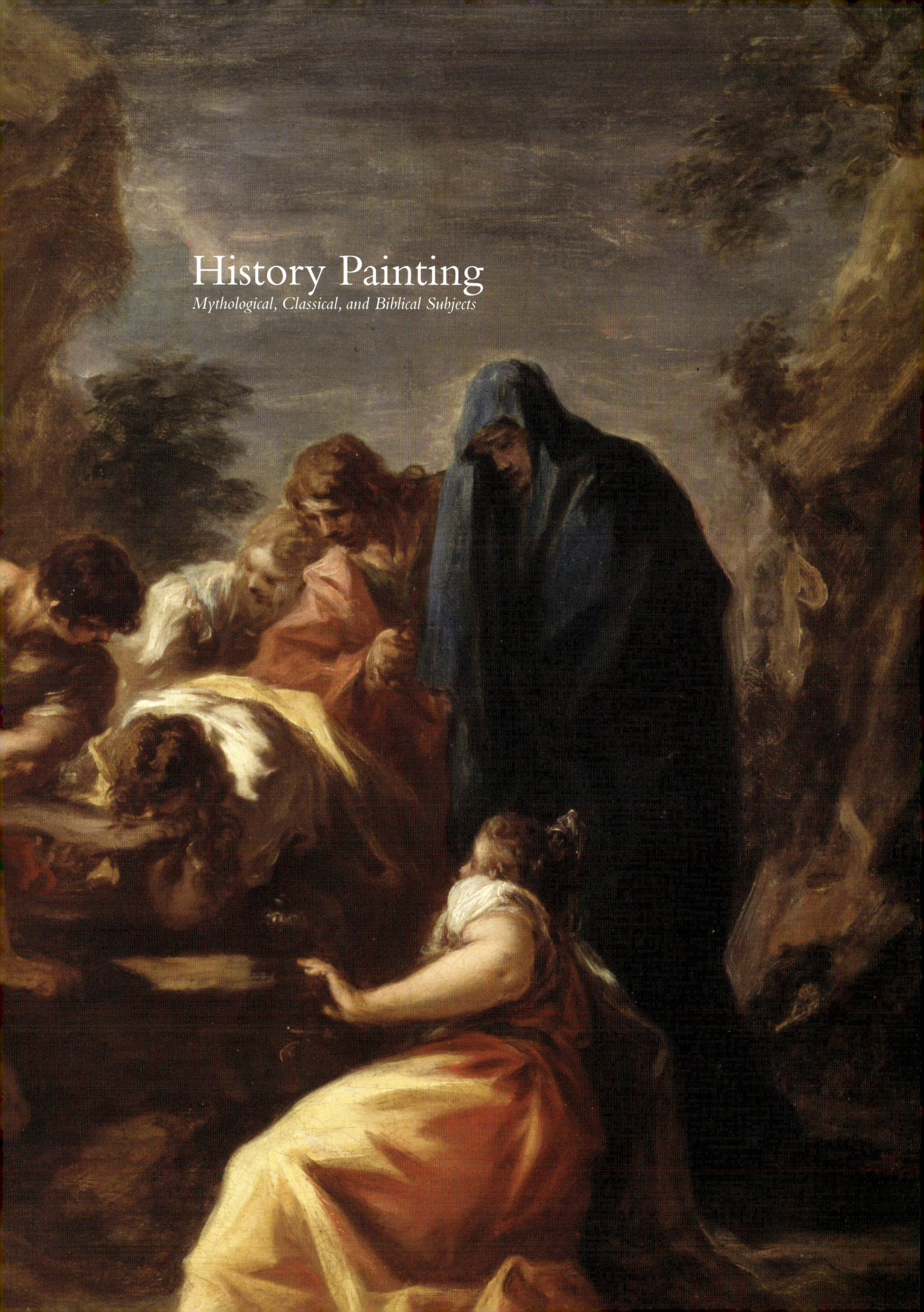

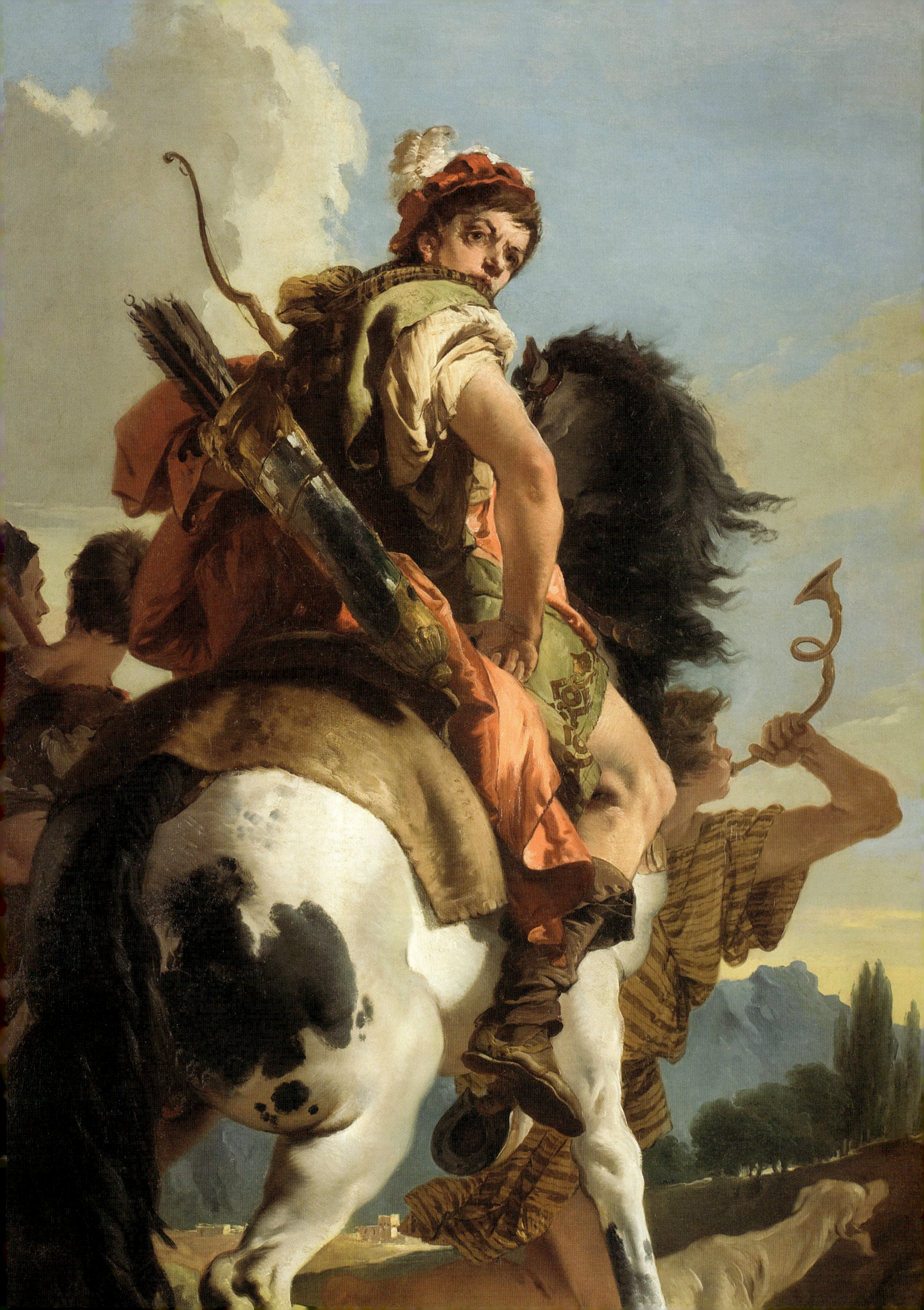

Tiepolo among the Titans

American Collecting of Venetian Eighteenth-Century History Painting

George Knox

In the annals of American collecting in the nineteenth and early twentieth century, the acquisition of Venetian history painting of the eighteenth century is little more than a footnote. American taste gave pride of place to works from Florence and the age of the Renaissance, and then to English portraiture and French decorative arts. Yet a handful of American buyers, with ample resources but with a modest commitment, for the most part, to things Venetian, acquired an astonishing array of masterpieces for their homes in the United States. By way of contrast, one may note that there is not now a single really important painting by Giovanni Battista Tiepolo (1696-1770) in England or in France, apart from the frescoes of the Musée Jacquemart-André. While this essay may not break much new ground, it offers a summary of a remarkable phase in American collecting.

Marble House, Newport, Rhode Island

We must begin with the Vanderbilts, the great American railway family, and their architect Richard Morris Hunt (1827-1895), the founding father of the American architectural profession, and the celebrated designer of the plinth of the Statue of Liberty and the façade of the Metropolitan Museum of Art. From 1888 to1892 Hunt was building the Marble House at Newport for William Kissam Vanderbilt (1849-1820). The house was inspired by the Petit Trianon at Versailles, with interiors supplied by the firm of Jules Allard *et fils* of Paris. It is a building entirely in the French style of *la Belle Époque*, with the exception of the ceiling in Mrs. Vanderbilt's bedroom, which is identified by Alessandro Bettagno as a fine work by the Venetian Antonio Pellegrini (1675-1741) from the Library of Ca' Pisani in Campo San Stefano in Venice.[1] This is not entirely surprising. Hunt was trained in Paris, and from 1855 to 1859 the Château de Ferrières was being built for the baron James de Rothschild (1792-1868) by William Paxton, of the Crystal Palace and Mentmore, with the great central room ornamented with the fine ceiling by Tiepolo, *The Triumph of Virtue*, from the Palazzo Angelo Vecchia at Vicenza, now in the Palazzo Isimbardi in Milan.[2]

Giovanni Battista Tiepolo (Italian, 1696-1770)
DETAIL: *Cacciatore a Cavallo (The Royal Hunt)*
(FIG. 14)

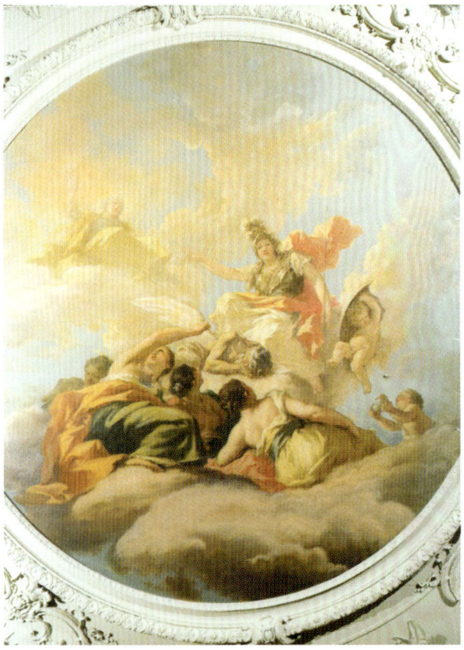

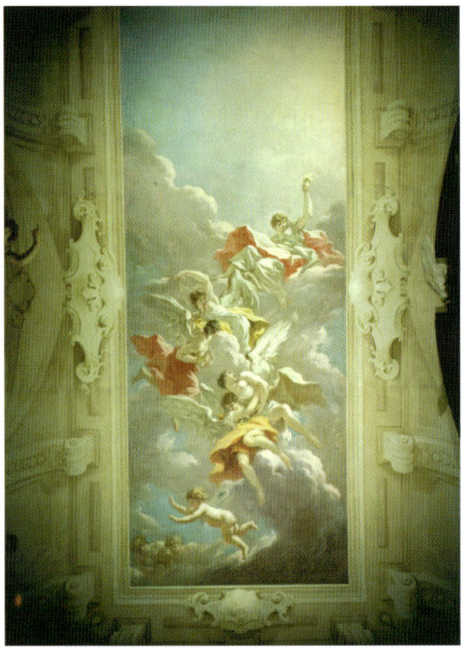

But this seems to have been something of a flash in the pan.[3] The Tiepolo frescoes of the Musée Jacquemart-André, from the Villa Contarini at Mira, were not found, purchased, and installed until 1893.[4]

Ca' Pisani was started in the early seventeenth century by the Pisani, apparently without an architect. After a somewhat inauspicious start and an earthquake in 1634, the building was pulled together and completed in 1720 by the architect Girolamo Frigimelica (1653-1732).[5] In about 1895 it became the seat of what is now the Conservatorio di Musica Benedetto Marcello, and it still retains the greater part of its eighteenth-century interiors.[6]

The Pellegrini ceiling in the Marble House depicts *Minerva and Immortality* (fig. 1), a most suitable theme for the decoration of a library.[7] It was followed to America by other items from Ca' Pisani.

Biltmore, Asheville, North Carolina

From 1890 until his death in 1895, Hunt was engaged in the construction of Biltmore for George Washington Vanderbilt (1862-1914), younger brother of William. George Vanderbilt was a man of strong intellectual and literary tastes. For his library, Hunt and Allard were able to supply a vast ceiling from the Ballroom of Ca' Pisani, *Aurora and the Hours* (fig. 2), which apparently was believed to be by Tiepolo, until it was attributed to Antonio Pellegrini by Antonio Morassi in 1962.[8] The ceiling is said to have been installed in 1894, but the library was, evidently, designed to receive it at a slightly earlier date.

Lino Moretti suggests that the ceiling left Venice in 1895, referring also to fifteen statues by Antonio Gai (1686-1769), which are discussed below.[9] He suggests that Parisian dealer Raoul Heilbronner was involved in the removal of both the ceiling of the library and the ballroom to Paris.

Other country houses of the Vanderbilt family of the period, and the several town houses in New York, do not appear to have been decorated with any further Venetian paintings. This seems to be the case in general, with the possible exception of the house of Edward Julius Berwind at 828 Fifth Avenue and 64th Street, designed by Nathan Clark Mellen, completed in 1896, with interiors by Jules Allard. The exterior essentially survives intact, while much of the interior shows attached wall paintings and ceilings still in position. However, legible photographs have yet to be found.

The Walters Art Museum, Baltimore, Maryland

The circumstances of the removal of the two ceilings from Ca'Pisani were noted in 2002 by Giuseppe Pavanello, who showed that four statues in the Walters Art Museum in Baltimore, the work of Antonio Gai, were part of a group of fifteen from the early 1720s that had ornamented the staircase of the palace. These had been sold to Raoul Heilbronner in the period 1890-92, together with the ceiling of the library, now in the Marble House. The statues were exhibited by Heilbronner in 1900[10] and appear to have been acquired

FIG. 1
Giovanni Antonio Pellegrini (Italian, 1675-1741)
Minerva and Immortality
Marble House, Newport, RI
Courtesy of The Preservation Society of Newport County

FIG. 2
Giovanni Antonio Pellegrini (Italian, 1675-1741)
Aurora and the Hours
Ceiling in the Library at Biltmore
Used with permission from The Biltmore Company, Asheville, North Carolina

shortly afterwards by Henry Walters (1848-1931), who, like the Vanderbilts, was a fabulously successful railway magnate.

It is hard to give names to these statues. It was once thought that they might be four of the nine muses, but such clues as are offered do not support this idea very effectively. Pavanello advances other suggestions, which do not clarify the situation a great deal,[11] and yet it is incredible that such a sumptuous and expensive scheme should not have meant something appropriate and uplifting. Giambattista Tiepolo, in the Gallery at Udine of the mid-1720s, introduces six standing prophetesses in niches, but identifies them clearly.[12] His drawings of similar figures at Trieste for the Villa Lochi at Biron of 1734 are similarly inscribed,[13] as is the later series of drawings for statues that belonged to Francesco Algarotti,[14] and this seems to suggest that such aids to identification were considered desirable. In fact the relationship between these painted figures by Tiepolo and contemporary sculpture was explored in two articles by Giuseppe Pavanello and Paola Rossi in 1998.[15]

One of the four, *Calliope, Muse of Epic Poetry* (?) (fig. 3), shows the left foot resting on a thin rectangular block, but this just seems to be a device to emphasize the *contraposto* stance. Little else distinguishes the figure from Baratta's *Sapienza* and Tarsia's *Liberalità* on the Valier monument in San Giovanni e Paolo, which employ the same device and use it to identify the piece.[16] More relevant to Calliope, muse of eloquence and epic poetry, is the open book she holds, one of the three great epics of antiquity. By contrast *Urania, Muse of Astronomy* (?) (fig. 4) is a much calmer figure, apparently gazing at a small globe in her left hand while holding a pair of dividers in her right, rendering her not unacceptable as Urania, muse of astronomy.

One may recall here that among the holdings of the Walters Art Museum is the very large canvas by Tiepolo, *Scipio Africanus Freeing Massiva* (fig. 5), purchased by Henry Walters in Rome in 1902.[17] Nothing is known of its origins, but the presence of a golden ornamental dolphin in the left background may point to the Dolfin family, possibly to their villa on the *terraglio,* between Mestre and Treviso, dating from the early 1720s.

The Elms, Newport, Rhode Island

For the next chapter in our study we must return to Newport, to the house known as The Elms, built by the architect Horace Trumbauer (1868-1938) in 1899-1901, for Edward Julius Berwind (1848-1936), mentioned above, who made a vast fortune in the coal industry.[18] The house was inspired by the Château d'Asnières, on the outskirts of Paris. In fact the original proposal was to bring the house over to Newport as a whole, but this was deemed impractical, and only the sculpture of the exterior was incorporated in the new building. Once again the whole reflected French taste of *la Belle Époque*, but the painted decorations were essentially a series of canvases taken from the portego of a relatively modest Venetian house of the late fifteenth century, Ca' Corner a San Tomà.[19]

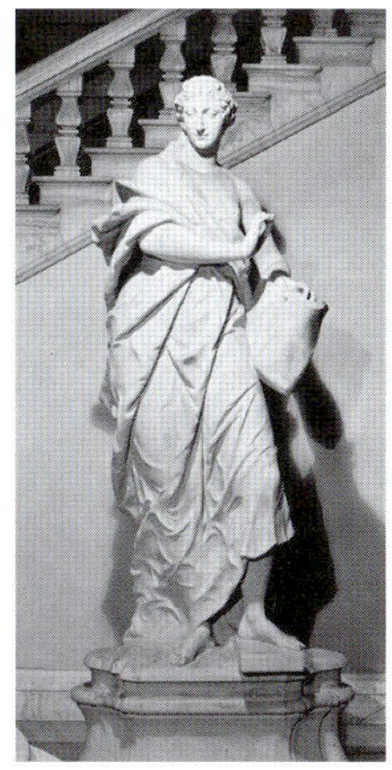

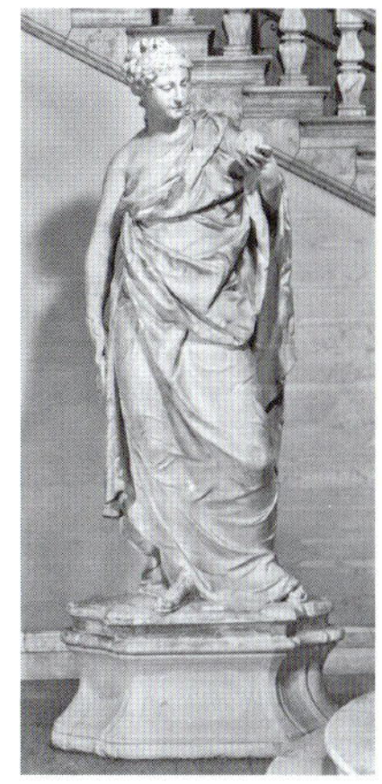

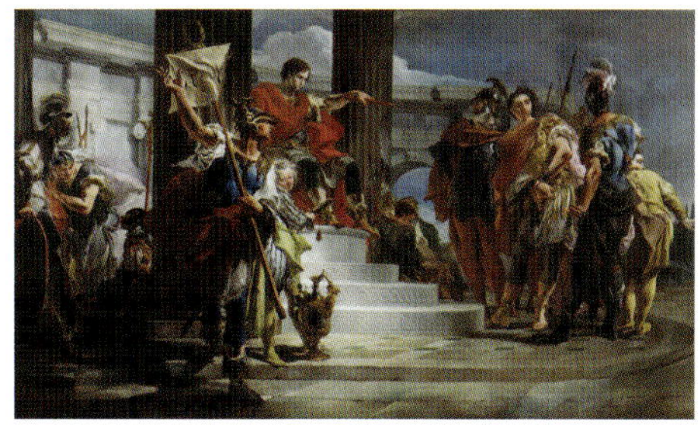

FIG. 3
Antonio Gai (Italian, 1686-1769)
Calliope, Muse of Epic Poetry (?)
Limestone, 119 11/16 in. (304 cm)
Photo copyright The Walters Art Museum, Baltimore

FIG. 4
Antonio Gai (Italian, 1686-1769)
Urania, Muse of Astronomy (?)
Limestone
Photo copyright The Walters Art Museum, Baltimore

FIG. 5
Giovanni Battista Tiepolo (Italian, 1696-1770)
Scipio Africanus Freeing Massiva
Oil on canvas, 110 x 191 15/16 in. (279.4 x 487.6 cm)
Photo copyright The Walters Art Museum, Baltimore

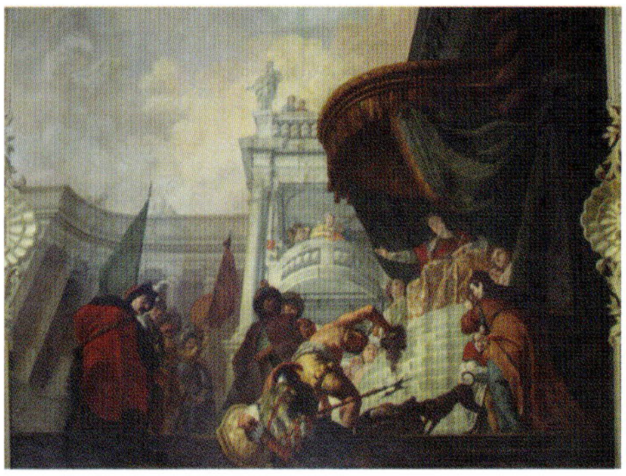

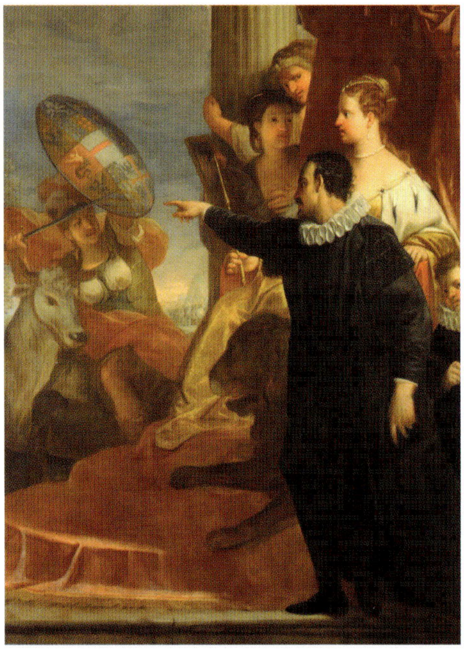

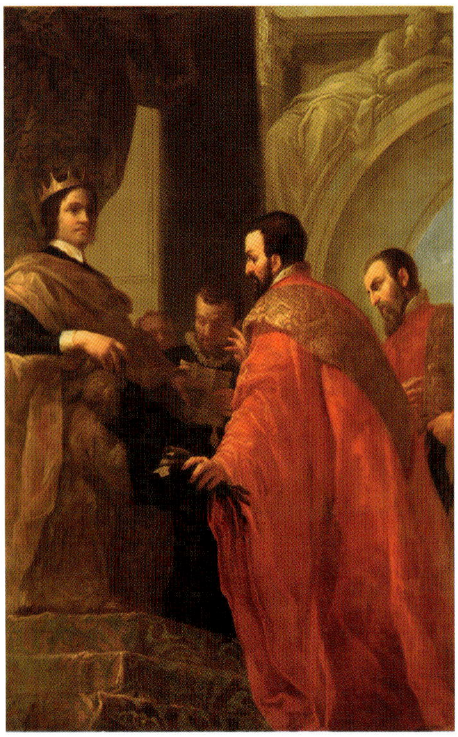

The circumstances of the acquisition are obscure, but once again the services of Jules Allard of Paris seem to have been involved. The works themselves, in their new setting, are briefly mentioned as by Tiepolo and Lazzarini in 1903, and again by Pompeo Molmenti in 1909, but this again was largely wishful thinking.[20]

The main group of canvases are ten in number: four large scenes depict episodes from the life of Scipio Africanus and six overdoor paintings illustrate the annals of the Corner family. These large scenes are glued to the wall and cannot be moved. The six overdoors were removed and sold in 1953, and were purchased by Wildenstein and Company. One was sold by Sotheby's in 2009 to a private collector, *Atropos*,[21] one remains with Wildenstein,[22] and the other four have found their way back to The Elms. Apart from these, there is a ceiling, greatly enlarged, in the hall, depicting *Queen Tomyris with the Head of Cyrus* (fig. 6) by Francesco Fontebasso, from Ca' Duodo a Sta. Maria del Giglio.[23]

The main group is recorded in an old photograph in its original setting,[24] which made it possible to identify the location. In The Elms it is divided between the hall—two of the large pictures making an effective pair—and the rest in the dining room, including the spaces for the six overdoors.

The attribution of these paintings has created some problems that are not entirely resolved. One of the overdoors, now back at The Elms, is listed by Vincenzo da Canal among the works of Gregorio Lazzarini, under the date 1700 (fig. 7),[25] which indicates an approximate date for the series. Another overdoor, also back at The Elms, can be given to Antonio Molinari (1655-1704), on the basis of two preparatory drawings at Düsseldorf (fig. 8).[26] In 1985-86 Catherine Monbeig Goguel pointed out that two further drawings by Molinari in the Louvre appear to be associated with another overdoor that I identified as *Caterina Cornaro receiving the surrender of a Turkish city*, with an attribution to Carlo Loth (1632-1698).[27] Since the principal figure wears full armour and the red hat of a *capitano generale da Mar*, clearly seen in the painting and in both drawings, this title cannot be right, and *A Cornaro receiving the surrender of a Turkish city* is preferred, but whether this permits an attribution of the third overdoor to Molinari (fig. 8) is another question.

One of the large canvases in the hall, *The Continence of Scipio* (fig. 9), was given by Alessandro Bettagno to Antonio Pellegrini, and this remains unchallenged.[28] The other, *Scipio Declining Regal Honours* (fig. 10), and another in the dining room, *The Triumph of Scipio* (fig. 11), I attributed to Paolo Pagani.[29] The second large painting in the dining room, *Syphax before Scipio*

FIG. 6
Francesco Fontebasso (Italian, 1707-1769)
Queen Tomyris with the Head of Cyrus
The Elms, Newport, RI
Courtesy of The Preservation Society of Newport County

FIG. 7
Gregorio Lazzarini (Italian, 1655-1730)
Francesco Corner defends Venice against the League of Combrai
The Elms, Newport, RI
Courtesy of The Preservation Society of Newport County

FIG. 8
Antonio Molinari (Italian, 1655-1704)
The Embassy of Marco Corner to the Emperor Charles V
The Elms, Newport, RI
Courtesy of The Preservation Society of Newport County

(fig. 12), was given to Giambattista Piazzetta.[30] These are disputed but no alternative consensus has emerged.[31]

However, the interest of this cycle of paintings does not lie so much in questions of attribution, but in the importance of the story of Scipio to Venetians. It is the theme of Petrarch's *Africa*, first printed in Venice in 1501-3, and soon after this we find it depicted in associated works for the Corner family by Mantegna and Giovanni Bellini.[32] Already Scipio is cast as the national hero of Italy, who saved it from Carthaginian domination. The story is then taken up by Giulio Romano and Penni in the shape of a series of tapestry designs, perhaps for the Emperor Charles V, but then appropriated by François Ier for the embellishment of the French Court for two hundred years under the title *Le Grand Scipion*. It was finally burned during the French Revolution, to recover the gold and silver that had been woven into it (see the note on Hearst Castle below).

Edward Berwind owned four of another less important series, deriving from designs by Giulio Romano, depicting the story of Cupid and Psyche, which were given by Julia S. Berwind to the Metropolitan Museum of Art in 1953 and hang in the Petrie Court.[33]

Meanwhile other sets of tapestry had been woven from the same *grands patrons*, at least one for the Zane family in Venice, and when the fashion for large history paintings in private houses developed in Venice around 1700, it was really a cheap alternative to tapestry, and the Scipio tradition sprang into new life.[34] This explains the background of the cycle of works collected from Ca' Corner a San Tomà and several others of the period, including the Tiepolo of Henry Walters, mentioned above.

Further evidence of Edward Berwind's interest in Venetian Settecento painting is shown by his purchase in 1912 of two of the three fine and monumental landscapes by Francesco Guardi from the Castello di Colloredo, which seem to have remained in the building until 1906 and then remained together in the Rothschild collection. The central scene passed to Charles Alexander of New York and to the Metropolitan Museum of Art in 1941. The two side pieces went to Edward Berwind and were given to the Met by Miss Julia A. Berwind in 1953, bringing the three pieces together again.[35]

Blairsden, Peapack-Gladstone, New Jersey

C. Ledyard Blair (1867-1949) was the grandson of John Insley Blair (1802-1899), president of sixteen railroad companies. Ledyard Blair was prominent as a banker and a yachtsman, and between 1898 and 1903 he built Blairsden, a mansion at Peapack-Gladstone, New Jersey. He also had a cottage, Honeysuckle Lodge, at Newport, Rhode Island.[36] Ledyard Blair made his purchase of three important Tiepolos from Ca' Zenobio in Venice in 1909. It is not clear in

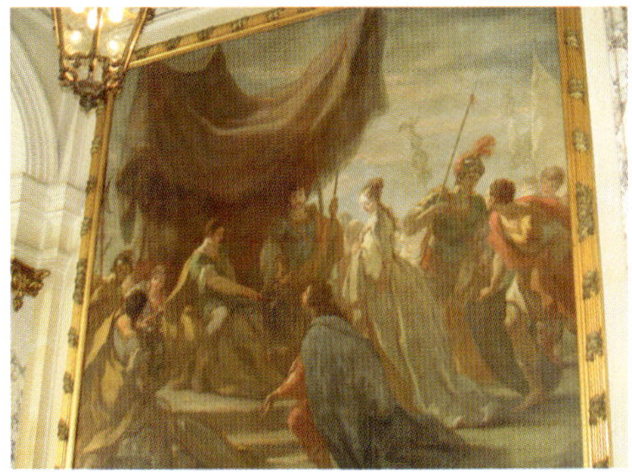

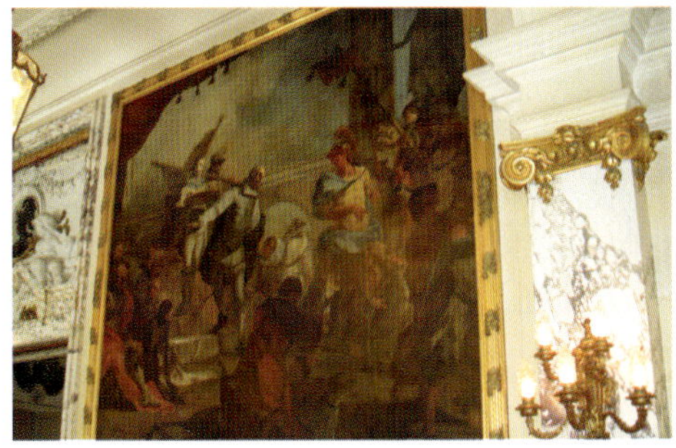

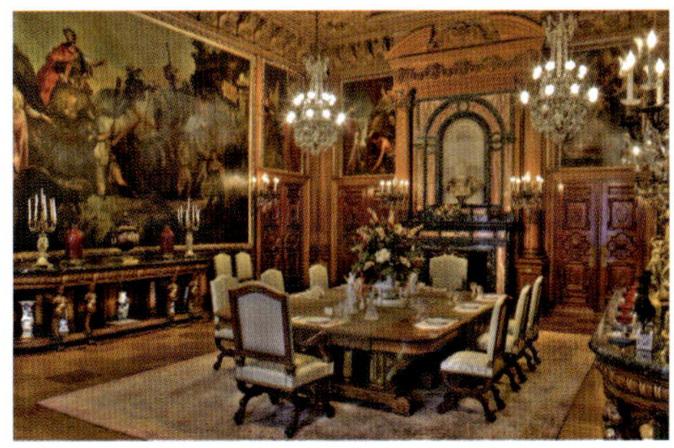

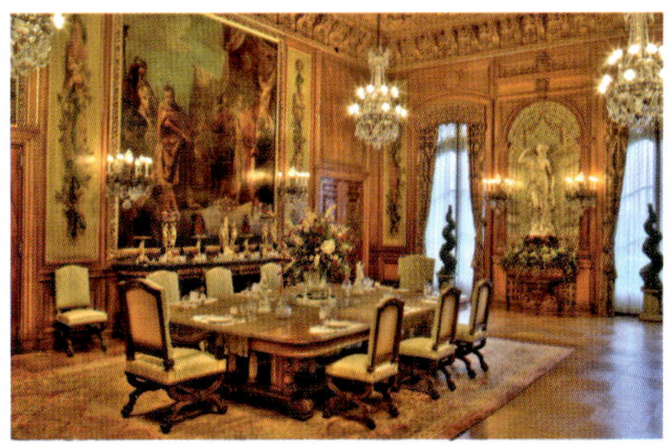

FIG. 9
Giovanni Antonio Pellegrini (Italian, 1675-1741)
The Continence of Scipio
The Elms, Newport, RI
Courtesy of The Preservation Society of Newport County

FIG. 10
Paolo Pagani (Italian, 1661-1716) (attribution)
Scipio Declining Regal Honours
The Elms, Newport, RI
Courtesy of The Preservation Society of Newport County

FIG. 11
Attributed to Paolo Pagani (Italian, 1661-1716)
The Triumph of Scipio
The Elms, Newport, RI
Courtesy of The Preservation Society of Newport County

FIG. 12
Attributed to Giovanni Battista Piazzetta (Italian, 1683-1754)
Syphax before Scipio
The Elms, Newport, RI
Courtesy of The Preservation Society of Newport County

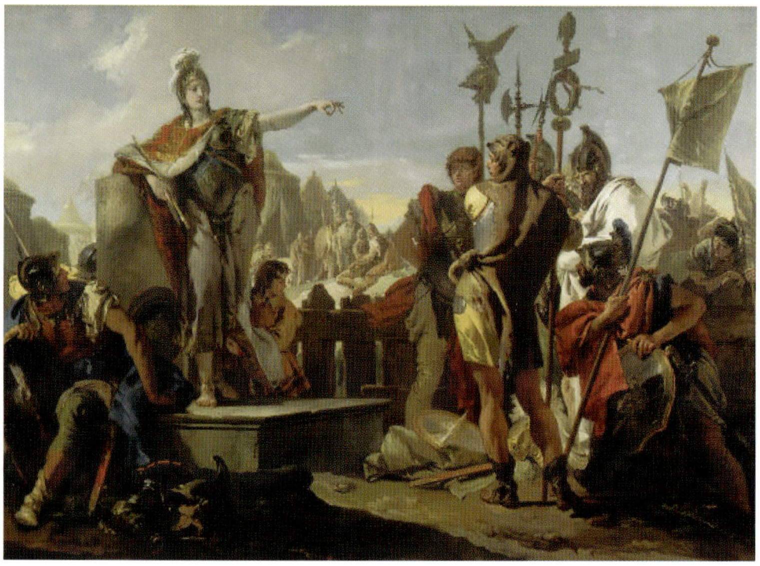

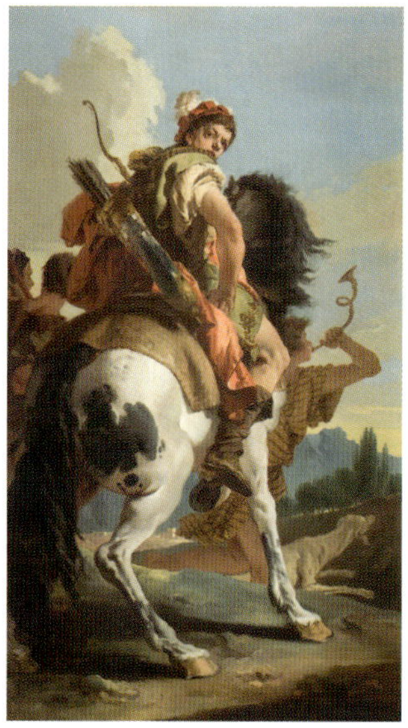

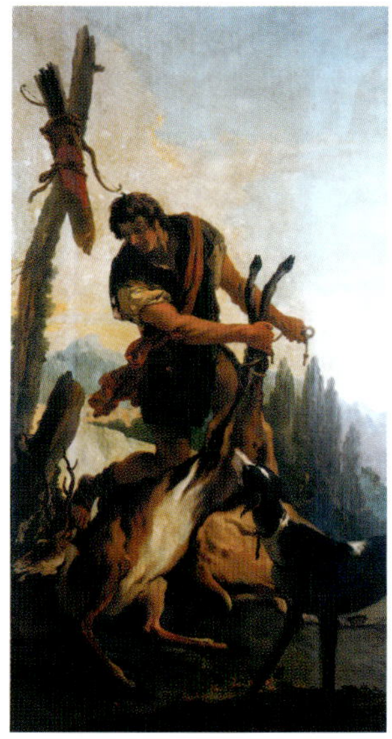

which of his houses they were placed. They remained with Ledyard Blair until his death and passed through the sale of works from his estate in New York in June 1950. The main picture, *The Allocution of Queen Zenobia* (fig. 13), went to Samuel Kress, and then to the National Gallery of Art, and the two smaller canvases, apparently fragments of *The Royal Hunt* (figs. 14, 15), to the Crespi collection in Milan. The canvases form part of a series by Tiepolo, *The Story of Queen Zenobia*, for Ca' Zenobio in Venice, which is described by da Canal as "one of his first works." It seems to have been dispersed in the 1840s, and comprised as well, *Queen Zenobia before Aurelian,* in the Prado, and *The Triumph of Aurelian* at Turin.[37]

Butterworth Center, Moline, Illinois

We must now turn away from this closely knit group of industrialists on the East Coast to examine later activity in the Midwest. William Butterworth (1866-1936) was the president of the John Deere company from 1907 to 1928, and his wife, Katherine (1866-1953), was the granddaughter of John Deere himself. They married in 1892. In 1917 they built a large addition to their house at 1105 8th Street in Moline, Illinois, to house a vast eighteenth-century Venetian ceiling painting, purchased from French and Company of New York. Inevitably it was assigned to Tiepolo, but by the time it came to my attention in the early 2000s, through the kindness of Janet Seiz, this hopeful notion was growing weak.[38] A wooden ceiling of the desired shape was constructed over the new library, and to this the canvas ceiling was glued permanently. On the death of Mrs. Butterworth in 1953, the contents of the house, a considerable collection of paintings and furniture, was sold, and the building became the Butterworth Center.

Tradition has it that in 1915, Mitchell Samuels, director of French and Company of New York, was staying in Venice at the Albergo Danieli. He was given

FIG. 13
Giovanni Battista Tiepolo (Italian, 1696-1770)
Queen Zenobia Addressing Her Soldiers
Oil on canvas, 102 15/16 x 144 in. (261.4 x 365.8 cm)
Samuel H. Kress Collection. 1961.9.41.
Image copyright National Gallery of Art, Washington

FIG. 14
Giovanni Battista Tiepolo (Italian, 1696-1770)
Cacciatore a Cavallo (The Royal Hunt)
Oil on canvas, 103¼ x 58¼ in. (262 x 148 cm)
Fondazione Cariplo, Milan, Italy

FIG. 15
Giovanni Battista Tiepolo (Italian, 1696-1770)
Cacciatore con Cervo (The Royal Hunt)
Oil on canvas, 103¼ x 58¼ in. (262 x 148 cm)
Fondazione Cariplo, Milan, Italy

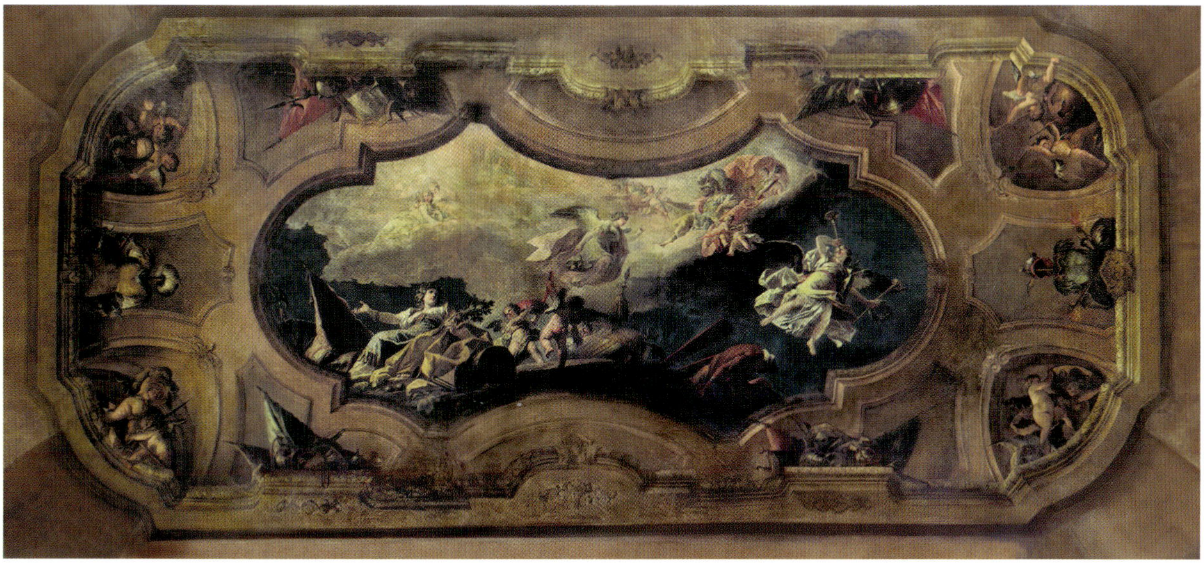

the small ballroom, which had a painted ceiling, though hidden by a velarium. It was said to depict the deeds of the Dandolo family, the original builders and owners of the building, which was now the most famous hotel in Venice. Perhaps because the hotel was planning to strip out the entire core of the building and replace it with a magnificent array of staircases in the Venetian-Byzantine style, which still exist, the hotel was happy to sell the ceiling and the elaborate wooden frieze that surrounded it to Mr. Samuels, who in short order sold the ceiling to the Butterworths at a price said to be $67,000. The wooden frieze went into stock and was later sold to William Randolph Hearst in 1923 (see below, under Hearst Castle).

In the eighteenth century, the second floor of Ca' Dandolo—the third floor in American parlance—was occupied by the Bernardo family, and their coat of arms is conspicuous in the upper central part of the ceiling, which must be given the title *The Glory of the Bernardo Family* (fig. 16). Old plans show a large central room on each of the main floors that answer to the description of a small ballroom, this providing ample confirmation of the story of the provenance of the ceiling.

The remaining problem is the identity of the painter. Large painted canvases covering the entire surface of a ceiling are something of a rarity in Venice, and this one is remarkable in that much of the surface is covered with a bold arrangement of painted coffering. This led to an attribution of part of the work to the Valeriani brothers, who were active in Venice in the 1720s and were specialists in *quadratura* of this serious and monumental character. They are celebrated for their later work at Stupinigi and Saint Petersburg. The figure painting of the great centerpiece and other smaller areas was assigned to Gaspare Diziani (1689-1767) at the suggestion of Giuseppe Pavanello, an attribution that is confirmed by the existence of a fine *bozzetto,* or oil sketch, in the collection of Egidio Martini in Ca' Rezzonico.[39] Diziani is an immensely prolific

FIG. 16
Gaspare Diziani (Italian, 1689-1767) and the Valeriani
The Glory of the Bernardo Family
The Butterworth Center, Moline, IL

Venetian painter and draughtsman, and Moline is fortunate to have one of the great Venetian ceilings of the early 1720s, an important representative work of major figures of the time. It may be compared with the ceiling at Biltmore by Pellegrini of the same period.

Hearst Castle, San Simeon, California

In the previous section, it was mentioned that the wooden frieze that surrounded *The Glory of the Bernardo Family* in Ca' Dandolo was sold to William Randolph Hearst (1863-1951) in 1923. Hearst Castle was begun in 1919 and building, under the direction of Julia Morgan, was never finished in Hearst's lifetime. The frieze now graces the main vestibule, which is to say the main entrance, of Hearst Castle at San Simeon.

From here the visitor passes into the great central hall, where hang the four great tapestries surviving from the second series of *Le Grand Scipion*, woven for Jacques d'Albon, maréchale de Saint-André. Not Venetian, it is true, but so immensely influential for Venetian painting, and so little known, that they must be noticed here.[40]

In discussing the theme of the story of Scipio in The Elms, it was necessary to point out the importance of *Le Grand Scipion* in France. It was no less celebrated in Venice, where there were several examples of later weavings of the seventeenth century. From there the themes were taken up by the history painters, making it the predominant theme for secular Italian history. Apart from the series at The Elms and the important example by Tiepolo at Baltimore, discussed above, there are important series in Ca' Vendramin Calergi, here given to Nicolo Bambini,[41] and the series of frescoes by Tiepolo in Palazzo Dugnani in Milan. The four tapestries of Hearst Castle are the fine survivors of the most important and influential series of secular tapestries of the sixteenth century.

Le Grand Scipion, of the 1530s, consisted of ten tapestries depicting *The Triumph of Scipio*, on designs by Giulio Romano, and twelve depicting *The Life of Scipio*, on designs by Luca Penni. The *tenture d'Albon,* which followed twenty years later, was a set of ten tapestries on *The Life of Scipio*, with four new items added. The four surviving items of this series depict *Scipio Saves His Father at the Battle of Ticino* (fig. 17), *The Battle of Baecula* (fig. 18), *Scipio Receives the Carthaginian Ambassadors* (fig. 19), and *The Continence of Scipio* (fig. 20).

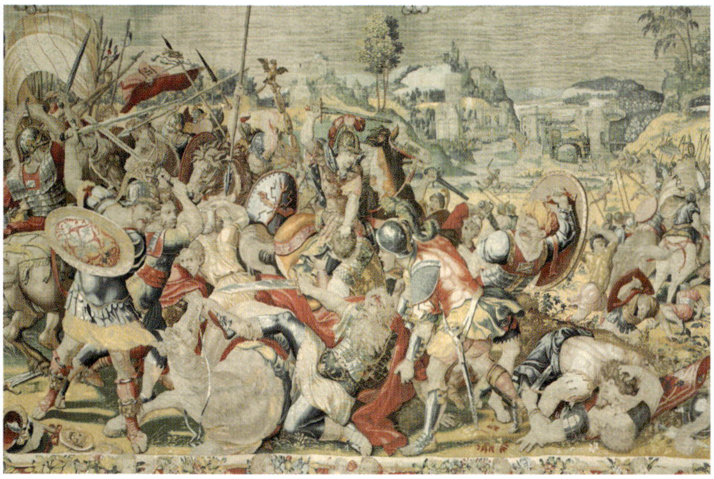

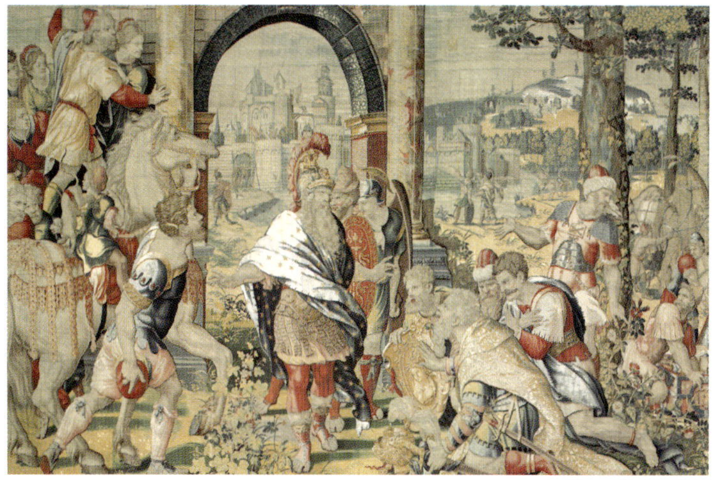

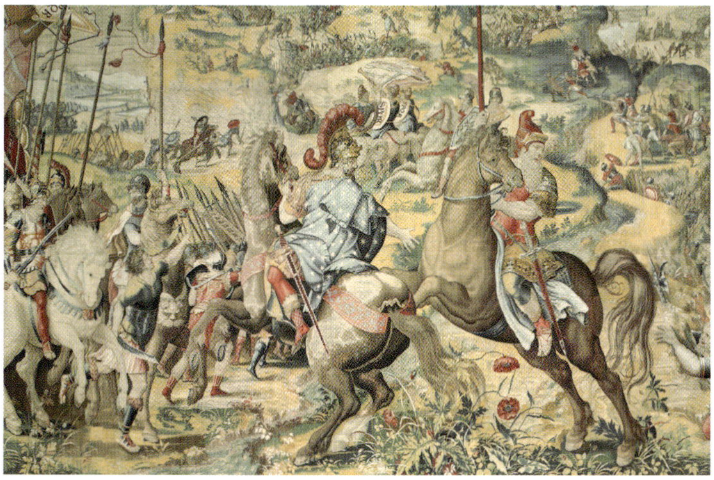

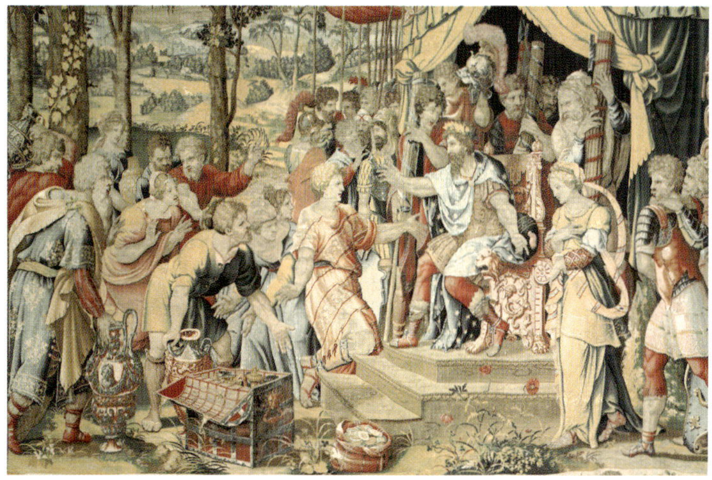

Vizcaya, Miami, Florida

No record has been noted of any contact between the Butterworths of Moline and Charles Deering (1852-1927) and his half brother James Deering (1859-1925) of Chicago, president and vice president respectively of International Harvester from 1902, though they represent two dominating corporations in the field of agricultural machinery. However, under the terms of James Deering's will, following his death in 1925, several important paintings were bequeathed to The Art Institute of Chicago, including a set of four magnificent canvases by Giovanni Battista Tiepolo (1696-1770), illustrating the story of Rinaldo and Armida (figs. 21-24), from Tasso's epic poem *La Gerusalemme Liberata.*

FIG. 17
Tapestry from the *tenture d'Albon* (Brussels, ca. 1550)
The Battle of Tessin
The Great Hall, Hearst Castle
Photograph by Victoria Garagliano/©Hearst Castle®/CA State Parks

FIG. 18
Tapestry from the *tenture d'Albon* (Brussels, ca. 1550)
The Engagement with Hasdrubal
The Great Hall, Hearst Castle
Photograph by Victoria Garagliano/©Hearst Castle®/CA State Parks

FIG. 19
Tapestry from the *tenture d'Albon* (Brussels, ca. 1550)
Scipio Receiving the Carthaginian Envoys
The Great Hall, Hearst Castle
Photograph by Victoria Garagliano/©Hearst Castle®/CA State Parks

FIG. 20
Tapestry from the *tenture d'Albon* (Brussels, ca. 1550)
The Continence of Scipio
The Great Hall, Hearst Castle
Photograph by Victoria Garagliano/©Hearst Castle®/CA State Parks

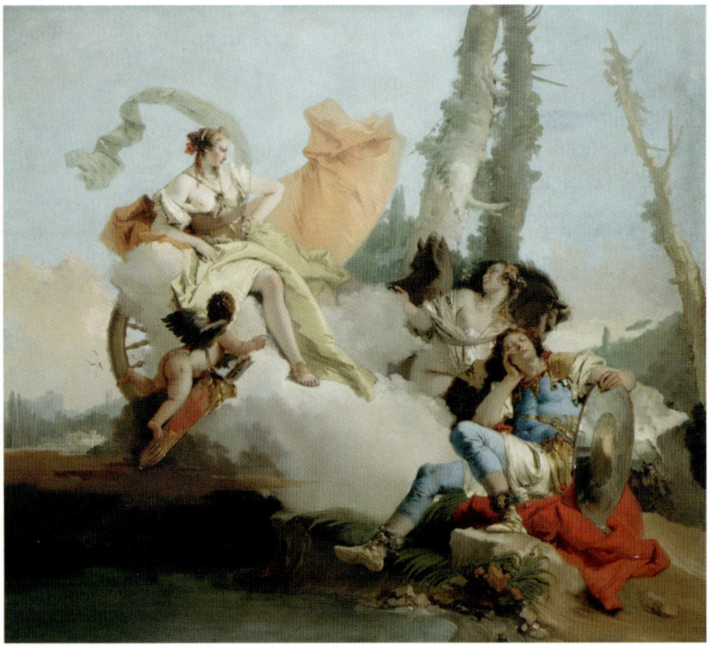

FIG. 21
Giovanni Battista Tiepolo (Italian, 1696–1770)
Rinaldo Enchanted by Armida
Oil on canvas, 73 11/16 x 85⅜ in. (187.5 x 216.8 cm)
The Art Institute of Chicago, Bequest of James Deering, 1925.700
Photography © The Art Institute of Chicago

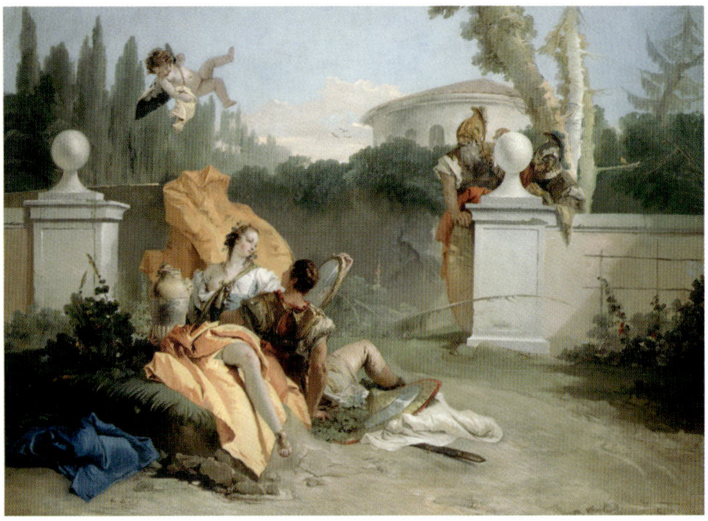

FIG. 22
Giovanni Battista Tiepolo (Italian, 1696–1770)
Rinaldo and Armida in Her Garden
Oil on canvas, 73½ x 102⅛ in. (186.7 x 259.4 cm)
The Art Institute of Chicago, Bequest of James Deering, 1925.699
Photography © The Art Institute of Chicago

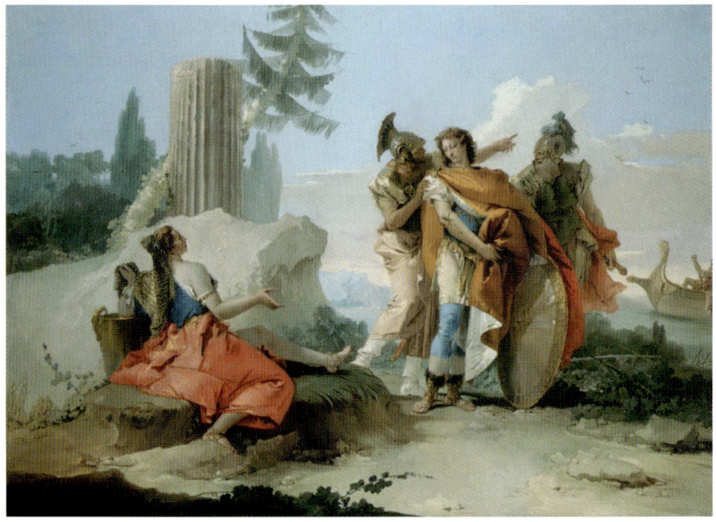

FIG. 23
Giovanni Battista Tiepolo (Italian, 1696–1770)
Armida Abandoned by Rinaldo
Oil on canvas, 73½ x 102⅛ in. (186.7 x 259.4 cm)
The Art Institute of Chicago, Bequest of James Deering, 1925.701
Photography © The Art Institute of Chicago

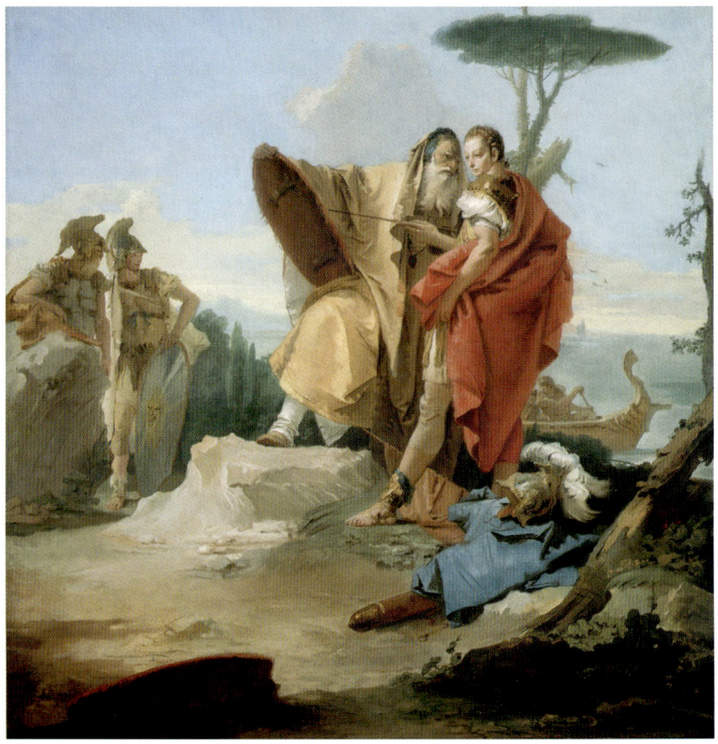

FIG. 24
Giovanni Battista Tiepolo (Italian, 1696–1770)
Rinaldo and the Magus of Ascalon
Oil on canvas, 72 x 74 in. (182.9 x 188 cm)
The Art Institute of Chicago, Bequest of James Deering, 1925.702
Photography © The Art Institute of Chicago

These have a somewhat complicated history. They are first recorded in the Serbelloni collection in, surprisingly, Ca' Pisano a San Stefano in Venice, at an uncertain date. By 1908 they were with Giulio Cartier in Genoa, and by 1912, with Charles Sedelmayer in Paris. By 1913 they are said to have been in Vizcaya, James Deering's fabulous house in Miami. This building, inspired by the Villa Rezzonico at Bassano del Grappa and now the Vizcaya Museum, was under construction from 1914-16, and it seemed very likely that the paintings may have been purchased with this project in mind. John Singer Sargent, a longtime friend of Charles Deering, visited the house in 1917 and made many watercolours of the house and its surroundings, but none seem to show interiors with the paintings in place,[42] nor do any of the period photographs of the interiors of Vizcaya, published by James T. Maher.[43] In fact, through the kindness of Flaminia Gennari Santori, it has become evident that the four Tiepolos never formed part of the decorations of Vizcaya, but were hung in James Deering's apartment in Chicago.

On the other hand, she has pointed out to me another link between Vizcaya and Tiepolo. In the gardens are two statues, inscribed *Ganimede* and *Leda*, of unknown origin, but attributed to the circle of the Marinali of Verona.[44] *Ganimede* (fig. 25) is clearly linked with a drawing by Giambattista Tiepolo (fig. 26), one of a series of seventeen known drawings out of thirty, recorded in an inventory of works belonging to Count Francesco Algarotti (1712-1764).[45] Even the lettering at the foot is the same as that of the drawing. The second, *Leda* (fig. 27), is equally clearly linked with a drawing by Domenico Tiepolo (1727-1804) in the Lehman collection (fig. 28),[46] which is evidently a copy of one of the missing drawings of the Algarotti series. Apart from a series of drawings in the Victoria and Albert Museum, which can be associated with two sculptured groups of *Rinaldo and Armida* that stand before the Villa Cordellina, these are the only drawings for sculpture that can actually be associated with a known piece,[47] thus proving that at least some of the designs were actually carved.

Flaminia Gennari Santori has also kindly brought to my attention the large Venetian ceiling in the casino or garden pavilion at Vizcaya. Measuring some 50′ by 30′, it consists of an elaborate architectural surround, possibly by the *quadraturista* Agostino Mengozzi-Colonna[48] with numerous figures inserted *en grisaille*, described as Tiepolesco, which may be given with some confidence to Jacopo Guarana (1720-1808) (fig. 29). All this in fresco, but with the central part of the decoration missing, was bought in fragments from Dino Barozzi in Venice in 1914. The casino was completed in 1920 and the missing central part of

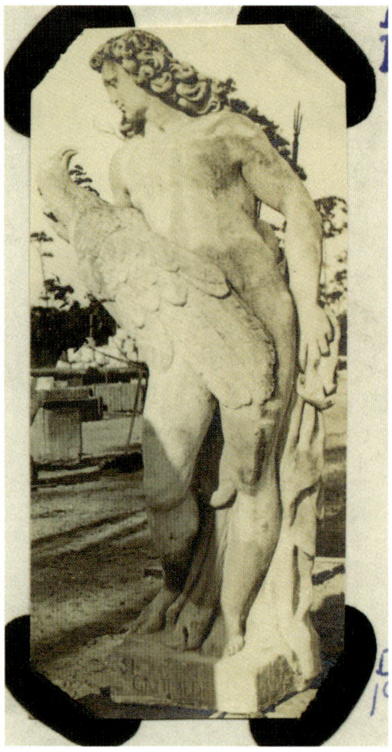

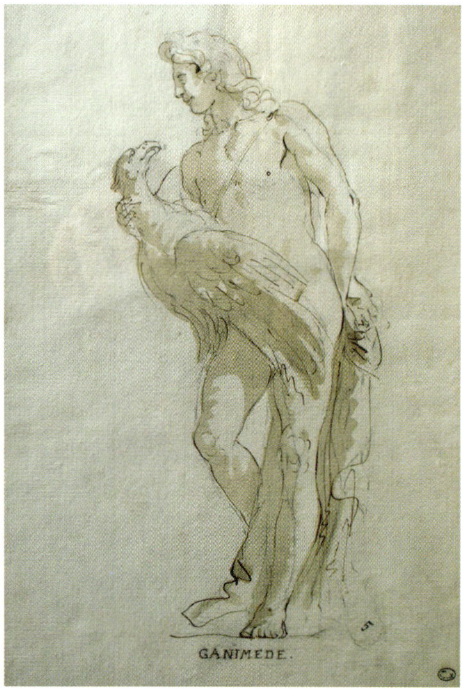

FIG. 25
Garden sculpture (Italian ca. 1750), after a drawing by Giovanni Battista Tiepolo; possibly from the workshop of Angelo Marinali (1654–1702)
Ganimede
Limestone, 84 x 27 x 27 in. (213.36 x 68.58 x 68.58 cm)
Vizcaya Museum and Gardens, Miami, Florida

FIG. 26
Giovanni Battista Tiepolo (Italian, 1696–1770)
Ganimede
Pen and brown ink, brown wash over black chalk,
$11\frac{3}{8}$ x $7\frac{5}{8}$ in. (29.0 x 19.5 cm)
Private Collection, Paris

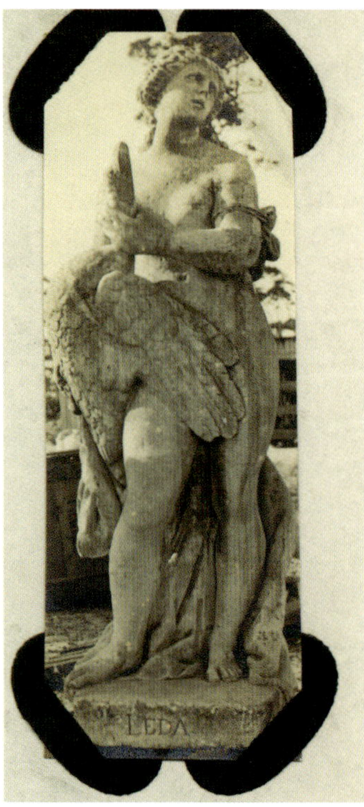

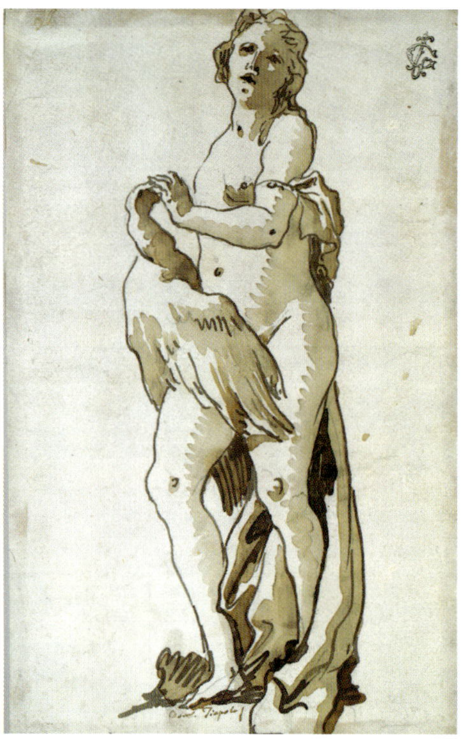

FIG. 27
Garden sculpture (Italian, ca. 1750), after a lost drawing by Giovanni Battista Tiepolo, (Italian, 1696–1770)
Leda and the Swan
Limestone
Vizcaya Museum and Gardens, Miami, Florida

FIG. 28
Giovanni Domenico Tiepolo (Italian, 1727–1804), after a lost drawing by Giovanni Battista Tiepolo
Leda, ca. 1747–1804
Pen and brown ink, gray wash, over black chalk,
10 x $5\frac{7}{16}$ in. (25.4 x 13.8 cm)
Robert Lehman Collection, 1975 (1975.1.493)
The Metropolitan Museum of Art, New York, NY, U.S.A.
Image copyright The Metropolitan Museum of Art/Art Resource, NY

the ceiling was completed in tempera by a young Swiss painter, Paul Thevanaz (1881-1921), with singularly happy results. Sadly, we have no information as to the origins of this fine monumental decoration, but it is presumably a work of the 1770s.[49]

In 1969 it was argued that the Chicago canvases were the major part of a larger complex representing the decoration of a room, including four vertical pieces in the National Gallery, London, three overdoors, two of them with the Norton Simon Foundation in Pasadena, and a ceiling, also in the Norton Simon Museum (fig. 30), all dateable ca. 1742. It was further proposed that the room might be identified as a grand apartment in the great Sansovino palace, Ca' Dolfin-Manin a Rialto, now the Banca d'Italia.[50]

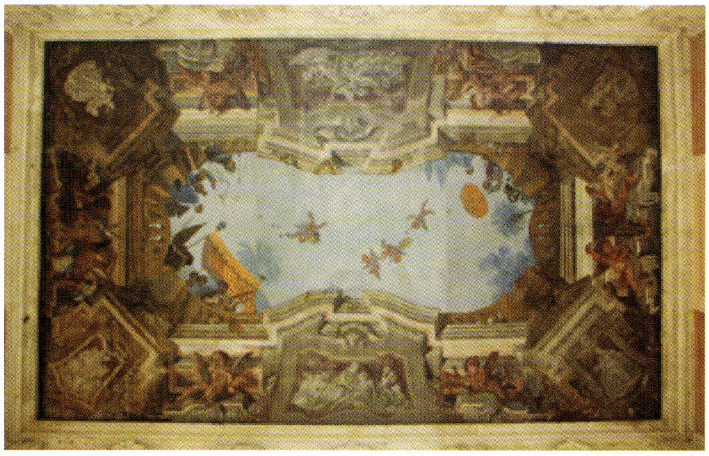

The ceiling has a particular interest since it was purchased in Venice, probably in the 1840s, by Edward Cheney (1803-1884), an Englishman whose fortune derived from the iron industry in Shropshire. In this way he prefigures the great American magnates. He lived in Venice for many years and visited the city frequently, and he built up a remarkable and varied collection.[51] An important group of Tiepolo oil sketches and nine albums of Tiepolo drawings were auctioned off at his death, with much else, but the ceilings remained at Cheney's Badger Hall until 1935, when they were sold to Contini-Bonacossi, from whom they passed to Norton Simon, to the National Gallery of Australia, and to the National Gallery of Art.

The link between the ceiling, which has a certain Manin provenance, and the rest of the paintings is questioned by Massimo Gemin and Filippo Pedrocco, and by William Barcham,[52] and the matter was further complicated by the discovery of documents by Giandomenico Romanelli describing a Tasso room by Tiepolo in Ca' Corner-Mocenigo a San Polo, dateable circa 1750.[53] This consisted of four large oblong compositions with Tasso subjects, together with overdoors and a ceiling. Romanelli suggested that this could well be the Tasso room that I had placed in Ca' Dolfin-Manin a Rialto and dated 1742. I have recently returned to this problem with a fine set of drawings by Giambattista on Tasso subjects in the Victoria and Albert Museum, which could well be connected with the Tasso room of Ca' Corner-Mocenigo.[54] The ceiling of this room may well be the *Peace and Justice* purchased by Nélie Jacquemart in Venice in 1893 and preserved in the Musée Jacquemart-André.[55] This is one of two ceilings from the Casa Reverdin in Venice. Reverdin is established as a factotum of the Corner family who purchased from them Ca' Corner-Mocenigo.[56]

FIG. 29
Jacopo Guarana (Italian, 1720-1808) and Agostino Mengozzi Colonna (Italian, 1725-1791)
[attribution recently suggested by George Knox]
Decorative ceiling with figure painting and quadratura
Fresco, detached and remounted on wood panels and distemper mounted on wood panels, overall dimensions 50 ft. x 29 ft. 8 in. (1467 x 888 cm); The border panels were acquired as "Tiepoleschi"; they are Venetian work, ca. 1770; The center panels were added by Paul Thevenaz (Swiss, 1891-1921), ca. 1920. Vizcaya Museum and Gardens, Miami, Florida

Conclusion

The bequest of James Deering of four great Tiepolos to the Art Institute of Chicago in 1925 marks the end of an era. Most of the great houses of the so-called "gilded age" have survived some initial neglect, and their future as public institutions is as secure as anything can be in this insecure age. From white elephants they have become geese laying golden eggs. But the process goes on, though without the assistance of the titans of American industry. We may note, as a recent development, the case of the two Tiepolo ceilings from the Palazzo Onigo at Treviso, which were removed to Milan in 1905, then to Paris, and were acquired, one by the Rhode Island School of Design in 1932, and the other by the Ringling Museum at Sarasota in 1940.[57] The focus now shifts to the great museums, and we find the Metropolitan Museum of Art creating a Tiepolo Room at the head of the main staircase, in which the three magnificent canvases from Ca' Dolfin a San Pantalon greet us and lead the way to the French, Italian, and Modern schools of painting.[58] Likewise the two vast and superb paintings by Giovanni Antonio Guardi (1699-1760), from his magnificent Tasso cycle,[59] on the staircase of the National Gallery of Art, welcome us and introduce us to the treasures to come within. This is the apotheosis of Venetian history painting of the Settecento.

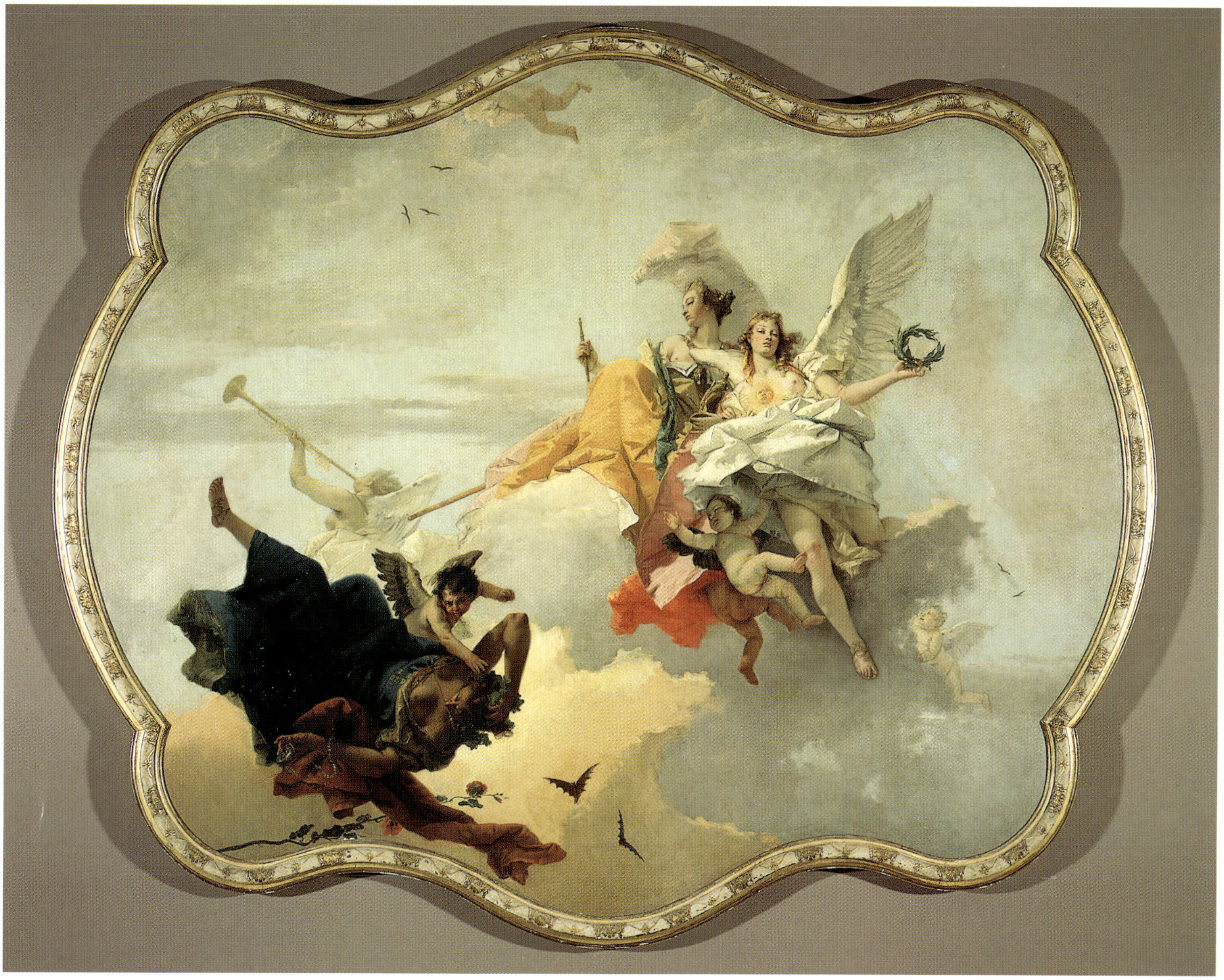

FIG. 30
Giovanni Battista Tiepolo (Italian, 1696–1770)
The Triumph of Virtue and Nobility Over Ignorance
Oil on canvas, 117¾ x 149¼ in. (299 x 379 cm)
The Norton Simon Foundation

Endnotes

1 Alessandro Bettagno, "Un soffitto ritrovato di Palazzo Pisani," in *Arte Veneta* 29 (1975): 224-6.

2 George Knox, *Giambattista and Domenico Tiepolo: A Study and Catalogue Raisonné of the Chalk Drawings* (Oxford, Clarendon Press, 1980: 23-25, pls.65-68).

3 For other details of Rothschild patronage, see George Knox, "Giambattista: A Forgotten Ceiling," in *Venezia—Arte e storia,* ed. Letizia Caselli, Jacopo Scarpa, Giordana Trovabene (Venice: Ateo Veneto, 2005: 132-9).

4 Stéphane Loire, "Tiepolo et le goût français depuis le XVIIIme siècle," in *Giambattista Tiepolo nel terzo centenario della nascità,* ed. Lionello Puppi (Venice: Quaderni di Venezia Artis, 1998: 291-9); Jean-Pierre Babelon and Nicolas Sainte-Fare Garnot, *Les Fresques de Tiepolo* (Paris: Noesis, 1998: 96-9), gives an excellent account of the discovery of the frescoes and their removal to Paris.

5 For the architecture of Ca' Pisani, see Remigio Massobello and Maria Tarla, "L'architettura di Palazzo Pisani" in *Il Conservatorio di Musica Benedetto Marcello di Venezia* 1876-1976: Centenario della Fondazione (Venice: Palazzo Pisani, Venezia, 1977: 109-33).

6 For a full description see Lino Moretti, "I Pisani di Santo Stefano e le opera d'arte del loro palazzo," in *Il Conservatorio,* 135-81. The ceiling in The Marble House is discussed and reproduced on pp. 178-9.

7 George Knox, *Antonio Pellegrini, 1675-1741* (Oxford: Clarendon Press, 1995: 165, pl. 131); citing a longer description of the painting by Pietro Edwards.

8 Antonio Morassi, in *Emporium* (1958): 195, pls. 1-5; Antonio Morassi, *A Complete Catalogue of the Paintings of G. B. Tiepolo* (London: Phaidon Press, 1962: 6); Knox, *Antonio Pellegrini,* 159-65, pls. 129, 130.

9 Moretti, "I Pisani," 173, pls. 41, 42; Knox, *Antonio Pellegrini,* pls.129-30.

10 Giuseppe Pavanello, "Antonio Gai Statues for Palazzo Pisani Discovered in Baltimore," *The Journal of the Walters Art Museum,* 60/61 (2002/4): 27-31.

11 The first of the four, as illustrated by Pavanello, *Euterpe?/Concordia?,* clearly shows a lady carrying the bundle of lictor's rods, a symbol associated with Justice.

12 Giovanni Battista Tiepolo is also known as Gianbattista or Giambattista Tiepolo; Aldo Rizzi, *I Tiepolo a Udine* (Milan: Electa, 1996: 54-56).

13 Giorgio Vigni, *Disegni del Tiepolo* (Padua: Le Tre Venezia, 1942: 8-22).

14 George Knox, "Some Tiepolo Drawings in the Collection of Francesco Algarotti: *30 lavés statues,*" in *Per l'Arte da Venezia all'Europa,* ed. Mario Piantoni, Laura de Rossi (Venice: Edizioni della Laguna, 2001: 471-4, pls. 677-87).

15 Giuseppe Pavanello, "Tiepolo e la scultura: della copia all'invenzione," in *Giambattista Tiepolo nel terzo centenario,* ed. Lionello Puppi (Venice: Il Poligrafo, 1998, 165-70); Paola Rossi, "Giambattista Tiepolo e la scultura del suo tempo," in *Giambattista Tiepolo,* 171-6.

16 Rossi in *Giambattista Tiepolo,* pls.1, 2.

17 It was part of the vast collection of works of art in the Palazzo Accoramboni, for which Walters paid one million dollars; George Knox, "Giambatttista Tiepolo in Baltimore: A Painting in Search of a Subject," *Apollo* (May 1996: 15-7); exh. cat., *Giambattista Tiepolo, 1696-1770* (New York: Metropolitan Museum of Art, 1996, 60-4).

18 For a full and sympathetic account of Trumbauer, see James T. Maher, *The Twilight of Splendor,* (Boston: Little, Brown and Company, 1975), in the chapter on Whitemarsh Hall. Maher planned to give an account of "The Elms" in a subsequent volume, *A Season of Splendor,* but this was prevented by his death.

19 George Knox, "Pagani, Pellegrini and Piazzetta: from Ca' Corner to 'the Elms,'" *Apollo* cx (November 1979): 428-37, pls. 1, 2.

20 Pompeo Molmenti, *Tiepolo* (Milan: Ulrico Hoepli, 1909: 284).

21 Knox, "Pagani," pl. 15.

22 Ibid., pl. XI.

23 Ibid., pl.17; Marina Magrini, "Il Fontebasso nei palazzi veneziani," in *Arte Veneta* 28 (1974): pl. 286, shows the ceiling in its original position; Marina Magrini, *Francesco Fontebasso,* (Venice: Neri Pozza, 1988: no. 111, pl.54).

24 Bettagno, "Un soffitto"; Alberto Craievich, *Antonio Molinari* (Soncino: Edizioni del Soncino, 2005: pl. 94a).

25 Vincenzo da Canal, *Vita di Gregorio Lazzarini* (Venice: G. A. Moschini, 1809: lvii); Knox, "Pagani," 1979, pl. 13.

26 Knox, "Pagani," pls.10, 11, 12; Craievich, *Antonio Molinari,* pls. 94c, 94d.

27 Knox, "Pagani," pl. 16; Monbeig Goguel, "Drawings by Antonio Molinari in the Louvre," Master Drawings 23-24, 1985-86, Bo. 28, pl. 48b; Sonja Brink, *Die Zeichnungen des Antonio Molinari* (Düsseldorf: Museum Kunst Palast, 2005, n.s. 27, 28; figs. 28a, 28b); Craievitch, *Antonio Molinari,* pls. 94d, 94e.

28 Bettagno, "Un soffitto"; Knox, "Pagani," pl. 3; Knox, *Giambattista Piazetta, 1682-1754* (Oxford: Clarendon Press, 1992: pl. 34); Knox, *Antonio Pellegrini,* pl. 31.

29 Knox, "Pagani," pl. 4, 5; Knox, *Giambattista Piazzetta,* pl. 35, 36; Knox, *Antonio Pellegrini,* pl. 32.

30 Knox, "Pagani," pl. 7; Knox, *Giambattista Piazzeta* 1982, pl. 37.

31 Lino Moretti, "Antonio Molinari rivisitato," *Arte Veneta* 33 (1989—Addendum): 69.

32 George Knox, "The Camerino of Francesco Corner," *Arte Veneta* 32 (1978): 70-84.

33 Inv. 53.225.8-11. Edith Standen, *European Post-Medieval Tapestries* (New York: Metropolitan Museum of Art, 1985: 294-307). I am grateful to Paul Miller of Newport for drawing my attention to the Berwind bequest.

34 Knox, *Giambattista Piazetta,* 16-17, pls. 18-25.

35 Federico Zeri and Elizabeth Gardner, *Italian Paintings, Venetian School* (New York: Metropolitan Museum of Art, 1973: 29-31, pls. 30-3). For a further note on these pictures, see George Knox, "An Italian Harpsichord and the Search for Nicolo Guardi," in *Arte/Documento* 17, 18, 19 (2003): 532-5.

36 See Wikipedia for useful notes on both men. Honeysuckle Lodge is currently for sale.

37 George Knox, "Giambattista Tiepolo: Queen Zenobia and Ca' Zenobio, *una delle prime sue fatture," Burlington Magazine* 121 (July 1979): 400-18; see Diane de Grazia and Eric Garberson, *Italian Paintings of the 17th and 18th Centuries,* (Washington, D.C.: National Gallery of Art, 1996: 309-17) for some alternative views.

38 Janet Seiz and George Knox, "Un soffitto attribuito a Gaspare Diziani e ai Valeriani al Butterworth Center di Moline," *Arte Veneta* 61 (2005): 228-32.

39 Egidio Martini, *Pittura veneta* (Rimini: Stefano Patacconi, 1992: 408-11 [reproduced in color].

40 Knox, *Giambattista Piazetta*, pls. 14-17.

41 George Knox, "Some notes on large paintings...," in *Atti... Ricci* (Udine: Electa, 1975: 96-105, pls. 98-100); Knox, *Giambattista Piazetta*, pls. 22-25.

42 See Google, under Vizcaya Sargent.

43 Maher, *Twilight of Splendor,* 159-214, pls. 147-158, gives an admirable account of the house and its owner.

44 Purchased from Eugene Glaentzer, in New York in 1913, as French. I am grateful to Flaminia Gennari Santori of Miami for this information.

45 George Knox, "Some Tiepolo Drawings in the Collection of Francesco Algarotti: *30 lavés statues*," in *Per l'Arte da Venezia all'Europa* (Venice: Edizioni della Laguna, 2001: 471-4, pls. 677-87, no. 5, pl. 5); George Knox, *A Panorama of Tiepolo Drawings* (Riemst: Gallery Kekko, 2008: pl. 19). A copy by Domenico Tiepolo (1727-1804), Giambattista's son, also a Venetian painter and printmaker, is also illustrated (fig. 19).

46 James Byam Shaw and George Knox, *The Robert Lehman Collection, VI: Italian Eighteenth-Century Drawings* (New York, The Metropolitan Museum of Art, in association with Princeton University Press, 1987: no. 136 [reproduced]). It also appears in *The scenes of contemporary life*, in *A Garden with statues*—see Adelheid M. Gealt & George Knox, *Scene di vita quotidiana…* , (Venice: Marsilio, 2005: pl. 45), and again in the *Divertimento per li ragazzi*, pl. 92, James Byam Shaw, *The Drawings of Domenico Tiepolo* (London: Faber & Faber, 1962: pl. 94).

47 George Knox, *Catalogue of the Tiepolo Drawings in the Victoria and Albert Museum*, (1st ed., London: HMSO, 1960: pls. 74-80, fig. V); Giovanni Mariacher, "Le sculture di Villa Cordellina." In *I Tiepolo e il Settecento Vicentino*, exh. cat. (Vicenza: Electa, 1990: 321-8).

48 Son of the quadraturista Gerolamo Mengossi-Colonna (1688-1772) who collaborated frequently with Giambattista Tiepolo. With Guarana, he signed and dated the very pleasant decorations of the Music Room of the Ospedaletto in 1776.

49 The invocation of the names of Agostino Mengozzi Colonna and Jacopo Guarana in this context is prompted by a reading of Ileana Chiappini di Sorio, "Affreschi settecenteschi veneziani: Palazzo Mocenigo", *Notizie di Palazzo Albani, III* (1974: pls. 13, 14, 15, 16)—erratum slip as: *Pttore Tiepoloesco della fine del sec. xviii; (Gian Domenico?)*; di Sorio, "Palazzo Pisani-Moretta… ," *Notizie di Palazzo Albani*, 1983, 264-73; di Sorio, "L'apothosi dei Foscarini nel Palazzo ai Carmini," *Arte/Documento* 23 (2007): 202-9.

50 George Knox, "The Tasso Cycles of Giambattista Tiepolo and Gianantonio Guardi," in *Museum Studies* 9 (Chicago 1978): 49-95.

51 Knox, *Catalogue of the Tiepolo Drawings*, 4-8; Knox, "Some notes on large paintings, 4-9; Tim Knox "Edward Cheney of Badger Hall: A Forgotten Collector of Italian Sculpture," *The Sculpture Journal* 16 (2007). George Knox, a biographical note on Edward Cheney, is awaiting publication by the Albertina, Vienna.

52 Massimo Gemin and Filippo Pedrocco, *Giambattista Tiepolo: I dipinti*, (Venice: Arsenale Editrice, 1993: 356-60, pls. 284-94, 381); William Barcham in exh. cat., *Giambattista Tiepolo*, 1696-1770 (New York: The Metropolitan Museum of Art, 1996: 134-47, no. 17 [numerous excellent illustrations]).

53 Giandomenico Romanelli, "Giambattista Tiepolo e i Cornaro di San Polo," in *Giambattista Tiepolo nel terzo centenario della nascità*, ed. Lionello Puppi (Venice: Il Poligrafo, 2008: 215-24).

54 George Knox, "The mystery of the Tasso Room of Ca' Corner," in *Un identità … in ricordo di Aldo Rizzi*, ed. Giuseppe Maria Pilo (Venice: Edizioni della Laguna, 2007: 339-42, pls. 499-501); Knox, *A Panorama of Tiepolo Drawings*, pls.39-42.

55 Morassi, *Complete Catalogue… Tiepolo*, pl. 398; Babelon and Garnot, *Les Fresques de Tiepolo*, 63, pl. 10—*Peace and Justice.*

56 The second ceiling, Babelon and Garnot, *Les Fresques de Tiepolo*, 65, pls. 8, 9—*The Apotheosis of Hercules*—may be given to Fabio Canal.

57 They are recorded *in situ* in two excellent photographs by Giovanni Ferretto—see Andrea Bellieni, "Da Treviso al USA: i soffitti di Palazzo Onigo," in *L'impegno e le conoscenza … in onore di Egidio Martini*, ed. Filippo Pedrocco and Alberto Craievich (Venice: Scripta, 2009: 299-309). The Providence ceiling, *Fame*, is given to Giambattista; the Sarasota ceiling, *Aurora*, is given to Domenico(?). I think that a strong case can be made for giving both ceilings to Domenico Tiepolo—cf. exh. cat., *Tiepolo* (Stuttgart: Stuttgarter Galerieverein e V, 1970: pl. 176); Aldo Rizzi, *Etchings of the Tiepolos* (London: Phaidon Press, 1971, pl. 64).

58 George Knox "Tiepolo Triumphant: The Roman Histories of Ca' Dolfin," *Apollo* (Nov. 1991): 301-10; Keith Christiansen, "The decorations for Ca' Dolfin," in exh. cat. *Tiepolo*, (New York: Metropolitan Museum of Art, 1996: 86-103); Keith Christiansen, "The Ca' Dolfin Tiepolos," *The Metropolitan Museum of Art Bulletin* (Spring 1998): 1-60.

59 Knox, "Tasso Cycles of Tiepolo and Guardi," pls. 28, 29; de Grazia and Garberson, *Italian Paintings of the 17th and 18th Centuries*, 147-57.

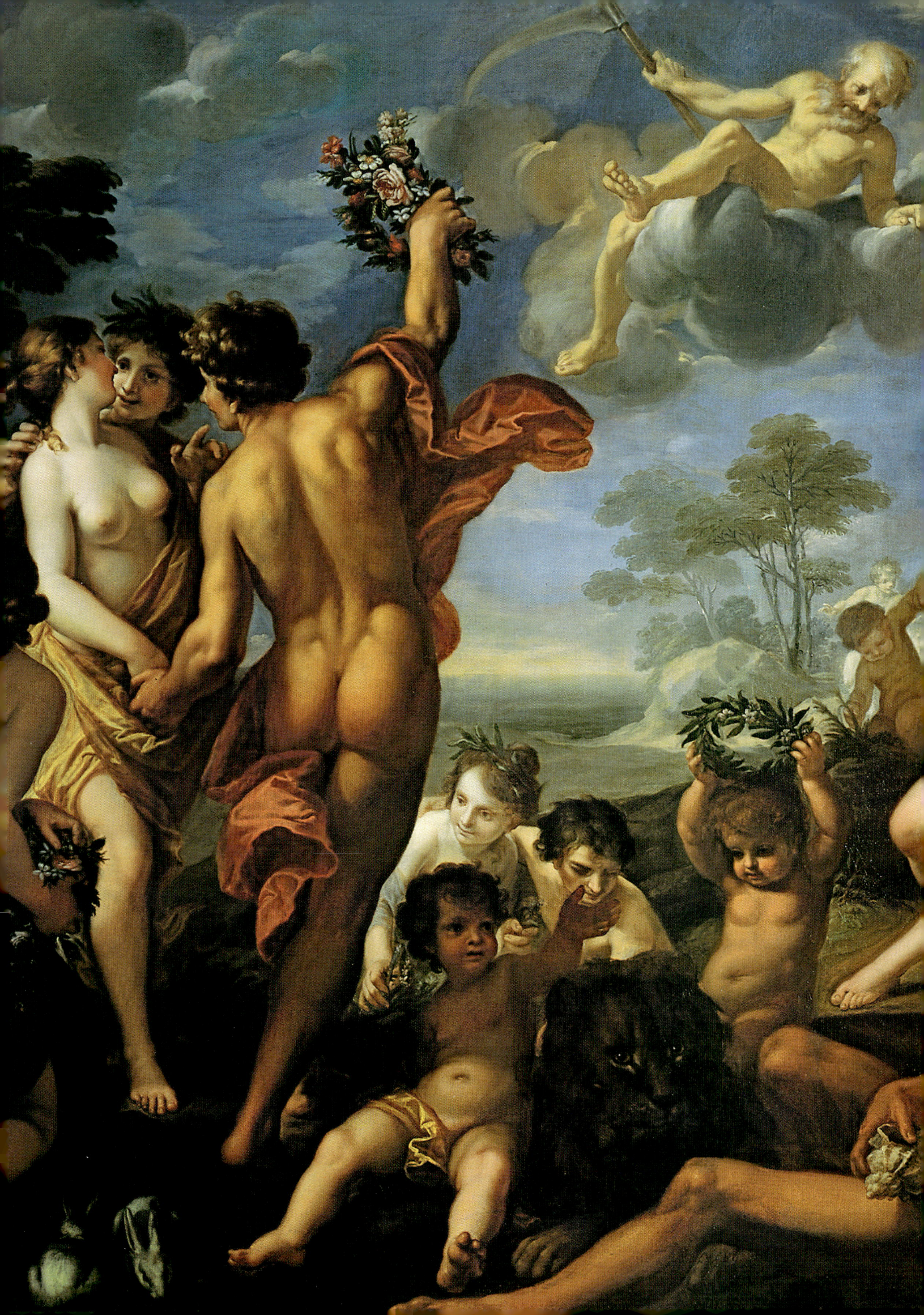

Parallels in Roman Baroque and Venetian Art

Allison Lee Palmer

Venice remains unique in both its artistic culture and its relationship to the rest of Italy, and this is particularly true in the eighteenth century.[1] From its origins as a cluster of fishing communities in the lagoon region along the northeastern Italic peninsula, the Republic of Venice grew into one of the most powerful maritime cities in the world. Its Byzantine heritage, proximity to northern Europe, and its political ideology—distinct from Central Italy and far from classical influences—made for a richly and decidedly unique history. Despite its differences from the rest of Italy, however, Venice, as the starting point for the crusades, maintained an important symbiotic relationship with the papacy and the rest of the Italic peninsula and was therefore important to the history of Italy from the Middle Ages, when the city was first called La Serenissima, onward. Monumental stone architecture and a thriving artistic culture emerged, and soon after, monumental altarpieces and historical paintings began to appear in churches, *scuole,* homes, and civic buildings across the city. In addition to these religious, historical, and mythological works, *vedute* paintings, a subject that originated in Rome, began to dominate the burgeoning Grand Tour art market in Venice.[2]

By the eighteenth century, a great stylistic variety could be found in Venice, with Rococo paintings appearing next to paintings done *alla Romana.*[3] Venetian artworks featuring mythological and religious scenes were often based on Roman Baroque sources, and painter Gregorio Lazzarini (1655–1730), one of the earliest eighteenth-century Romanists working in Venice, epitomizes this type of painter. Lazzarini's connections to Rome were cultivated by his instruction with Genovese painter Francesco Rosa (?–1687), who had completed a number of commissions in Rome before returning to Venice to work.[4] Lazzarini is represented in this exhibition by his large mythological painting called alternatively *The Golden Age* or *A Bacchanal,* ca. 1700 (cat. 10), which reveals a crisply delineated pastoral scene that was likely created for a Venetian villa or palace, where it would have covered the major portion of an audience hall or drawing room.[5] The scene depicts several groups of young, semi-clad dancing figures, some crowned with laurel branches, while Father Time appears above to remind the youth of the fleeting aspect of time.

Gregorio Lazzarini (Italian, 1655–1730)
DETAIL: *The Golden Age (A Bacchanal),* ca. 1700
(CAT. 10)

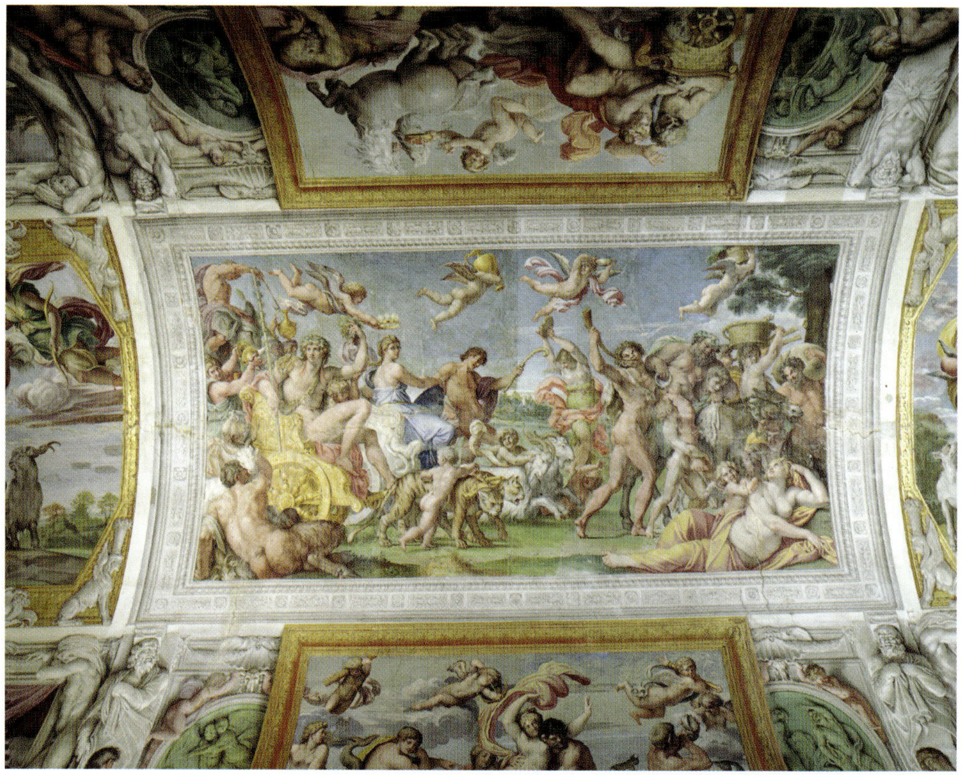

FIG. 1
Annibale Carracci (Italian, 1560–1609)
The 'Galleria di Carracci' (Carracci Hall) detail of the *The Triumph of Bacchus,* 1597–1604; Fresco
Palazzo Farnese, Rome, Italy/ The Bridgeman Art Library

The painting is similar in theme to Venetian Renaissance painter Titian's *Bacchanal of the Andrians* (1523–25; Madrid, Prado Museum), which was part of a cycle of paintings commissioned for the private home of the Duke of Ferrara, but the *vanitas* subtext of Father Time, absent in Titian's celebratory scene, is one that emerged in the Baroque Counter-Reformation. Stylistically, the image is consistent with the work of Annibale Carracci (1560–1609), whose classical Baroque monumental ceiling fresco, *The Triumph of Bacchus,* in Rome was begun in 1597 (fig. 1). Carracci's work forms the central image of the *Loves of the Gods* series painted in the gallery of the Farnese Palace in Rome.[6] The subject from Ovid's *Metamorphoses,* which dates to the first century A.D., was introduced at the Medici Neoplatonic Academy in Florence during the Renaissance and quickly became popular throughout Central Italy. Ovid's text was the primary source of information for over two hundred mythological tales, many of which focus on the themes of love, loyalty, and change. Carracci's monumental fresco cycle, which established a stylistic shift away from Mannerism and toward a widely popular classicizing Baroque style, featured a series of scenes surrounding the central *Triumph* that featured the lovers Jupiter and Juno, Diana and Endymion, Hercules and Iole, Venus and Anchises, and several others, set in square panels separated by medallions, and framed nude male caryatid figures done in grisaille to resemble sculpture. While the muscularity of these figures recalls the Renaissance *ignudi* in Michelangelo's Sistine ceiling frescoes, Annibale Carracci also studied classical sarcophagi to cultivate his own restrained "grand manner" *quadro riportato* ceiling. A century later, Lazzarini's oil on canvas *Bacchanal*, one of several bacchanal scenes he painted for various domestic settings in the Veneto, reveals a mixture of classical grandeur with a more frivolous and sentimental character that anticipates the Rococo.

Venetian painter Sebastiano Ricci also worked in the late Roman Baroque painting tradition, as seen in his mythological painting of *Diana and Endymion* (ca. 1717-20) in this exhibition (cat. 16).[7] Ricci traveled extensively and brought back to Venice an international approach to painting that incorporated Roman classicism in the manner of Pietro da Cortona (1596-1669) with a softly saturated Venetian color. In this painting, we find the idea of Platonic love and ideal beauty expressed by Diana, who encounters the beautiful, youthful shepherd Endymion.[8] The scene, set in the soft moonlight, depicts the barely clad Endymion reclining asleep on a red robe while Diana, accompanied by her dogs and surrounded by cupid figures, leans over a softly painted rock and gazes at Endymion. The scene anticipates her kiss, which solidifies her love for Endymion. While Nicolas Poussin's version from 1630 in the Detroit Institute of Arts reveals a more linear approach to this mythological love scene, the tenebrism of Ricci's work draws upon the Caravaggisti traditions in Rome blended with a sweetness and sentimentality found in the Rococo.

Antonio Bellucci was perhaps the first Venetian artist to work extensively in Northern Europe, where his mingling of the Roman Baroque and Rococo was embraced in England, Vienna, and Düsseldorf.[9] Bellucci's religious image, the *Adoration of the Magi* (ca. 1700) in this exhibition (cat. 3), reveals a scene that draws equally from Venetian Renaissance and Roman Baroque works. The clearly delineated painting reveals the Virgin and Christ Child to the left, seated on a humble wooden platform and adored by a Magus kneeling before them, while two other Magi arrive to the left of the scene, one looking out to the viewer while the African Magus arrives on horseback. The rich colors and the dramatic silhouettes recall Titian's style of painting, and indeed the playful Christ Child who holds the Virgin's mantle above his head is a clear quotation from Titian's *Pesaro Madonna* (1519-26; Venice, Church of Santa Maria Gloriosa dei Frari). At the same time, the anatomy of the semi-clad muscular servant and the close attention paid to the tactile qualities of the satins and silks reveal the influence of such Romanists as Carlo Maratti (1625-1713), whose *Baptism of Christ*, commissioned in 1695 (Rome, Santa Maria degli Angeli), reveals a similar use of *chiaroscuro* to define the muscular body of Christ.[10]

Finally, Giovanni Battista Tiepolo, who trained with Lazzarini but was also influenced by his Venetian elders Ricci and Giovanni Battista Piazzetta,[11] is perhaps the best-known Venetian painter to receive international acclaim for his work across northern Italy in Udine, Bergamo, and Milan, and then in Würzburg and Madrid.[12] Tiepolo was known for his large works, which include an oil-on-canvas mythological scene of *Juno Triumphant, as Queen of the Air* (ca. 1735), featured in this exhibition (cat. 20). Here we see an image *di sotto in sù* that reveals Juno, the Roman goddess of marriage, seated in a majestic pose on her chariot pulled by peacocks, which were her main attribute from the Hellenistic era onward. Stories of Juno, found in Ovid's *Metamorphoses*, were revived in the Renaissance, and they typically focused on her as the jealous wife of Jupiter who sought revenge upon his various consorts. In this painting, Juno looks down upon Luna while Luna, swirling in the clouds below, holds an image of the moon encircled by clouds above her head. The Renaissance version of Luna was Diana, sometimes conflated with Selene, all of whom were considered the goddess of the moon, last seen in Ricci's painting of *Diana and Endymion* in this exhibition (cat. 16).

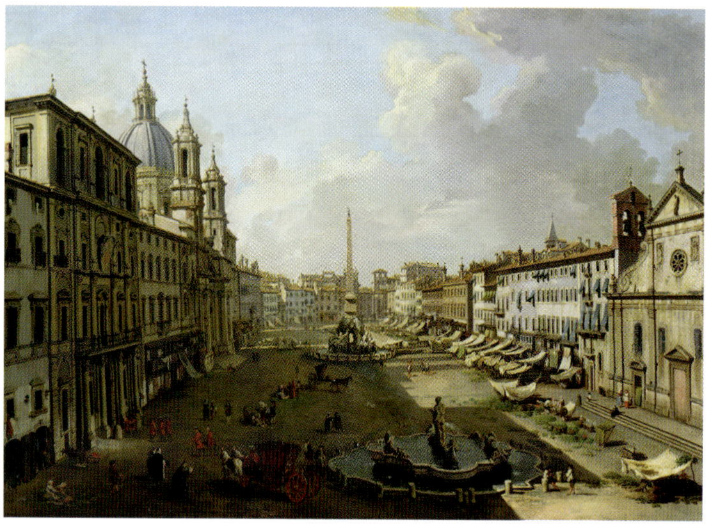

Images of both Jupiter and Juno and Diana and Endymion became very popular across Italy after their appearance in Annibale Carracci's Baroque Farnese fresco cycle and remained popular subjects through the eighteenth century in Venice.

In addition to the monumental religious and mythological scenes found in Venice in the eighteenth century, another important category of artworks, one for which Venice is perhaps best-known, is the *veduta,* or "view" painting. *Vedute* paintings and engravings are also numerous in this exhibition.[13] Such works can be either topographically accurate or more imaginary, and the fantasy-driven landscapes are called *capricci,* or *vedute di fantasia.* The first vedute were created in Rome by Northern European Renaissance artists working in Italy who were drawn to the classical landscape tradition and created either panoramas or closely detailed views of the land, some of which included Roman ruins, in an idealized format called the Italianate landscape.[14] Like the large-scale religious and mythological scenes found in Venice, these eighteenth-century landscape paintings also drew upon Ovid's *Metamorphoses* and express in visual form Ovid's poetic descriptions of the ideal landscape settings in which his mythological narratives unfolded. These classical landscapes were replete with wooded areas, springs, rolling hills, and golden lighting, and in adapting these images to the Venetian urban context, it was specifically the effects of light on water, the atmospheric qualities, and the golden lighting that were most effectively used in vedute.

FIG. 2
Giovanni Paolo Pannini, or Panini
(Italian, 1691/2–1765)
The Piazza Navona in Rome, ca. 1760s
Oil on canvas
Musée des Beaux-Arts, Nantes, France/The Bridgeman Art Library

The market for this genre expanded rapidly from the Renaissance through the Baroque era, as the recognizable landscape was a source of pride to the rising national identity of the newly prosperous mercantile communities in both northern Europe and Italy. The eighteenth-century vedute were similar in conception to earlier "views," but they were specifically connected to the "Grand Tour" tourist trade and therefore reflected an acknowledgement of the *dilettanti* lifestyle and an enlightened, intellectual way of viewing the world. Vedute artists congregated in the most popular cities of the Grand Tour itinerary, including Rome, Naples, and Venice, which by the mid-eighteenth century was the largest producer of vedute.

Roman Baroque artists, such as Giovanni Battista Falda (1640-1678) and eighteenth-century Roman printers Giovanni Paolo Pannini (1691-1765), Giovanni Battista Piranesi (1729-1778), and Giuseppe Vasi (1710-1782), all made etchings and engravings of Rome that were copied and marketed widely, and it was specifically the Venetian architectural engraver Antonio Visentini (1688-1782) who helped to introduce this medium to Venice.[15] Pannini's style in particular influenced the later views of Bellotto and Canaletto.[16] Especially noteworthy is Pannini's *Piazza Navona* (1760s; Nantes, Musée des Beaux-Arts), which reveals a scenic view of one of the most important tourist destinations in Rome from the eighteenth century onward (fig. 2). In this oil painting, Pannini elongates the piazza into a raking view that aggrandizes the square. The Baroque church of Sant'Agnese rises up to the left of the painting as the viewer looks north, and market stalls dot the open area between the lines of buildings. A vast blue sky hangs over the image.

In Venice the Canale and Guardi families, led by Antonio Canaletto and Francesco Guardi, were the most successful families in this line of work. Included in the Venetian school of vedute in the *La Serenissima* exhibit are Antonio Canaletto, Francesco Guardi, Bernardo Bellotto, Luca Carlevarijs, and Michele Marieschi (1696-1743). This exhibition features Canaletto's *View of the Molo, Venice* (cat. 33), from ca. 1725, which reveals an idyllic image of the quay on the south side of Piazza San Marco. The loosely and softly painted view shows the Grand Canal on the left and a raking view of the Doge's Palace to the right, while the orthogonal roofline of the palace draws the viewer's eye back to Baldassare Longhena's Baroque church of Santa Maria della Salute. The still, clear sky provides a calm backdrop to this image of Venice, and it is this restrained, classical tone that establishes a link to Ovid. Carlevarijs's view *The Molo, Venice, Looking West* (cat. 40), from ca. 1709, also featured in this exhibition, provides the same vista but in a more tightly painted image that reveals details such as the unique brickwork on the Doge's Palace to the right, fashionable people milling around the square, and the dock to the left. Longhena's church is loosely painted in the distance. Finally, Guardi's *View of the Dogana and Santa Maria della Salute* (cat. 42), from 1767-69, provides a rustic image of the canal with a mixture of fishing boats, gondolas, and merchant boats unloading cargo down from the Piazza San Marco, while the loosely painted background reveals the ever-present Longhena church.

Focused on Venetian religious and genre paintings and prints, the *La Serenissima* exhibition reveals the rich stylistic variety of eighteenth-century art in Venice; a variety that takes its cue from Rome, but also reflects the unique history of the city as a cultural crossroads between southern and northern Europe, between the east and the west, and identified by its marshlands, canals, and seaports, as well as by its art and architecture, which rivaled that of major cities across Europe.

ENDNOTES

1 See *The Glory of Venice: Art in the Eighteenth Century,* ed. Jane Martineau and Andrew Robinson, exh. cat. (London: Royal Academy of Arts and Washington D.C.: National Gallery of Art, 1994), and Michael Levey, *Painting in Eighteenth-Century Venice* (Ithaca, N.Y.: Cornell University Press, 1959, 1980), for the two main overviews of Venetian art of this era.

2 See Bruce Redford, *Venice and the Grand Tour* (New Haven: Yale University Press, 1996), for this historical overview.

3 Johannes Wilde, *Venetian Art from Bellini to Titian* (Oxford: Clarendon Press, 1974) and Mark Roskill, *Dolce's Aretino and Venetian Art Theory of the Cinquecento* (New York: New York University Press, 1968) are the main sources for Renaissance art in Venice.

4 Gregorio Lazzarini receives scant attention, but an overview of his life can be found in Vincenzo da Canal's, *Vita di Gregorio Lazzarini* (Vinegia: Dalla Stamperia Palese, 1809).

5 The painting was traditionally attributed to Luca Giordano, but was changed to Gregorio Lazzarini in 1982 by Sydney Freedberg (see S. E. Cushing and D. B. Dearinger, *Acquired Tastes: 200 Years of Collecting for the Boston Athanaeum* [Boston: Boston Athanæum: 189, n.54] for this attribution).

6 The main source on this fresco cycle remains Charles Dempsey's *Annibale Carracci, the Farnese Gallery* (New York: G. Braziller, 1995).

7 Jeffrey Daniels, *Sebastiano Ricci* (Hove: Wayland, 1976), remains the standard catalogue and bibliography of Ricci's work.

8 See George Knox, "Sebastiano Ricci at Burlington House: A Venetian Decoration 'alla Romana,'" *Burlington Magazine* 127, no. 950 (Sept. 1985): 601-9, for another possible Diana scene.

9 Fabrizio Magani, *Antonio Bellucci: catalogo ragionato* (Rimini: S. Patacconi, 1995) is one of the few publications on the artist.

10 Francis H. Dowley, "Carlo Maratti, Carlo Fontana, and the Baptismal Chapel in Saint Peter's," *Art Bulletin* 47, no. 1 (1965): 57-81, is the first study focused on this painting. Carlo Maratti, considered a classical Baroque painter similar to Guido Reni and Andrea Sacchi, lacks a recent monographic study.

11 The main monography on Piazzetta is George Knox, *Giambattista Piazzetta, 1682-1754* (Oxford: Clarendon Press, 1992).

12 Tiepolo is the most thoroughly researched of these Venetian artists. The exhibition catalogue *Giambattista Tiepolo, 1696-1770* (New York: Metropolitan Museum of Art, 1996) and Filippo Pedrocco, *Tiepolo: The Complete Paintings* (New York: Rizzoli, 2002), are two well-illustrated recent sources, while the exhibition catalogue *Venice in the Age of Canaletto,* ed. Alexandra Libby, et. al. (Memphis: Brooks Museum of Art, 2009), is the most recent source.

13 See Filippo Pedrocco and Susan Scott, *Venetian Views* (New York: Rizzoli, 2002), for an overview of the subject.

14 See *The Rome of Piranesi: The Eighteenth-Century City in the Great Vedute,* eds, Mario Bevilacqua, et. al. (Rome: Fondazione Cassa di Risparmio di Roma, 2006), for the Roman vedute.

15 John McAndrew, *Antonio Visentini* (Farnborough Hants: Gregg International, 1974) and J. G. Links, *Views of Venice by Canaletto, engraved by Antonio Visentini* (New York, 1971).

16 Alessandro Brogi, *Canaletto e la veduta: Gaspar van Wittel, Giovanni Paolo Pannini, Luca Carlevarijs, Michele Mareschi, Bernardo Bellotto, Francesco Guardi* (Milan: Il Sole 24 ore, 2007).

Antonio Bellucci (Italian, 1654-1726)
DETAIL: *Adoration of the Magi*, ca. 1700
(CAT. 3)

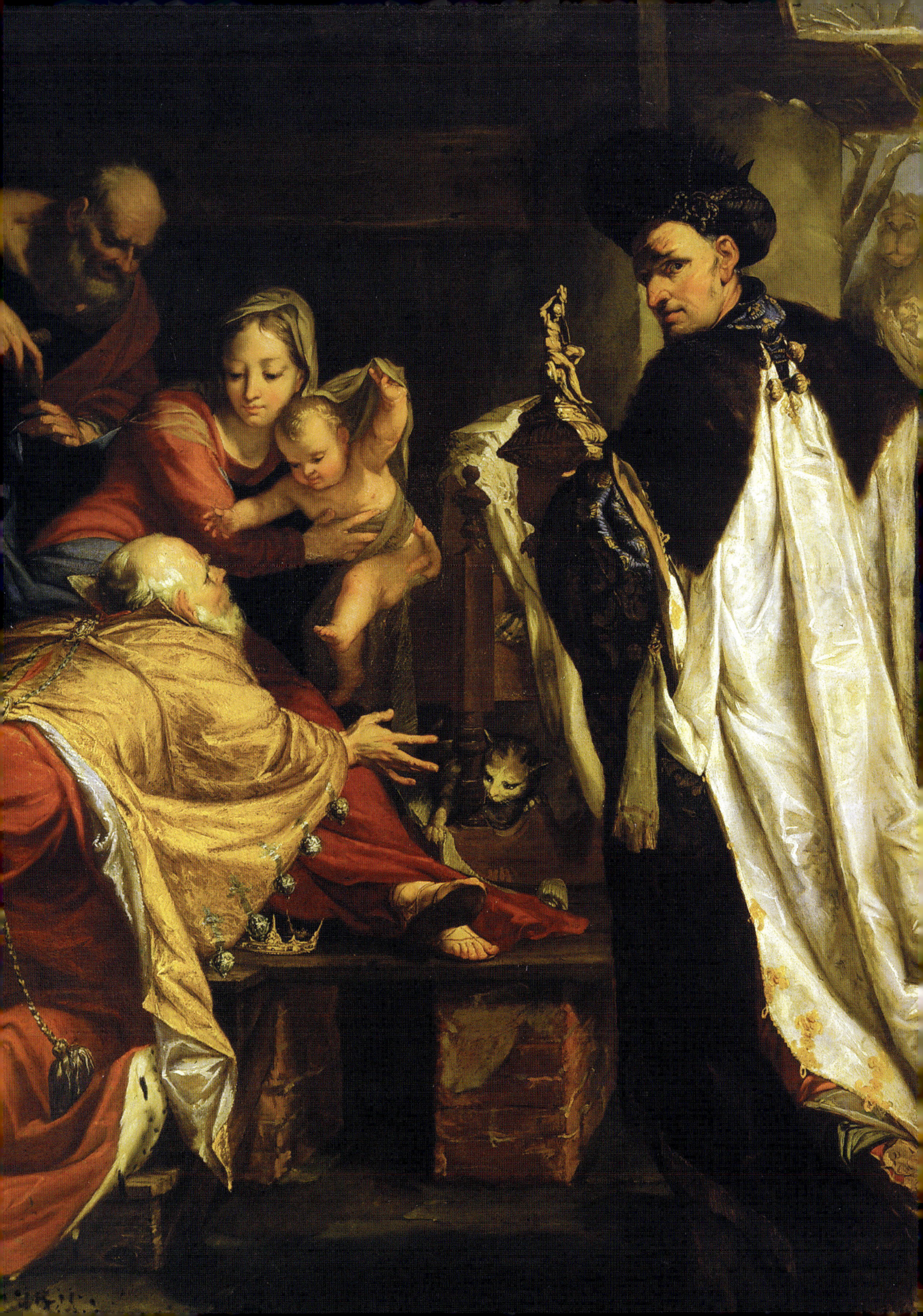

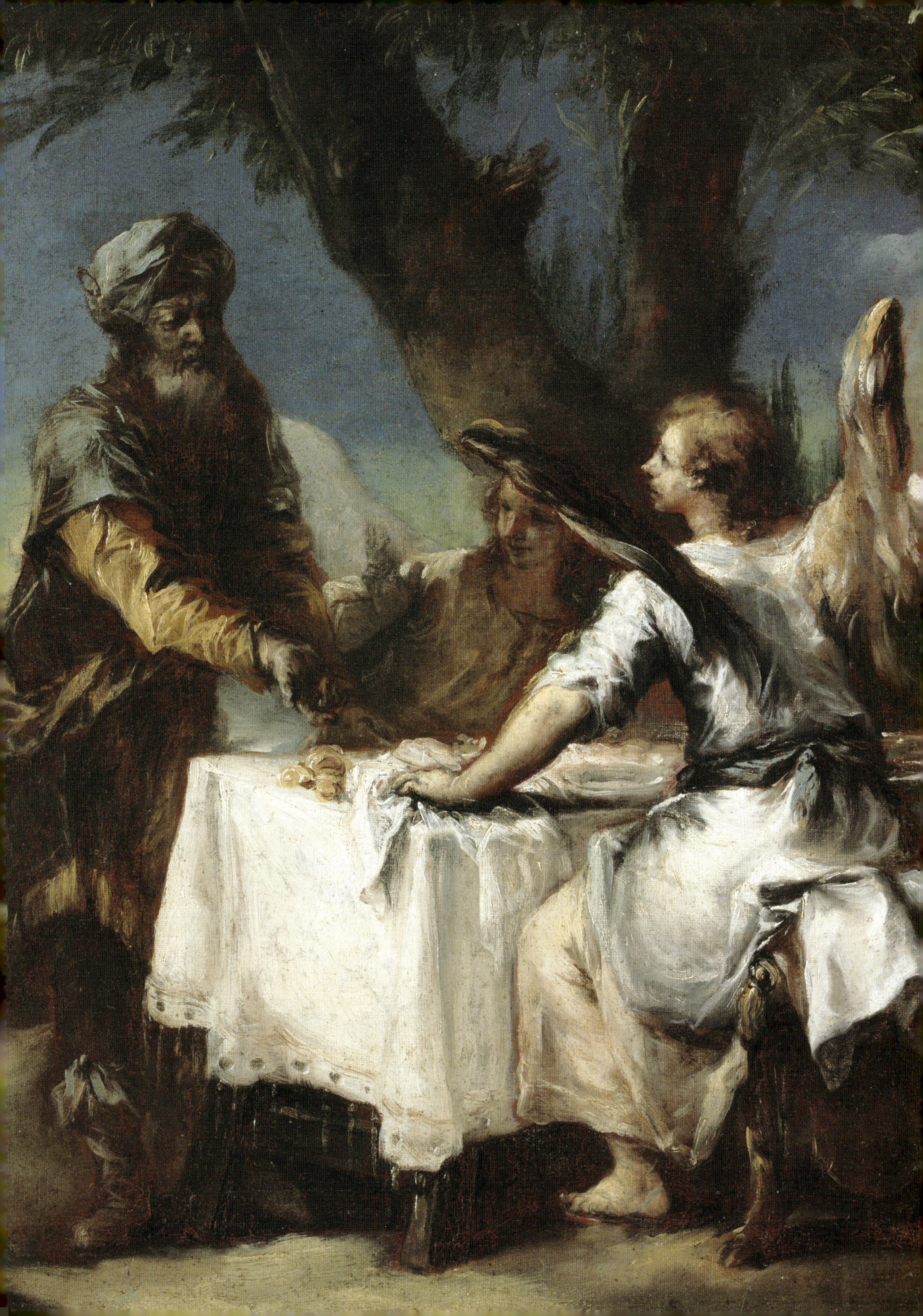

Francesco Guardi's Biblical Paintings in the Cleveland Museum of Art

Jon L. Seydl

Although he is best known today as a view painter (see cats. 42 -44), Francesco Guardi (1712-1793) only turned to this genre in the 1750s. Prior to that point he had focused primarily on history and religious painting, which he had learned in the studio of Antonio Guardi (1699-1760), his elder brother, with whom he worked closely until his sibling's death. The Guardis, unlike most of the artists represented in this exhibition, never strayed far from Venice, and their patrons were likewise from the area, rather than international visitors or foreign courts. Francesco never created subject pictures in large quantities, although they were part of his oeuvre across his career, even after his success as a view painter.

Three of the four pictures in the Guardi series from Cleveland depict episodes from the life of the Old Testament figure of Abraham, beginning with *The Angels Appearing to Abraham* (cat. 6). According to Genesis 18, Abraham met three men at midday and, recognizing that they were angels, humbly bowed down to them with his face touching the ground. The encounter incongruously takes place before a marble, classicizing portico in which a woman lurks, presumably his wife, Sarah.

The second work, *Abraham Welcoming the Three Angels* (cat. 7), interprets a later verse in the same chapter. After their initial meeting, Abraham graciously offers to feed the angels and wash their feet. Following the meal, they announce that his wife, Sarah, long past menopause, will soon bear a son, fulfilling a promise God had made earlier to Abraham. The artist presents the moment of revelation, the angels resplendent in their pastel gowns and feathery wings, with Sarah learning the news while hiding behind their cottage door.

The Sacrifice of Isaac (cat. 8) presents the most familiar narrative from Abraham's life. Testing the elder man's faith, God demands that Abraham go out to the countryside and sacrifice his only son, Isaac. Leaving his servants, seen in the far distance at left, Abraham places Isaac on an altar, and at the very moment he lifts his arm to kill his son, an angel intervenes, staying his hand.

Francesco Guardi (Italian, 1712-1793)
DETAIL: *Abraham Welcoming the Three Angels*, ca. 1750s
(CAT. 7)

The final work, *Tobias and the Angel* (cat. 9), by contrast, derives from the apocryphal book of Tobit. The blinded Tobit sends his son Tobias from Assyria to retrieve family money in the distant region of Media. The angel Raphael, in the guise of a distant relative, offers to accompany the young man on his journey. Bedding down along the Tigris River, Tobias is attacked by a fish leaping out of the water, but Raphael instructs the boy to kill it by hand, later extracting organs from the animal with which Tobias would eventually cure his father's blindness. The pairing of the stories of Abraham and Tobias is not common in Venetian art, but they each deal with similar themes: obedience inspired by faith, hospitality and caregiving, the relationships of fathers and sons, and the intercession of angels.

The Neumann Gallery in Vienna presented all four works in 1937 as by Francesco Guardi, suggesting a date in the 1750s. Antonio Morassi affirmed that attribution and date the same year, which nearly all scholars since that time have maintained, with the exception of Morassi himself, who reversed his position in 1951, subsequently arguing that Antonio Guardi was the author. The question reopened in 1992, with Mitchell Merling considering all four works to be by Francesco, while Diane de Grazia believed that two independent hands executed the series, Francesco Guardi and an assistant in the studio.[1]

De Grazia rightly observed considerable inconsistencies across the four pictures, raising questions of authorship. For example, in *Isaac*, wispy, evanescent strokes form the angel's wings, melding with the clouds, whereas Raphael's wings are darker, more concretely described, and painted with blunter strokes. Abraham's beard, profile, and hairline also differ considerably in each painting. Likewise, the angels, while rather homogenous in *The Angels Appearing to Abraham*, have more individualized hair color and facial features in the second work. The setting of the first two paintings also drastically differs, one scene taking place before a grand marble building, the other in front of a humbler wooden structure—even though the biblical text implies a similar setting for both moments. On the other hand, other details unmistakably solidify connections between the works, such as Sarah's identical position in the first two pictures—surreptitiously beholding the events portrayed in each from the extreme right.

Two factors set significant hurdles for attribution. The first is the condition of the paintings, whose surfaces have been abraded by earlier cleanings, leaving thicker paint layers nearly intact, while the thin layers of glazes, an essential component of Francesco's characteristic flickering brushwork, have been damaged considerably.[2]

The other complicating factor is that Guardi closely based his paintings on the work of earlier artists, emulating not only his predecessors' compositions but also their techniques. Therefore, inconsistency was, in one sense, the aim of the series. The works demonstrate his ability to replicate a variety of styles within a language still recognizable as Francesco Guardi, a playful game for Guardi and his patron, turning the entire series into a kind of capriccio. *The Angels Appearing to Abraham* derives from a ca. 1717 painting by Antonio Balestra (1666-1740) in Sona, near Verona (although more likely adapted from Pietro Rotari's later engraving, whose format Guardi follows more precisely).[3] *The Sacrifice of Isaac* adapts a composition by Giovanni Battista Piazzetta (1683-1754), probably his ca. 1735 interpretation of the subject, now in the Gemäldegalerie Alte Meister in Dresden (although in this case, the vertical format of the source image demanded that Guardi invent an extensive landscape setting).[4] Finally, *Tobias and the Angel* looks to a work by significantly earlier artist Domenico Fetti (1588/89-1623), also now in Dresden, but painted during Fetti's brief Venetian career and probably still available to the younger painter in a Venetian collection. The muted palette, more solid figures forms, lush vegetation, and blunt brushwork—quite distinct from the other paintings—show Guardi adapting to Fetti's early Baroque manner.[5] From these three examples, it is likely that the fourth picture also derives from a source in Venetian painting, not yet identified.

Importantly, the brothers began their careers in the employ of Count Matthias von der Schulenberg, and to a lesser extent, Giovanni Benedetto Giovanelli, both key Venetian patrons who each commissioned the Guardis to paint copies of works by earlier Venetian artists. In 1934 Morassi sought to connect *Isaac* (and only this picture) to a painting of that subject in a 1731 document connected to Giovanelli. This document, however, lacks a clear connection to the work in question, and in any event the Cleveland pictures all date much later on the basis of style. These paintings should not be understood as copies, but variations in the style of other artists, and while these works draw on Francesco's early work as a copyist, they represent a departure from this early practice.

Although the original setting for the Cleveland series is not known, the imbalance of subjects may indicate that the group might have once included even more paintings. Although Abraham and Tobit were not often paired in Venetian eighteenth-century art, a key precedent appears in Francesco Guardi's own early work, where *The Sacrifice of Isaac* and *Tobias and the Angel* join a set of biblical subjects, including the Judgment of Solomon, the Expulsion from Paradise, Joseph Sold by His Brothers, and Christ and the Samaritan Woman.[6] However, these works, from the start of the artist's career, were stylistically coherent and do not emulate other artists' styles.

Endnotes

1 Correspondence and notes in curatorial files.
2 Treatment reports, Marcia Steele, June 16, 1994, and loan examination reports, Dean Yoder, June 29, 2009.
3 Marco Polazzo, *Antonio Balestra: pittore Veronese del Settecento* (Verona: Il Segno, 1990: 96-7).
4 George Knox, *Giambattista Piazetta, 1682-1754* (New York: Oxford University Press, 1992: 176, 178).
5 Eduard A. Safarik, *Domenico Fetti, 1588/89-1623* (Milan: Electa, 1990: 55-8).
6 Antonio Morassi, *Guardi: Antonio e Francesco Guardi* (Venice: Alfieri, 1973: vol. 1, 338-9; vol. 2, figs. 190-1, 945-8).

Provenance

Baroness Valeria Groedel/Gredel (Budapest, Hungary); Neumann Gallery (Vienna, Austria), 1937; Alessandro Brass (Venice, Italy), by 1951; sold through Francesco Pospisil (Venice, Italy), to the Cleveland Museum of Art, 1952.

Bibliography

Cleveland Museum of Art, *The Cleveland Museum of Art Catalogue of Paintings*, vol. 3. Cleveland: Cleveland Museum of Art, 1982, with prior bibliography.

CAT. 1

Jacopo Amigoni (Italian, ca. 1685–1752)

Aeneas Appearing Before Queen Dido, ca. 1729

Oil on canvas, 62⅞ x 46$^{1}/_{16}$ in. (160 x 117 cm)
Collection of the Art Gallery of Greater Victoria, British Columbia, Canada
Gift of Mr. and Mrs. G.B. Benson, 1966.058.001

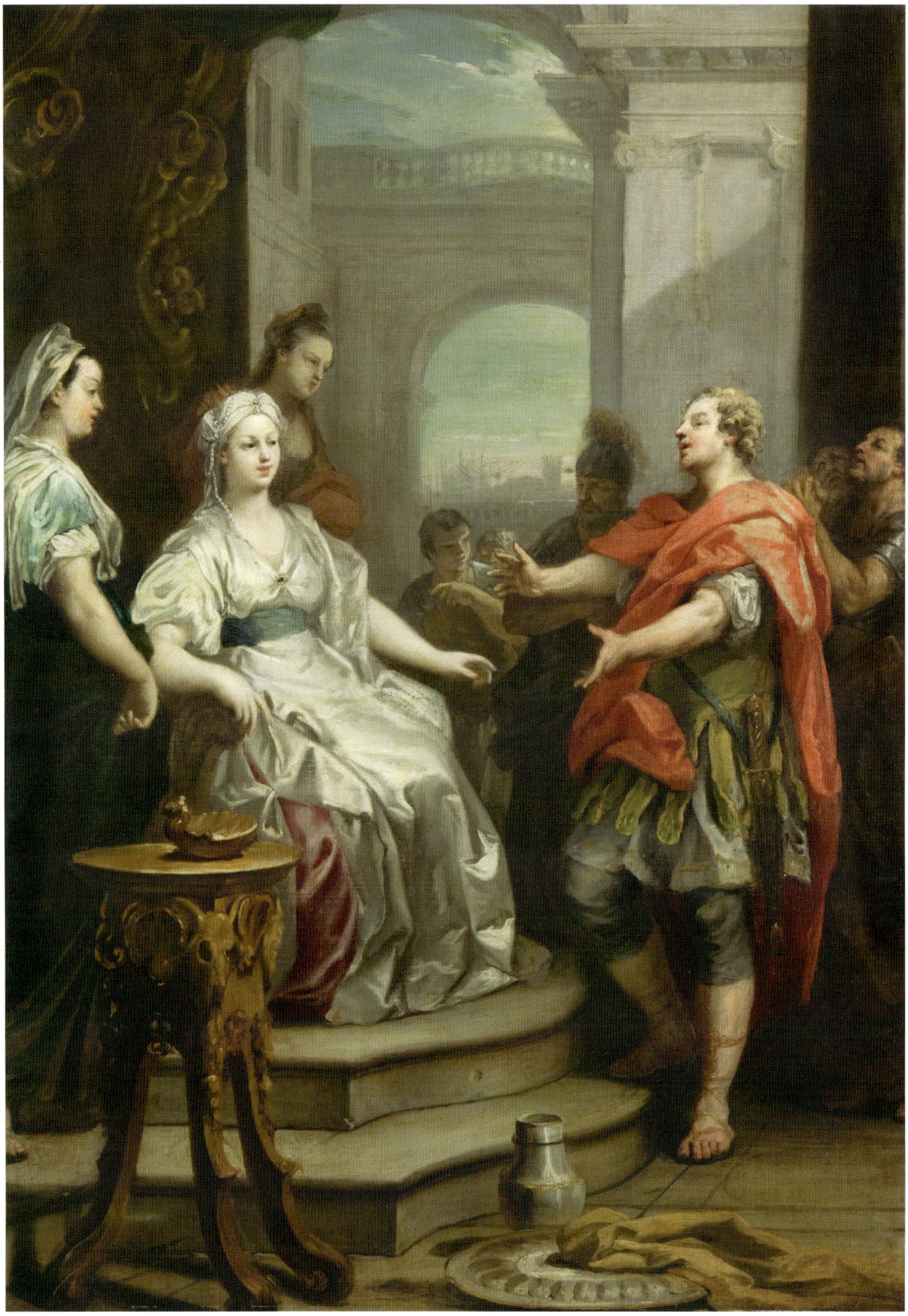

This painting had no attribution or history prior to its discovery in the vaults of the Art Gallery of Greater Victoria. Nothing new has been said about it since its exhibition at the Vancouver Art Gallery more than twenty years ago. It is not mentioned in the monograph on Amigoni, published by Annalisa Scarpa Sonino in 1994.[1]

Amigoni's beginnings are obscure. Horace Walpole says that he was born in Venice in 1675, which would make him an exact contemporary of Giovanni Antonio Pellegrini (1675-1741). A lost document, apparently belonging to his last years, claimed that he was born in Naples in 1682, which is generally more acceptable as to date. Walpole states that he was a pupil of Antonio Bellucci (1654-1726) in Düsseldorf, which seems quite likely, though his mature style seems to owe a lot to France.[2] He spent most of his very active career away from Venice, in Bavaria, London, and Madrid. In London he became close to the world of opera, marrying in 1738 the singer Maria Antonia Marchesini and forming a close friendship with Farinelli, the celebrated *castrato*, who arrived in London in 1734 and who was later instrumental in bringing him to Madrid in the last phase of his career.

The present picture is clearly an operatic scene. Illustrating an episode in Book I of the *Aeneid*, in which Aeneas comes to the court of Queen Dido of Carthage clothed in invisibility. At the appropriate moment, he miraculously appears before the queen. Dido takes his sudden appearance remarkably calmly, but Aeneas has already launched into his introductory aria.

The central position of Virgil in English culture is underlined by John Dryden's translation of Books 1 and 2 of the *Aeneid* and by Henry Purcell's *Dido and Aeneas*, but in the 1730s it was probably the celebrated libretto of Pietro Metastasio, *Didone abbandonata*, that lay behind Amigoni's visualisation of the scene.

Other, later representations of the Dido story may be noted, for example Tiepolo's fresco in the Virgil Room of the Villa Valmarana of 1757, in which a slightly later episode is shown.[3] To avert the wiles of Juno, Venus arranges that Cupid shall be presented to Dido, disguised as Ascanius, Aeneas's son, so that he may inspire the queen with passion for the father. This properly occurs at the banquet, which fills the closing pages of Book 1 of the *Aeneid*. Giustino Menescardi, in the frescoes of Ca' Crotta of 1766, shows both scenes,[4] but his *Aeneas Appearing Before Queen Dido* hardly matches the drama of the present picture. His *Banquet* on the other hand, has a brio, which is sadly lacking in the Tiepolo design.

George Knox

Notes

1 Annalisa Scarpa Sonino, *Jacopo Amigoni* (Soncino: Edizioni dei Soncino, 1994).
2 For an analysis, see Scarpa Sonino, *Jacopo Amigoni*, 15, 16.
3 Massimo Gemin and Filippo Pedrocco, *Giambattista Tiepolo: i dipinti, opera complete* (Venice: Arsenale Ed., 1993: 444, pl. 447).
4 Giuseppe Pavanello, "Giustino Menescardi frescante a palazzo Crotta," *Arte/Documento* 13 (1999): 280, 281, pls. 3, 4.

Exhibition

Vancouver Art Gallery, *Eighteenth Century Venetian Art in Canadian Collections*, 1989, cat. no. 7.

Bibliography

Gemin, Massimo, and Filippo Pedrocco, *Giambattista Tiepolo: i dipinti, opera complete*, 444, pl. 447. Venice: Arsenale Ed., 1993.
Scarpa Sonino, Annalisa. *Jacopo Amigoni*. Soncino: Edizioni dei Soncino, 1994.
Pavanello, Giuseppe. "Giustino Menescardi frescante a palazzo Crotta." *Arte/Documento* 13 (1999): 280, 281, pls. 3, 4.

CAT. 2

GIUSEPPE ANGELI (Italian, 1712–1798)
Diana, with Wings, Holding an Arrow and a Bow, and the Head of Cupid, ca. 1745
Oil on canvas, 20⅞ x 27⅝ in. (53 x 70 cm)
Collection of Mr. A. G. Khamneipur, Canadian Art Collector

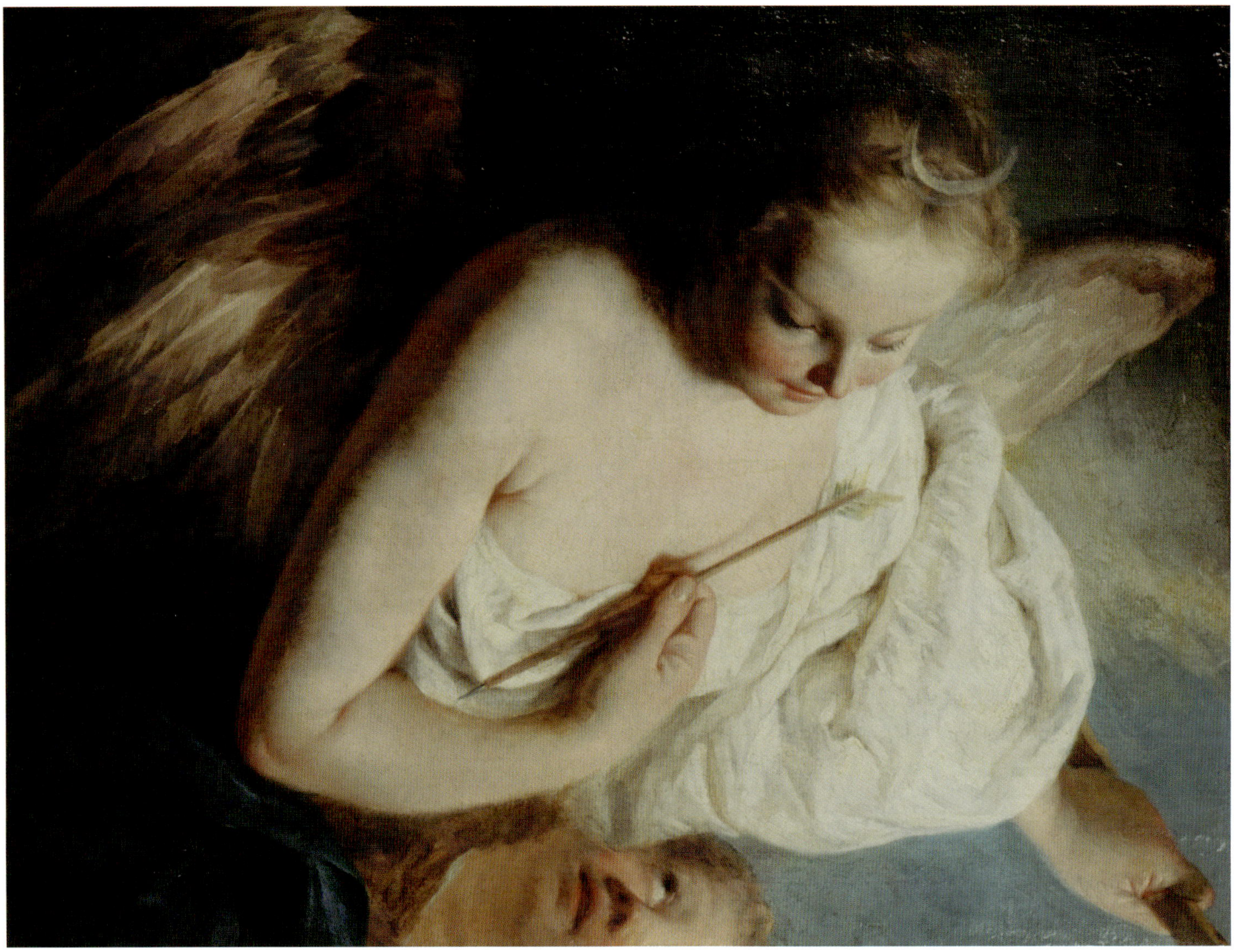

This canvas is apparently a fragment of a ceiling, and it was purchased with an attribution to Pellegrini. It is here attributed to Giuseppe Angeli, the most important follower of Giambattista Piazzetta. So far as we know, Piazzetta painted only one religious ceiling and no secular ceilings in the course of his career, whereas secular ceilings in Venetian palaces by Angeli are still to be found in Ca' Barbaro and Ca' Pisani. Mythological subjects are also extremely rare among Piazzetta's work though some evidence of them can be traced among the drawings. It may be compared with the Mars and Venus in the British Museum, and perhaps even more effectively with the Diana and Actaeon at Brussels,[1] and the Endymion which is recorded in an engraving by Berardi.

The present canvas is quite typical of Angeli, who enjoyed a successful career. His ceilings for Ca' Pisani-Moretta were paid for in the course of the summer of 1744.[2] On August 25, 1745, he is mentioned as the director of the school of Piazzetta; in 1751 he is Prior of the Collegio dei Pittori; in 1754 he is entrusted with the task of finishing Piazzetta's canvas for the High Altar of the Pieta, left unfinished at his death; in 1756 he is the professor of drawing at the Venetian Academy.

A winged Diana is illustrated by Cartari as Diana Cinthia or Luna,[3] following a description by Pausanias of a statue at Corinth in antiquity. This would appear to be the source of the image here.

Addendum 2010:
In fact one can go a little further and suggest that the present picture may be a fragment of a *Luna and Endymion*. One may note that Angeli painted a ceiling on this theme for Ca' Barbaro-Curtis in Venice, which is not dissimilar. It is dateable to 1742-45 and provides a suggested date of ca. 1745 for this picture.[4]

George Knox

Notes

This entry first appeared as catalogue number 14 in the Vancouver Art Gallery exhibition, *Eighteenth Century Venetian Art in Canadian Collections,* curated by George Knox, October 6, 1989–January 1, 1990. The Vancouver Art Gallery has kindly given the Oklahoma City Museum of Art permission to reproduce the entry.

1 *Piazzetta, a bicentenary exhibition*, catalogue by George Knox (Washington, D.C.: National Gallery of Art, 1983: cat. nos. 4 and 6). Krückmann considers the British Museum drawing and the corresponding Pordenone sketch to be works of Benkovich after a lost Piazzetta.
2 Ileana Chiappioni di Sorio, "Palazzo Pisani-Moretta: restauri e decorazioni (Angeli, Piazzetta, Tiepolo, Guarana)," *Notizie di Palazzo Albani* (1983): 268, figs. 1, 2.
3 Vincenzo Cartari, *Imagini delli Dei de gl' Antichi* (Venice, 1647: 60; reprint Graz, 1963).
4 Mariana Mollenhauer Hanstein, *Giuseppe Angeli und die Venezianische Malerei des Settecento* (Ph.D. diss., Rheinischen Friederich-Wilhelms-Universität, Bonn, 1986, pl. 21). This study also establishes the birth date of Giuseppe Angeli: October 8, 1712 (p. 17). He was baptized in the Abbazia di San Gregorio.

Provenance

Purchased at the Gallery Voltaire, Paris, ca. 1972. Vancouver, A. G. Khamneipur.

Exhibition

Vancouver Art Gallery, *Eighteenth Century Venetian Art in Canadian Collections*, 1989, cat. no. 14.

Bibliography

18th Century Venetian Art in Canadian Collections. Vancouver Art Gallery, no. 14 (1989).

CAT. 3

Antonio Bellucci (Italian, 1654-1726)

Adoration of the Magi, ca. 1700

Oil on canvas, 78 x 105 in. (198.1 x 266.7 cm)
The Sarah Campbell Blaffer Foundation, Houston, 1979.24

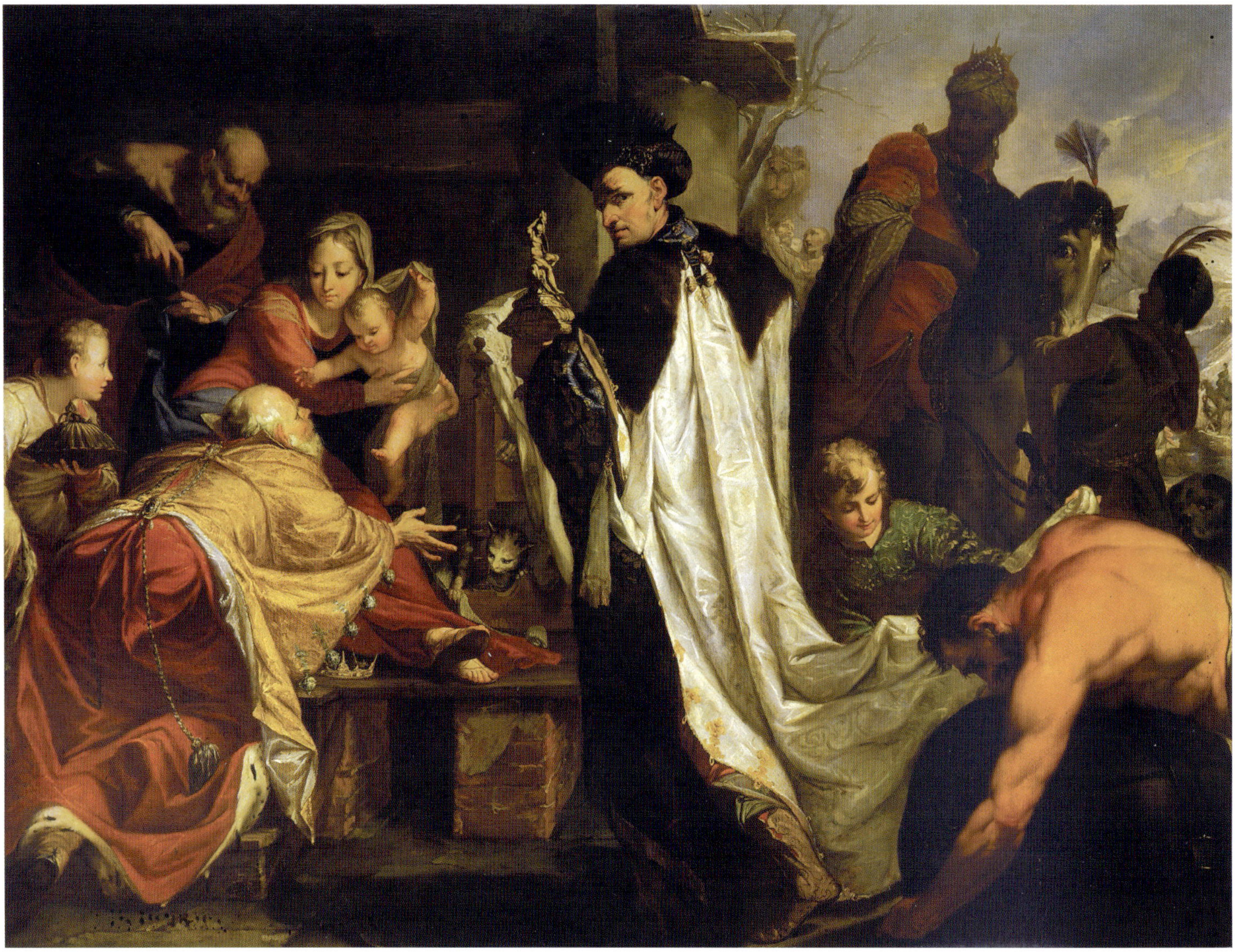

Antonio Bellucci, Gregorio Lazzarini, and Antonio Molinari were all pupils of Pietro Liberi (1605-1687). Together they carry the traditions of Venetian painting into the eighteenth century, but unlike the others Bellucci spent some thirty years away from Venice, in Vienna, Düsseldorf, and London. As a young man, he worked with them in Ca' Correr a San Zan Degolà[1] and Ca' Moro-Lin a Santa Sofia,[2] and in the great church of San Pietro di Castello.[3]

Bellucci left Venice for Vienna in 1692 and painted numerous ceilings for the Palais Lichtenstein. In 1706 he moved to Düsseldorf, working ten years for the Elector Palatine; he painted numerous works for Bensberg, working in association with the younger Pellegrini.[4] In 1716, on the death of his patron Jan Willem von der Pfalz, he moved to London for six years, working for the Duke of Chandos at Canons[5] and at Buckingham House.[6]

Nothing is known of this handsome canvas, prior to its acquisition by Bernard Cohen of the Trafalgar Galleries in London in June 1968. In 1973 it was published by Eric Young as by Antonio Bellucci, with a suggested early date of 1682, a position that is supported by Fabrizio Magani in his monograph of 1995. Teresio Pignatti describes it as "one of Bellucci's mature masterpieces, and a superb example of the decorative yet spiritual approach of the late Baroque in Venice." He also discusses that striking central figure of the king in black and white, as a self-portrait of Bellucci himself. Compared with this, the rest of the composition sinks into comparative insignificance.

George Knox

Notes

1 George Knox, *Giambattista Piazzetta, 1682-1754* (Oxford: Clarendon Press, 1992: pls. 11-3; George Knox, "Bellucci, Lazzarini and Molinari: the mythologies of Ca' Correr," *Ex Fumo Lucem: Baroque Studies in Honour of Klara Garas* (Budapest: Museum of Fine Arts, 1999: 237-50).
2 See cat. no. 10, Lazzarini in this volume.
3 Knox, *Piazzetta*, pls. 8-10.
4 See George Knox, *Antonio Pellegrini* (Oxford: Clarendon Press, 1995: chap. 4).
5 His work for the Chapel at Canons, the ceilings, and perhaps the design of the stained glass windows, have been moved to the church at Great Whitley in Herefordshire, according to Francis Watson, "A Venetian Settecento Chapel in the English Countryside," *Arte Veneta* 8 (1954): 295-302.
6 His great ceiling for Buckingham House, for which, Horace Walpole tells us, he was paid £500, is lost, but it appears to be recorded in part in an engraving by J. B. Pine (see Sacheverell Sitwell, *British Architects and Craftsmen* (London: B.T. Batsford, 1945: pl. 1).

Provenance

Trafalgar Galleries, June 1968.

Bibliography

Young, Eric. "Antonio Bellucci in England and Elsewhere," *Apollo* 117 (1973): 495-6.
Pignatti, Teresio. *Five Centuries of Italian Painting*, 185-7. Houston: The Sarah Campbell Blaffer Foundation, 1985.
Magani, Fabrizio. *Antonio Bellucci*, pl. 7, fig. and color pl. Rimini: Stefano Patacconi, 1995.
Clifton, James, ed. *Venetian Painting from the Sarah Campbell Blaffer Foundation*, pl. 6. Houston: Museum of Fine Arts, 1995.

CAT. 4

Francesco Fontebasso (Italian, 1707–1769)

Family of Darius Before Alexander, 1750

Oil on canvas, 50⅛ x 65⅛ in. (127.32 x 165.42 cm)

Dallas Museum of Art. Gift of Colonel C. Michael Paul, 1964.110

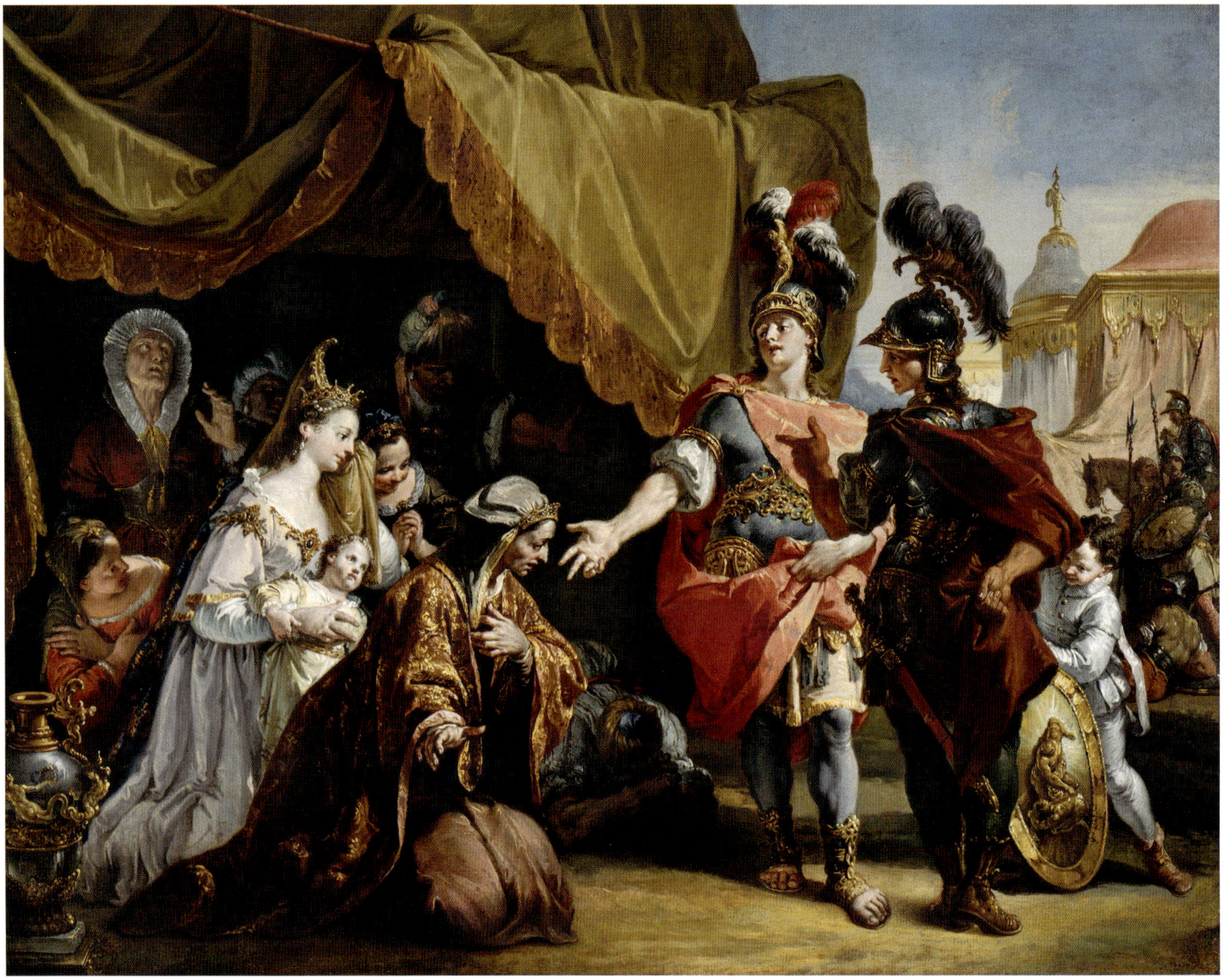

In 333 B.C., Alexander the Great defeated the Persian Emperor Darius III at the Battle of Issus. The monarch fled, and Alexander and his best friend, the general Hephaestion, visited the tent of the vanquished Persian, where the imprisoned family still remained. Queen Sisygambus, the mother of Darius, deceived by Hephaestion's bearing, knelt before him to offer the deference due the victor, believing the general to be Alexander. In the moment depicted by Fontebasso, Hephaestion redirected the family's attention to Alexander, who forgave the queen for her error, accepted her supplication, and encouraged her to rise. By stressing Alexander's humility, restraint, grace, and magnanimity, the story demonstrates good leadership and dignified behavior in victory.

The story is derived from several ancient sources available in the eighteenth century: *The Bibliotheca historica* by Diodorus Siculus (17.37.5), *The Anabasis of Alexander* by Arrian (2.12.31), and *Historiae Alexandri Magni* by Quintius Curtius Rufus (3.12.17). However, in eighteenth-century Venice, the subject would also have been known through operas as well as paintings, including an influential 1565-1567 interpretation by Veronese, then in the Palazzo Pisani (National Gallery, London). Gaspare Diziani (1689-1767) and Giovanni Battista Tiepolo referred to this precedent in their own interpretations, the latter for a well-known fresco at the Villa Cordellino near Vicenza. All three works likely served as starting points for Fontebasso's own version.

After apprenticing with Sebastiano Ricci, Fontebasso worked in Rome and Bologna. By the 1730s, he was back in Venice and fell under the sway of Giovanni Battista Tiepolo, whose career he sought to emulate, in fresco and oil painting as well as drawing. Nonetheless, the experience of Arcadian Rome never left Fontebasso, whose paintings always retained a solidity and a greater use of light and dark contrasts, qualities that give his work a more concrete and grounded quality. The painting here adopts the formal, grandiloquent gestures associated with Tiepolo's large historical works, gestures that almost overpower this smaller cabinet picture. Fontebasso brings a unique level of anecdotal detail, rarely seen among Venetian painters of this period, to his interpretation of the subject—carefully describing such minutiae as the armor mounts, jewelry, and exotic headdresses—along with his characteristic bright, saturated colors; firmer sense of contour; and thick impasto.

Fontebasso returned to this subject several times. In 1962 Rodolfo Palluchini published two related oil sketches, one for this work and the other for *The Banquet of Cleopatra* (both private collection, Lugano), suggesting that the compositions were considered pendants. However, the subsequent connection of the two pictures remains shadowy, since the extant paintings differ strikingly in terms of scale and finish, and versions of Fontebasso's *Cleopatra* have also been paired with other subjects. A possible preliminary sketch for the Dallas painting appeared at Christie's, Milan (November 29, 2006, lot 60), and a smaller sketch sold at Sotheby's, New York (January 15, 1993, lot 101).

Jon L. Seydl

PROVENANCE

Possibly Wildenstein and Company (New York, New York); C. Michael Paul, 1901-80 (New York, New York); by gift to the Dallas Museum of Art, 1964.

BIBLIOGRAPHY

Magrini, Maria. *Francesco Fontebasso,* 135, cat. no. 40. Venice: Neri Pozzi Editore, 1988, with previous bibliography.

CAT. 5

LUCA GIORDANO (Italian, 1632–1705)

The Meeting of Venus and Adonis, 1652–53

Oil on canvas, 81 3/16 x 60 15/16 in. (206.1 x 154.5 cm)
Collection of the Vancouver Art Gallery, Vancouver Art Gallery Acquisition Fund, VAG 86.192
Photo: Rachel Topham, Vancouver Art Gallery

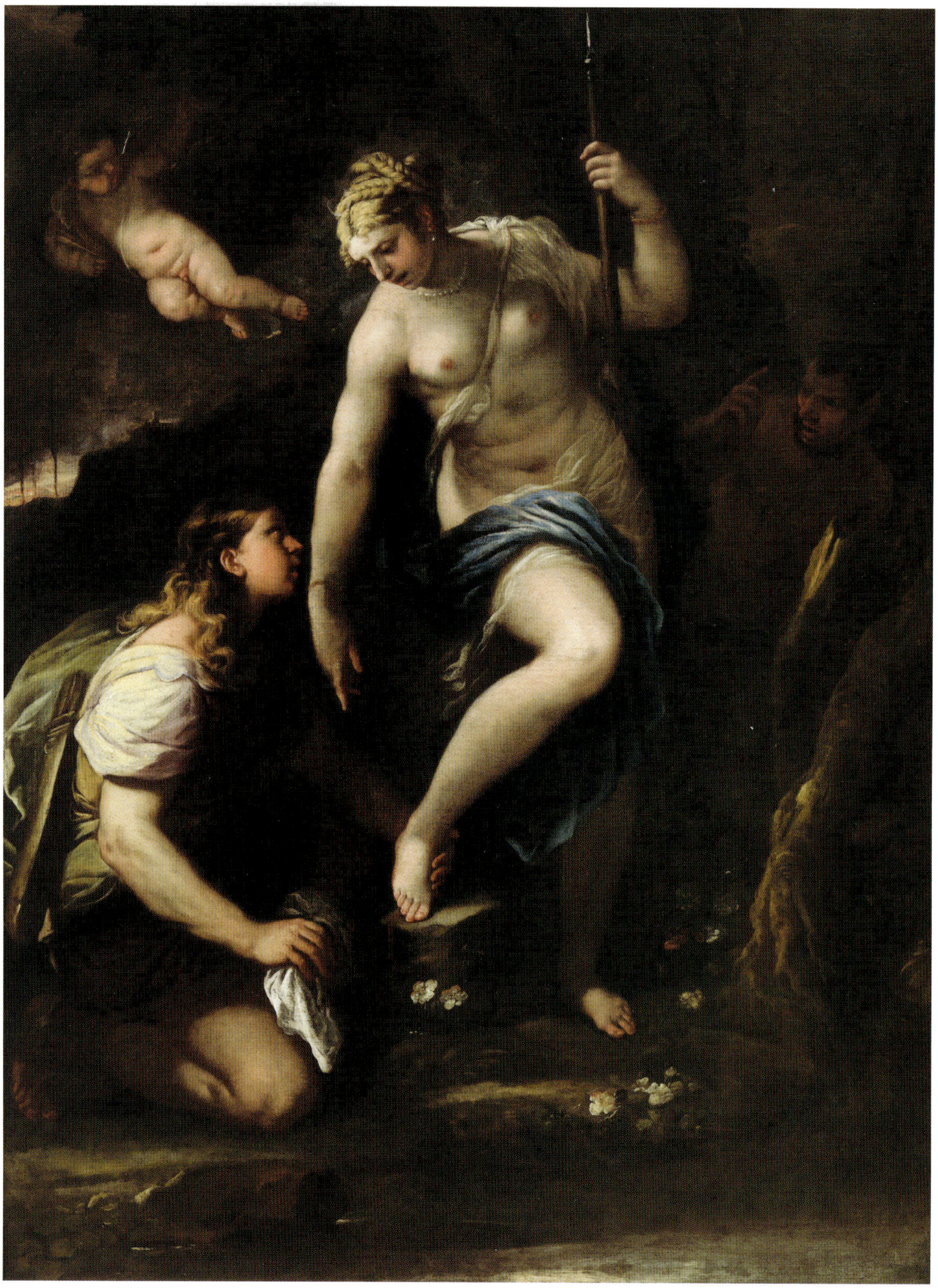

Luca Giordano and Francesco Solimena (1657-1747), though both Neapolitans, were warmly welcomed and deeply influential in Venice, from the mid-1650s onwards, until well into the eighteenth century. It is therefore not inappropriate to preface this exhibition with a deeply Venetian painting by Luca.

When the picture was sold at Christie's, it bore the title *Diana and Actaeon*, indicated by the crescent moon on the lady's brow, but otherwise hard to reconcile. In fact, it is a complete visualisation of the meeting of Venus and Adonis, as it is described in Canto III of the *Adone* of the Cavaliere Marini. Giambattista Marino (1569-1625) came from Naples and was the most celebrated poet of his day in Italy, and the *Adone*, his most famous work, was first published in Paris in 1623, with a dedication to Queen Marie de Medici. In stanzas 61-122 of Canto III, he describes how Venus decides to disguise herself as Diana, before her encounter with Adonis. On her way to the assignation, she tears her foot on a rose, which is why roses are white, and pink, and red. Adonis staunches the wounds with a cloth and, indeed, all the elements in the picture can be traced to the poem.

Luca came to Venice at the age of twenty. The picture owes much to his first awakening enthusiasm for sixteenth-century Venetian painting, for Tintoretto and Veronese. Venice was also a centre of enthusiasm for the poetry of Marino, and Filippo Zanimberti (1585-1636) is recorded as painting the story of Venus and Adonis after Marino, now sadly lost, in the great room of Ca' Loredan in Campo San Stefano. Luca enjoyed several important commissions in Venetian churches on this early visit, but this picture has a more personal significance. He was a good-looking lad, and evidently Adonis is a self-portrait of the young painter, kneeling reverently before the presiding deity of his country, the mother of Aeneas, under whose protective eye the fugitives from Troy came to Italy and founded Rome.

George Knox

Provenance

Christie's sale, April 19, 1985, lot 93; Christie's sale, October 24, 1986, lot 97.

Exhibition

Vancouver Art Gallery, *Eighteenth Century Venetian Art in Canadian Collections*, 1989, cat. no. 1.

Bibliography

Knox, George. "A New Italian Painting for Vancouver: *The Meeting of Venus and Adonis* by Luca Giordano." *RACAR* (1988): 85, 86, illus. on front cover.

Knox, George. "Bellucci, Lazzarini, Molinari: The Mythologies of Ca' Correr," in *Ex Fumo Lucem, Baroque Studies in Honour of Klara Garas*, 237-50, pl. 5. Budapest: Museum of Fine Arts, 1999.

CATS. 6 and 7

FRANCESCO GUARDI (Italian, 1712–1793)
The Angels Appearing to Abraham, ca. 1750s
Oil on canvas, 22¼ x 29⅝ in. (56.5 x 75.5 cm)
The Cleveland Museum of Art
Mr. and Mrs. William H. Marlatt Fund, 1952.235.3

FRANCESCO GUARDI (Italian, 1712–1793)
Abraham Welcoming the Three Angels, ca. 1750s
Oil on canvas, 22¼ x 29⅝ in. (56.5 x 75.5 cm)
The Cleveland Museum of Art
Mr. and Mrs. William H. Marlatt Fund, 1952.235.4

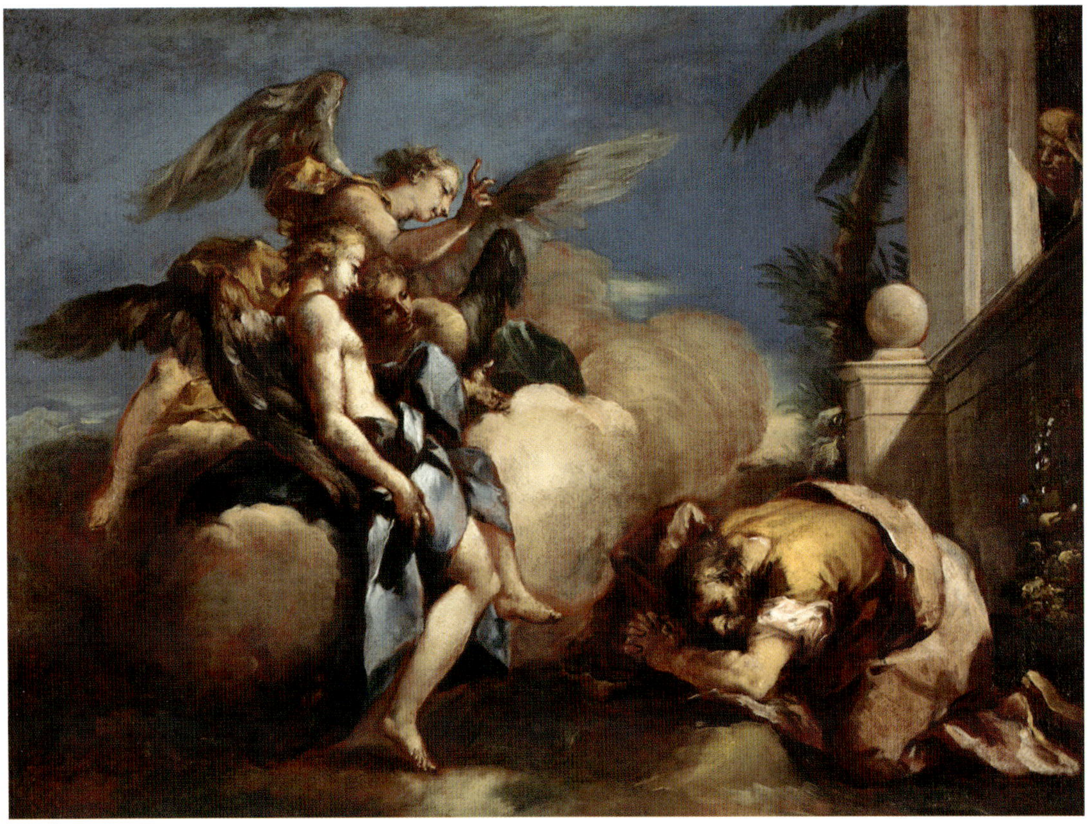

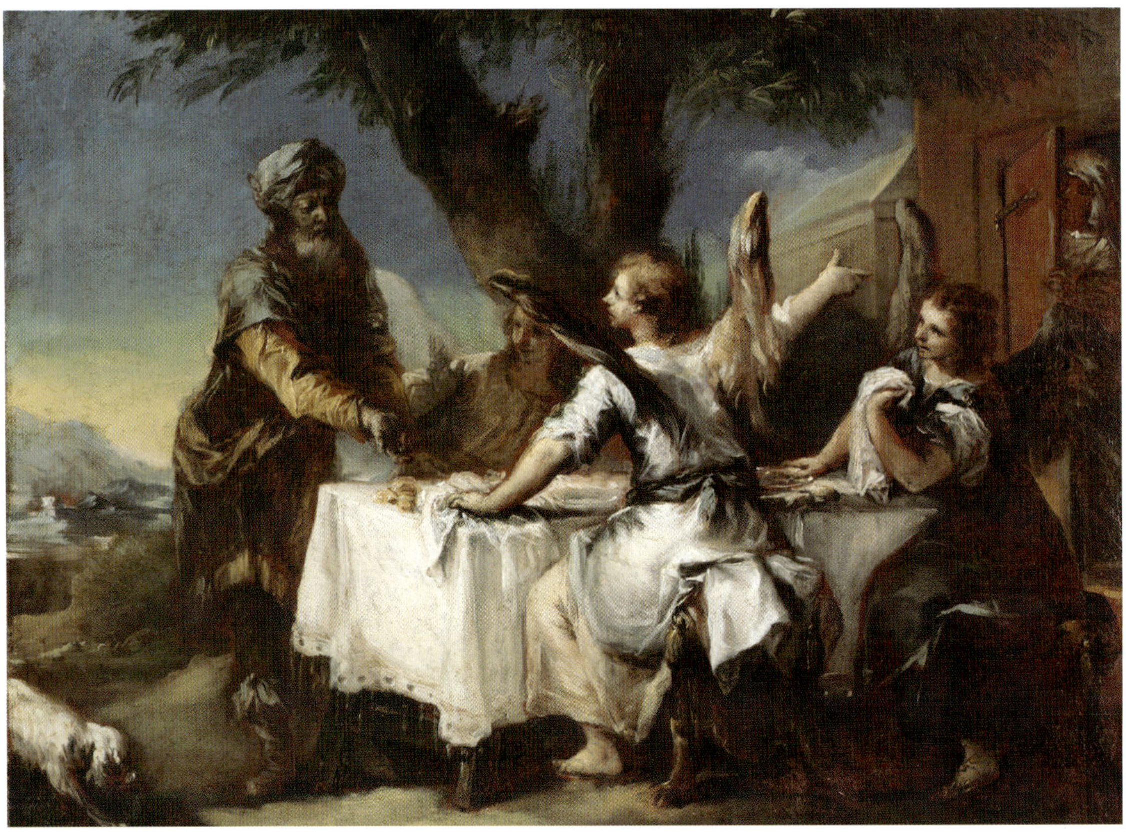

CATS. 8 and 9

Francesco Guardi (Italian, 1712-1793)
The Sacrifice of Isaac, ca. 1750s
Oil on canvas, 22¼ x 29¾ in. (56.5 x 75.5 cm)
The Cleveland Museum of Art
Mr. and Mrs. William H. Marlatt Fund, 1952.235.1

Francesco Guardi (Italian, 1712-1793)
Tobias and the Angel, ca. 1750s
Oil on canvas, 22¼ x 29¾ in. (56.5 x 75.5 cm)
The Cleveland Museum of Art
Mr. and Mrs. William H. Marlatt Fund, 1952.235.2

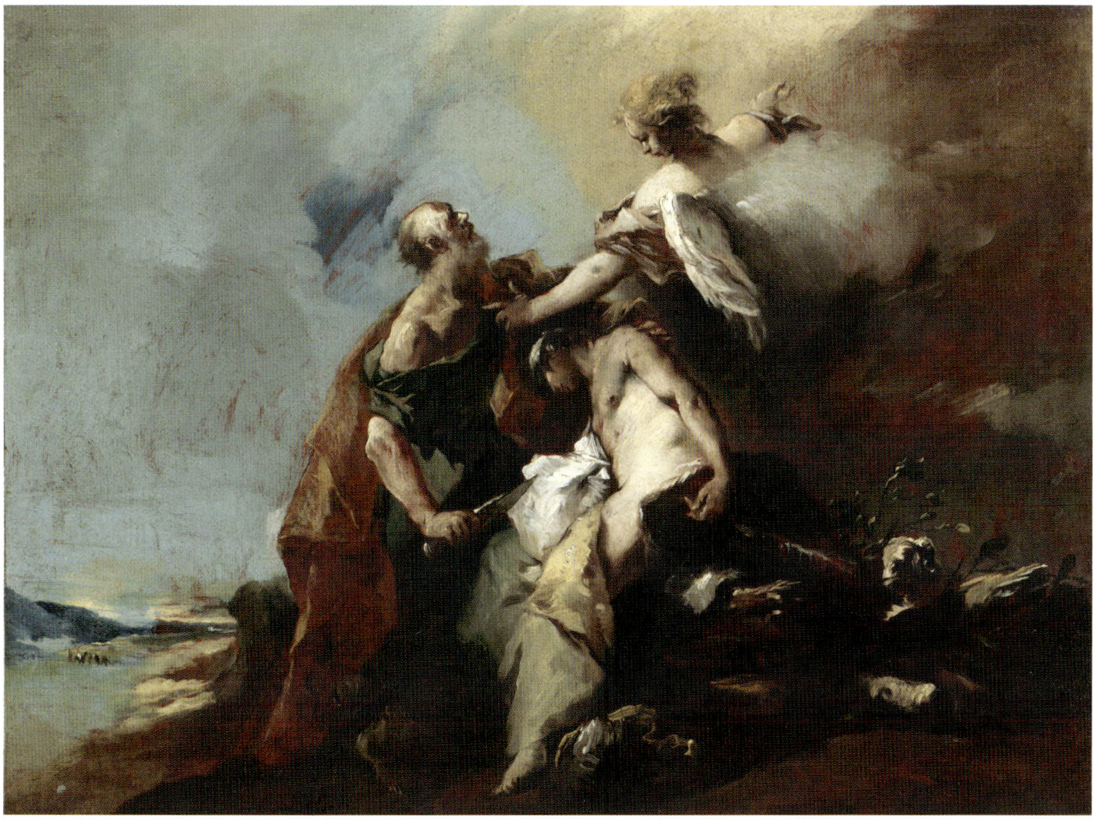

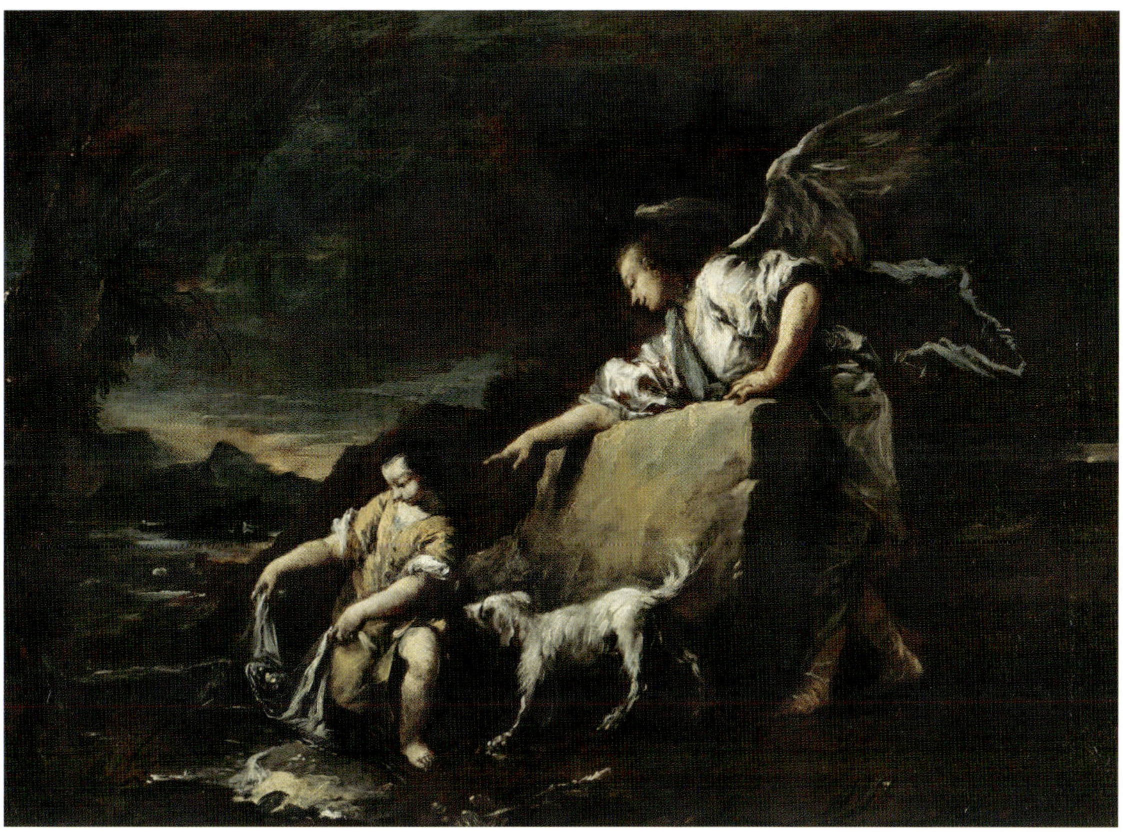

CAT. 10

GREGORIO LAZZARINI (Italian, 1655–1730)

The Golden Age (A Bacchanal), ca. 1700

Oil on canvas, 94 x 144 in. (240.4 x 366.5 cm)

The Boston Athenæum. Gift of George Washington Wales, 1861, as by Luca Giordano

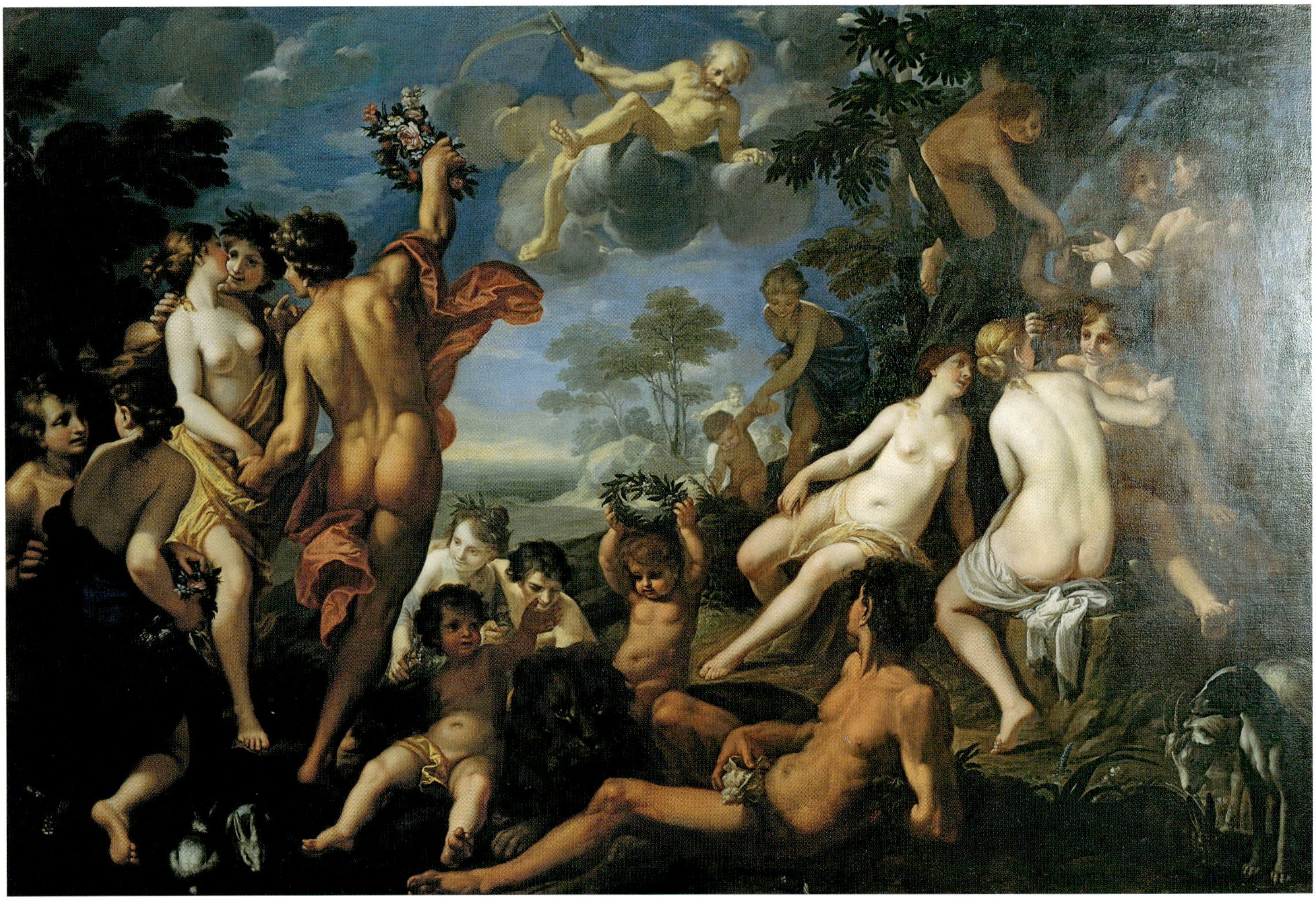

No systematic study of Lazzarini has yet appeared, but after the death of Pietro Liberi in 1687, he was one of the leading figures in Venetian painting, together with Antonio Bellucci and Antonio Molinari, who acted as a team on several projects in the 1680s and 1690s. Among these projects was the decoration of Ca' Moro Lin on the Grand Canal for Liberi. Part of this decoration, a *Bacchanal* now in the Civico Museo Correr,[1] offers convincing support for the attribution of the present picture to Lazzarini. It is one of a series of *Bacchanales* painted for the palace by Lazzarini.[2] Several of these were engraved by Giuseppe Wagner.[3]

It is not possible to identify this canvas positively as part of the decoration of Ca' Moro Lin, but meanwhile it is perhaps possible to redefine the subject as *A Bacchanal*, rather than *The Golden Age*, as heretofore listed. It shows a dancing couple on the left, with a third man crowned with laurel between them, on the right is a group of three naked nymphs, perhaps the Three Graces, in the central area, men, women, and putti lie on the ground, with more laurel crowns, while above, in the sky, Father Time, with his scythe, adds a sombre note to the otherwise joyous proceedings. This corresponds roughly with an item listed by Vicenzo da Canal, under the year 1696.[4]

This large and extremely handsome painting evidently was created for the decoration of one of the principal rooms of a great Venetian palace or villa. One must imagine it covering the full surface of a wall, perhaps between two doorways with overdoors, above a dado about three feet high, raising it above tables and other furniture, and reaching the cornice of the ceiling above.[5] The traditional attribution to Luca Giordano, in itself not a bad guess, was adjusted to Gregorio Lazzarini with the assistance of Sydney J. Freedberg about 1982.[6]

George Knox

Notes

1 Teresio Pignatti, *Il Museo Correr di Venezia* (Venice: Neri Pozza, 1960: 125–6, fig. 1,019); Egidio Martini, *La pittura veneziana del settecento* (Venice: Edizioni Marciane, 1964: pl. 9).
2 Recorded by Vincenzo da Canal in his, *Vita di Gregorio Lazzarini*, printed in Venice by G. A. Moschini, 1809.
3 Finarte sale, Milan, October 24, 1989, lots 64a, 64b, with the Wagner engravings reproduced.
4 Da Canal, *Vita di Gregorio Lazzarini*, lvi, 1696, Pel Marchese Ghirardini di Verona: *un Bacchanal con Pastori, che danzano e suonano, con puttini e paese.*
5 For old photographs illustrating this arrangement in Ca' Corner a San Tomà and Ca' Bollani a Sant'Aponal. see Alessandro Bettagno, "Un soffitto ritrovato da Palazzo Pisani;" *Arte Veneta* 29 (1975): 224–6; and George Knox, "Some notes on Francesco Fontebasso," in *Pittura veneziana ... Egidio Martini* (Venice: Arsenale Editore, 1999: 249)
6 D. B. Dearinger, in *Acquired Tastes: 200 Years of Collecting for the Boston Athenæum*, ed. S. E. Cushing & D. B. Dearinger (Boston: Boston *Athenæum*, 2006: 189–90, pl. 54).

Bibliography

Da Canal, Vincenzo. *Vita di Gregorio Lazzarini*, written in 1732. Venice: G. A. Moschini, 1809.
Pignatti, Teresio. *Il Museo Correr di Venezia*. Venice: Neri Pozza, 1960.
Martini, Egidio. *La pittura veneziana del settecento*. Venice: Edizioni Marciane, 1964.
Bettagno, Alessandro. "Un soffitto ritrovato da Palazzo Pisani;" *Arte Veneta* 29 (1975): 224–6.
Knox, George. "Some notes on Francesco Fontebasso," in *Pittura veneziana ... Egidio Martini*, 249. Venice: Arsenale Editore, 1999.

CAT. 11

Giustino Menescardi (Italian, ca. 1720–1776)

The Holy Family and the Holy Dove Appearing to S. Francesco di Paola, ca. 1750

Oil on canvas, 31½ x 22 in. (79 x 55 cm)
University of Toronto Art Centre, Malcove Collection, M82.17

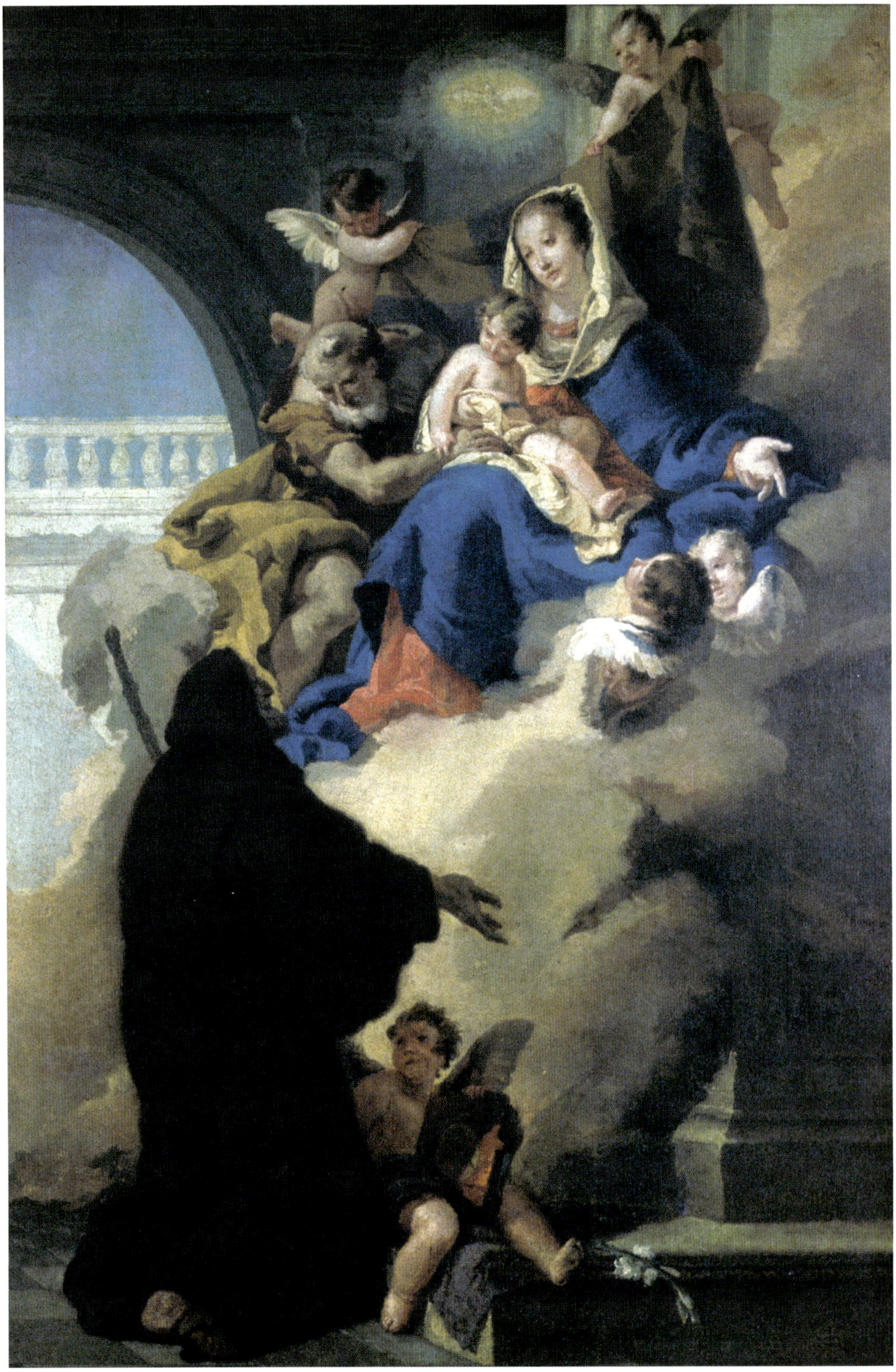

No systematic account of Menescardi has yet appeared. He came from Milan and no doubt joined the Tiepolo studio when Giambattista was in that city in 1738 or 1740. He is one of the three Tiepolo apprentices, apart from members of the family, who were able to establish themselves in successful independent careers. Several of his works are noted by Antonio Morassi, and a preliminary checklist of his paintings and drawings appeared in 1996.[1] Since then there has been modest progress in Menescardi studies. In September 1997, two small Alexander paintings were exhibited at Thessalonika, and in 1999 Giuseppe Pavanello rediscovered and published the frescoes of Ca' Crotta in the Lista di Spagna of 1766.[2] Menescardi is listed in the *Fraglia dei Pittori* from 1751 until 1776. The finest of his works in the United States, indeed his masterpieces, are the two large canvases at the Cleveland Museum of Art, *Horatio Defending Rome Against the Etruscans* and *The Wounded Horatio Swimming the Tiber.*[3]

S. Francesco di Paola was a popular saint in eighteenth-century Venice, with a large church dedicated to him in the Via Garibaldi. This small devotional picture shows him typically as an old man in a black monk's habit, with a staff and a book, the Rule of the Minims. The staff usually bears in a small glory the letters *CAR*, for *Caritas* (Charity), but in this case that emblem is held by the putto at the saint's knee.

George Knox

Notes

1 Antonio Morassi, *A Complete Catalogue of the Paintings of G. B. Tiepolo, Including Pictures by His Pupils and Followers Wrongly Attributed to Him* (London: Phaidon Press, 1962: passim); George Knox, "The Drawings of Giustino Menescardi," *Arte/Documento* 10 (1996): 208-20.

2 *The Family of Darius before Alexander, Alexander at the Temple of Jupiter Ammon*, 62.4 x 89.7 cm. Exhibited: London, Trafalgar Galleries, 1996, pl. 13; Salonika, *Alexander the Great in European Art* (Organization for the Cultural Capital of Europe, Thessalonika, 1997, pls. XI.10, XI. 11); Giuseppe Pavanello, "Giustino Menescardi frescante a palazzo Crotta," *Arte/Documento* 13 (1999): 278-83.

3 These have not been adequately published. Morassi, *A Complete Catalogue*, 9, as "certainly by Menescardi," (not illustrated); Massimo Gemin and Filippo Pedrocco, *Giambattista Tiepolo: i dipinti: opera complete* (Venice: Arsenale, 1993: 504, pls. 12, 13), as *opere attribuite*, with small reproductions; Knox, "Drawings of Giustino Menescardi," 213.

Exhibition

Vancouver Art Gallery, *Eighteenth Century Venetian Art in Canadian Collections*, 1989, cat. no. 15.

Bibliography

Knox, George. "The Holy Family and the Holy Dove appearing to S. Francesco di Paola." In *The Malcove Collecton*, ed. Sheila Campbell, 384-5. Toronto: University of Toronto Press, 1985.
Knox, George. "The Drawings of Giustino Menescardi." *Arte/Documento* 10 (1996): 213.

CAT. 12

Giovanni Antonio Pellegrini (Italian, 1675-1741)

The Entombment, 1719

Oil on canvas, 38½ x 50½ in. (97.79 x 128.27 cm)
Bequest of John Ringling, 1936, Collection of The John and Mable Ringling Museum of Art, the State Art Museum of Florida, a Division of Florida State University, SN176

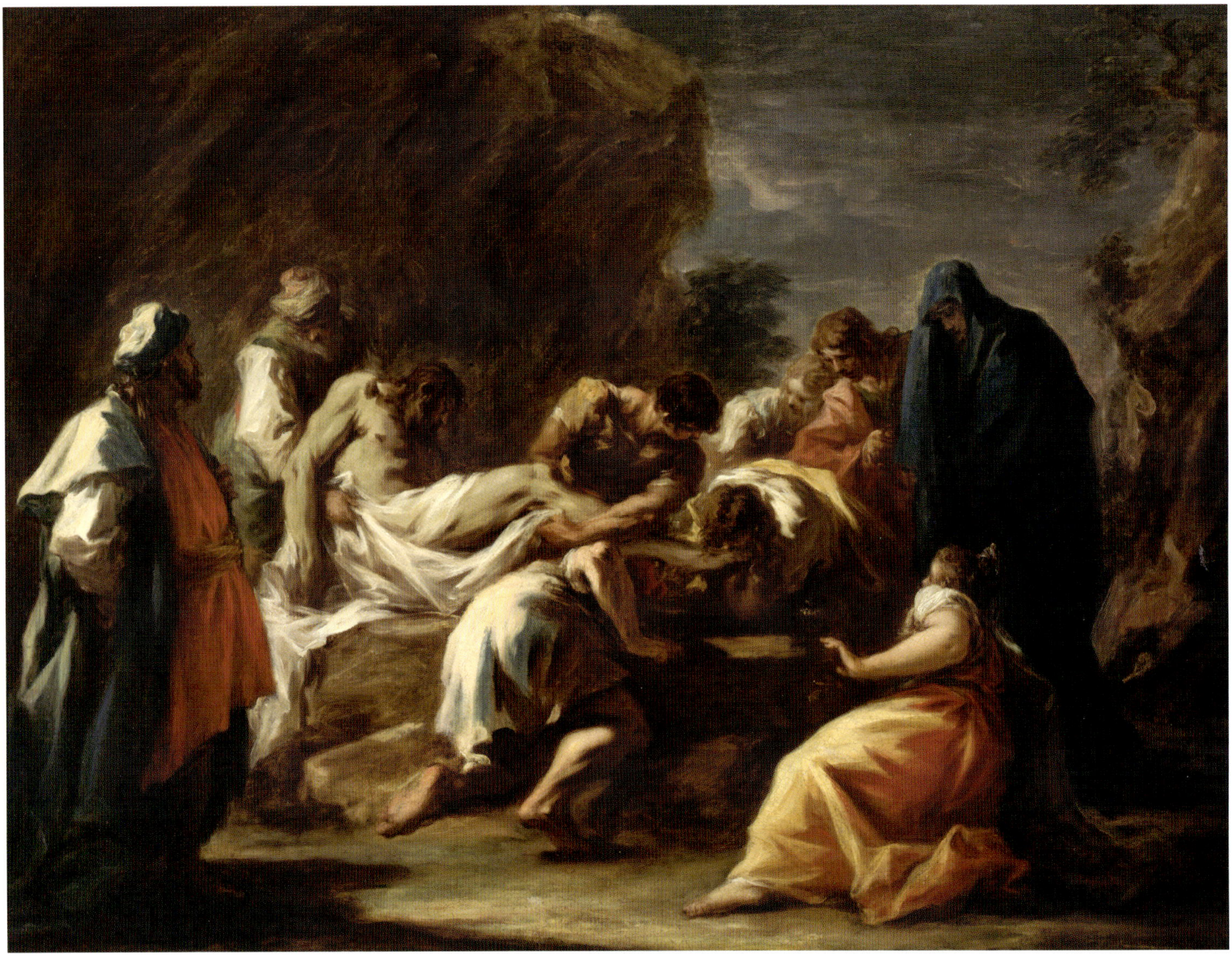

This canvas presents problems, exacerbated by the lack of an opportunity to study the picture firsthand before writing this entry. The first appearance in a collection in Wales may suggest a date in one of the English periods, either 1708-13 or 1719, but Pellegrini seldom painted religious subjects in England. Moreover the composition could very well be one of a set, though there do not seem to be any other obvious candidates.

There is a clear link with the three subjects in the Capella Molin of Santa Maria del Giglio, dateable to 1698-1700, one of them being an Entombment.[1] The Capella Molin is in fact a mortuary chapel with a door to the street as well as a door into the church, which is a familiar element in Venetian churches, often decorated with schemes of The Passion of Christ. A good example is the Capella del Crocifisso at San Polo, with decorations by the young Domenico Tiepolo, circa 1717, culminating in an Entombment.[2] Another even more imposing example is the series of eight canvases painted by Domenico for the church of San Felipe Neri in Madrid in 1772, again leading up to an Entombment.[3]

The strong enfilading light from the left seems to be typical of works following Pellegrini's visit to Rome in 1701-2.[4]

George Knox

Notes

1 George Knox, *Antonio Pellegrini* (Oxford: Clarendon Press, 1995: pls. 17-9).

2 George Knox, *Giambattista and Domenico Tiepolo: A Study and Catalogue Raisonné of the Chalk Drawings* (Oxford: Clarendon Press, 1980: 31-8, pls. 76-119).

3 Knox, *Giambattista and Domenico*, pls. 267-97.

4 Knox, *Antonio Pellegrini*, pls. 21-7.

Provenance

Lt. Col. H. B. T. Hughes, Kimmel Park, Wales; Sotheby's sale, July 1929.

Bibliography

Gregori, Mina. "Osservazioni a proposito degli abbozzi del Pellegrini," in *Paragoni* 131 (1960): 61-70.

Pallucchini, Rodolfo. *La pittura veneziana del '700*,. pl. 36. Venice: Istituto per la collaborazione culturale, 1960.

Martini, Egidio. *La pittura veneziana del '700*, 51. Venice: Edizioni Marciane, 1964.

Catalogue, pl. 102, as dateable 1719. Sarasota, Fla.: The John and Mable Ringling Museum, 1976.

Knox, George. *Antonio Pellegrini, 1675-1741*, 381. Oxford: Clarendon Press, 1995.

CAT. 13

Giovanni Battista Piazzetta (Italian, 1683–1754)

Madonna and Child Appearing to Saint Philip Neri, ca. 1725

Oil on canvas, 44¼ x 25 in. (112.4 x 63.5 cm)
National Gallery of Art, Washington, Samuel H. Kress Collection, 1961.9.82 (1634)

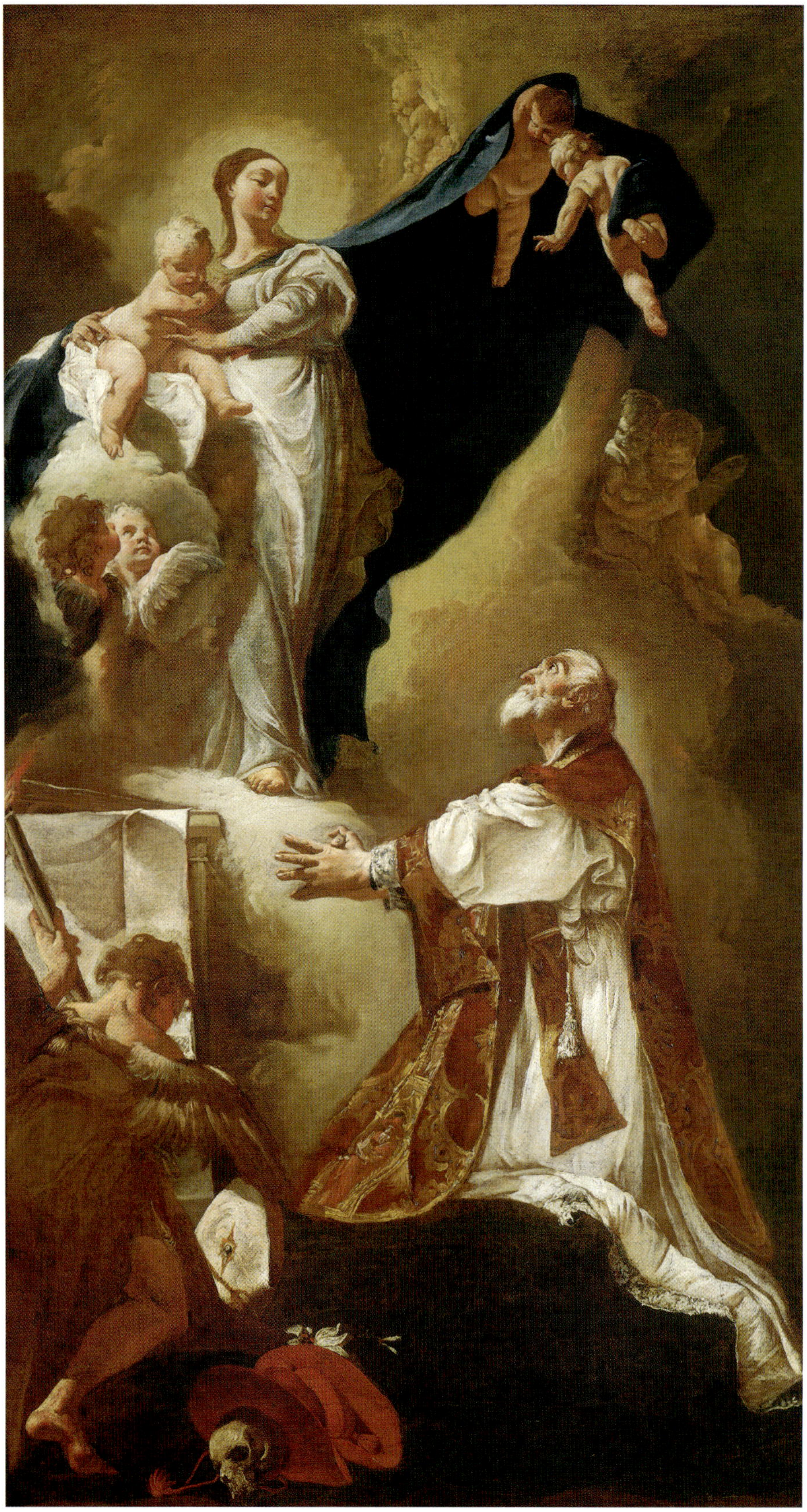

Piazzetta was the son of a distinguished wood carver in Venice and became one of its leading history painters, rivalling Giambattista Tiepolo. Apart from an early period of study in Bologna, he travelled little and devoted himself to oil painting, drawing, and book illustration. He was also an inspired teacher and became the first President of the Venetian Academy of Painting.

Since its sudden appearance in Rome in 1941, this picture has been recognized as an important example of the work of Piazzetta, related to his celebrated altarpiece in the Church of the Fava, Santa Maria della Consolazione, in Venice,[1] which was commissioned in 1725 and paid for in 1727. The exact relationship is still a little unclear, and Eric Garberson, in a long and careful discussion, debates whether it should be regarded as a *bozzetto*, a preliminary sketch; a *modello,* a more careful sketch to be shown to the patron; or a *ricordo,* made after the altarpiece as a record of the work. The matter involves another version of the work at Salzburg, which has some claim to be a bozzetto.[2] The present work is so close to the finished picture that Garberson proposes it to be a ricordo.[3]

Such questions may be left to specialists, allowing us to turn to the remarkable qualities of the work. Piazzetta, throughout his work, is devoted to a calm realism. He has an uncanny way of turning the miraculous into an unremarkable everyday event. San Filippo Neri kneels in prayer on the steps of an altar. He fills the lower terrestrial square of the composition. The Virgin is a statue standing on the altar that has come to life. With a twisting stance and a swirling blue cloak born aloft by putti, she fills the upper celestial square of the composition with movement and light. The two squares overlap around the head of St. Philip, but Piazzetta keeps the two figures separate, one on the left, the other on the right of the central divide.

Piazzetta seems to have had some special devotion to Philip Neri, a saint of everyday simplicities, who is usually shown in plain black cassock. The altarpiece marks his first great success in Venice, when he was in his early forties, and his only etching, apart from the celebrated *Self-portrait* (fig. 1),[4] is a record of the *La Madonna della Fava* (fig. 2).[5] And when Piazetta died, he was buried in the Fava, in the tomb of his friend Giovanni Albrizzi.

George Knox

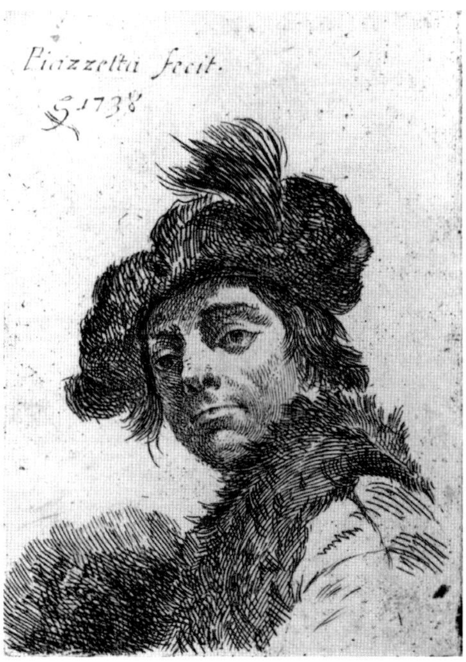

FIG. 1
Giovanni Battista Piazzetta (Italian, 1683-1754)
Self-portrait, 1736
Etching, unique first state
Vienna, Albertina

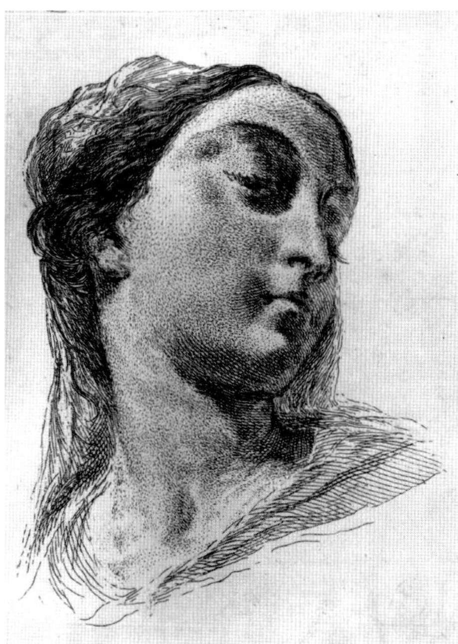

FIG. 2
Giovanni Battista Piazzetta (Italian, 1683-1754)
La Madonna della Fava
Etching, unique impression
Vienna, Albertina

Notes

1 George Knox, *Giambattista Piazzetta, 1682-1754* (Oxford: Clarendon Press, 1992: pl. 81); Diane de Grazia and Eric Garberson, *Italian Paintings of the Seventeenth and Eighteenth Centuries* (Washington, D.C.: National Gallery of Art, 1996: fig. 1).
2 Knox, *Giambattista Piazzetta,* pl. 79; de Grazia and Garberson, *Italian Paintings,* fig. 2.
3 Knox, *Giambattista Piazzetta,* pl. 80; de Grazia and Garberson, *Italian Paintings,* fig. 3.
4 George Knox, *Piazzetta* (Washington, D.C.: National Gallery of Art, 1983: pl. 107).
5 Knox, *Piazzetta,* pl. 108.

Provenance

Private collection, Rome, by 1941; Samuel H. Kress Foundation, New York.

Bibliography

Knox, George. *Giambattista Piazzetta, 1682-1754*, 98-107. Oxford: Clarendon Press, 1992.
de Grazia, Diane, and Eric Garberson. *Italian Paintings of the Seventeenth and Eighteenth Centuries*, 207-12. Washington, D.C.: National Gallery of Art, 1996.

CAT. 14

Giovanni Battista Pittoni (Italian, 1687–1767)

Saints Presenting a Devout Woman to the Virgin and Child, 1720s

Oil on canvas, 67¾ x 53⅜ in. (172 x 135.5 cm)

The Cleveland Museum of Art. Leonard C. Hanna, Jr. Fund, 1982.36

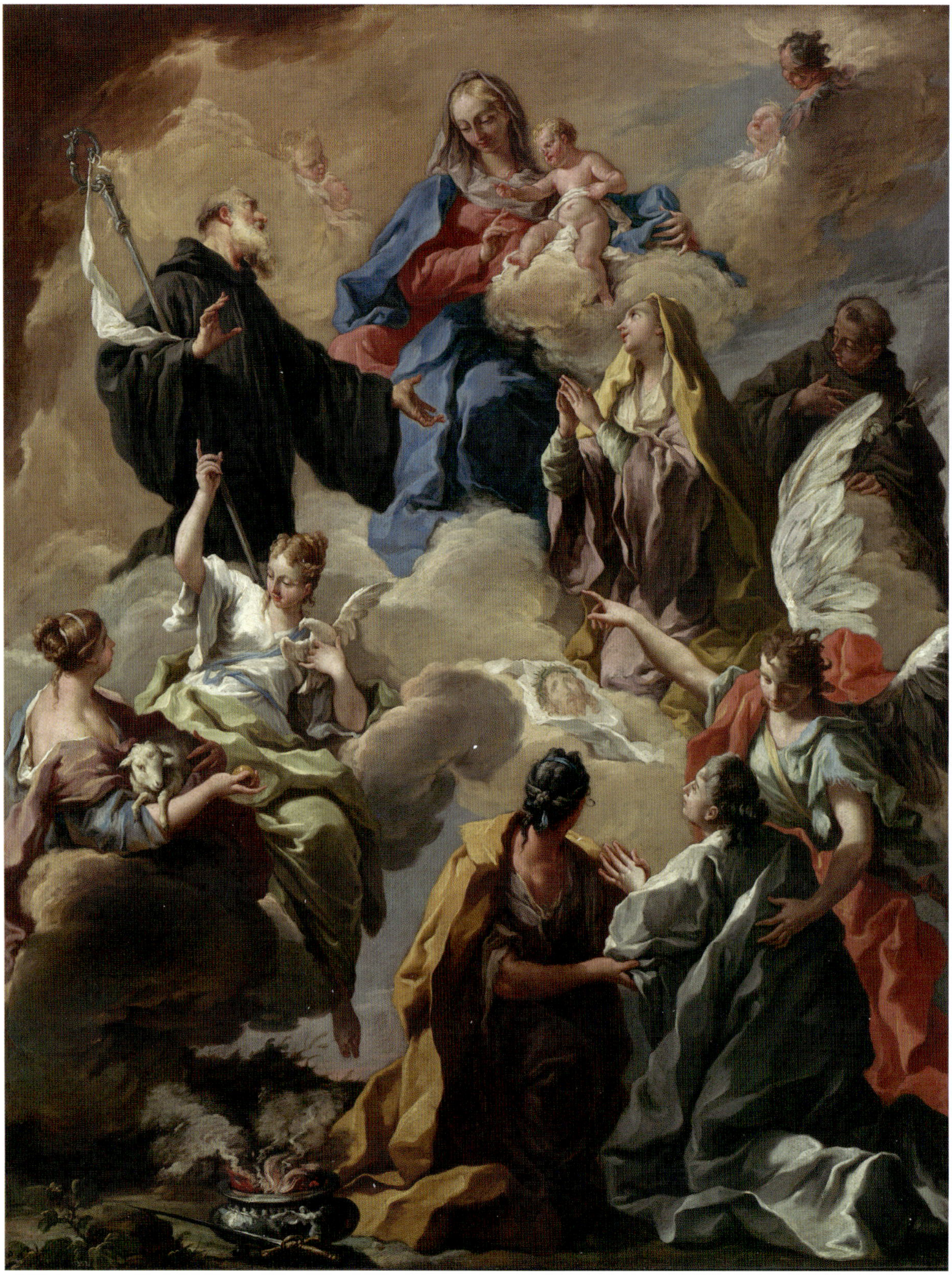

This work by Giovanni Battista Pittoni (also known as Giambattista Pittoni) is characteristic of the Venetian Rococo style seen at the beginning of the eighteenth century. In it a devout woman, at lower right, is presented to the central Virgin and Child by an angel and Saints Lucy, Agnes, Scholastica, Benedict, Veronica, and Anthony of Padua. To the left of the woman, St. Lucy is identified by her wide-sleeved robe, the cauldron, and the sword, which pierced her neck, lying at her feet. Next to Lucy is St. Agnes, carrying a lamb (*agnus* in Latin), the underdrawing of which appears through the paint, showing that the animal's leg has changed position and that Pittoni must have experimented with the painting's composition.[1] St. Scholastica holds the dove, symbolic of the account of her death in which her brother, St. Benedict, witnessed her soul flying up to Heaven in the form of a dove. St. Benedict wears a Benedictine habit and holds his traditional T-shaped crosier, which signifies an abbot. Below the Madonna at center is St. Veronica, wearing a simple robe and head scarf and kneeling before the cloth bearing Christ's face. St. Anthony of Padua, in his Franciscan habit and holding a lily stalk, appears behind St. Veronica in a pose of adoration.[2] Pittoni's paintings often include Franciscan saints, perhaps due to his own devotional identity or more likely at the request of the patron.[3]

This particular grouping of saints does not appear in any of Pittoni's other paintings. The size of this group, with ten figures, is also rare for Pittoni, as generally only three or four saints appear with the Virgin and Child.[4] The saints in this group come from different time periods and are generally unrelated to each other, except that Benedict and Scholastica are siblings. The grouping probably had special meaning to the patron, although the original location and patronage of this work have not yet surfaced, so the specific context is not yet known. Giambattista's career began during the early eighteenth-century in the workshop of his uncle Francesco Pittoni (1645-1724), who, though undistinguished among Venetian painters, painted in the heavy and dramatic manner that prevailed in eighteenth century Venice. Giambattista's hand can be seen in some of Francesco's works, as the energetic handling of drapery and the animated facial expressions and graceful poses of the figures are characteristic of Giambattista's paintings.[5]

By the mid-1720s, Pittoni was a peer to accomplished Venetian painters such as Sebastiano Ricci, Pellegrini, Piazzetta, and Giambattista Tiepolo. The light-saturated and roseate palette of Ricci and Pellegrini attracted Pittoni, though at the same time, he developed his own elegant style of figural arrangements. By studying the work of Venetian and foreign painters, Pittoni developed a style that had an affinity with the French Rococo.[6] Rodolfo Pallucchini considered Pittoni representative of "the most international moment in Venetian Settecento painting, although he did not leave Venice to transverse Europe."[7] The painting here exemplifies the Venetian Rococo in its elegant composition, soft treatment of light, broad, richly colored brushstrokes, and the balletic, graceful poses of the figures.[8]

Pittoni was admired by his fellow painters in Venice and served as president of the Venetian Academy from 1758 to 1760 and again in 1763.[9] Giovanni Battista Piazzetta stated, "*Se io avessi figlioli per genio amici della pittura, non vorrei che avessero altro maestro che Giambattista Pittoni*" ("If I had children with a talent for painting, I would not want them to have any teacher other than Giambattista Pittoni").[10]

Ana Dieglio

Notes

1 Franca Zava Boccazzi, *Pittoni* (Venice: Alfieri Publishing, 1979: 187).
2 For identification of the saints, see *Encyclopedia of Saints* by Clemens Jockle (London: Alpine Fine Arts Collection, Ltd., 1995).
3 Boccazzi, *Pittoni*, 187.
4 For examples of Pittoni paintings with smaller groupings of saints, see *Madonna and Child with Saints Peter, Paul, and Pius V* in the Church of Corona, Venice (Boccazzi, *Pittoni*, fig 45), *Madonna and Child with Saints Nicholas of Bari and Anthony of Padua* in the Duomo, Venice (Boccazzi, *Pittoni*, fig. 383), and *Madonna and Child with Saints Rose of Lima, Domenic, Bonaventure, and Carlo Borromeo* in the Nat Leeb Collection, Paris (Boccazzi, *Pittoni*, fig. 419).
5 Dwight C. Miller, "Review: Pittoni: L'opera completa by Franca Zava Boccazzi," *The Art Bulletin* (New York: College Art Association) 64, no. 4 (Dec. 1982): 673.
6 Ibid.
7 Philip Pouncey, "Review: I disegni di Giambattista Pittoni by Rodolfo Pallucchini," *The Burlington Magazine for Connoisseurs* 88, no. 521 (Aug. 1946): 205.
8 Jane Martineau and Andrew Robison, eds., *The Glory of Venice: Art in the Eighteenth Century* (London: Royal Academy of Arts, 1994 and Washington, D.C.: The National Gallery of Art, 1995: 130).
9 Ibid., 486.
10 Miller, "Review: Pittoni," 673.

Provenance

Thought to have come from the chapel of a now-demolished palace in Belluno, Italy. Eugene Broerman (1860-1930), sold, Galerie Georges Giroux (Brussels, Belgium), March 21, 1927, as a work by Giambattista Tiepolo, 65.000 francs written in auction catalog margin as price, purchaser unknown. In the Piccoli Collection, Venice, 1933; Listed in Benefit of L'Oevre Nationale de Service Social aux Familles Mililtaires auction catalog, Galerie Fievez (Brussels, Belgium), June 23-24, 1941, price and purchaser unknown. Baron André Descamps (Brussels, Belgium) appears as owner of work in Cleveland Museum of Art Curatorial Files, date and price of purchase unknown. Newhouse Galleries (New York, New York), sold to the Cleveland Museum of Art, 1982.

Exhibition

The Cleveland Museum of Art, *The Year in Review*, 1983, cat. no. 15, repr.

Bibliography

Galerie Fievez, Brussels, *Catalogue d'une vente publique* [organized for the benefit of L'oeuvre Nationale de Service Social aux Familles de Militaires] (June 23-24, 1841): 48, no. 232, pl. VI.
Galerie Georges Giroux, Brussels, *Catalogue of the Collection of Eugene Broerman* (March 21, 1927): 48, no. 24, pl. 17 (as Tiepolo).
Pittoni, Laura Cogiola, "Pseudo influenza francese nell'arte di Giambattista Pittoni," in *Rivista della citta di Venezia* 12, no. 8 (August 1933): 410, no. 23.
Arslan, W., "Breve nota su Pittoni," *Bolletino d'Arte* 36, ser. 4 (1951): 30, n. 6.
Pittoni, Laura Coggiola, *Opera inedite, revendicate a poco note di Giambattista Pittoni*, 31, fig. 35. Venice: Tipografia del Gazzettino Illustrato, 1953.
Ruggieri, Ugo, *Corpus Graphicum Bergomense; Disegni inediti di collezioni bergamasche*, Vol. I: *Collezioni Private*, 29, MF440 (drawing). Bergamo, Monumenta Begomensia, 26, 1969.
Boccazzi, Franca Zava, *Pittoni*, 187. Venice: Alfieri Publishing, 1979.
Cleveland Museum of Art Bulletin (Jan. 1983), reproduced on pp. 1, 14.
Martineau, Jane, and Andrew Robison, eds., *The Glory of Venice: Art in the Eighteenth Century*, 130, 486. London: Royal Academy of Arts, 1994 and Washington, D.C.: The National Gallery of Art, 1995.

CAT. 15

Giovanni Battista Pittoni (Italian, 1687–1767)

The Vision of Saint Anthony of Padua, ca. 1730

Oil on canvas, 30⅞ x 23⅛ in. (78.6 x 58.7 cm)

The San Diego Museum of Art, Gift of Anne R. and Amy Putnam, 1948:3

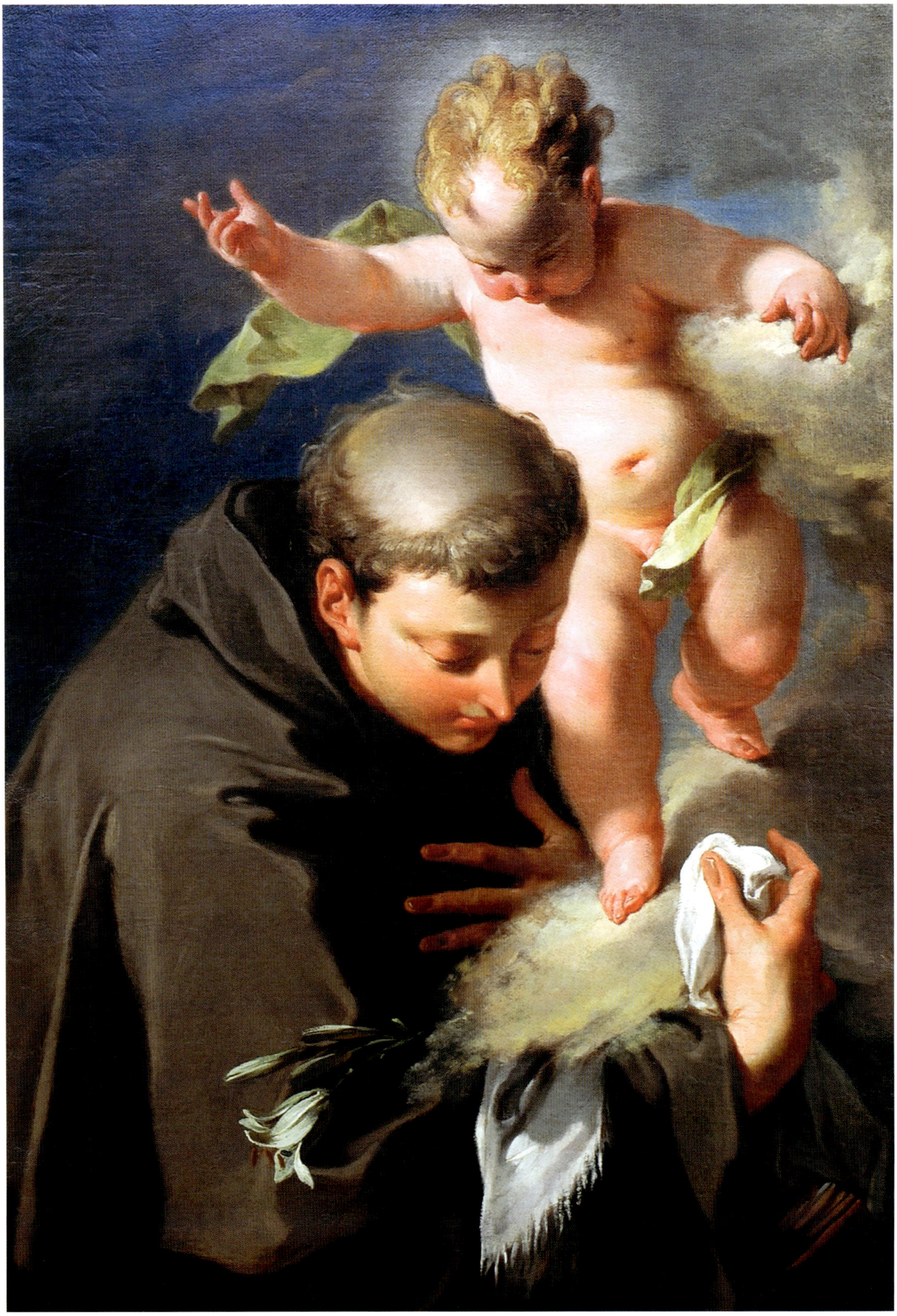

Giovanni Battista Pittoni, also known as Giambattista Pittoni, is an artist to whom the accidents of history have been unkind. Versatile and technically proficient, he might have been the leading Venetian artist of his day if he had been born a generation earlier. He was instead the contemporary of Piazzetta and Tiepolo, from whose shadows he has never quite emerged. Yet, while Pittoni's early work shows some of Piazzetta's quixotic power, and his later work the luminosity of Tiepolo, he is an artist of a different stamp from either of them, with a light Rococo touch more closely akin to contemporary French painters. The sources of this style remain a subject of debate: some scholars propose that Pittoni accompanied his uncle (and first master) Francesco Pittoni (1645-1724) during the latter's trip to France in 1720, whereas others argue that Pittoni's apparent Frenchness was acquired indirectly through artists like Ricci or Pellegrini.

The qualities of Pittoni's mature style, whatever their source, are all apparent in *The Vision of St. Anthony*, ranging from the intimate tone of the composition, to the attenuated and expressive hands of the saint, to the liquid strokes of paint that define glints of light on the fingernails, ears, noses, and hair of the figures. These highlights are far more visible after the painting's recent conservation treatment. Freeing the work of a yellowed varnish and extensive overpaint (underneath which much original paint was still intact), the restoration also brought to light the subtle colors now visible in the clouds beneath the child's feet. Pittoni has been accused of an inability to paint convincing psychological drama, but we here witness an inventive pictorial conceit: for the moment depicted is not the height of the vision when the saint looks upward at the child, but rather the first moments as the vision appears and Anthony drops the book—it tumbles out of the lower right corner of the painting—from which he had been reading or praying. The recent restoration of the painting has also revealed that when it was long ago relined, the tacking edges had been opened flat and painted, enlarging the canvas. This was presumably done to make the painting fit the frame it was given when in the Crawford collection. A new frame now covers the extensions and returns the composition to its original painted dimensions, enhancing its intimate feel.

Pittoni frequently repeated his compositions, and another version of this painting was formerly in the Donà collection in Venice and later in the Vigolo collection at Vicenza, but its present whereabouts are uncertain.[1] The note on the reverse of the painting's old frame explained that it was thought to be by Elisabetta Sirani (1638-1635) when acquired in Venice in 1825, and according to inscriptions on the photograph in the Witt Library, the painting was later given to Jacopo Amigoni (1682-1752) before correctly reattributed to Pittoni by a "B.S.M." A related drawing in the Louvre (inv. no. 5276) is there catalogued as by Pittoni, but it is instead one of a set of copies after Pittoni made by Anton Kern (German, 1709-1747), who worked with Pittoni from ca. 1725-35.[2] Kern's drawing nonetheless supports Zava Boccazzi's dating of the painting to the late 1720s.

John Marciari

Notes

1 L. Cogglioli Pittoni, "Pseudo influenza francese nell'arte di Giambattista Pittoni," *Rivista della città di Venezia* (August 1933): 410.

2 Alice Binion, *I Disegni di Giambattista Pittoni*, Corpus Graphicum, Vol. 4 (Florence, La Nuova Italia, 1983: 83).

3 A handwritten note affixed to the back of the painting's old frame records this provenance.

4 The painting was not among those in the Crawford sale at Christie's, London, October 11, 1946, but was presumably sold around the same time.

5 Zava Boccazzi was unaware that the ex-Crawford painting (her cat. no. 252) is the canvas now in San Diego and mistakenly thought it another version.

Provenance

James Lindsay, later 24th Earl of Crawford (1783-1869), purchased at Venice in 1825;[3] by descent to David Alexander Robert Lindsay, 28th Earl of Crawford and 11th Earl of Balcarres (1900-1975), until ca. 1946-48;[4] Jacob M. Heimann, New York and Los Angeles, from whom acquired by The San Diego Museum of Art.

Bibliography

Frederickson, Burton B., and Federico Zeri. *Census of Pre-Nineteenth-Century Italian Paintings in North American Public Collections,* 167, 374, 632. Cambridge, Mass.: Harvard University Press, 1972.

Boccazzi, Franca Zava. *Pittoni,* 159, cat. nos. 178, 183, 252. Venice: Mondadori Electa, 1979.[5]

Brezzo, Steven L., *et al. San Diego Museum of Art: Selections from the Permanent Collection,* 141. San Diego: The San Diego Museum of Art, 1993.

CAT. 16

SEBASTIANO RICCI (Italian, 1659-1734)

Diana and Endymion, ca. 1717-20

Oil on canvas, 49 3/16 x 70 3/8 in. (125 x 178.7 cm)
Princeton University Art Museum, Museum purchase, bequest of Gilbert S. McClintock, Class of 1908, and gift of Mr. and Mrs. Harry L. Tepper, by exchange, y1964-167
Photo: Bruce M. White

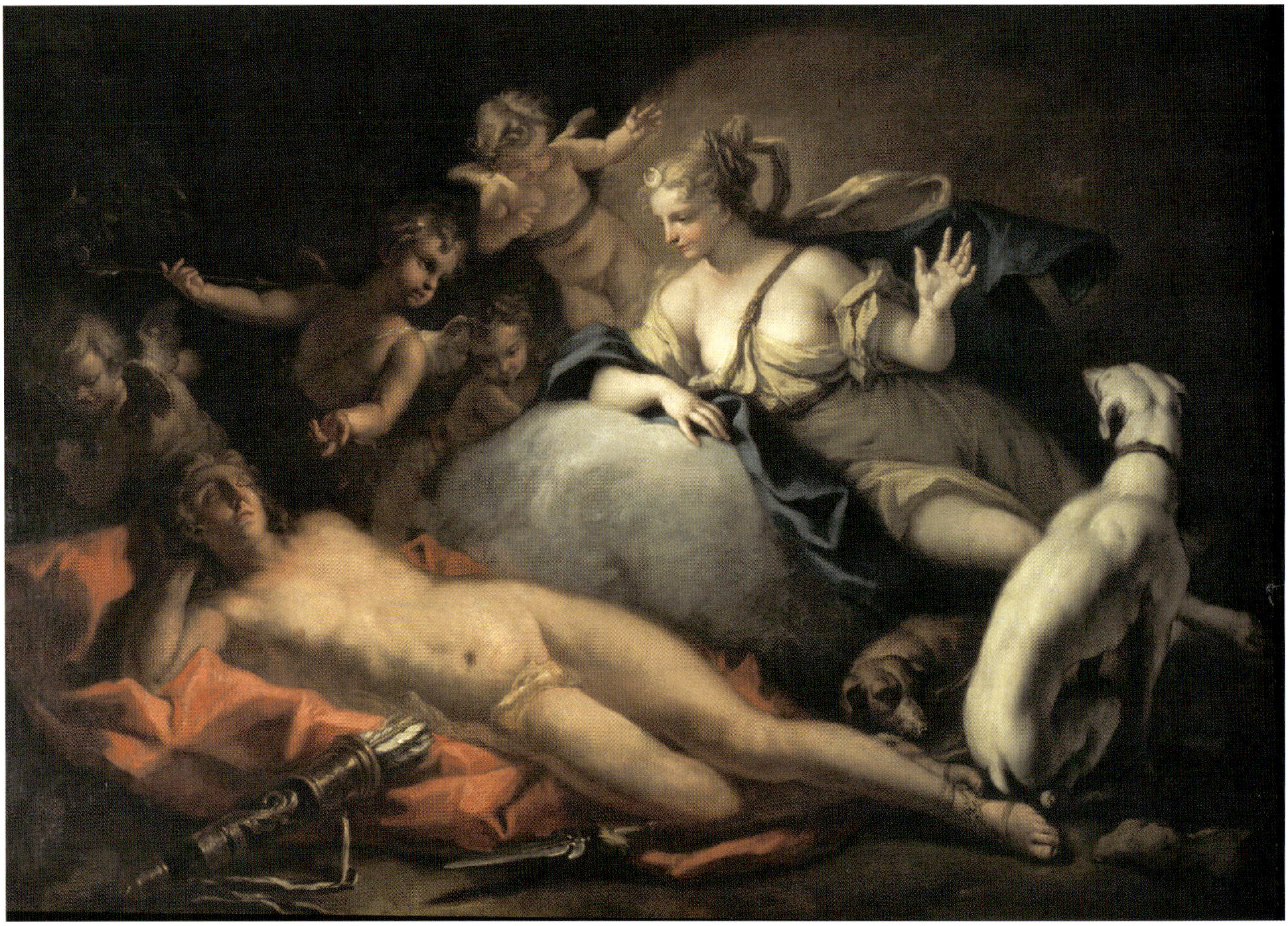

The story of Endymion has its roots in classical antiquity and appears in an immense variety of accounts. However, from the Renaissance forward, interpretations generally coalesce around the goddess of the moon falling in love with the hunter or shepherd Endymion, who, in order to stay in this state forever, falls into an eternal sleep, in which he is visited by the goddess. In Ricci's version, Endymion reclines on an orange-red cloak, his elegant, nude body displayed for the viewer. Emphasizing the depth of his slumber, Endymion rests atop his spear, quiver dropped by his side, and hunting dogs waiting at his feet. The moon goddess, identified by her lunar headdress, has descended from the heavens on a cloud, gazing adoringly upon the young man, while lifting her proper left hand in a formal gesture of surprise. Four cupids articulate the narrative's contours. At far left, a putto holds a bow, while his neighbor points an arrow directly at the goddess as he gestures to Endymion. A third putto gazes down at the sleeping hunter, mimicking the goddess's gaze with a knowing smile, while the last cupid points to the deity.

By presenting the goddess as the putti's target, Ricci presents an interpretation that—rather than drawing on the classical sources for the myth, such as Apollodorus, Pausanias, and Hyginus—owes more to contemporary literary and musical interpretations of the story. In early modern Europe, the goddess became identified with Diana, the virgin goddess of the moon and the hunt, and Cupid took on a pivotal role in the story, inflaming Diana's love. The link between literary accounts and visual representations of Endymion already had a considerable legacy by Ricci's era, including a well-known 1620 sonnet by Giovanni Battista Marino, based on a work of art in the poet's own collection. Endymion subsequently became a popular subject for the stage. Although no documentation links the artist to specific productions, Ricci must have been intimately familiar with a number of them, given his involvement in set design throughout his career. His extensive international travel and his position as a celebrated artist in such cities as Venice, Rome, London, and Paris also surely exposed him to many stagings, potentially including such works as two interpretations by Alessandro Scarlatti, a pastoral poem by Alessandro Guidi written for Queen Christina of Sweden, a libretto by Francesco de Lemene (set to music by Paolo Magni and Giacomo Griffini), and especially Pietro Metastasio's 1720 libretto, first scored the following year by Domenico Sarro and presented by at least twenty-seven other composers across the eighteenth century.[1]

These narratives generally centered around a conflict between chastity and love, or passion and reason, and follow the basic elements of the Arcadian reform movement, key to the musical and literary works mentioned above: simplicity, clarity, and a reasoned balance of invention with verisimilitude. Ricci had earlier interpreted the subject of Endymion while in England (1713, Chiswick House), but as part of a larger, lighthearted program about the loves of the gods, which reinterpreted the amorous themes of Annibale Carracci's Farnese Palace ceiling in Rome from the 1590s.[2] By contrast, the Princeton work, with its circular chain of figures, emphasizes Diana being struck by the arrows of love, the moment in which chastity becomes destabilized, and it addresses the biting irony of falling in love with someone who will remain forever present, but inaccessible. For this more contemplative interpretation, Ricci chose an altogether more sober tone, from the muted palette and subdued handling to Diana's serious expression and the putti's restraint.

This painting only came to the attention of scholars in 1964, when it was acquired by Princeton and published as a work of Sebastiano Ricci from the first decade of the eighteenth century. Recently Annalisa Scarpa has convincingly redated the work based on its rapport with the Diana in the Palazzo Taverna in Rome, also noting the close correspondence of the greyhound in this painting with the dog in the Getty picture (cat. 17), placing this work between 1717 and 1720. As Betsy J. Rosasco has observed, the position of Endymion may also draw on the 1668 version of the subject by Giovanni Battista Gaulli (1639-1709), which Ricci could have easily seen while in Rome, where it stood in the Palazzo Colonna from 1694, a place where Ricci executed important ceiling paintings.[3]

Jon L. Seydl

Notes

1 For a more comprehensive list of works of art on Endymion, see the entry in *The Oxford Guide to Classical Mythology in the Arts 1300-1990s*, 2 vols. (New York: Oxford University Press , 1993, I: 373-82). For a more in-depth analysis of some of the most important performances in the late seventeenth and eighteenth centuries, see Bruno Forment, "Moonlight on Endymion: In Search of 'Arcadian Opera,' 1688-1721," *Journal of Seventeenth-Century Music* 14, no. 1 (2008). May 28, 2010. http://www.sscm-jscm.org/v14/no1/forment.html. Wendy Heller (email May 23, 2010) also offered useful suggestions.

2 George Knox, "Sebastiano Ricci at Burlington House: A Venetian Decoration 'Alla Romana'" *Burlington Magazine* 127, no. 990 (September 1985): 600-9.

3 Email May 13, 2010; Robert Enggass, *The Painting of Baciccio, Giovanni Battista Gaulli, 1639-1709* (University Park, Penn: Pennsylvania State University Press, 1964: 156-7, fig. 5).

Provenance

Robert Draper (Miami, Florida), sold to the Princeton Museum of Art, 1964, by exchange with the bequest of Gilbert S. McClintock, Class of 1908, and the gift of Mr. and Mrs. Harry L. Tepper.

Bibliography

Scarpa, Annalisa. *Sebastiano Ricci*, 286-87, cat. no. 400. Milan: Bruno Alfiere, 2006, with prior bibliography.

CAT. 17

Sebastiano Ricci (Italian, 1659-1734)

Diana and Her Dog, 1717-20

Oil on canvas, 29⅛ x 21⅞ in. (74 x 55.6 cm)
The J. Paul Getty Museum, Los Angeles, California

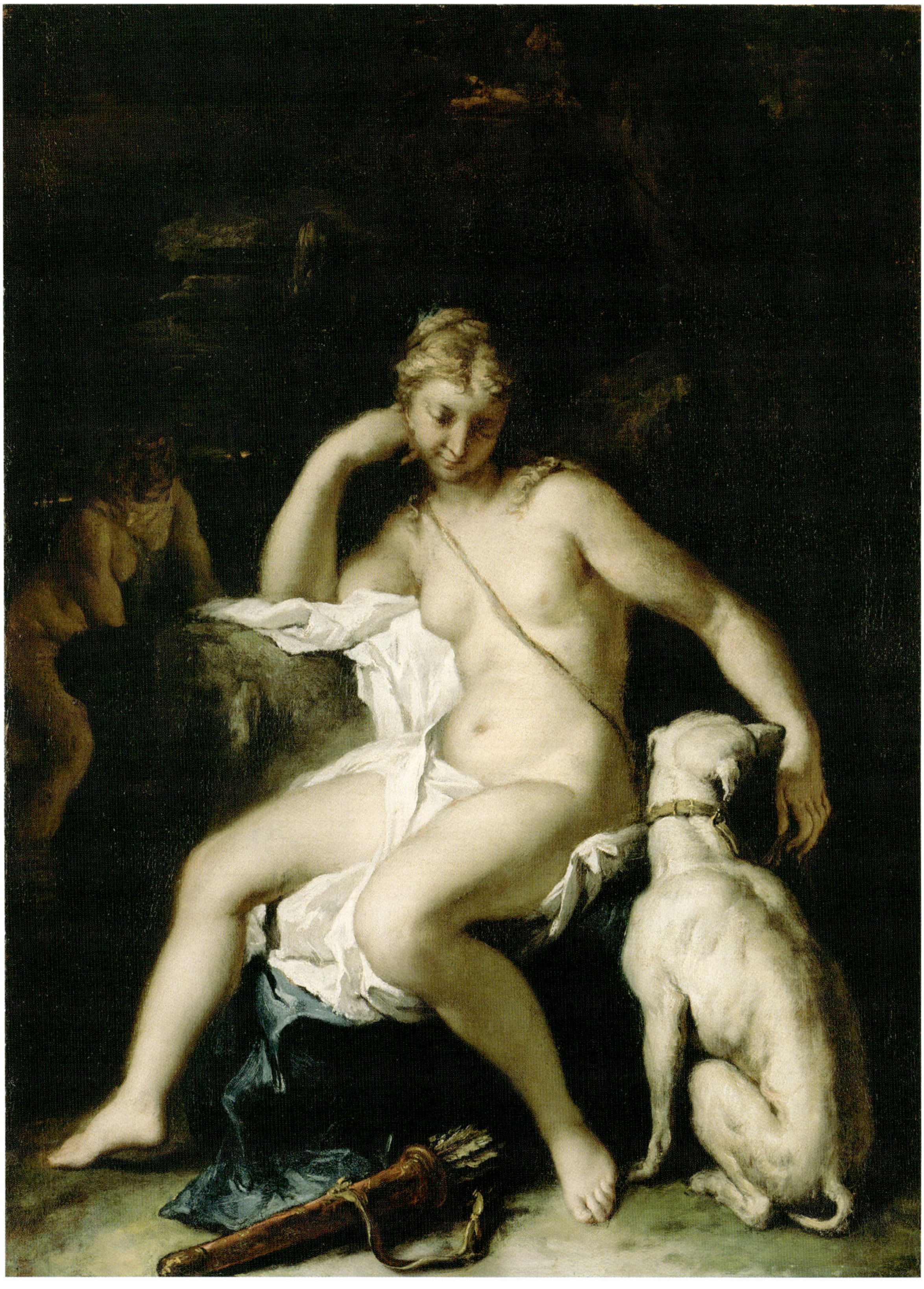

Diana, the Roman goddess of the moon and the hunt, sits on a rock in a dark, sylvan setting, caught in a moment of reflection, quiver at her feet. The virgin deity distractedly holds the leash of a lithe, muscular greyhound, resting on its haunches, while one of her attendants strides into the middleground at left, her action in distinct contrast to Diana's pensive leisure.

Sebastiano Ricci, one of Venice's greatest narrative painters, rarely painted single mythological figures, and this picture is uncharacteristically spare and muted for the artist. Perhaps for this reason, the painting first appeared on the market in 1970 with an attribution to the Venetian painter Jacopo Amigoni (ca. 1685–1752). Jeffrey Daniels first published the painting as Ricci in 1976, an attribution sustained by David Jaffe and Annalisa Scarpa. Scarpa further connected this unsigned work to Ricci because of its similarity in style and subject matter to a significantly larger painting of Diana in the Palazzo Taverna in Rome, where an attendant and dog also accompany the goddess, who, in contrast to the Getty picture, actively strides forward in the act of hunting.

The dog's nervous glance off to the left refers obliquely to the story of Diana and Acteon, a hunter who came upon Diana and her attendants bathing in the woods. When he was discovered spying upon the women, the goddess transformed Acteon into a stag, and his dogs turned on the hunter and killed him. Common since the Renaissance, the subject justified the display of beautiful, nude women, while simultaneously reflecting on the risks of this visual pleasure. With Ricci's subtle allusions only the dog seems aware of a viewer, leaving the goddess entirely at rest, displayed openly for the viewer.

Ricci's creamy, tactile brushwork emphasizes the pleasure of beholding Diana's body. The impastoed edge of the white drapery highlights the curve of the goddess's breast, abdomen, and thighs, while Ricci dragged beige and brown paint lightly across her torso to represent her bow strap. Likewise, the goddess's pinwheel form almost makes contact with her dog, the gap between the paw and foot as well as the nose and wrist tantalizingly drawing attention to the sense of touch.

The Roman version of this subject has been plausibly dated to the period of 1717 to 1720, when Pietro Gabrielli, an important Roman patron of Ricci, owned the palazzo. For this reason, Scarpa has questioned the ca. 1705–10 date, and has reasonably considered it painted in 1717–20.

Jon L. Seydl

Provenance

Leicester Art Gallery (London, England), sold to a private collector; Private collector, sold, Sotheby's, London, June 24, 1970, lot 3, to J. Paul Getty. J. Paul Getty, 1892–1976 (Malibu, California, and Sutton Place, Surrey, England), upon his death, held in trust by the estate; Estate of J. Paul Getty, distributed to the J. Paul Getty Museum, 1978.

Bibliography

Scarpa, Annalisa. *Sebastiano Ricci,* 233, cat. no. 257. Milan: Bruno Alfiere, 2006, with prior bibliography.

CAT. 18

Sebastiano (Italian, 1659-1734) and Marco (Italian, 1676-1730) Ricci

Death of Saint Paul the Hermit, 1700-10

Oil on canvas, 37 x 54 in. (94 x 137.2 cm)

Spencer Museum of Art, University of Kansas, Gift from the Samuel H. Kress Study Collection, 1960.0055

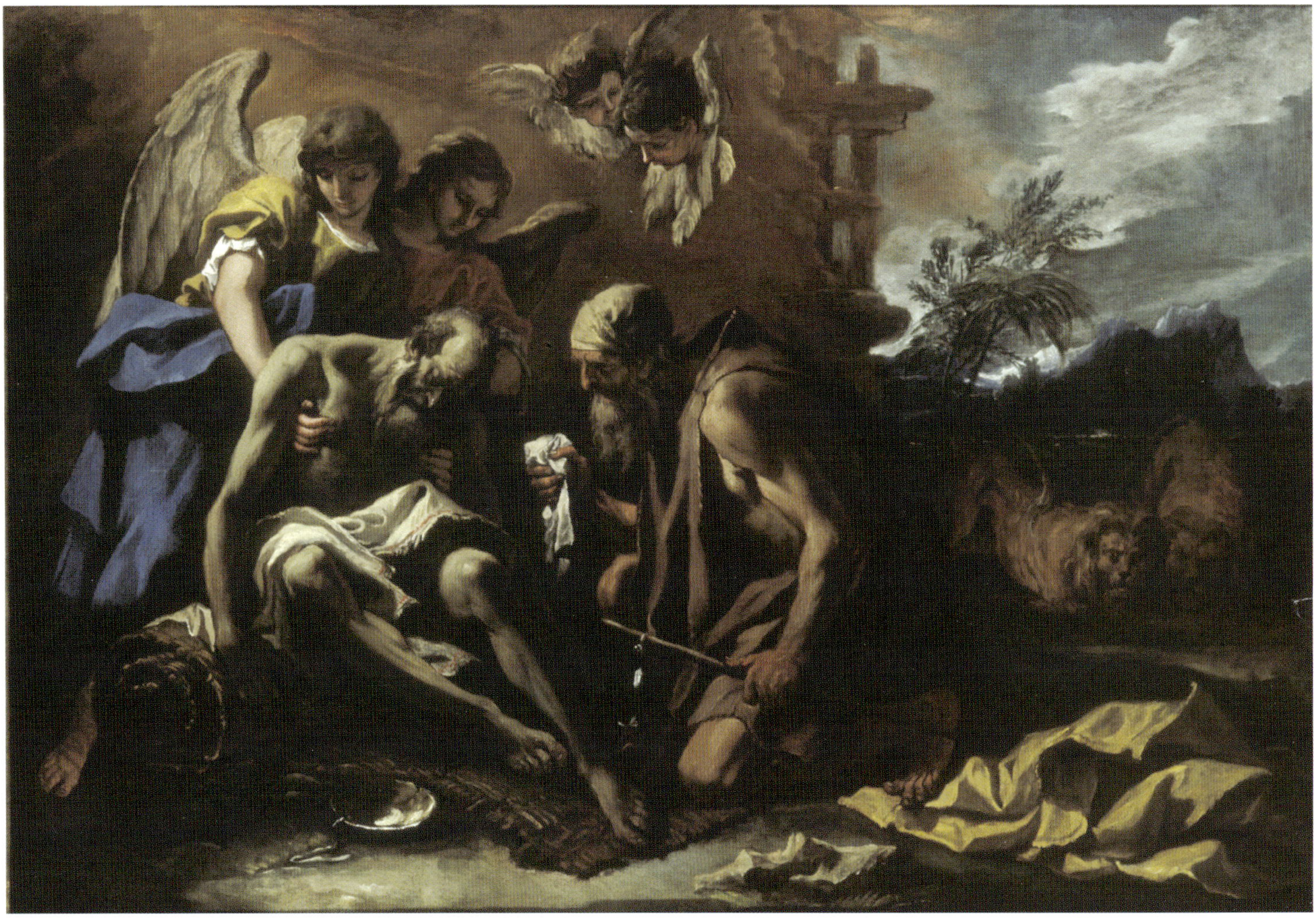

Sebastiano Ricci is an important figure in Venetian history painting during the first third of the eighteenth century, and his work was celebrated throughout Europe. After long periods of study and early activity in Parma and Rome, he returned to Venice at the age of forty. Even after that he traveled extensively to Vienna and Florence, and above all to London, where he stayed from 1712 to 1716. He brought into Venetian painting something of the classicism of central Italy, as exemplified by Pietro da Cortona (1596-1669) and, even more importantly, that of sixteenth-century Venice, as exemplified by Paolo Veronese (ca. 1528-1588), which in the course of time became an important element in the art of Tiepolo.

The story of Saint Paul the Hermit, said to be the founder of the anchorite tradition in early fifth-century Egypt, and his younger contemporary, Saint Anthony Abbot, founder of the monastic traditions of early Christianity, was written down very soon after their death by Saint Jerome and must be essentially a matter of history. Anthony believed himself to be the original anchorite of the desert, but God directed him to journey into the wilderness to find a precursor. After various adventures, he found Paul, who had lived quietly all his life in a cave with a palm tree and a spring of water nearby, sustained by a raven that brought him half a loaf of bread each day. After they had a little talk, the raven came by with a whole loaf of bread for the pair of them. The next morning, Paul, aware of his approaching death, sent Anthony back across the desert to fetch a cloak in which he wished to be buried. When Anthony returned, he found Paul dead and wondered how he was going to dig a grave for him. This task was then performed by two friendly lions. The essential elements of the story are depicted in Ricci's picture: Paul's body is held up by angels on the left, in the manner of a pietà; Anthony and the cloak fill the central area; the lions dig the grave in a landscape, possibly by Marco Ricci (1676-1730), Sebastiano's nephew, on the right.

Although the relics of Paul were preserved in Venice, from 1240 until 1381, and Anthony was universally popular, there is little that seems Venetian about this picture, and it appears to have been painted in Florence in 1706-7.[1] It reflects a spirit of stoicism, which pervades certain aspects of the work of Salvator Rosa (1615-1673) and Alessandro Magnasco (1667-1749), and the celebration of the simple life as depicted in the work of Giuseppe Maria Crespi (1665-1747). It may remind us of the pervasive influence down through the ages of Camaldoli, lost in the mountains west of Florence above Vallombrosa, and the Camaldolensian fathers who continue the solitary path of Paul the Hermit.

George Knox

Note

1 The case for a dating in the Florentine period is argued in George Knox, "Sebastiano Ricci's St Anthony Abbot attending the body of St Paul the Hermit." *The Register of the Spencer Museum of Art* 6 (Lawrence: University of Kansas, 1991: 63 ff.)

Provenance

Edman sale, Christie's, July 17, 1925, lot 96, as Jan Lys; H.V. Clark; Berlin, Galerie Fritz Rothman, as Sebastiano Ricci; Milan, Galli; Samuel H. Kress, New York, 1950.

Exhibition

Wertheim Galleries, Berlin, 1927, with the present title.

Bibliography

Shapley, Fern Rusk. *Paintings from the Samuel H. Kress Collection: Italian Schools, XVI-XVIII Century*, 129-30, pl. 249. London: Phaidon Press, 1973.

Daniels, Jeffery. *Sebastiano Ricci*, cat. no. 129, pl. 77. Hove: Wayland, 1975.

Knox, George. "Sebastiano Ricci's St Anthony Abbot attending the body of St Paul the Hermit." *The Register of the Spencer Museum of Art* 6, nos. 8, 9: 57-72. Lawrence: University of Kansas, 1991.

CAT. 19

GIOVANNI BATTISTA TIEPOLO (Italian, 1696–1770)

Queen Tullia Commands Her Coachman to Drive over the Body of Her Father, 1722

Oil on canvas, 16⅞ x 29⅛ in. (43 x 74 cm)
Private Collection, Vancouver, Canada
Image courtesy of Rachel Topham

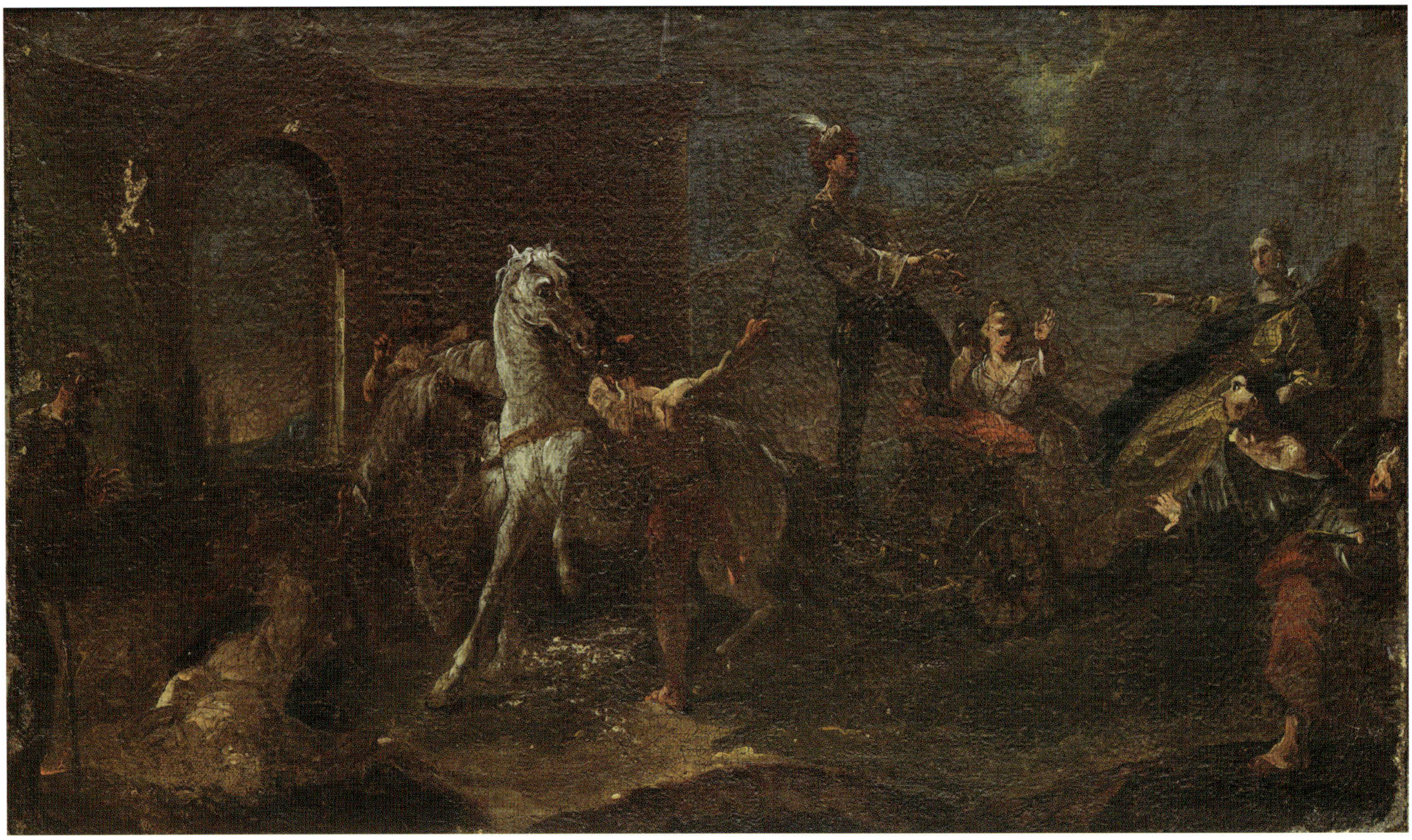

Giovanni Battista Tiepolo is the dominating history painter of eighteenth-century Venice, and indeed of Italy. In his early years, he won celebrity for large-scale secular oil paintings for private houses in Venice, depicting Roman history and other uplifting subjects for a serious clientele. This market collapsed around 1730 with the spread of the more relaxed Rococo style, and Giambattista found commissions in Milan and in the decoration of Venetian villas, often in fresco, developing a dazzling new style that quickly won international esteem, leading to the masterpieces of the Würzburg years, 1751-3. In the last phase of his life, he created magnificent decorations for the Royal Palace at Madrid. Tiepolo was also a great religious painter, and a prolific and superb draughtsman.

The present oil sketch is typical of his preparatory studies for large compositions and belongs to the early 1720s. The story of Tullia is told by Livy, 1.48, and by Ovid in the *Fasti VI*, 569-636. She was the daughter of Servius Tullius, the sixth king of Rome, who contrived the murder of her sister and her own husband, so that she might marry Tarquin, her brother-in-law. She then induced him to depose her father, so that he became the seventh and last king of Rome. After the assassination of the good Servius Tullius, the driver of her chariot came upon his body lying in a Roman street, and pulled up, but Tullia ordered him to drive on—over the body of her father. The subject is understandably rare in art, but it is found in another small painting by Tiepolo in the Simon collection in Berlin, published by Antonio Morassi in 1934 and not seen since.[1]

The painting, though not in perfect condition, is evidently a *bozzetto*, or preliminary oil sketch for a very large picture of which we have no record. It is comparable with the bozzetto in the Marinotti collection in Milan[2] for the painting in the Baltimore *Scipio Africanus Freeing Massiva* (see fig. 5 of Knox's essay in this catalogue), which could even be a pendant for this work, illustrating vice as opposed to virtue.

George Knox

Notes

1. Antonio Morassi, *A Complete Catalogue of the Paintings of G. B. Tiepolo* (London: Phaidon Press, 1962: pl. 301).
2. Massimo Gemin and Filippo Pedrocco, *Giambattista Tiepolo: i dipinti* (Venice: Arsenale Editrice, 1993: pl. 19); George Knox in *Arte/Documento* 22: pl. 3, as *Scipio Africanus Frees Massiva*.

Provenance

Dorotheum sale, Vienna, March 21, 2002, pl. 431.

Bibliography

Knox, George, "Giovanni Battista Tiepolo, *Queen Tullia commands her coachman to drive over the body of the father,*" *Arte/Documento* 22 (2007): 214-7.

CAT. 20

Giovanni Battista Tiepolo (Italian, 1696–1770)

Juno Triumphant, as Queen of the Air, ca. 1735

Oil on canvas, 91½ x 86 in. (213 x 231 cm)

Sarah Campbell Blaffer Foundation, Houston, 1983.4

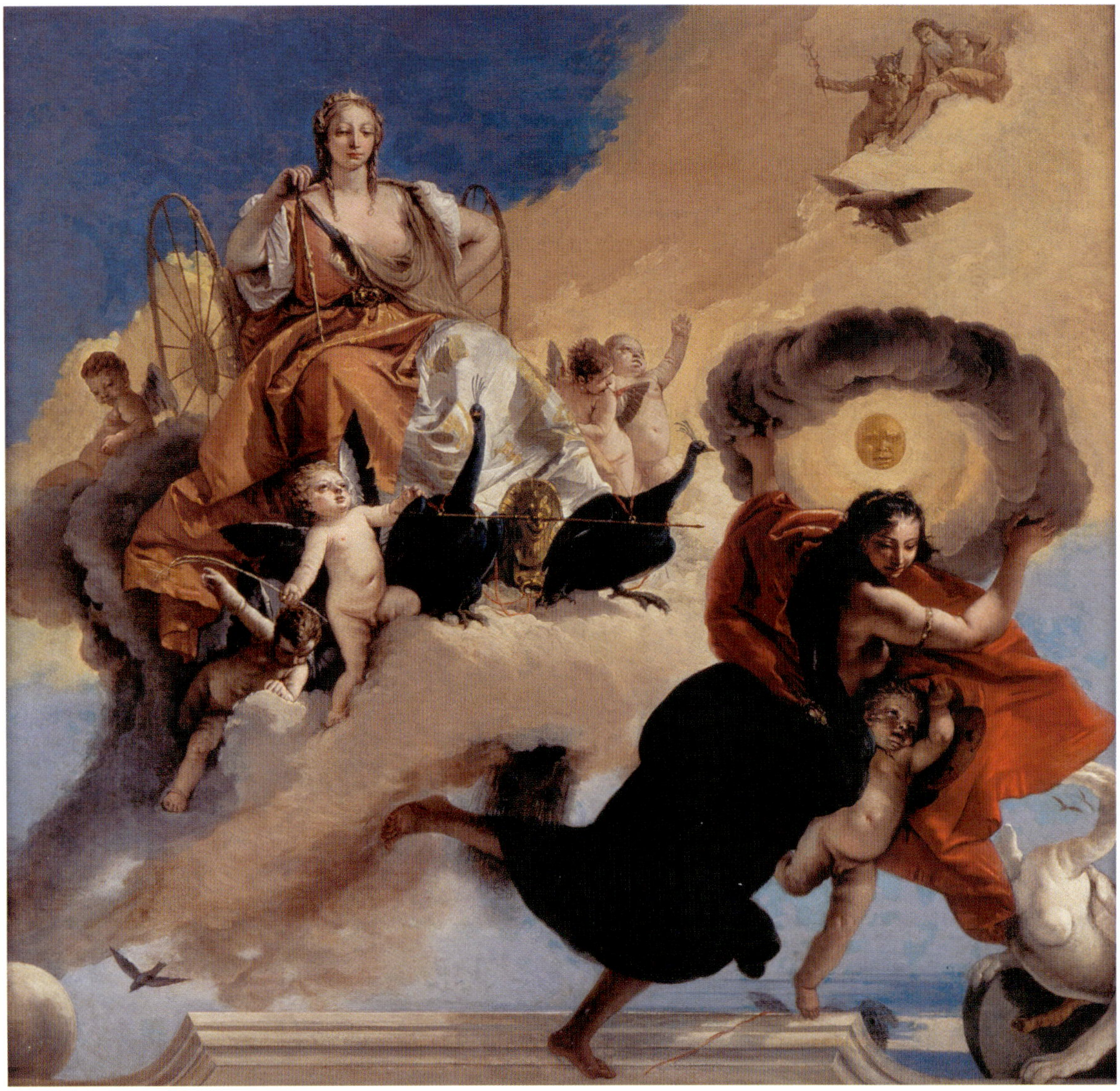

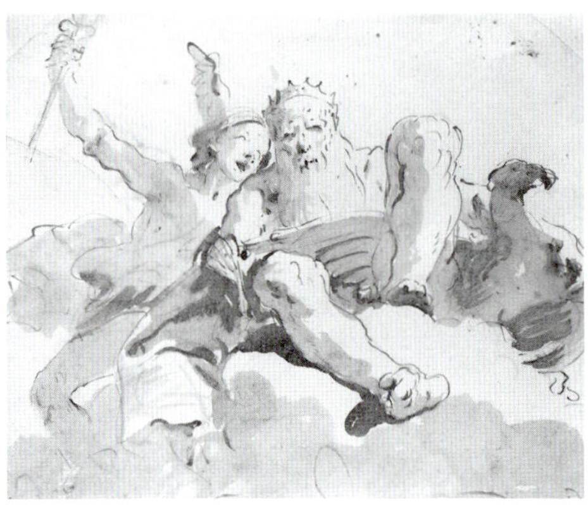

FIG. 1 Giovanni Battista Tiepolo (Italian, 1696–1770)
Jupiter and Mercury
Pen and wash, 7⅝ x 9½ in. (19.5 x 24 cm)
Roux sale, Charpentier 1936, lot 85, location unknown

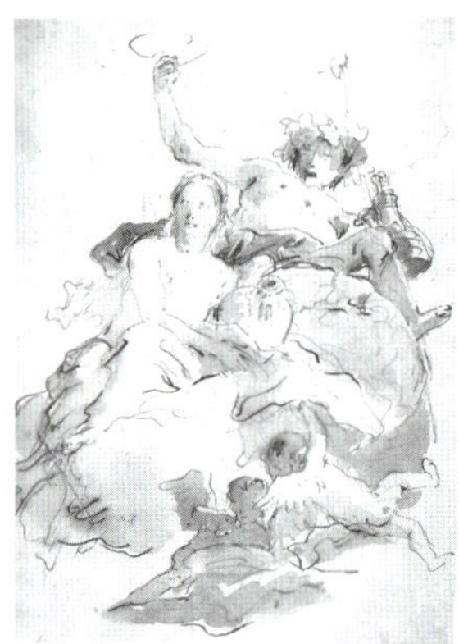

FIG. 2 Giovanni Battista Tiepolo (Italian, 1696–1770)
Bacchus and Ariadne
Pen and wash, 9⅞ x 8⅛ in. (20 x 17.5 cm)
Exh. cat., *Tiepolo et Guardi* (Paris: Galerie Cailleux, 1952: pl. 6); location unknown

This canvas is one of a set of three: a pendant, *The Triumph of Bacchus,* is in the National Gallery of Art, and a much wider, central item, *The Triumph of Amphitrite*, is at Dresden. The three, apparently painted for an unidentified Venetian palace, present intricate problems, which are thoroughly discussed by Diane de Grazia.[1] She suggests sources for the iconography, which seems to represent three of the four elements in the pages of Vincenzo Cartari's *Le immagini degli dei.*[2]

The unity of the three canvases is attested by uniform decorative elements *en grisaille,* on either side of each, and a strip of masonry along the lower edge. In each work these elements were largely painted out at an uncertain date. In the case of the *Bacchus*, Diane de Grazia has published an X-ray showing these decorative elements still visible, though painted out,[3] and a photograph of the *Amphitrite*, showing these elements now restored.[4] In the *Juno* painting, some of these architectural elements can still be seen along the lower edge. Such elements, serving a similar purpose, are also found in Sebastiano Ricci's decorations for the staircase at Burlington House of 1712–14,[5] which suggests some Venetian prototype and indicates that our three canvases may have decorated a staircase. Something quite similar is found in Tiepolo's own fresco decorations on the Scipio theme for the Palazzo Dugnani in Milan of 1731,[6] some ten years earlier than the date generally proposed for the present work, and an earlier dating in the mid-1730s may be considered. However, it may well be that these decorative elements were painted over in the Tiepolo studio at a comparatively early stage, well before the canvases were removed to the Villa Girola, which was acquired by Francesco Artaria in 1798. One may note, on the left in the *Bacchus*, an elderly lady wearing a mural crown; she appears in vestigial form in the X-ray and is completed after the grisaille elements are painted over. This figure is taken directly from the 1647 Italian edition of Cartari, where it is illustrated with a woodcut representing *La Gran Madre.*[7] As "Mother Earth," she reinforces the subject of this painting as representing the element *Earth.*

The present canvas is taken to represent Air. Cartari describes Juno, in her chariot drawn by peacocks, as "queen of the sky, dominatrix of the air."[8] Even more authoritative than Cartari, for Tiepolo, must be Bernard de Montfaucon—"*Il dit aussi comme Ciceron, Macrobe, Martianus Capella et plusieurs autres que Junon est la même chose que l'air.*"[9]

The dark, smiling woman descending before her also represents Air, as described by Cesare Ripa, "over her head is a sun whose rays mix with her hair," with a wreath of clouds and, not a bat, but a bird, perhaps a swallow, a lark, or a nightingale.[10] The presence of Mercury and Jupiter, and Jupiter's eagle, watching from a distance, may be accounted for by another passage in Montfaucon to the effect that Jupiter rules the upper air and Juno the lower air.[11]

Several drawings are associated with this project.[12] One may also note that Jupiter and Mercury are represented in a drawing (fig. 1), which helps to confirm a date in the mid-1730s, and in another drawing, for the *Bacchus and Ariadne* (fig. 2).[13]

A letter from Tiepolo dated 1764, published by Giovanni Marino Urbani de Gheltof, written to an unidentified correspondent in Venice,[14] refers to a cartoon for an Amphitrite, painted for the correspondent's father *di buon memoria* many years before. The phrase "of good memory" may imply that the father is dead, otherwise one might think of the eminent lawyer Carlo Cordellina (1702–1791), for whom Tiepolo worked in his palace in Vicenza and in his Villa at Montecchio Maggiore, nearby. Cordellina also had a palace in Venice in Campo San Maurizio.

George Knox

Notes

1 Diane de Grazia and Eric Garberson, *Italian Paintings of the Seventeenth and Eighteenth Centuries* (Washington, D.C.: National Gallery of Art, 1996).
2 Vincenzo Cartari, *Le imagini degli dei* (Venice: G. Zilletti, 1571: passim).
3 Diane de Grazia in de Grazia and Garberson, *Italian Paintings,* 302, fig. 1.
4 Ibid., 304, fig .2.
5 George Knox, "Sebastiano Ricci at Burlington House: A Venetian Decoration *alla Romana,*" (*Burlington Magazine* 127 (Sept. 1985: 601–9).
6 Michael Levey, *Giambattista Tiepolo: His Life and Art* (New Haven and London: Yale University Press, 1986: pls. 65, 66); Massimo Gemin and Filippo Pedrocco, *Giambattista Tiepolo: i dipinti: opera complete* (Venice: Arsenale Editrice, 1993: pls. 107–9).
7 Vincenzo Cartari, *Imagini delli dei de gl'antichi* (Venice: Tomasini, 1647: 110; facsimile reprint, Graz: Akademische Druck und Verlagsanstalt, 1963: 111).
8 Ibid., 97. Even more authoritative than Cartari, for Tiepolo, must be Bernard de Montfaucon, *L'antiquité expliquée et représentée en figures, vol. 1* (Paris F. Delaulne, 1719: 55): *"Il dit aussi comme Ciceron, Macrobe, Martianus, Capella et plusieurs autres que Juno nest la même chose que l'air."*
9 Montfaucon, *Antiquité expliquée,* vol. 1, 55.
10 Cesare Ripa, *Baroque and Rococo Pictorial Imagery*, ed. Edward Maser (New York: Dover, 1971: cat no. 8). Unfortunately she is there described as "a pretty young girl dressed in draperies of transparent white, with wings on her shoulders," but the traditional identification as Luna (Selene), going back to Heinrich Modern, "Les peintures de Tiepolo a la Villa Girola," (*Gazette des Beaux-Arts* 27 [1902]: 477–88, ill. page 483) and Pompeo Molmenti, *G. B. Tiepolo: la sua vita e le sue opera,* 1909: 278, must be abandoned. An alternative, more general title might be *An Allegory of Air.*
11 Montfaucon, *Antiquité expliquée,* vol. 5, 212.
12 James Byam Shaw and George Knox, *The Robert Lehman Collection*, vol. 6 (New York: The Metropolitan Museum of Art, 1987: pl. 76); Jacob Bean and William Griswold, *18th Century Italian Drawings in The Metropolitan Museum of Art* (New York: The Metropolitan Museum of Art, 1990: pl. 226).
13 Roux sale, Charpentier 1936, lot 85, pen and wash, 19.5 x 24 cm; Richard Owen, Paris; Colnaghi 1952, no. 30. A similar study for the Bacchus was with Zacharie Birtschansky in Paris; exh. cat. *Tiepolo et Guardi* (Paris: Galerie Cailleux, 1952: no. 23, pl. 6), pen and wash, 20 x 17.5 cm).
14 Discussed by Diane de Grazia in *Italian Paintings of the Seventeenth and Eighteenth Centuries* (Washington, D.C.: National Gallery of Art, 1996: 301).

Provenance

Venetian palace; Franceco Artaria, Villa Girola, Lake Como, from January 16, 1798, until 1870; Auguste Artaria, Vienna; Charles Sedelmayer, Paris, 1911; William Robert Timken and Lillian Guyer Timken; bequeathed to the Metropolitan Museum of Art, 1959; deaccessioned 1981; Colnaghi.

Bibliography

Modern, Heinrich. "Les peintures de Tiepolo a la Villa Girola," *Gazette des Beaux-Arts* 27 (1902): 477–88, ill. page 483.
Molmenti, Pompeo. *G. B. Tiepolo: la sua vita e le sue opera,* 277–80, ill. page 279. Milan: Ulrico Hoepli, 1909.
Pignatti, Terisio. *Five Centuries of Italian Painting, 1300–1800,* 190–2. Houston: The Sarah Campbell Blaffer Foundation, 1985.
de Grazia, Diane, and Eric Garberson. *Italian Paintings of the Seventeenth and Eighteenth Centuries*, 301–8. Washington, D.C.: National Gallery of Art, 1996.

CAT. 21

Giovanni Battista Tiepolo (Italian, 1696-1770)

Jesus and the Barren Fig Tree, 1752-53

Oil on canvas, 33¼ x 78½ in. (83 x 189 cm)
Private Collection, Vancouver, Canada
Photo courtesy Vancouver Art Gallery

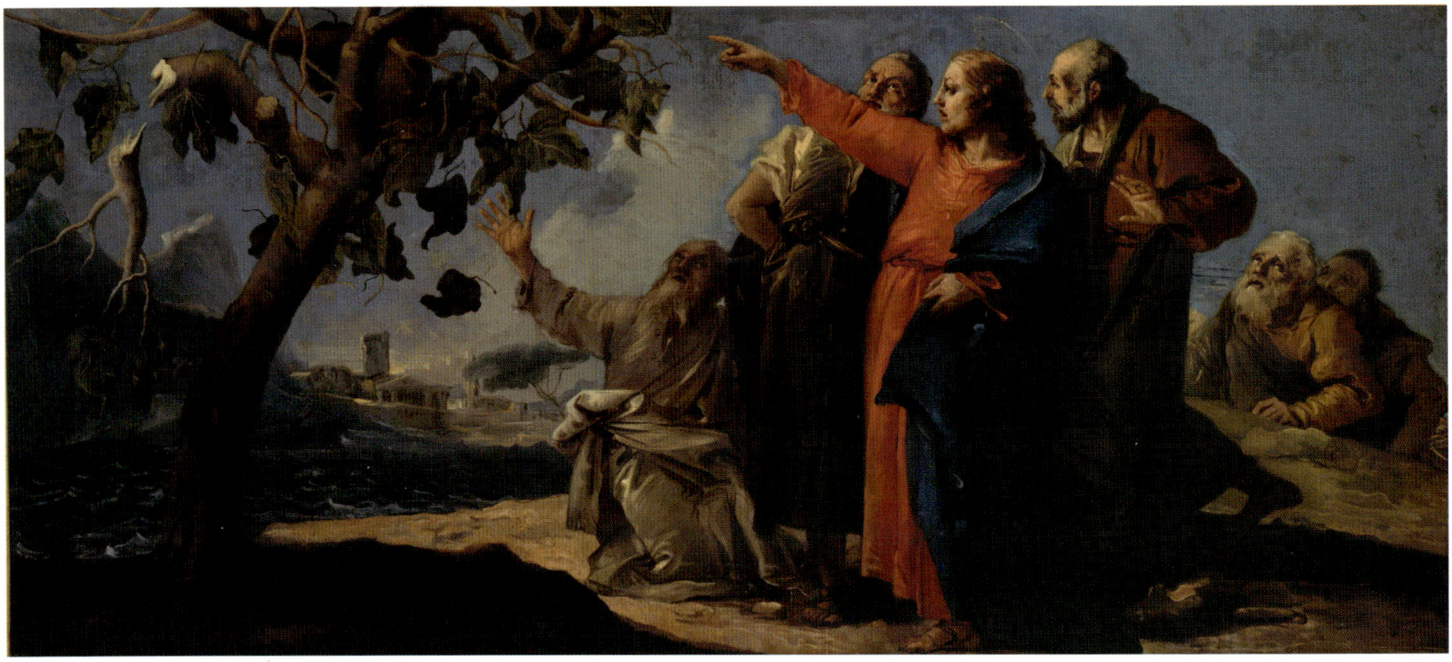

In spite of some general scepticism, and its rough treatment by Peter Krückmann, this painting may deserve more careful consideration as an important product of the Tiepolo studio in the Würzburg years, 1750–1753. First of all, it descends from a pen drawing at Stuttgart that was attributed to Giambattista in 1970.[1] When the painting emerged from obscurity ten years later, it was evident from its shape and character that it was designed as an overdoor. It is very similar in size to a characteristic painting by Domenico Tiepolo in the Thyssen collection, *Jesus Cleansing the Temple*, which appeared to be the lone survivor of a set of four overdoors that were painted for the central room of the Lustschlosslein at Veitshochheim, just outside Würzburg.[2] In Mark 11:12-22 the two themes are interwoven as parts of the same story, and in spite of slight differences in height and total differences in style, the two paintings seem to belong together. *Jesus Cleansing the Temple* is a typical Domenico composition and is unequivocally Domenico's style, as opposed to the present picture and the drawing that precedes it, which seem equally characteristic of Giambattista's work.

There is another difference: Jesus Cleansing the Temple is one of the most popular themes of New Testament imagery,[3] whereas Jesus and the Barren Fig Tree, though it appears in different forms in all three of the synoptic gospels,[4] is one of the rarest. In fact one may cite only two examples of the later theme in the history of Western Art, both German in origin, in two illuminations of the *Deutsche Bilderbibel* and in a woodcut by Urs Graf.[5] Certainly both subjects show Jesus in an unusually aggressive light, and even if the fig tree is to be interpreted as the old tradition of the synagogue, now held to be outworn, it barely justifies the wanton destruction of an innocent tree.

We do not know the exact circumstances of this commission, but it seems clear that some adviser who had a taste for recondite subjects recommended the theme. Domenico was baffled. Giambattista made a careful drawing based upon the Urs Graf woodcut—a type of drawing that he often used when a design was to be executed by another hand. But on this occasion, bearing in mind the importance of a commission for the Prince-Bishop's Summer Palace, I suggest that Giambattista went further, and that he painted the picture himself.

George Knox

Notes

1 George Knox and Christel Thiem, *Tiepolo: Zeichnungen von Giambattista, Domenico und Lorenzo Tiepolo … Handzeichnungen* (Stuttgart: Staatsgalerie, 1970: pl. 5). Domenico writes on the verso: *J. B. Tiepolo, prix. 3 fl. C.M. No. 2694.* The price, 3 Florins, is unusually high, and the attribution, I think, unique. Peter Krückmann in *Tiepolo in Würzburg* (Würzburg: Residenz *Würzburg*, 1996: pl. 130) ignores Domenico's inscription and his attribution of the drawing to his father.

2 Adriano Mariuz, *Giandomenico Tiepolo* (Venice: Alfieri, 1971: pl. 40). Mariuz assigns the painting to the Würzburg years, but does not make the link with Veitshochheim. A visit to the Summer Palace makes the link entirely plausible. Krückmann does not make the link with Veitshochheim or with Domenico's painting.

3 Adelheid Gealt and George Knox, *Domenico Tiepolo: A New Testament* (Bloomington: Indiana University Press, 2006: pls. 172–73).

4 Matthew 21:18–22, *Jesus Curses the Fig Tree*; Mark 11:12–22, combined with *Jesus Cleansing the Temple*; Luke 13:6–9, as *The Parable of the Barren Fig Tree*.

5 See Gealt and Knox, *Domenico Tiepolo,* 14–15. The theme does not appear among the known images of the 315 recorded of the series of Domenico's New Testament illustrations; *Deutsche Bilderbibel aus dem spatter Mittelalter* (Konstanz: J. Thorbecke, 1960: pls. 24a, 24 verso); see *The Illustrated Bartsch* (96 volumes, Norwalk, Conn: Abaris Books, 1978: 2f, pl. 459), for the Urs Graf woodcut.

Provenance

B. Coureau, IB Pall Mall Place, London SW; Christie's sale, July 12, 1912, lot 68; Sotheby's sale, April 16, 1980, pl. 210, as G. D. Tiepolo.

Exhibitions

Vancouver Art Gallery, 1989, pl. 10, as G. B. Tiepolo; Hannover and Düsseldorf, 1991, pl. 80D, as Giovanni Domenico Tiepolo.

Bibliography

Gemin, Massimo, and Filippo Pedrocco. *Giambattista Tiepolo: i dipinti, opera completa,* 511 [*opere attribuite*: 57]. Venice: Arsenale, 1993.

Krückmann, Peter. *Tiepolo in Würzburg*, 1, under cat. no. 130, reproduced p.186, as *Moglicherweise handelt es sich bei Ihm eine grössere Copie eines verlorener Originale von Domenico.* Würzburg: Residenz *Würzburg*, 1996.

CAT. 22

GIOVANNI BATTISTA TIEPOLO (Italian, 1696-1770) and Studio
St. Charles Borromeo Meditating on the Crucifix (fragment), 1767-69
Oil on canvas, 48½ x 44⅛ in. (123.19 x 112.08 cm)
Cincinnati Art Museum, John H. Emery Fund, 1924.178

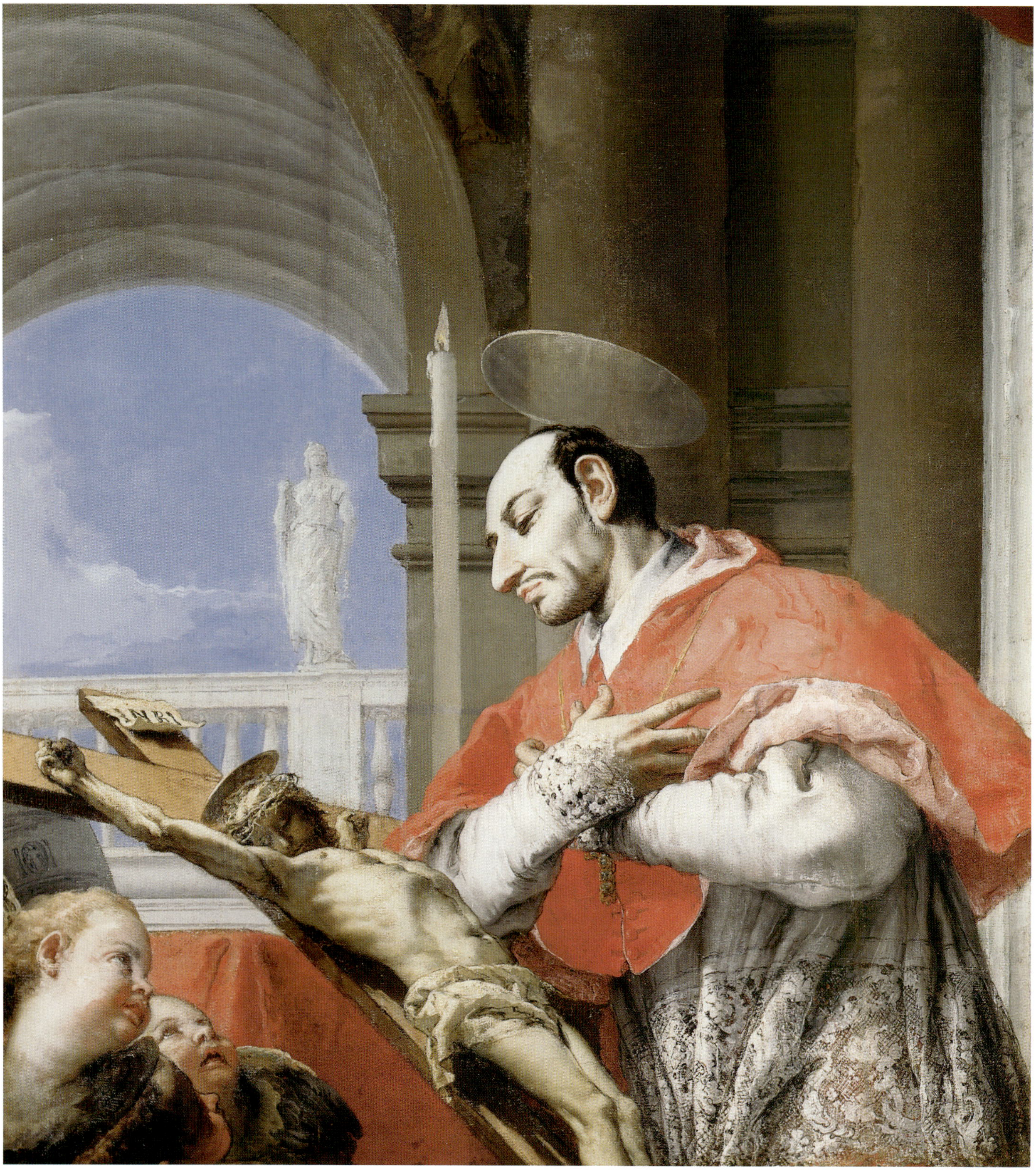

St. Charles Borromeo (1534-1584) was one of the pivotal figures of the Counter-Reformation, the Catholic reform movement that arose in response to the Protestant Reformation. Archbishop of Milan and founder of the Oratorian order, Borromeo transformed lay education and consolidated the power of the parish. Here, however, Tiepolo emphasizes spiritual over political qualities, with the saint gazing on a sculpted crucifix, subtly tinted to suggest the object is coming alive through his intense prayer.

This work is a fragment of a larger altarpiece, one of seven Tiepolo created for San Pascual Baylon, a church newly built at the request of Spain's King Charles III for the Alcantarine order (a Spanish Franciscan reform movement) in Aranjuez. The series—the first complete set of altarpieces commissioned from the painter—became one of Tiepolo's most significant commissions in Spain, where he was called in 1762 to work for the king, and where he remained for the rest of his career.

The court evidently selected the topics for the altarpieces, probably choosing Borromeo because he was both a protector of the Franciscans and the namesake of the king. The saint's meditation on the crucifix was also especially appropriate for this particular church, given the Alcantarines' special devotion to the Eucharist. For this high-profile commission, Tiepolo prepared a striking oil sketch (Courtauld Institute of Art, London), along with at least two known preliminary drawings (Albertina, Vienna, and private collection).

Tiepolo's altarpieces were quickly replaced by a series developed by Anton Raphael Mengs (1728-1779), another major court painter in Madrid, whose more sober and authoritative Roman style might have appealed more to the king's developing taste than the more mystical and expressive Venetian interpretation by Tiepolo. For reasons never directly expressed, the Borromeo altarpiece—unlike the artist's other works for the church—was never installed, nor was its alternative location documented. In any event, several of the Aranjuez altarpieces were later cut into fragments (Courtauld Institute of Art, London; Detroit Institute of Arts; and Prado, Madrid), presumably, like this work, all transformed into smaller and more saleable easel pictures.

For such a large commission, Tiepolo surely would have depended heavily on his studio to execute the final works, and the painting here demonstrates considerable input by assistants. The brushwork is uncharacteristically flat, nor is the fussy handling of the lace and facial features (which would have been seen from a great distance) typical of the artist's direct hand.

Jon L. Seydl

Provenance

Commissioned by King Charles III of Spain, 1716-1788, for San Pascual Baylon (Aranjuez, Spain), 1767; Baron Alfonse, 1831-1898, and Baroness de Ruble (Paris, France), by 1885; Trotti and Company (Paris, France), about 1900, sold to Knoedler, 1923. Knoedler (New York, New York), sold to the Cincinnati Museum of Art, 1924.

Bibliography

Spike, John T. *Italian Paintings in the Cincinnati Art Museum*, 82-85. Cincinnati: Cincinnati Art Museum, 1993.

Seydl, Jon L. *Giambattista Tiepolo: Fifteen Oil Sketches*, 58-63, 76-9. Los Angeles: The J. Paul Getty Museum, 2005, with prior bibliography.

CAT. 23

Giovanni Battista Tiepolo (Italian, 1696–1770)

Madonna of the Goldfinch, ca. 1762–70

Oil on canvas, 24⅛ x 19⅞ in. (61.1 x 50.3 cm)

National Gallery of Art, Washington, Samuel H. Kress Collection, 1943.4.40 (541)

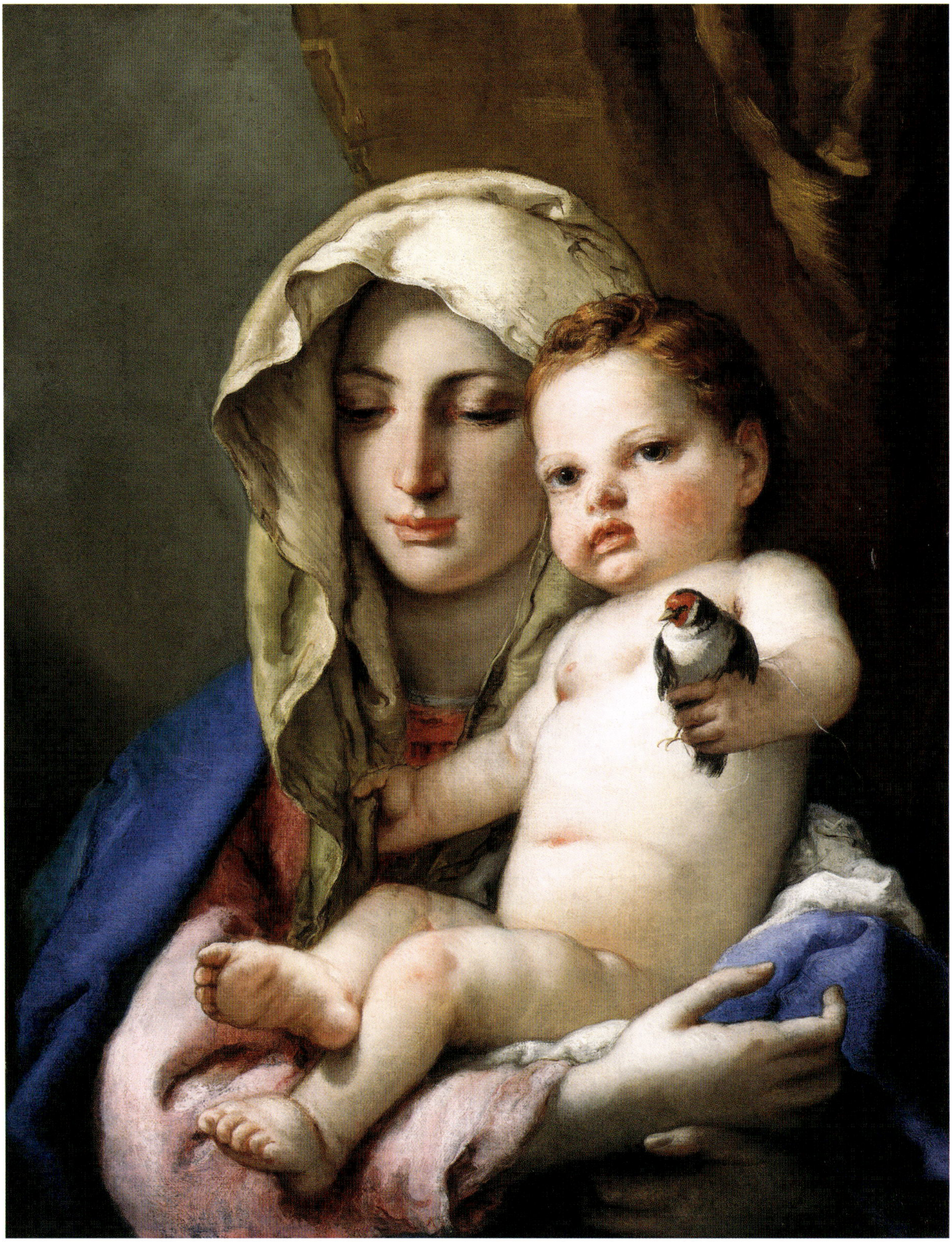

Diane de Grazia, in a long and careful essay, describes the different opinions that have been put forward about this picture, raising doubts about its status and authenticity, and its relationship to another similar painting from the collections of Jacques Seligman & Co. in New York that has been lost to sight since a sale in 1948.[1]

A salient fact that must be noted is that the present picture is not a copy of the Seligman canvas. A copyist follows his model closely, whereas here the painter seems to remember the earlier picture somewhat vaguely, making innumerable variations as his memory and his present thoughts serve him.

It is noted that the theme is found in a drawing by Giambattista at Oxford, in which the child grasps the bird firmly with both hands.[2] This again is a loose variant with many differences, but it would seem certain that it precedes the Seligman design. The drawing is associated with several similar sheets at Bassano[3] and a drawing from the Holland-Martin collection[4] that do not include the goldfinch, but collectively they suggest a date no later than the mid-1750s for the group of drawings and the Seligman picture.

Then there is a further drawing in Madrid, a study in red chalk, that is clearly a careful copy of the present painting.[5] It studies the head and drapery of the Virgin carefully, and with equal care it omits any trace of the child, stopping short wherever the child enters the design. The drawing is very reasonably assigned to Giambattista's younger son, Lorenzo, and to the years that the Tiepolo family spent in Madrid, from 1762 until Giambattista's death in 1770.

There is evidence that paintings from the Drago collection originated in Spain,[6] so our proposal here is that the present charming devotional work may be accepted as an authentic painting by Giambattista Tiepolo of the Spanish period.

George Knox

Notes

1 Diane de Grazia and Eric Garberson, *Italian Paintings of the Seventeenth and Eighteenth Centuries* (Washington, D.C.: National Gallery of Art, 1996: fig. 1).
2 Exh. cat. Savile Gallery, London, 1930, pl. 27.
3 Exh. cat. *Disegni del Museo Civico di Bassano* (Venice: Fondazione Giorgio Cini, 1956: cat nos. 60-65.
4 Holland-Martin sale, Christie's, New York, May 20, 1966, lot 105; Sotheby's, New York, June 6, 1981, pl. 79.
5 Museo del Prado, F.A. 707; George Knox, *Giambattista and Domenico Tiepolo: A Study and Catalogue Raisonné of the Chalk Drawings* (Oxford: Clarendon Press, 1980, M. 184); Christel Thiem, *Master Drawings* (1984: pl. 41), as Lorenzo; exh. cat. *Lorenzo Tiepolo* (Madrid: Museo Nacional del Prado, 1999: pl. 39), as Lorenzo.
6 de Grazia and Garberson, *Italian Paintings,* 288 n.1.

Provenance

Principe del Drago, Rome; Samuel H. Kress Foundation, New York.

Bibliography

de Grazia, Diane, and Eric Garberson, *Italian Paintings of the Seventeenth and Eighteenth Centuries*, 285-9. Washington, D.C.: National Gallery of Art, 1996.

CAT. 24

Giovanni Domenico Tiepolo (Italian, 1727-1804)

The Building of the Trojan Horse, mid-1770s

Oil on canvas, 88¼ x 154 in. (224.16 x 391.16 cm)
Wadsworth Atheneum Museum of Art, Hartford, CT. The Ella Gallup Sumner and Mary Catlin Sumner Collection Fund, 1950.658
Photo credit: Wadsworth Atheneum Museum of Art/Art Resource, NY

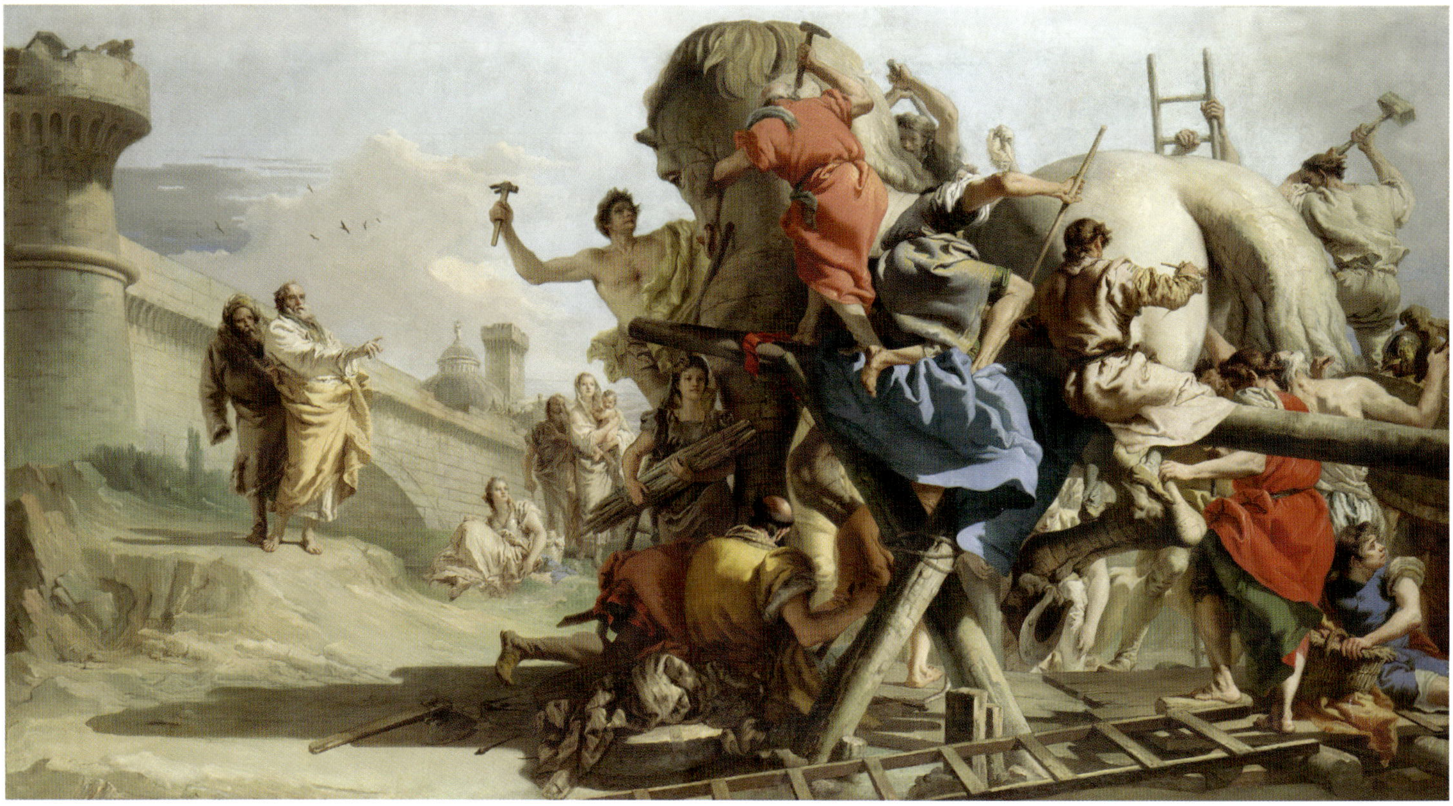

Domenico Tiepolo is somewhat overshadowed as a painter by his celebrated father Giambattista, but he developed his own distinctive style at an early stage. He appears to have, in some degree, retired from painting after 1783, in his mid-fifties. Domenico was also very prolific as a draughtsman and an etcher. He accompanied his father to Würzburg and to Spain, and after his father's death in 1770 in Madrid, Domenico maintained the family studio in Venice with success for more than a decade.

This fine painting is perhaps his master work as a secular easel painter. It is the single known survivor of a set of at least three items, which are known in the form of sketches: two in the National Gallery in London, *The Building of the Trojan Horse* and *The Trojan Horse Enters Troy,*[1] and one that is now preserved in the Sinebrychoff Gallery at Helsinki, depicting *The Fall of Troy*.[2]

The story of the Fall of Troy is told at length by Aeneas to Queen Dido in Book II of *The Aeneid*, but we have no information about any other source that Domenico may have used, either literary or pictorial. Nor do we have any indication of the patron or the original location of the paintings or the sketches. All we have is a general consensus that this remarkable undertaking should be dated in the mid-1770s.

We also have a fine series of drawings in the Correr Museum, one of which bears on the verso a study for the Accademia *Abraham and the Angels* of 1773, which may provide a more precise indication of date.[3]

George Knox

Notes

1 Michael Levey, *National Gallery Catalogues: The Seventeenth and Eighteenth Century Italian Schools* (London: National Gallery, 1971: 238-40). Levey reports rumours that all three large paintings survived in France into the twentieth century; Adriano Mariuz, *Giandomenico Tiepolo* (Venice: Alfieri, 1971: pls. 268-69).

2 Mariuz, *Giandomenico Tiepolo* (Venice: Alfiere, 1971: pl. 271), as formerly d'Atri collection, Paris; George Knox, *Giambattista and Domenico Tiepolo: A Study and Catalogue Raisonné of the Chalk Drawings* (Oxford: Clarendon Press, 1980: pls. 306-8).

3 Knox, *Giambattista and Domenico Tiepolo*, pls.298-301.

Provenance

Count Pignatelli; Château de Fervoz, Namur; Seligman 1913; Lennie Davis; Charpentier sale, December 17, 1938, lot 6.

Bibliography

Morassi, Antonio. *A Complete Catalogue of the Paintings of G. B. Tiepolo, Including Pictures by His Pupils and Followers Wrongly Attributed to Him*, 14, as Domenico. London: Phaidon Press, 1962.

Mariuz, Adriano. *Giandomenico Tiepolo*, pl. 270. Venice: Alfieri, 1971.

Knox, George. *Giambattista and Domenico Tiepolo: A Study and Catalogue Raisonné of the Chalk Drawings*, pls. 300-5. Oxford: Clarendon Press, 1980.

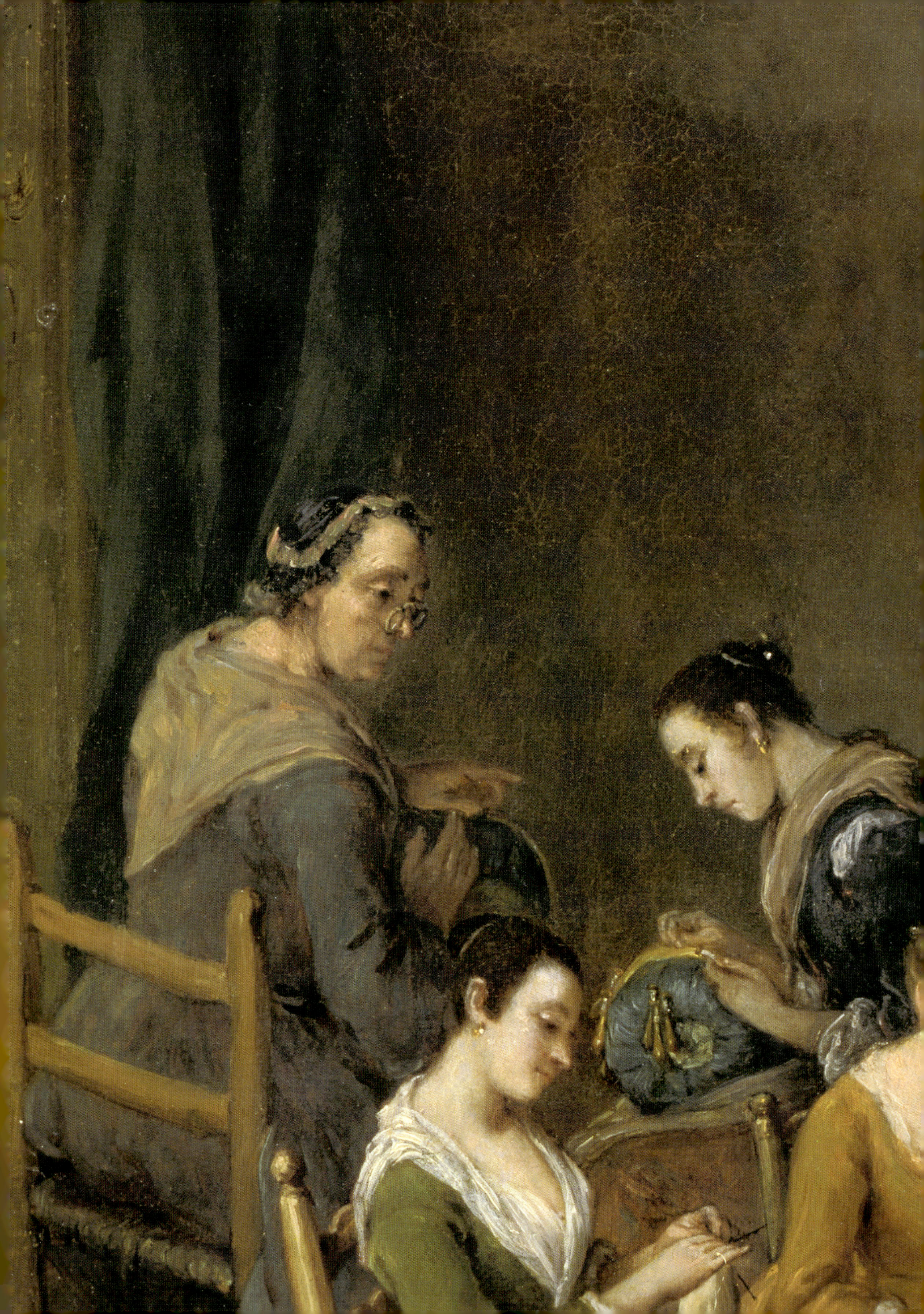

Genre and Portrait Painting

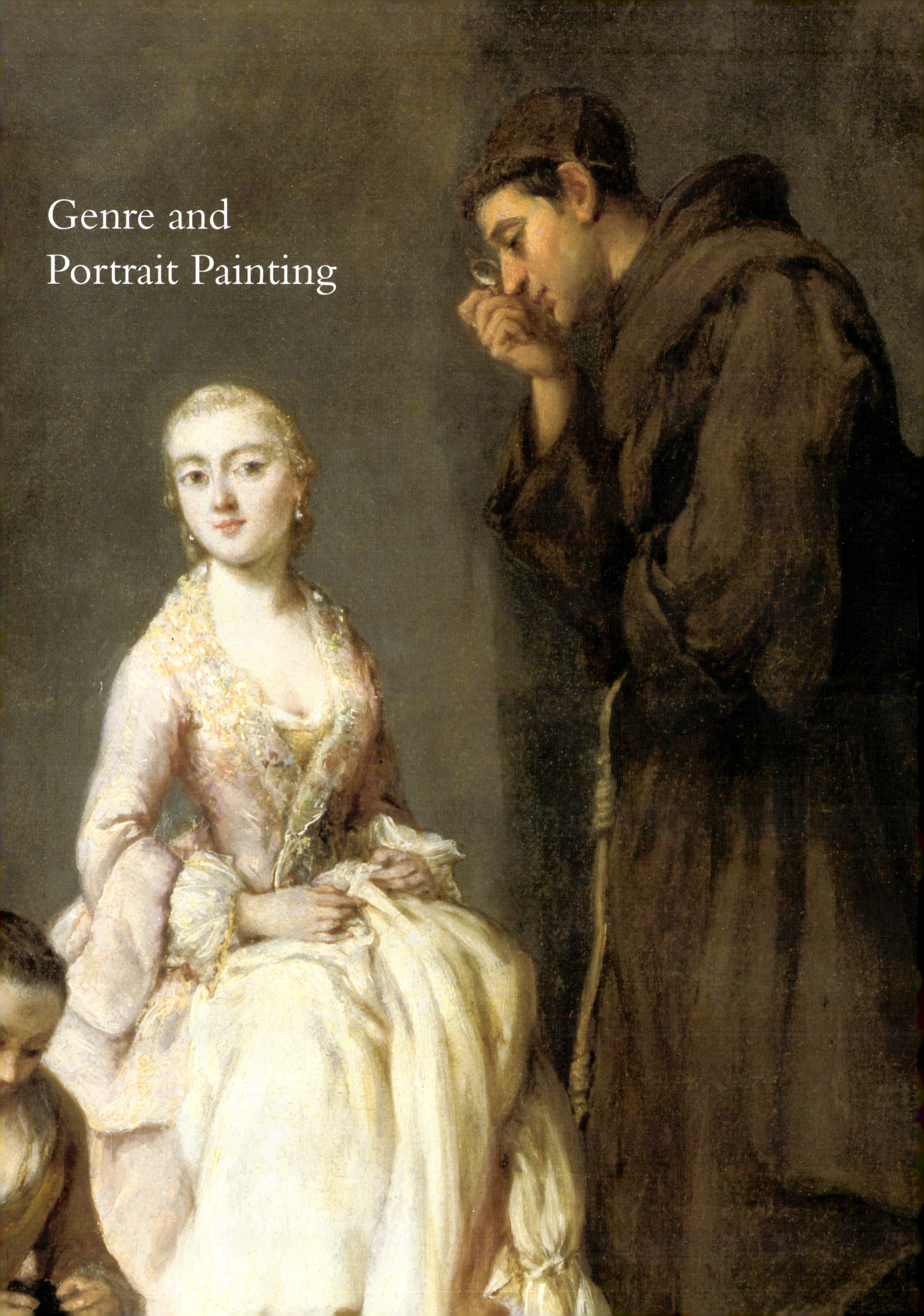

CAT. 25

Giuseppe Maria Crespi (Italian, 1665–1747)

Portrait of a Woman Holding a Mask, ca. 1700

Oil on canvas, 32 x 26 in. (81.28 x 66.04 cm)
Oklahoma City Museum of Art. Gift of Mr. and Mrs. S. T. Fee, Mr. and Mrs. Howard Melton, Mrs. Omar Milligan, Mr. and Mrs. Richard L. Sias, and Mr. and Mrs. John A. Taylor, 1978.046

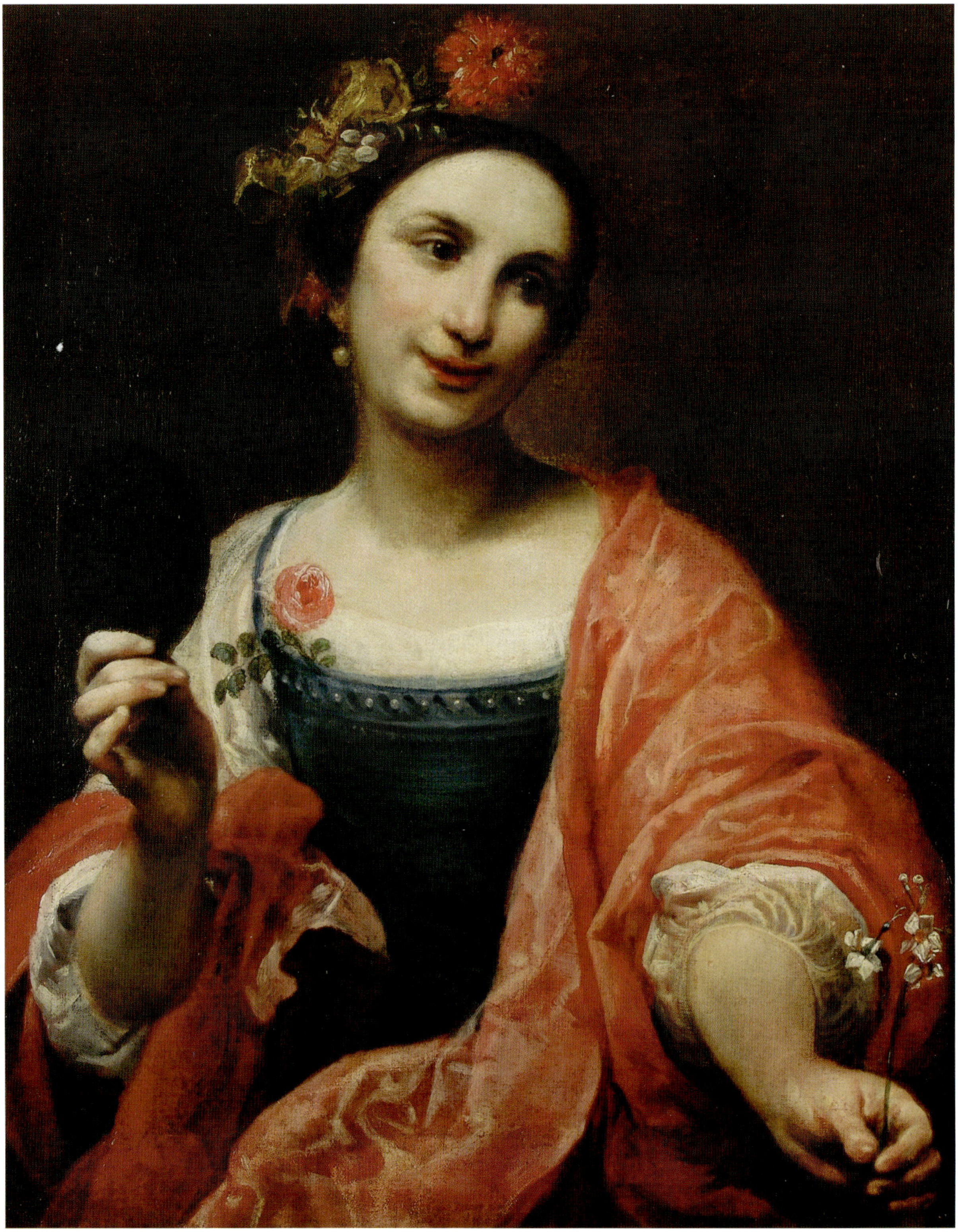

Giuseppe Maria Crespi was born in Bologna, studied with local Bolognese artists, and traveled to Venice to study the paintings of Titian and Veronese. Crespi's mature painterly manner exhibits the early influence of the seventeenth-century Venetian colorists and the Bolognese use of chiaroscuro. It is said that Pietro Longhi's (1702-1785) teacher Antonio Balestra (1666-1740) found his student's figure studies as well as his historical (religious) paintings unsuitable and sent him to Bologna to study with Crespi. The intimacy and humor of Crespi's interior genre paintings made a lasting impression on Longhi (cat. 26) and influenced his manner of portraying his subjects.[1] This painting relates to a number of his half-length portraits of pretty young women, sometimes holding a flower or wearing flowers in their hair, as well as his similar emblematic portraits personifying the arts.[2] This type of half-length portrait of coquettish and fashionably dressed young women appears in the later related paintings of the 1760s by the Venetian artists Giovanni Domenico Tiepolo (cat. 31) and Pietro Rotari (cat. 30), who may well have known Crespi's genre portraits. A mask of the kind held by the sitter in this Crespi painting was called a *moretta* and was worn only by women, on all occasions, by both aristocrats and commoners. Women wearing this mask also appear in the works of Giovanni and Domenico Tiepolo, Pietro Longhi, and others. In the Crespi portrait, the combination of the mask, held in one hand, and the flower, in the other, has been taken to represent the "image of the narcissus, suggestive of self-absorption, and the mask, emblem of deceit, [which] gives it a moralizing tone, though one rendered with a light touch typical of the artist."[3]

Hardy George

Notes

1 Michael Levey, *Painting in Eighteenth-Century Venice,* 3rd ed. (New Haven and London: Yale University Press, 1994: 137).

2 Giuseppe Maria Crespi, *Woman with a Dog,* in the Joe and Emily Lowe Art Gallery at the University of Miami; *Woman with a Rose and a Cat,* Pinacoteca Nationale, Bologna; *Allegory of Architecture,* Rome, Galleria Nationale d'arte antica; *Allegory of Painting, Sculpture, and Music,* Pommersfelden, Schönborn Galerie. See Mira Pajes Merriman, *Giuseppe Maria Crespi* (Milan: Rizzoli Editore, 1980: 294 ff).

3 "In the case of the *Portrait of the Woman Holding a Mask,*" writes Edgar Munhall, "the artist seems to have utilized Cesare Ripa's *L'Iconologia* as a source for his subject … the character of a mask in one hand and a narcissus in the other—just as Crespi's subject does." Cesare Orlandi's text describes her thus: "a young woman attired in an elaborate style, with a simpering and delicate face, dressed in fabrics of various colors. She holds in one hand a narcissus and in the other a mask." The dark oval mask depicted by Crespi was called a *morreta* referring to the black head of a tufted duck of that name. Invented in Venice but mass-produced in Bologna as well, they were made originally of wax, then of painted cardboard, silk, and linen. They were worn only by women and, as part of the eighteenth-century craze for masks, on all imaginable occasions by young and old. Munhall, "Giuseppe Maria Crespi, *Portrait of a Woman Holding a Mask,*" in *Oklahoma City Museum of Art: Selected Paintings and Sculpture from the Collection* (Oklahoma City: Oklahoma City Museum of Art, 2007: 54-5).

Provenance

Dr. F. Haussmann, Berlin; Jacob M. Heimann, New York, 1944; Mr. and Mrs. Arthur Erlanger, 1962; Sotheby Parke Bernet Ltd., New York. Sale # 4136, Date: 6/7/78, lot 243. Purchaser Gimpel-Weitzenhoffer, New York, for the Oklahoma Museum of Art; Oklahoma City Art Museum, a merging of the Oklahoma Museum of Art and the Oklahoma Art Center. Registrar's Work Sheet dated 4/9/90. Assession # 1978.46 / Old # 78.3.

Exhibitions

Weisbaden, *Nassauisches Landesmuseum, Italienische Malerei des 17 und 18 Jahrhunderts,* May and June 1935 (illus.), Bologna, 1938.

Baltimore Museum of Art, *Three Baroque Masters,* April 28 to June 4, 1944, cat. no. 27 (illus.).

New York, Finch College Museum of Art, *Baroque Painters of Bologna and Neighboring Cities,* February 27 to April 8, 1962, cat. no. 29.

Bibliography

Ripa, Cesare. *L'Iconologia, I.* Perugia: Stamperia di Piergiovanni Constantini, 1764.

Voss, Hermann, "Spätitalienische Gemälde der Sammlung Haussmann," In *Zeitschrift für Bildende Kunst,* Vienna: Öesterreich Galerie Belvedere, 1931-2.

"Maschera." In *Encylopedia Italiana di Scienze, Lettere et Arti,* XXII. Rome: Istituto della Enciclopedia Italiana, 1934.

Italianische Maleri des 17. und 18. Jahrhunderts. Exh. cat. Wiesbaden: Nassauisches Landesmuseum, 1935.

Lasareff, V. "Studies on Giuseppe Maria Crespi," *Pantheon* (Jan. 1939): 1-2.

Three Baroque Masters: Strozzi, Crespi, Piazzetta. Exh. cat., pl. 27. Baltimore: The Baltimore Museum of Art, 1944.

Baroque Painters of Bologna. Exh. cat., pl. 29. New York: Finch College Museum of Art, 1962.

Merriman, Mira Pajes, *Giuseppe Maria Crespi,* Milan: Rizzoli Editore, 1980.

Spike, John T. *Giuseppe Maria Crespi and the Emergence of Genre Painting in Italy.* Exh. cat. Fort Worth: Kimbell Art Museum, 1986.

Munhall, Edgar, "Giuseppe Maria Crespi, *Portrait of a Woman Holding a Mask,*" *Oklahoma City Museum of Art: Selected Paintings and Sculpture from the Collection.* Oklahoma City: Oklahoma City Museum of Art, 2007.

CAT. 26

Pietro Longhi (Italian, 1702-1785)

The Temptation, ca. 1750

Oil on canvas, 29¼ x 25⅛ in. (74.93 x 63.82 cm)
Wadsworth Atheneum Museum of Art, Hartford, CT.
The Ella Gallup Sumner and Mary Catlin Sumner Collection Fund, 1931.188
Photo credit: Wadsworth Atheneum Museum of Art/Art Resource, NY

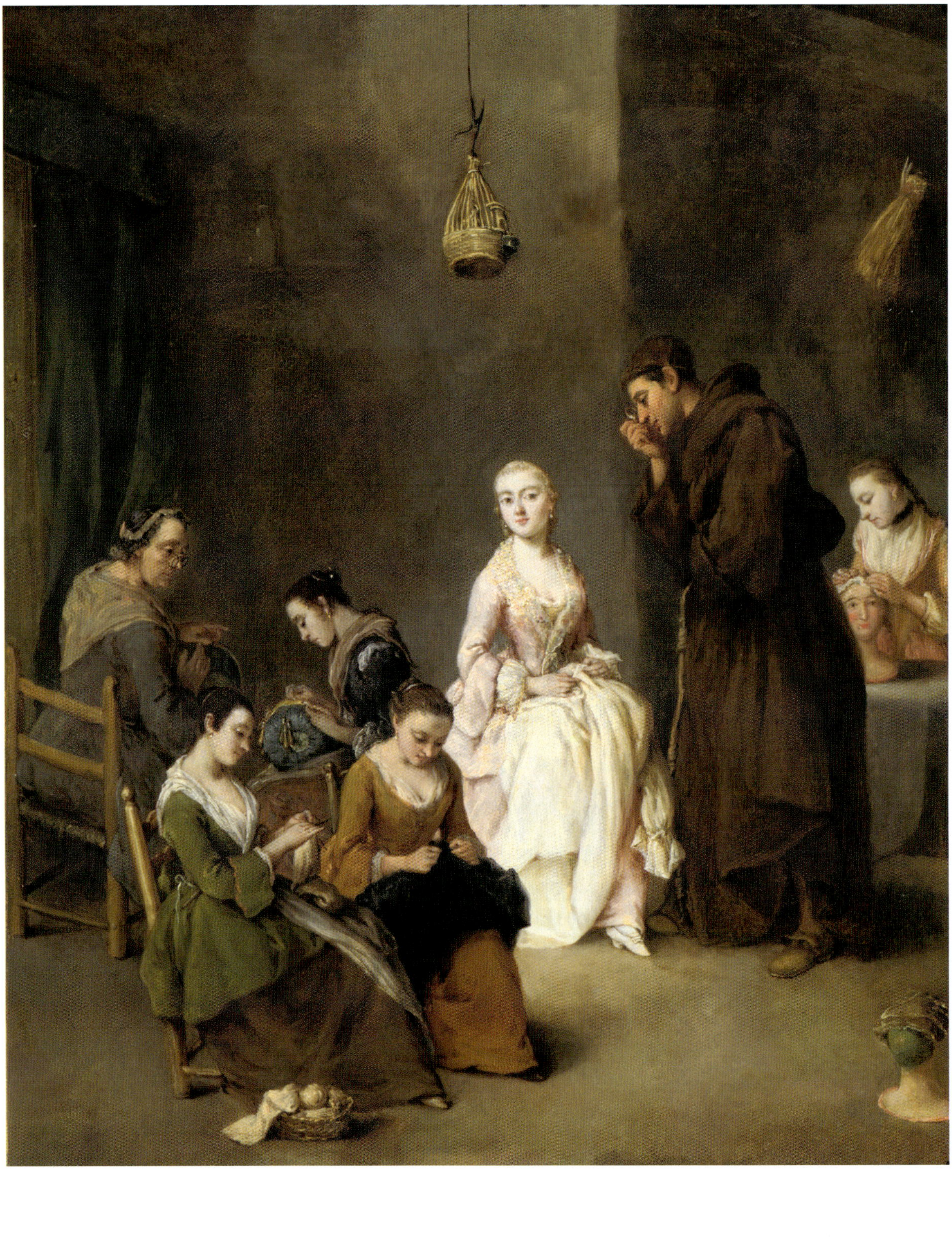

Pietro Longhi's best-known works take the lives and leisure pursuits of the Venetian upper classes as their subjects, but *The Temptation* is one of a number of related paintings that focus instead on seamstresses and shop girls, often with a subtext of seduction or at least of illicit glances and actions. The Hartford canvas depicts the interior of a millinery shop. An old woman keeps a watchful eye on the younger girls sewing at left, and a girl at far right is equally engaged in her task. At center, however, we see a more smartly dressed young woman who holds fabric in her lap but shows little interest in work. Yet, she is ignored by the other women in the scene and does not appear to be a customer. In contrast to the inattention of the other women, the monk gazes intently at her, using a glass to study her décolletage all the more carefully. This seems a familiar mockery of clerical "attention," but it does not help us understand the central woman's place in this scene. Perhaps she is a lazy apprentice, more interested in trying on finery and in making her way in the world than in her work, and thereby requiring counsel from the local cleric (who turns out himself not to be as focused on his occupation as one might desire). As Rolf Bagemihl has noted with regard to a similar painting, *The Letter* at the Metropolitan Museum of Art, "needlework has often been the occupation of a virtuous woman. But by the same token it was also the corrective to be applied to those who were not in that state."[1] The birdcage (or more aptly, caged bird) above the young woman's head is a familiar symbol for desired freedom and, like her gaze out of the picture and beyond the confines of her surroundings, would seem to support the idea that, one way or another, the young woman at center is soon to leave the industrious and virtuous world of the shop. As is so very often the case with Longhi, however, the scene resists a simple or single reading.[2]

Lightly titillating, ambiguous narratives such as this one were Longhi's mainstay, and the Hartford painting is one of a group of works in which the artist reused and recombined a number of common motifs. The above mentioned, *The Letter* in New York, shows a similarly dressed seamstress approached by a procuress and an older man, variously identified as an abbé or a bureaucrat; the same figures reappear in the more dramatic *Seduction* from the Crespi collection in Milan. Another well-dressed seamstress stares similarly out of the picture from beneath a birdcage in *The Needlework School* at Ca' Rezzonico, while the monk reappears in *The Music Lesson* at the Staatliche Museen in Berlin, where he stares intently at a young female singer. Rather than a series of works created at one time or for one client, however, these and the other paintings with common themes should be understood to illustrate Longhi's working practice. Indeed, it was precisely through the subtle manipulation of familiar themes and situations that Longhi won such an avid following among his Venetian contemporaries.

John Marciari

Notes

1 Rolf Bagemihl, "Pietro Longhi and Venetian Life," *Metropolitan Museum Journal* 23 (1988): 242.

2 As noted in cat. no. 27, recent scholarship on Longhi has emphasized the frequent difficulty in understanding the artist's subject matter.

Provenance

Prince Alberto Giovanelli, Venice; Adolf Loewi, Venice; from whom purchased by the Atheneum in 1931.

Bibliography

Ravà, Aldo. *Pietro Longhi*, 99. Florence: Alinari, 1923.

Morassi, Antonio, "Una mostra del Settecento veneziano a Detroit," *Arte Veneta* 7 (1953): 55.

Moschini, Vittorio. *Pietro Longhi*, 24. Milan: A. Martello, 1956.

Pignatti, Terisio, trans. Pamela Waley. *Pietro Longhi: Paintings and Drawings*, 76, pl. 100. London: Phaidon, 1969.

Pignatti, Terisio., *L'opera completa di Pietro Longhi*, cat. no. 73. *Classici d'Arte* 75. Milan: Rizzoli, 1974.

Sohm, Philip L., "Pietro Longhi and Carlo Goldoni: relations between painting and theatre," *Zeitschrift für Kunstgeschichte* 45 (1982): 269.

Bagemihl, Rolf, "Pietro Longhi and Venetian Life," *Metropolitan Museum Journal* 23 (1988): 243.

Cadogan, Jean K. *Wadsworth Atheneum Paintings. Vol. 2, Italy and Spain: Fourteenth through Nineteenth Centuries*, 168. Hartford, CT: The Antheneum, 1991.

CAT. 27

Pietro Longhi (Italian, 1702–1785)
The Concert (The Mandolin Recital), ca. 1755–60

Oil on canvas, 23 x 18¾ in. (58.4 x 47.6 cm)
Fine Arts Museums of San Francisco, Gift of Kathryn Bache Miller, 1964.71

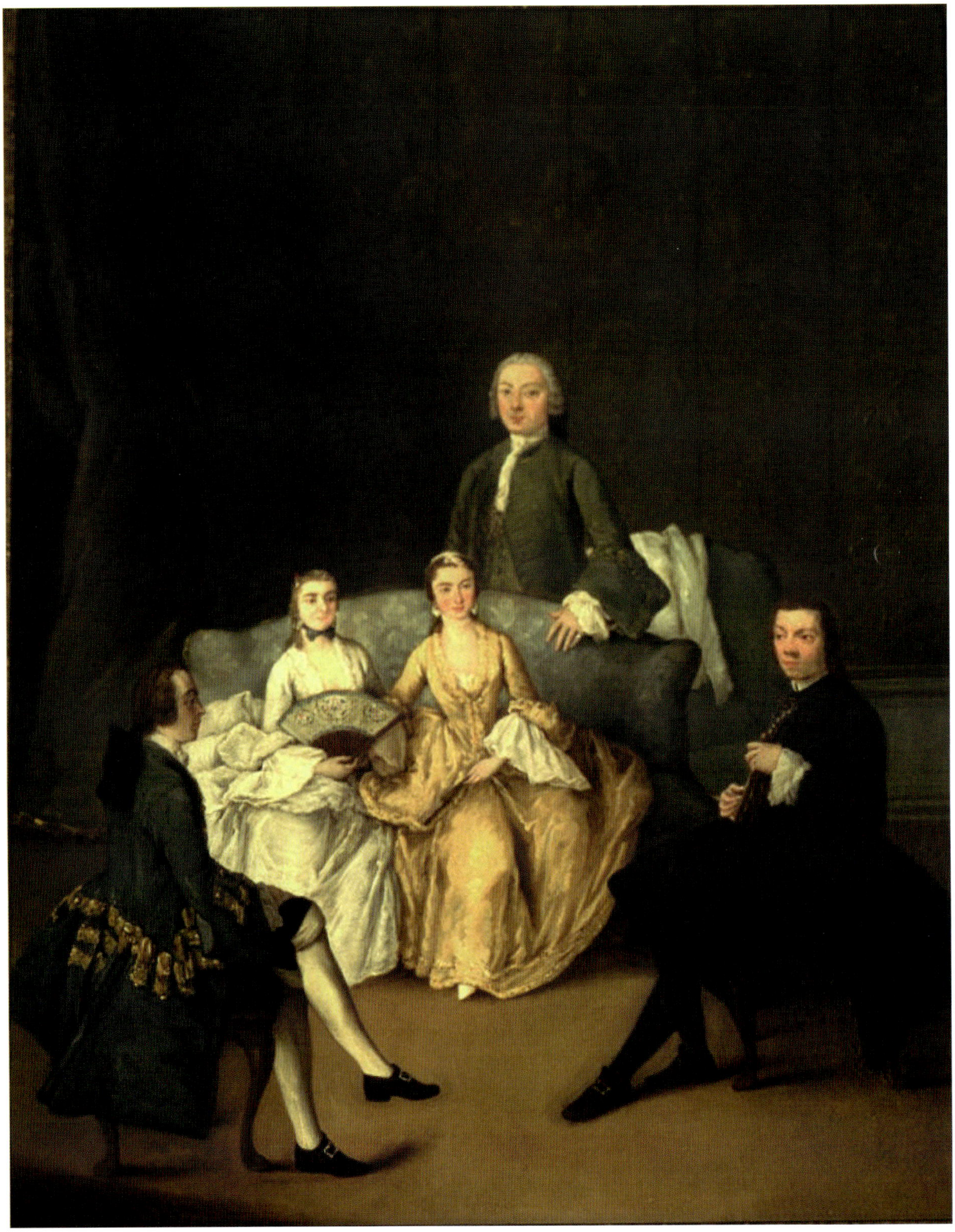

Pietro Falca, known as Pietro Longhi, is reported to have received his initial training under Antonio Balestra (1666-1740), but Longhi's own early efforts in the late Baroque style of his master met with notable disapproval. Longhi then spent time in Bologna and while there was much influenced by the genre scenes of Giuseppe Maria Crespi (1665-1747). Returning to Venice, Longhi made a career of painting small works that documented Venetian life. Rather than the ceremonies and pageants recorded by Canaletto, Carlevarijs, and others, however, Longhi's works showed private concerts, games of cards, seductions, and other indoor entertainments. These studies of the minor dramas and foibles of ordinary life were a novelty in Venetian painting, but they find a close parallel in the innovative works by Longhi's contemporary, the playwright Carlo Goldoni.[3] As Longhi's son, the painter Alessandro Longhi (1733-1813), explained in a biography of his father, Pietro Longhi "wished to amuse" in creating his paintings of "conversations, arrangements, with the games of love and of jealousy."[4] These delicate delights won a broad following. Longhi was immensely popular in his day and enjoyed broad patronage especially from Venetian patricians.

The Concert is one of several hundred similarly sized interior views produced by the artist. One is struck at first glance by the seemingly naïve quality of these works, with their slightly weightless figures loosely organized on a shallow stage. Upon closer examination, however, and particularly with a recently cleaned and well preserved example like the present canvas, the subtle genius of the artist comes to life. The entrancing color harmonies—in the jacket of the standing figure, for example—and the delicate dabs of paint that delineate highlights and patterns bespeak a careful, if unusual, painterly technique. Even more importantly, small details such as the direction of a figure's glance, a grasped skirt, or a gesturing hand often lend surprising candor and pungency to these small stories. This is not to say, however, that the narratives are always clear. On the contrary, the more recent scholarship on Longhi has noted how often the subjects or meanings of his pictures have resisted explanation.[5] *The Concert* is no exception. Putting the musician aside for the moment, one cannot help but wonder about the relationship of the other four figures. Are they a family group, with a proud father standing behind the couch? Is the young man at left a brother or a suitor? His attitude and pallid skin suggest a cool demeanor, and the direction of his stare, at the musician rather than the women, would seem to argue against an amorous role. In contrast, the black-garbed musician glances sideways at the women, and one wonders whether his tight lips, rosy cheeks, and red-rimmed eyes result from the effort of his performance or from some other passion. As is so often the case for Longhi's works, characterized by ambiguity and gentle irony more than caricature or biting satire, the ultimate reading of the scene remains a mystery.

John Marciari

Notes

1 Another of the paintings by Longhi formerly in the Papadopoli collection, the *Masked Party in a Courtyard* at the Saint Louis Art Museum (inv. no. 32:1939), was acquired by Saint Louis from the Paul Drey gallery in 1939. The Saint Louis painting bears a date of 1755 on the back of the original canvas, which could also plausibly be the date of the ex-Papadopoli painting in San Francisco.

2 Teresio Pignatti, *Petro Longhi: Paintings and Drawings: Complete Edition* (London: Phaidon Press, 1969: 93), gives the provenance as "formerly in the Papadopoli collection," and notes that it "may belong to the group of conversation pieces formerly in the Perera Collection." Kathryn Bache Miller (1896-1979) was the daughter of New York financier and notable art collector Jules Bache (1861-1944), but it is not known when she acquired the painting or whether it came from her father's collections. Contrary to Pignatti's supposition, the San Francisco painting is not one of the paintings from the collection of Lionello Perera, which were acquired at the December 17-19, 1917, sale of Elia Volpi's collection at the American Art Galleries.

3 See especially Philip L. Sohm, "Pietro Longhi and Carlo Goldoni: relations between painting and theatre," *Zeitschrift für Kunstgeschichte* 45 (1982): 256-73.

4 Alessandro Longhi, *Compendio delle Vite de' Pittori Veneziani* (Venice: Alessandro Longhi, 1762).

5 In addition to Sohm, "Pietro Longhi," see also Rolf Bagemihl, "Pietro Longhi and Venetian Life," *Metropolitan Museum Journal* 23 (1988): 233-47.

Provenance

Count Nicolò Papadopoli, Venice, to 1922?; (possibly Paul Drey, New York, ca. 1939);[1] Kathryn Bache Miller; by whom given to the Fine Arts Museums of San Francisco.[2]

Bibliography

Ravà, Aldo. *Pietro Longhi,* 38. Florence: Alinari, 1923.

Bacchelli, Ricardo, and Roberto Longhi. *Teatro e immagini del settecento italiano,* 116. Milan: Radio Italiana, 1953.

Pignatti, Terisio. *Pietro Longhi: Paintings and Drawings,* 93, pl. 197. Trans. Pamela Waley. London: Phaidon, 1969.

Pignatti, Terisio. *L'opera completa di Pietro Longhi,* cat. no. 149. *Classici d'Arte* 75. Milan: Rizzoli, 1974.

CAT. 28

Domenico Maggiotto (Italian, 1713–1794)

Head of a Girl with a Spindle, ca. 1735–40

Oil on canvas, 18¾ x 14¾ in. (47.6 x 37.5 cm)
Bequest of John Ringling, 1936, Collection of The John and Mable Ringling Museum of Art, the State Art Museum of Florida, a Division of Florida State University, SN183

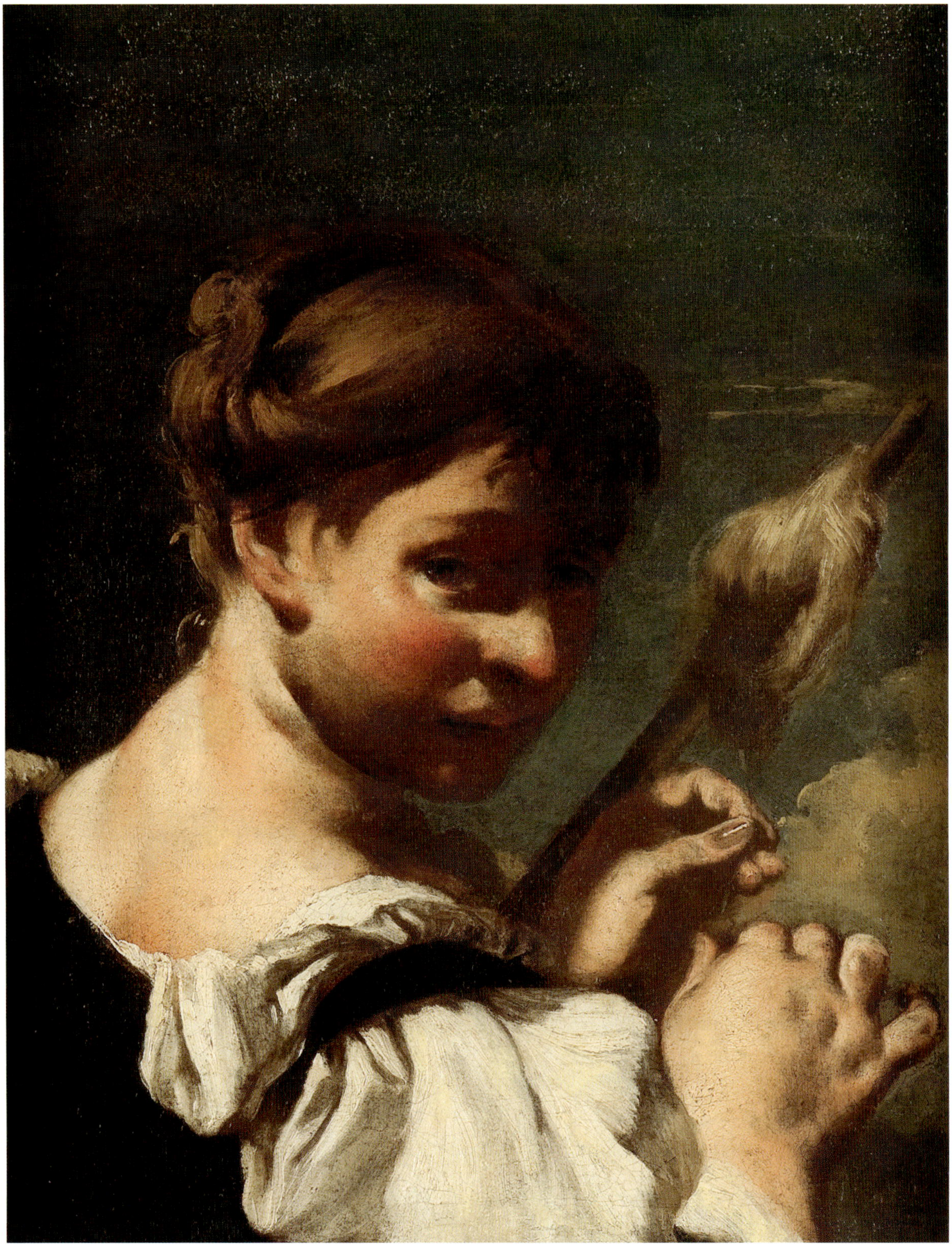

The young woman in this portrait holds a spindle, the rounded stick used to twist yarn in wool spinning. Dressed as a Venetian *popolana*, or peasant girl, she is evidently a domestic servant.[1] She engages the viewer with a casual turn of the head, her soft eyes and parted mouth charmingly conveying the impression that this brief encounter is unexpected but not unwelcome. Although she is a peasant, she is no prosaic. Indeed, this image bears little kinship with conventional European genre painting, which largely focused on low or base subject matter.

Genre painting was little explored in Venice before the early 1700s. Yet, during the eighteenth century, as tastes increasingly turned toward private life, an interest developed in pictures of intimate, domestic scenes. Rather than depicting low culture, however, Venetian genre painting tended to be scenic and pleasing and to assume a level of fantasy that was characteristic of Venetian art in general. Only a handful of artists capitalized on this burgeoning market; one of them was Domenico Maggiotto. A student of the Venetian genre master Giovanni Battista Piazzetta (1683-1754), he relied heavily on the expressive formulas developed by his teacher. Pictures featuring bust- or half-length portrayals of quotidian figures are most typical in Piazzetta's oeuvre, as are strong modeling, an "aggressive" naturalism, a chiaroscuro reminiscent of the Baroque, and a certain Arcadian sentimentality.[2] Particular to Maggiotto's work is the dense use of warm browns and hot reds—evident here in the young woman's face and hair.[3] A plasticity of form and strong chiaroscuro are also characteristic of Maggiotto, particularly his early style (late 1730s-40s), which is often considered to be his most successful.[4]

Alexandra Libby

Notes

Acknowledgment: This entry was first published in the exhibition catalogue *Venice in the Age of Canaletto* (Memphis Brooks Museum of Art, 2009). Reprinted with permission of the author, Alexandra Libby.

1 For Venetian dress and the popolana, see Giuseppe Morazzoni, *Il Mobile Veneziano del '700* (Milan: G. G. Görlich, 1931: pl. 94); and Maria Angela Bulgarelli, "Profilo di Domenico Maggioto," *Arte Veneta* (1973): 223.

2 Rodolfo Pallucchini, *La pittura veneziana del Settecento* (Venice: Istituto per la Collaborazione Culturale, 1960: 62).

3 On a 1969 visit to the Ringling, Terisio Pignatti, vice-director of Musei Civici Veneziani d'Istoria e dell'Arte, pronounced this picture to be by "Domenico Maggiotto. Definitely" (Ringling Museum Curatorial files). Disregarding Pignatti, Burton B. Fredericksen and Federico Zeri, in their 1972 *Census of Pre-Nineteenth-Century Italian Paintings in North American Public Collections* (637), cited the painting as a work by Piazzetta. The first firm attribution to Maggiotto came four years later, in Peter Tomory's catalogue of Italian paintings in the Ringling Museum collection (98). However, William E. Suida had suspected as early as 1949 that Maggiotto might have painted it (see Suida, *Catalogue of Paintings: The John and Mable Ringling Museum of Art* [Sarasota, Fla.: The John and Mable Ringling Museum of Art, 1949: 155]).

4 Pietro Zampetti, *A Dictionary of Venetian Painters, vol. 3* (Leigh-on-Sea: F. Lewis, 1970: 65).

Provenance

Elia Volpi (1858-1938), Palazzo Davanzati, Florence, by 1917; (sold, American Art Association, New York, December 17, 1917, no. 439, as by Piazzetta); John Ringling (1866-1936), Sarasota, 1917-36.

Bibliography

Vilas, Curtis N., and Naomi R. *A Guide to the Collection: The John and Mable Ringling Museum of Art*, 67, no. 246 (as by Piazzetta). Chicago: C. D. Heller, 1942.

Suida, William E. *Catalogue of Paintings: The John and Mable Ringling Museum of Art*, 155, no. 183 (as by Piazzetta). Sarasota, Fla.: John and Mable Ringling Museum of Art, 1949.

Fredericksen, Burton B., and Federico Zeri. *Census of Pre-Nineteenth-Century Italian Paintings in North American Public Collections*, 163, 637 (as by Piazzetta). Cambridge: Harvard University Press, 1972.

Tomory, Peter. *Catalogue of Italian Paintings before 1800*, 98, no. 96 (as by Maggiotto). Sarasota, Fla.: John and Mable Ringling Museum of Art, 1976.

Ferrazza, Roberta. *Palazzo Davanzati e le collezioni di Elia Volpi*, 119, fig. 117. Florence: Centro di, 1994.

Libby, Alexandra. *Venice in the Age of Canaletto*, 126-127, cat. 30. Memphis: Memphis Brooks Museum of Art, 2009.

CAT. 29

GIOVANNI BATTISTA PIAZZETTA (Italian, 1682–1754)

Portrait of Giacomo in a Fur Hat, 1745

Oil on canvas, 32½ x 24⅞ in. (82.55 x 62.99 cm)
University of Arizona Museum of Art & Archive of Visual Arts,
Gift of Samuel H. Kress Foundation, 1961.013.024

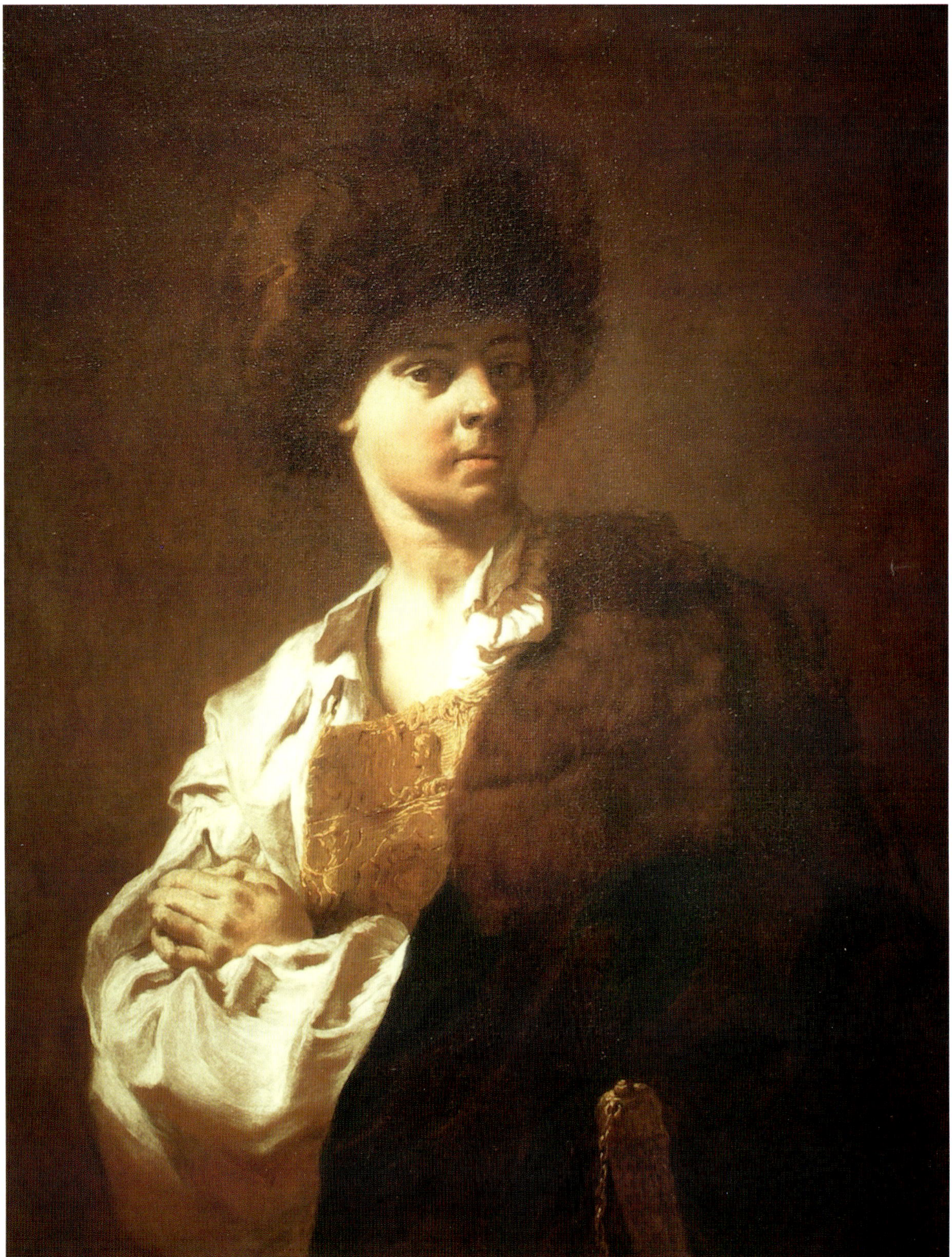

Rodolfo Pallucchini and Adriano Mariuz point out that the young man in this painting is the same as the one in the Cologne *Pastorale*,[1] for which Marshal Schulenburg made a final payment in April 1745. This persuasively suggests a date for the present picture.

There is a fine study for the head of the young man of the Cologne picture in the Fogg Art Museum,[2] and in 1983 it was suggested that several of these heads might be identified as studies for Piazzetta's wife, Rosa, and their children.[3] The drawing in question was identified as *A Portrait of* (Piazzetta's eldest son) *Giacomo at Twenty Years of Age,* 1745.[4] Hence, it would seem that the sitter in this picture is likewise Giacomo, and this is a portrait of him at the same age.

Pallucchini describes the sitter as, "a young man in a fur hat." Mariuz describes him as, "a youth in Polish costume," and associates him with the painting at Springfield,[5] *A Boy in Polish Uniform*, who is sometimes thought to be a young sculptor but is certainly around the age of Giacomo, about seventeen, as is the Dresden *Young Standard Bearer*,[6] which is dated perhaps 1742.[7]

George Knox

Notes

1 Rodolfo Pallucchini, *Piazzetta* (Milan: Aldo Martello, 1956: 81–3; color pl. 18).
2 Pallucchini, *Piazzetta,* 145.
3 George Knox, *Piazzetta* (Washington, D.C.: National Gallery of Art, 1983: 24–34).
4 Knox, *Piazzetta,* 19.
5 Adriano Mariuz, *L'opera completa del Piazzetta* (Milan: Rizzoli, 1982: 85, color pl. 31).
6 Mariuz, *L'opera … Piazzetta,* 87, color pl. 30.
7 George Knox, *Giambattista Piazzetta* (Oxford: Clarendon Press, 1992: 186, pl. 142).

Provenance

Rambaldi, Bologna, 1934; Contini-Bonacossi, Rome 1950; Samuel H. Kress Foundation, New York; to Tucson, 1987.

Bibliography

Pallucchini, Rodolfo. *Piazzetta*, pl. 85. Milan: Aldo Martello, 1956.
The Samuel H. Kress Collection at the University of Arizona, pl. 21. Tucson: University of Arizona Museum of Art, 1957.
Shapley, Fern Rusk. *Paintings from the Samuel Kress Collection*, pl. 271. London: Phaidon Press, 1973.
Mariuz, Adriano. *Piazzetta*, pl. 94, color pl. 40. Milan: Rizzoli, 1982.

CAT. 30

PIETRO ROTARI (Italian, 1707–1762)

Young Woman with a Sprig of Jasmine, ca. 1756–62

Oil on canvas, 18¼ x 15¼ in. (46.4 x 38.8 cm)

Museum of Art and Archaeology, University of Missouri-Columbia. Gift of the Samuel H. Kress Foundation, 61.82

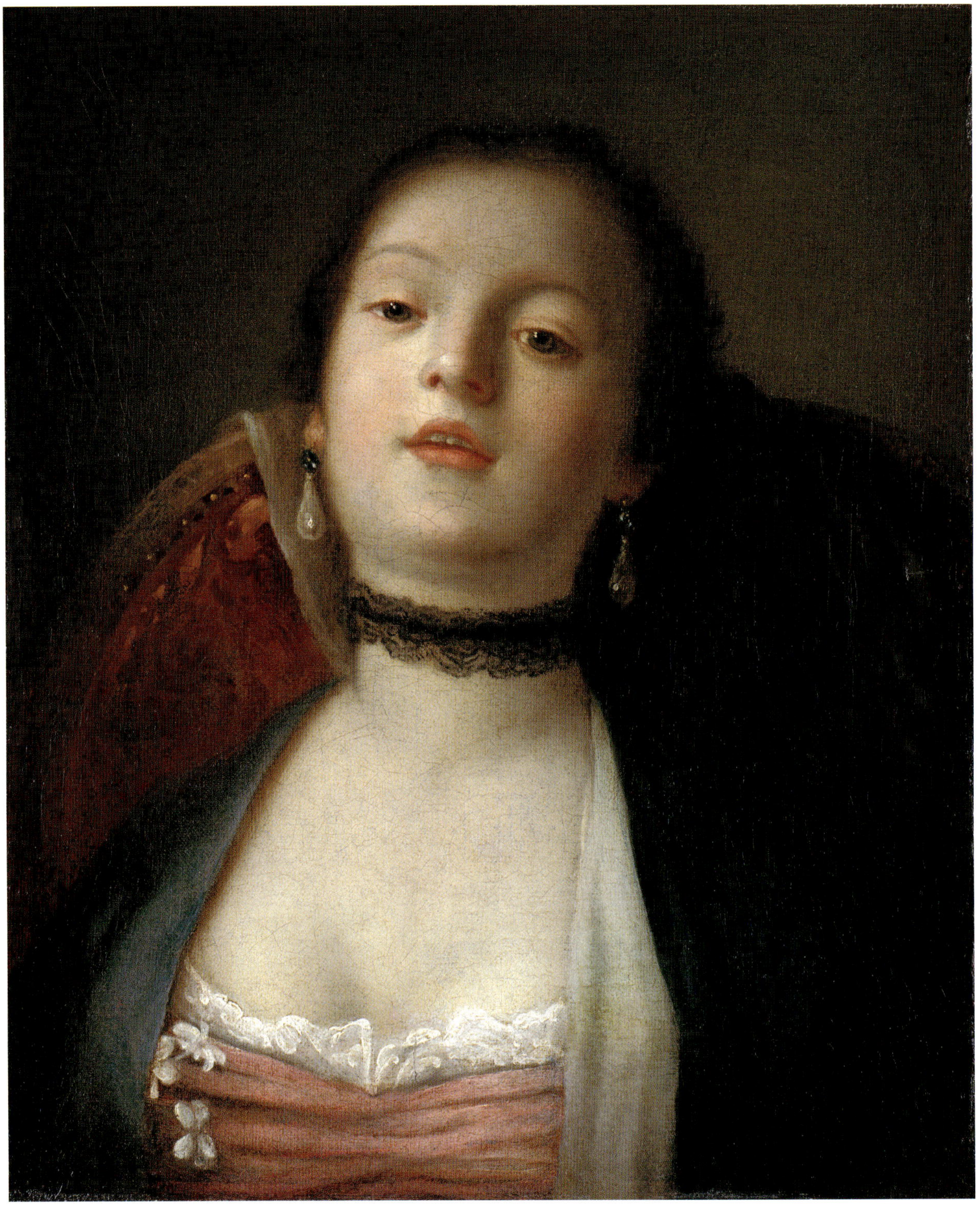

Rotari's first significant training came with Antonio Balestra (1666-1740) in his hometown of Verona, then with Francesco Trevisani (1656-1746) in Rome and Francesco Solimena (1657-1747) in Naples, where he seems to have first established an independent career. His career would unfold in this peripatetic vein, subsequently working in Verona, then Vienna, Dresden, and St. Petersburg—the latter three positions all for royal courts. Rotari's encounter with the intense likenesses of Jean-Etienne Liotard (1702-1789) in Vienna, and later the pastels of Rosalba Carriera (1675-1757) in Dresden, would have a major impact on the artist, who increasingly moved away from his early multi-figured altarpieces to concentrate on tightly observed single figures. These works at first came mostly in the forms of portraits and scenes of daily life, and then in groups of character studies, largely of young women. Rotari reached the acme of this genre in St. Petersburg, where he executed 638 paintings in this vein, including this work. Although Rotari appears to have used only eight models for the set in Russia, these works are all graceful variations on a theme, bringing his smooth handling, intense focus, and light-hearted sensuality to bear on an extended Enlightenment taxonomy of characters—all within a carefully calibrated range of subtle emotions and social types.

In this work, tightly cropped in an unidentifiable space, a young woman leans back into a chair covered in watered silk. Her dark cloak, opened to reveal a simple, low-cut, ruched bodice, is trimmed with transparent white lace. A few white jasmine blossoms tucked into her pink bodice dangle over her proper right breast, a detail that picks up the gleaming white of her extravagant pearl earrings—easily visible with her dark hair pulled back. A band of black lace at the woman's throat draws attention to her long, exposed neck, contrasting strikingly with her pale skin. Her heavy-lidded eyes gaze directly at the viewer, and her open mouth, revealing teeth, at once conveys an openness to our gaze as well as a remote interiority. Rotari's visible, tactile brushstrokes, seen especially in the lace dancing along her décolletage, as well as the rich glazes used in the lips, earrings, and eyes, extend this sensual, reflective mood, activating the sense of touch.

As Judith Mann and Leslie Griffin Hennessey have recently observed, there are at least seventeen versions of this composition, many connected to the studio of François Boucher (1703-1770), a number of which circulated as prints. Given the movement of images and artists between Paris and St. Petersburg in this period, pinning down the source of this image as the invention of a specific artist has proven difficult. However, Mann rightly observes that the woman's stiff pose is better suited to sitting in a chair than reclining on a pillow (the common distinguishing feature of the French images), suggesting that Rotari probably developed the subject first.

Jon L. Seydl

Provenance

Catherine II, Empress of Russia, 1729-1796 (St. Petersburg, Russia), ca. 1756-62; Arnold Seligmann, Rey & Co. (New York, New York); Paul Drey (New York, New York), sold to the Samuel H. Kress Foundation, 1948; Samuel H. Kress Foundation, transferred to the Museum of Art and Archaeology, University of Missouri-Columbia, 1961.

Bibliography

Sullivan, Edward J., and Ruth Ann Krueger, eds. *The Taft Museum: Its History and Collections.* Vol. 1, 286-89. New York: Hudson Hills Press, 1995.

Land, Norman E., ed. *The Samuel H. Kress Study Collection at the University of Missouri Museum of Art and Archaeology, University of Missouri-Columbia,* 80-86. Columbia, Mo., and London: University of Missouri Press, 1999, with prior bibliography.

CAT. 31

Giovanni Domenico Tiepolo (Italian, 1727-1804)

Head of a Woman, 1762-70

Oil on canvas, 23⅞ x 19⅛ in. (60.4 x 48.6 cm)
The Cleveland Museum of Art. Gift of Harry D. Kendrick, 1952.541

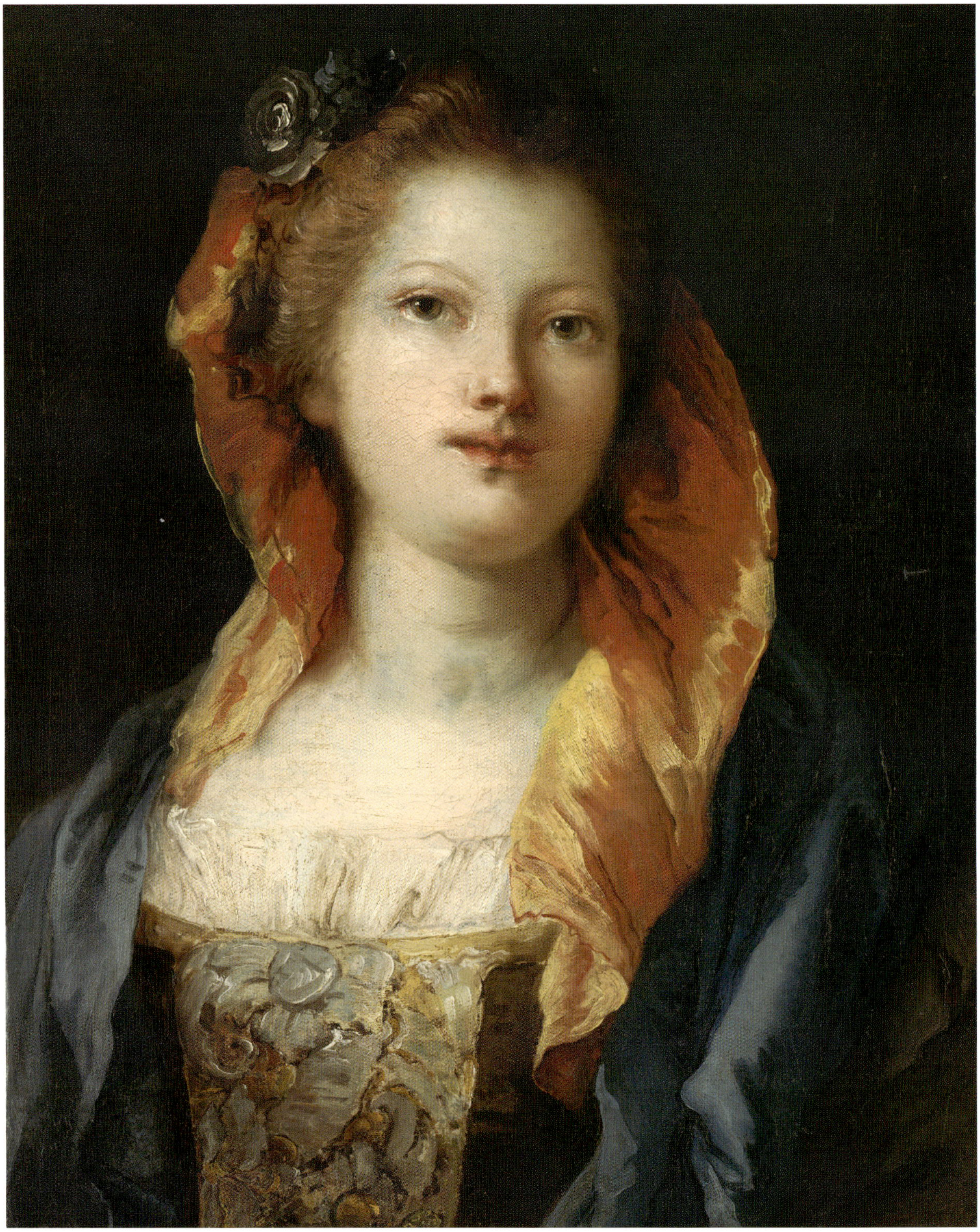

Commanding the generously scaled canvas, a woman looks directly out at the beholder, shoulders pulled back, her soft skin and green eyes set off by the sophisticated palette of the garments. A stiff lace fringe crests her cream and goldenrod brocaded dress, and a simple azure cloth covers her bare shoulders. A shimmering red-orange textile, shot through with yellow, surrounds her head, tucked under the blue drape without covering her reddish-brown hair, which is loosely pulled back with a blue ribbon and a flower. Despite the expanse of exposed skin, her firmly set jaw and lips, erect pose, and cool gaze convey a magnificent beauty rather than any playfulness or easy availability to the viewer.

While the woman's features may well have been drawn from life, her garments seem to be a fanciful variation on late eighteenth-century costume. This painting thus emerges from an eighteenth-century Venetian tradition of bust-length images of women in fancy dress, set in no particular location. Artists such as Rosalba Carriera (1675–1757) and Pietro Rotari (see cat. 30) had established the general typology in the eighteenth century, although their playful and understated approach to the genre turns into something altogether more dramatic and bold in Giovanni Domenico's hands.

The artist's father, Giovanni Battista Tiepolo, created a group of fancy dress portraits in the 1750s. Such sensual and playful images of women have a long history in Venice, where the art of depicting beauties and courtesans in painting extends back to the Renaissance. The elder Tiepolo also painted a series of old men and philosophers, among other types of men, again pictures not generally linked to specific sitters. These latter paintings connect to a long-standing Baroque tradition, including the versions by Giovanni Battista Piazzetta. Attesting to the popularity and importance of his father's works, the younger Tiepolo created variations on these genres for several decades, most significantly in the 1757–58 (published 1770–74) *Raccolta di Teste* (Collection of Heads), a two-volume set of etchings after his father's paintings in this vein, as well as numerous paintings of his own, that responded to a clear market for this genre.[1] Although the works produced in the tight-knit Tiepolo studio were always close to one another, Giovanni Domenico distinguishes himself from his father by using more solid forms and less dramatic handling, as well as giving his figures a more remote air. Unlike Carriera or even Giovanni Battista Tiepolo, the younger artist's works in this genre rarely can be understood as allegorical, for they have no props that would permit such a symbolic reading.

Attributed to Giovanni Battista Tiepolo upon its discovery in the 1920s, Antonio Morassi considered it the work of Giovanni Domenico, an attribution that has held to the present day. The painting's first recorded owner said the work had been discovered in a Spanish private collection, and this putative connection has led scholars to date the work to Giovanni Domenico Tiepolo's period in Spain (he moved there with his father in 1762 to work for the court in Madrid). Attempts to connect the costume to Spanish dress of the 1760s have not been convincing, but the most persuasive argument for an Iberian connection came from George Knox, who noted that nearly all the published images of women in fancy dress by the younger man have some provenance connection to Spain and their handling closely resembles that used for his philosophers, which were painted at the same time.[2]

Jon L. Seydl

Notes

1 George Knox, "'Philosopher Portraits' by Giambattista, Domenico, and Lorenzo Tiepolo," *The Burlington Magazine* 117 (March 1975): 147–55, cat. no. 864.

2 George Knox, *Giambattista and Domenico Tiepolo: A Study and Catalogue Raisonné of the Chalk Drawings* (Oxford: Clarendon Press, 1980).

Provenance

Richard Owen, died 1951 (Paris, France), by 1925, sold to Thomas Agnew & Sons, 1927; Thomas Agnew & Sons (London, England), sold to Henry Gordon Dalton, 1929; Henry Gordon Dalton, 1862–1939 (Cleveland, Ohio), upon his death, by inheritance to his nephew, Harry Dalton Kendrick; Harry Dalton Kendrick, died 1958 (Cleveland, Ohio), by gift to the Cleveland Museum of Art, 1952.

Bibliography

Cleveland Museum of Art, *The Cleveland Museum of Art Catalogue of Paintings*, vol. 3, 432–34, cat. no. 189. Cleveland: Cleveland Museum of Art, 1982, with prior bibliography.

Christiansen, Keith, ed. *Giambattista Tiepolo, 1696–1770*, 256–57, fig. 84. New York: Metropolitan Museum of Art, 1996.

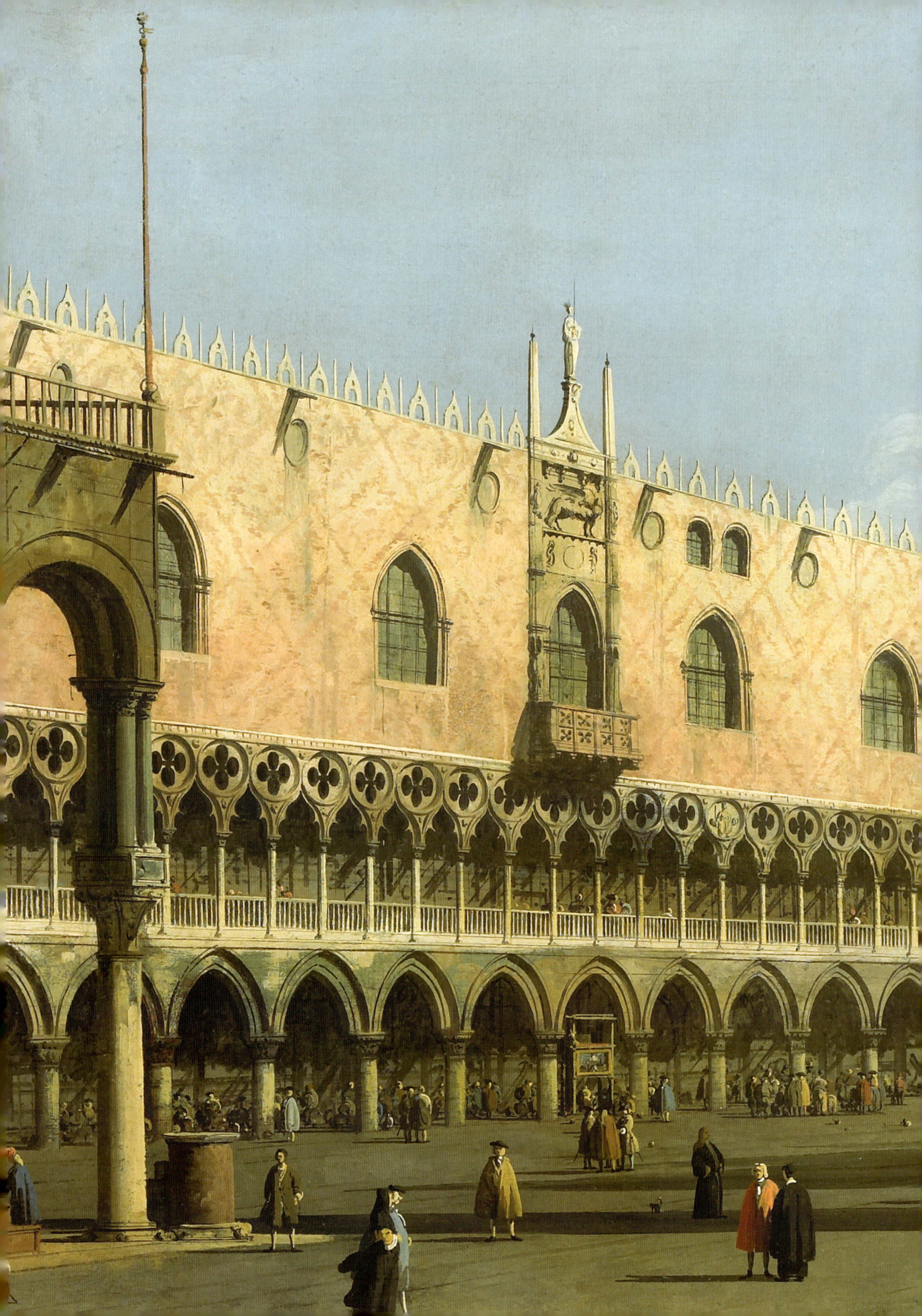

View Painting

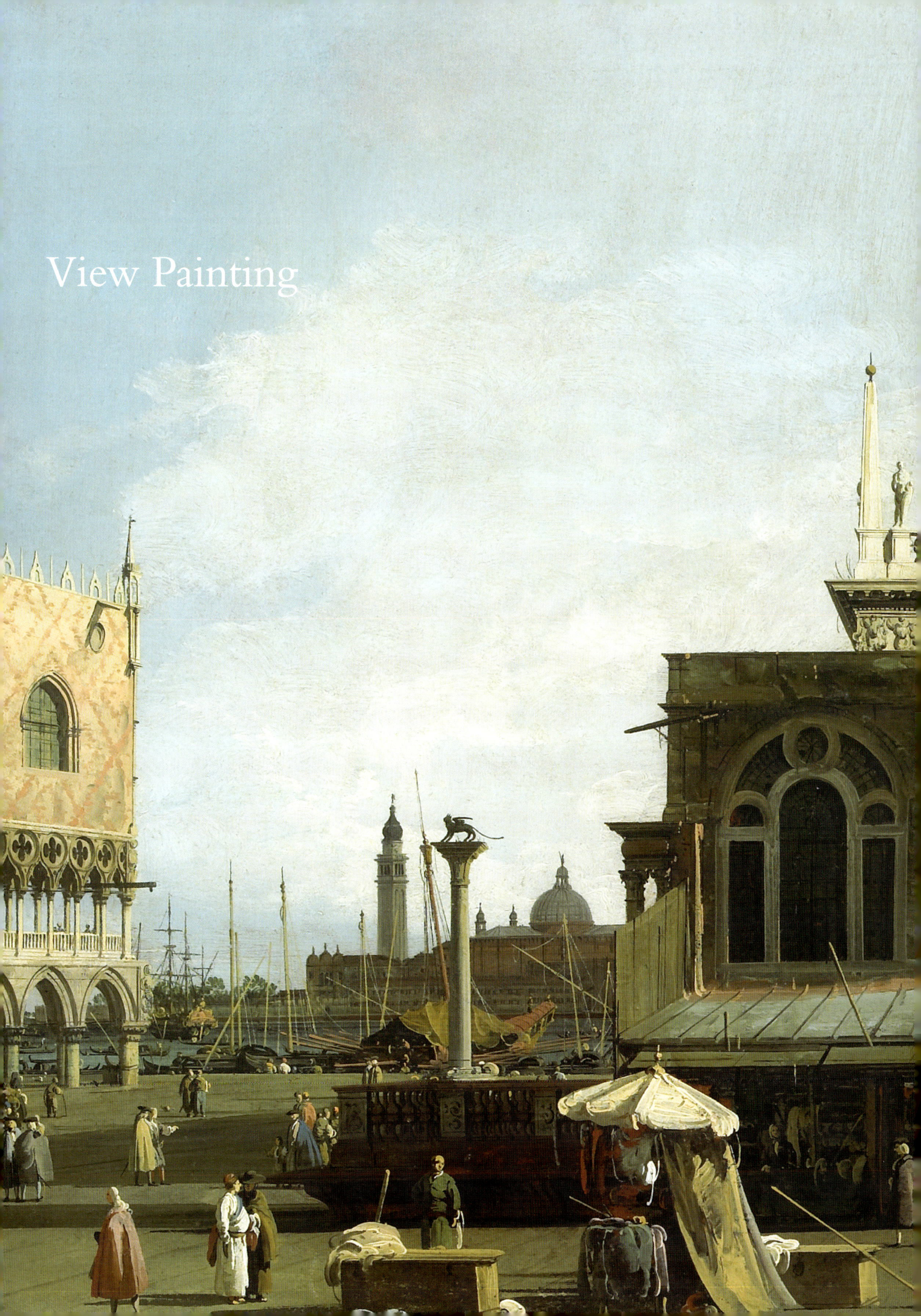

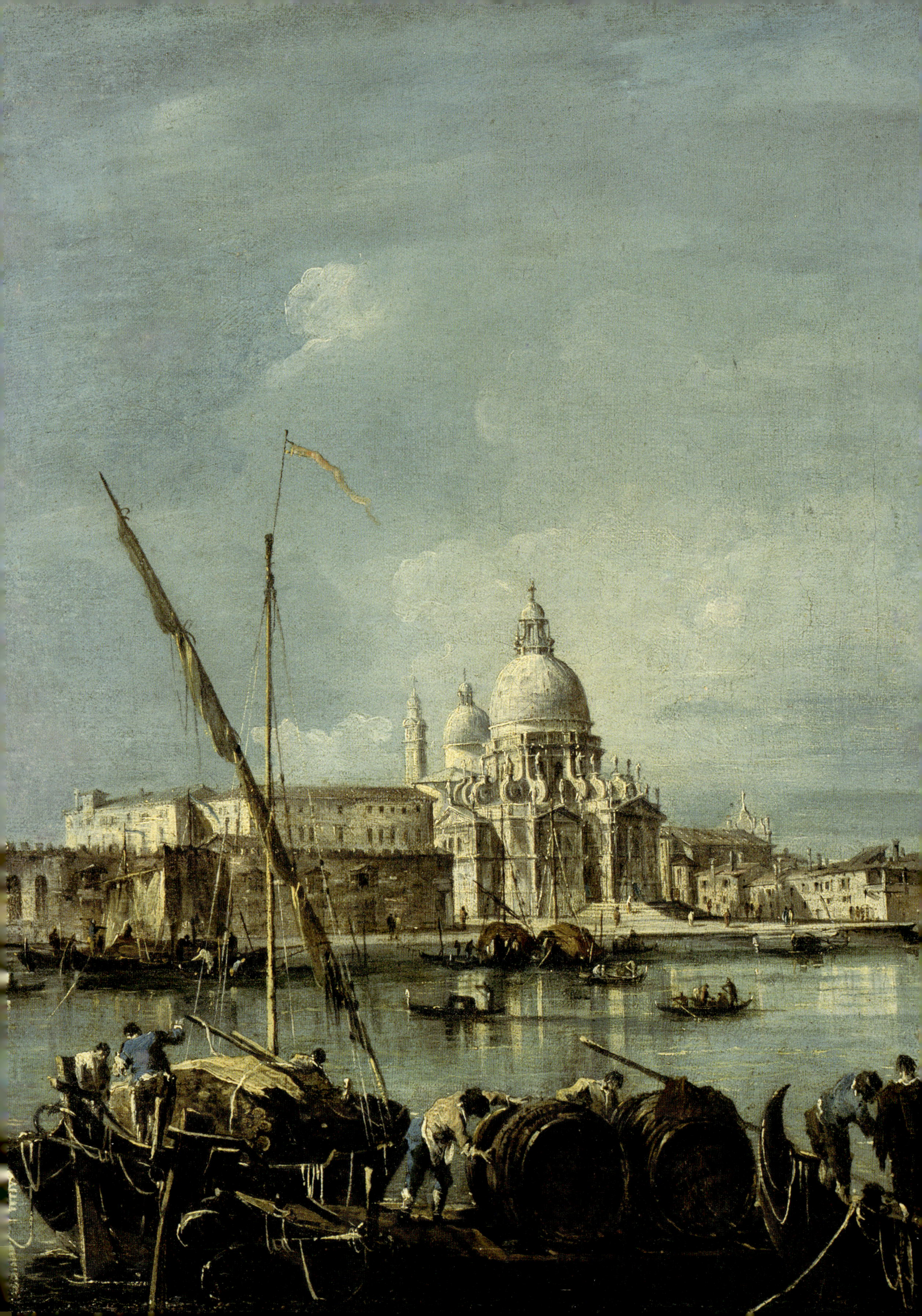

Venetian Views by Carlevarijs, Canaletto, and Guardi

Attributions, Dating, and a Bit of History

Andria Derstine

In 1882, because of the thousands of paintings and descriptions of the city that had saturated the popular imagination, the writer Henry James wryly noted that there was "notoriously nothing more to be said" about Venice.[1] Almost 130 years later, given the profusion of writings about Venetian art (and specifically about eighteenth-century view painting) that began in the late nineteenth century and continue to today, one is tempted to agree. So much has been written about the works of Canaletto and Guardi especially, that it is difficult to say anything new. One constant about their works—and to a lesser extent, those of their predecessor Carlevarijs—is the amount of difficulty scholars have had in grappling with their attribution and dating. Another theme in recent decades is the knowledge that can be gained about the artists' painting practices through technical examination, and how this can help in attribution and dating. These issues are important for our understanding of these three prolific artists.

Venetian views may be said to have begun on May 27, 1703, when Luca Carlevarijs (1663-1730) published his collection of engravings of the city, entitled *Le Fabriche, e Vedute di Venetia disegnate, poste in prospettiva et intagliate ...*, with a frontispiece stating that they were created specifically to make the wonders of the city better known to foreigners. Despite the fact that paintings had been made in prior centuries recording city festivals or the receptions of notables, and although views of the city had been painted by the Dutchman Gaspar van Wittel (1652/3-1736), also known as Vanvitelli, and the German Joseph Heintz (ca. 1600-1678), Carlevarijs, both in the scope of his engravings, and in his subsequent view paintings, was the first Venetian artist to champion, and to take up his brush to paint, pure views of the serene city on the lagoon.[2]

Carlevarijs was born in Udine, part of the mainland territory of the Venetian Republic, on January 20, 1663. The son of an artist and architect, he became adept at both architecture and mathematics, arrived in Venice proper in 1679, and was painting well before the turn of the century. Among his earliest dated works are three paintings commemorating the receptions of foreign ambassadors to the Republic, which each contain views.[3] His earliest dated

Francesco Guardi (Italian, 1712-1793)
DETAIL: *View of the Dogana and Santa Maria della Salute*, 1767-69
(CAT. 43)

paintings that were views proper—that is, made without the added motive of an ambassadorial reception—whose whereabouts are securely known today, are two in Lucca that were likely painted in 1706 for a patron, Stefano Conti, of that city, and a set of four from 1709, the only such set of four that remain together. Two of this set are in the present exhibition, *The Molo, Venice, from the Bacino di San Marco* (cat. 39) and *The Molo, Venice, Looking West* (cat. 40); their two companions depict *The Bacino with the Dogana and the Isola di San Giorgio* and the *Piazza San Marco.*

While today the heavily clouded (if often sherbet-colored) skies, colorful, larger-scale figures, and beautiful if somewhat prosaic handling of Carlevarijs can be readily discerned from the works of Canaletto and Guardi, such was not always the case. When these four works were at Stoneleigh Abbey, their home from at least 1771 and quite possibly for decades earlier (as they may have been ordered in Italy by the third Baron Leigh as early as ca. 1709), they were described in an early twentieth-century guide to the collection as "four views of Venice in the style of Canaletto" with a note that "some experts think they are by Guardi."[4]

That they are by Carlevarijs is not in doubt today, but their dating has presented an issue. A painted cartouche on the right-most pier of the lower level of the Doge's Palace in *The Molo Looking West* contains the text "L / DCC / IX" but is partially obscured by tape masking the painting's edge. When the paintings were sold to Robert Lehman in 1954, this was interpreted forthrightly as 1709, and when Aldo Rizzi catalogued them in 1967 he gave them a date of "ca. 1710."[5] In 1987 and again in 2001 scholars noted that the text presupposes a masked "C" following the "L" (for Luca Carlevarijs) as well as a masked "M," and that therefore the full text could equally be "L (C) (M) / DCC (X) / IX," giving a possible date of 1719.[6] Charles Beddington has argued persuasively for a 1709 dating on the grounds of style and of their presumed purchase by the third Baron Leigh while he may have traveled in Italy ca. 1709-10. It seems that "XIX" would more naturally be kept together rather than awkwardly split, so an original text of "L (C) (M) / DCC / IX," or 1709, makes more sense. It is instructive to be able to compare this painting with the later (probably ca. 1725-27) view of *The Molo Looking West* (cat. 41), in which the handling is less precise and the features not as detailed.

The contrast between those two works of Carlevarijs shows that by his late years, he was no longer painting with the smooth, liquid touch seen in his works from earlier in the century. He was struck with progressive paralysis in 1728 and died in February 1730.[7] But a new star was already on the rise, and several of Carlevarijs's patrons were already defecting to the newcomer, Giovanni Antonio Canal (1697-1768), better known as Canaletto, by the mid-1720s. Among them was the aforementioned Stefano Conti, a wool and silk merchant from Lucca, who had, as early as 1706, commissioned Carlevarijs to produce three view paintings.[8] Nineteen years later, in 1725, Conti asked his agent, the painter Alessandro Marchesini, to procure him two more works by the artist. Marchesini's reply is telling: he wrote on July 14, 1725, that Carlevarijs had been surpassed in public esteem by Antonio Canal, "who amazes absolutely everyone here who sees his works, which are similar to Carlevarijs's, but in which one sees the sun shining."[9]

The torch had been passed to Canaletto, whose works in many ways define our present view of Venice and our conception of what the city looked like in the eighteenth century. Born in October 1697, to a family of artists and scenographers, he collaborated in the family business and developed a great sense for perspective, theater, and how best to create an appealing scene.

One of his early works, painted ca. 1725, has recently been "rediscovered" and is emblematic of the dating and attribution problems that have dogged so many Venetian views. Examination by a conservator was crucial in surmounting the difficulties inherent in attempting to create a secure chronology for an artist who made over a thousand works, including paintings and drawings. The *View of the Molo, Venice* (cat. 33) was initially considered by W. G. Constable, the doyen of Canaletto studies and the first to undertake the mammoth task of systematically cataloguing Canaletto's immense oeuvre, as an original work by the artist from ca. 1730.[10] By 1954 he had changed his mind, writing to William Suida at the Kress Foundation: "After careful study and much hesitation, I've reluctantly come to the view that it is not by Canaletto and is probably a work of the earlier 19th century. This view is based mainly on the character of the brush work and the drawing."[11]

Constable had examined it in person a year earlier and felt the architecture to be "scratchy and thin" and the figures "impressionist and sketchy," although twice before, when studying it through photographs from the Witt Library and the Museum of Fine Art in Boston, he had accepted it as an original Canaletto.[12] In the first edition of his important two-volume catalogue of the artist, published in 1962, he held to his 1954 opinion and went further, stating that it is "perhaps by an early nineteenth-century imitator."[13] In 1973, Fern Rusk Shapley called it "attributed to Canaletto" and noted that an X-ray taken of the work "tends to support the opinion that this painting may be by a follower rather than by Canaletto himself."[14] As Katharine Baetjer notes in her excellent 2006 study of the painting, this is curious, as what the X-ray revealed was a large *pentimento* at lower right and the extension of the composition towards the right, both of which indicate that the artist was working out his ideas on the canvas, rather than copying another's work.[15]

The painting benefited greatly from a 1997-98 technical examination and treatment by conservator Elise Effman, who published her findings along with Baetjer's in 2006. She identified underpainting, very similar to that of Canaletto works known to be from the late 1720s, and wrote that the artist's "sheer exuberance and texture of the paint application" conforms in all respects to Canaletto's works of that period, as do other aspects of the painting, such as the method used to lay in the ground. The use of an early version of the Prussian blue pigment additionally shows it to be an eighteenth-century, not nineteenth-century, work. The pentimento and extension of the composition also conform to Canaletto's practice in other works of the 1720s. Moreover, Effman discovered the use of a particular black substance, similar to ink, which is used in the architectural details and certain shadows and found in other Canaletto paintings of the 1720s, that he did not use later in his career, as well as figures underpainted with black, a practice he used until ca. 1727.[16] These aspects of handling, technique, and materials, in concert with a careful comparison of the work with known paintings of the 1720s, led both Baetjer and Effman to conclude that Constable's first opinion—that the painting is an authentic, early Canaletto—was correct. Their work is a model for the type of collaboration between curators and conservators that continues to grow, which will no doubt provide more important rediscoveries.

Indeed, a precursor to their work is a joint 1992 publication by Nancy Minty and Sandra Lawrence, another curator/conservator team, who examined Toronto's *The Molo Looking West* by Carlevarijs, as well as its *The Bacino di San Marco from the Piazzetta* by Canaletto (fig. 1), a work whose attribution has also been questioned. The painting was purchased as a Canaletto by J. P. Richter for Ludwig Mond in 1891, but when Richter published it in 1910 he had demoted it to "School of Canale," stating, "The plan, the formal design of this picture, is Canale's but that which makes Canale supreme among the painters of Venice is absent: *brio*, atmosphere, and the glow and sparkle of light," suggesting that it might be by Bernardo Bellotto (1722-1780), the artist's nephew.[17] Constable and J. G. Links, however, have consistently given the painting to Canaletto, while noting its "cool tone" and "long grey shadows."[18] Nancy Minty and Sandra Lawrence believe that the "autumnal afternoon sun casting long shadows ... helps to confirm the attribution to Canaletto,"[19] even as they note the presence of multiple layers of varnish that were present on the work when Richter saw it—since removed—that would have caused it to appear darker than it is. Richter's attribution to Bellotto was also rejected by that artist's cataloguer, Stefan Kozakiewicz,[20] and today it is fully accepted by scholars as a Canaletto.

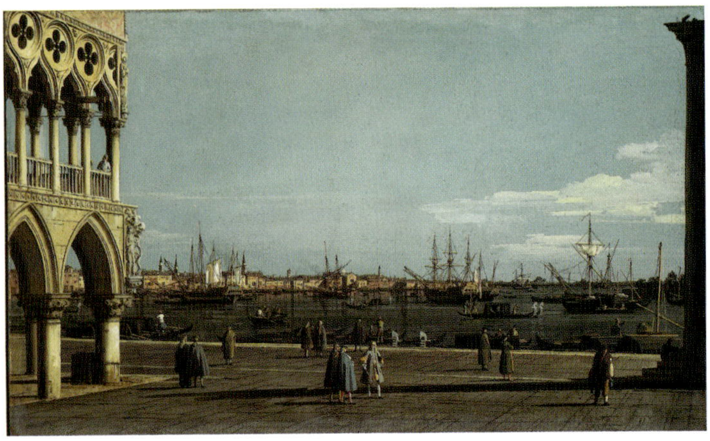

FIG. 1
Canaletto (Giovanni Antonio Canal) (Italian, 1697-1768)
The Bacino di San Marco, from the Piazzetta, ca. 1735
Oil on canvas, 19¼ x 32¼ in. (48.8 x 81.8 cm)
Art Gallery of Ontario, Toronto. Gift of the Ludwig Mond Estate, 1926. © 2010 AGO

The other Canaletto paintings in this exhibition, most of which have been dogged by attribution and dating issues, have not received the same in-depth consideration as the Columbia and Toronto paintings. Happily, in the case of Houston's *The Grand Canal near the Rialto Bridge, Venice* (cat. 34), its attribution has never been questioned, and documentary evidence conclusively proves that it was painted by August 22, 1730, when a "Mr. Smith"—certainly Joseph Smith (ca. 1674-1770), Canaletto's primary patron and agent—was paid for two works, which were subsequently sent to Hugh Howard.[21] Indeed, this painting, and its pendant, *The Entrance to the Grand Canal,* are the only known works for which it is certain that Smith acted as the artist's agent, among the many for which he acted that part.

The Canaletto painting from the Metropolitan Museum of Art, *Venice: Santa Maria della Salute* (cat. 35), was part of the collection of the Minneapolis Institute of Arts for twenty years, from 1938 to 1958, before it was withdrawn and sold. That museum published it in 1938 as "all that we have come to expect from the artist."[22] William Suida, in a note dated Sept. 1, 1939, wrote that he thought it a "first quality" work, and when it was catalogued by Constable, and later by Federico Zeri as part of the Metropolitan collection, there were no doubts as to its authenticity.[23] The reason for its deaccession from Minneapolis is unclear, but it may simply have occurred because it is not a particularly exciting view—the Minneapolis 1938 publication noted, "There is nothing exciting in this scene, except insofar as Venice itself excites," and commented on its "everyday aspect," contrasting it with the "vivacity, the brilliant light, and the sumptuous qualities" of Guardi's views of Venice.[24] J. G. Links, who took up the difficult task of cataloguing Canaletto's works following Constable's death, wrote to Katharine Baetjer at the Metropolitan in 1992 that although its figures are "stiff," he had little doubt that Canaletto composed the work, as its viewpoint is unique to the artist and his followers were not capable of changing a Canaletto viewpoint and then also copying his style.[25]

Allentown's beautiful *The Piazzetta: Looking South* (cat. 36), a painting from around 1740-46, has also had its share of doubts concerning attribution. A former Kress painting, Constable noted in 1929, from a Witt photograph, that it "may be OK" (i.e., may be a Canaletto). When he saw the painting in person in January 1953, he felt that it was "by Canaletto, but dull and mechanical."[26] The following year, in the same letter to William Suida cited above, Constable further demoted it: "I was able to study this picture on several occasions and came to the conclusion that it is a studio piece in the sense that Canaletto had helpers in painting it. This view is based on certain tricks in the painting of the figures and the architecture which are not characteristic of Canaletto himself as I know him."[27] Naturally this was the view that was published in the 1962, 1976, and 1989 editions of his catalogue of the artist's work, where it appears as a "studio work of the 1740s, mechanical in quality."[28] Fern Rusk Shapley, who had commented negatively with regard to the Columbia painting's X-ray in her 1973 catalogue of the Kress collection, similarly questioned this painting's execution and the "poor condition" that she felt its X-ray revealed.[29] However, in 1989, while preparing the major Canaletto exhibition held that year at the Metropolitan Museum of Art, Katharine Baetjer accepted the work, quite rightly, as entirely by Canaletto, noting the "freedom and expressive quality of the brushwork, particularly in the foreground passages depicting vendors and the details of the canal in the background."[30] In the subsequent supplement to Constable and Links' *Canaletto* catalogue, the negative view dating to 1953-54 was rectified, with the comment that "the composition appears to be by Canaletto and the work no more mechanical than is usual at the period."[31]

The two small *capricci* from Springfield seen here, *Farmhouse on the Venetian Mainland* (cat. 37) and *Villa and Ruins by a River* (cat. 38) have never been doubted as original works by the artist, although no one except Antonio Morassi, in 1953, has hazarded to date them. Morassi, reviewing the exhibition in Detroit in which they appeared, called them "a bit summary, but with a rapid, flying touch, and with a slight grayish tone, from the artist's last decade (and in truth, a bit mannered)."[32]

Just as Marchesini's 1725 comments about Canaletto's rising prominence mark a clear transition between his career and that of Carlevarijs, a diary entry by Pietro Gradenigo ushers in the next phase of Venetian view painting. On April 25, 1764, Gradenigo wrote, "Francesco Guardi, painter from the contrada of Santi Apostoli on the Fondamente Nove, good student of the famous Canaletto, very successful by means of the *camera ottica* in depicting on two not small canvases, ordered by a foreign Englishman, the views of Piazza San Marco towards the church, and the Clocktower, and of the Rialto Bridge, and the left-hand buildings towards Cannareggio, today exhibited them in the Procuratie Nove, to universal applause."[33] Given that Guardi was over fifty years old at the time, scholars were unsure for years whether to take it as literal that he was Canaletto's student, or whether Gradenigo meant merely that he painted in Canaletto's general manner. It does, however, seem possible that Guardi studied with Canaletto prior to the latter's 1746 trip to England, especially since his early view paintings (the earliest known is dated 1756) strongly recall the works of Canaletto in the 1730s and 1740s,[34] and he could equally have worked with him after Canaletto's return to Venice in 1756. As with Canaletto's rise to prominence just as Carlevarijs was declining in the late 1720s, Guardi's rise coincides with Canaletto's final decade, the 1760s.

Francesco Guardi was born on October 5, 1712, in Venice, to a family that had been ennobled by the Habsburgs in 1643. His father was a painter who had probably worked in Austria before settling in Venice in 1702, and his elder brother, Antonio, became one as well. After their father's death in 1716, Antonio took over as both caregiver and teacher to his four-year-old brother, and the two were known to have worked together from the 1730s, primarily as copyists; it is certainly also very likely that each was encouraged by and may have studied with their brother-in-law, Giambattista Tiepolo, who married their sister in 1719.

With Francesco Guardi, problems of attribution and dating are, not surprisingly, similar to those surrounding works by Canaletto. Guardi, too, produced over a thousand works, including paintings and drawings. Moreover, there was much discussion in the mid- and late 1960s as to whether certain early works should be attributed to him or to his elder brother. And for paintings made toward the end of his life, there has been confusion about whether certain works were created with the assistance of his son, Giacomo (1764–1835). The Guardi painting from Toledo in this exhibition, *San Giorgio Maggiore, Venice* (cat. 44), has not been questioned in terms of its attribution, but has provoked concerns about its date and a possible intervention by Giacomo. In 1953 Morassi considered it a work of the 1770s, whereas in 1970 Barry Hannegan believed it to date after 1780.[35] The problem might have been cleared up by the presence of what seems to have been a monogram and date, painted on the left end of the front of San Giorgio Maggiore's terrace, which was visible in 1954 and was again studied in 1975. Just prior to the painting entering the museum in 1952, it was cleaned, at which point the text became visible, possibly reading "F [G] / 179[1 or 4]." William Hutton, then a curatorial assistant at the museum, wrote to ask the opinion of Francis Watson at the Wallace Collection, noting that "the inscription must have always been faint and applied with the most minute and fine brush possible," and that while the final figure looked like a "4," as Guardi died in 1793 it must be a "1," with a line of masonry coursing intersecting it to create the effect of a four. Watson responded that the date appeared to be "1794," which was "quite incomprehensible," with the only guess he could hazard being that the painting "remained unfinished or almost finished in Guardi's studio at his death" and that Giacomo fiddled about with it in the succeeding years, putting the finishing touches on it in 1794—although he couldn't tell whether there were any signs of Giacomo's handling in the work.[36] A second campaign to decipher the marks was made in 1975, and it was felt that enough remained to change the date to "ca. 1791."[37] What is left of the barely visible black markings in this area, as shown in a recent image (fig. 2), do not provide any further clarification, but the painting is of high quality and, taking everything together, should most likely be dated ca. 1780–91.

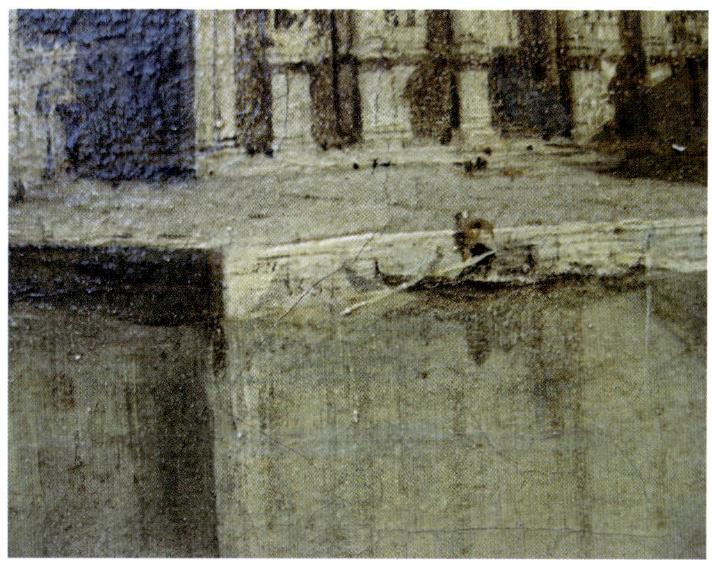

FIG. 2
Francesco Guardi (Italian, 1712–1793)
DETAIL: *San Giorgio Maggiore, Venice*, ca. 1790
(CAT. 44)

In his correspondence, Watson additionally made the point that it would be very unusual to find a Guardi signature on a late work, as that was a practice he primarily used early in his career, when he was trying to establish a name for himself as a view painter. Such is the case with the beautiful *View of the Dogana and Santa Maria della Salute,* from Kansas City, in this exhibition (cat. 42), which is signed, on the end of the barrel at lower right, "Guardi" and dates to ca. 1767-69.

In addition to the works from Toledo and Kansas City, this exhibit includes two other works by Guardi—one early, and one from his middle period. Each of these has been the subject of further difficult attribution and dating issues. The *Regatta at the Rialto Bridge*, at the Sarah Campbell Blaffer Foundation in Houston (cat. 43), dates to the 1770s and spent the years from 1906 to 1980 ensconced at the Metropolitan Museum of Art under varying attributions: it was first unquestionably "a large and important painting by Guardi ... [with] all the characteristics of Guardi's brilliant style very strongly developed, and it has, moreover, a certain suavity in the treatment of tone, which deserted him in his later years. He shows himself here very decidedly as a pupil of Canaletto. Few of his works have a greater breadth of handling or more dignity of tone."[38] While today we might take issue with this work being particularly "Canalettesque," we can not argue with the comment on the breadth of handling, as the brush strokes seem to flicker across the canvas. In 1914 it was still considered a Guardi, but in 1940 was demoted to a "copy after Guardi," after a similar, smaller, work that the Rijksmuseum had acquired in 1936.[39] This opinion was repeated by Morassi in his 1973 catalogue, and again by Luigina Rossi Bortolatto in 1974, who went further, calling it likely a nineteenth-century copy.[40] With that, the stage was set for it to be deaccessioned in 1980 from the Metropolitan (which was left, however, with no small number of Guardi paintings) and eventually sold to the Blaffer Foundation in 1983. In the process leading up to that purchase, the foundation did due diligence, checking with Sydney Freedberg, who gave his opinion that it was "absolutely autograph," and with Giuliano Briganti, who likewise said that it was "without any doubt an autograph work of the highest quality of Francesco Guardi," and noted that Federico Zeri concurred in that opinion, having changed his mind from an earlier dismissal of the work.[41] Conservation tests were undertaken, with the result that it was found to have all the qualities of handling and pigment composition—including the same sort of Prussian blue used in the eighteenth century and referred to in the examination of the Canaletto from Columbia—that an authentic Guardi should have. Pinpoint pricks were found on the work, connecting it to one of his workshop procedures of using a large drawing to provide a tracing of a specific view, for transfer to a canvas.[42] In the technical examination, much reference was made to the 1970 examination and publication of findings about Guardi's handling and pigments that accompanied the Chicago, Toledo, and Minneapolis exhibition in that year. In 1970, it was the intent of that exhibition's organizers to conduct a thorough technical examination of all the works, but, due to lack of time, only two paintings, a Guardi and a Cavallucci, were examined and published.[43]

While we may disagree with the writer who noted in the 1906 Metropolitan Museum of Art *Bulletin* that Guardi's painting at the Blaffer resembles the work of Canaletto, in the painting from Yale in this exhibition the resemblance with works by Canaletto is striking—so striking in fact, that it has been considered as by that artist, or his school, to this day. *Venice, The Molo and the Riva degli Schiavoni, Looking East* (cat. 45), however, is quite possibly an early work by Guardi, from the late 1750s, done in the period when he was significantly influenced by the works of the older master.[44] It can be compared in its general handling and treatment of rooflines, figures, dogs, and water with three of Guardi's early views recently displayed in Treviso, and its exhibition here, as well as further study of Guardi's early period, should eventually allow a definitive conclusion to be reached.[45]

Whereas Canaletto was celebrated during his lifetime, Guardi's fame didn't really begin to grow until the mid- to late-nineteenth century, and the era's nascent taste for impressionistic, loose, and sketchy works clearly played its part. Such favor was not yet apparent in the early nineteenth century: in May 1819 the Secretary of the Venetian Academy of Fine Arts wrote the Governor of the Venetian provinces that the export of some of Guardi's works to an Englishman should be halted, as they were "very distinguished works of their kind." The governor, however, disagreed, stating that Guardi was not among artists "who enjoy great fame," and the loss of the paintings from Venice would not be felt.[46] Though not highly valued in his own lifetime (certainly not to the extent of Canaletto's), Guardi's works have in the twentieth and twenty-first centuries again found that "universal applause" that was his on that April day in 1764.

Guardi died on January 1, 1793. Ninety years had passed since the publication of Carlevarijs's engravings, which had ushered in a tremendous period of growth and creative achievement in Venetian view painting. In a scant four years this proud city—an independent republic that had stood on its own for over a thousand years—fell to Napoleon and was then soon traded by the French to the Austrians, marking a definitive end to a chapter in its history. Although Venice would continue to be painted in the nineteenth century, by such important artists as Turner and Monet, it would never again be portrayed on the scale of the preceding century, and most later paintings would be done predominantly by foreigners.

Indeed, by the early nineteenth century, a palpable shift in the attitude towards topographical and view painting could be felt. In a lecture at the Royal Academy, the painter Fuseli said that topographical painting was "that kind of landscape which is entirely occupied with the tame delineation of a given spot," and that it was "the last branch of uninteresting subjects."[47] But Carlevarijs, Canaletto, and Guardi, as well as Bellotto, transcend topography. In their work, whether through charming figures, minute detail, or the scintillating manipulation of light, we constantly confront Venice anew. And to be able to see Venice through their eyes, we have benefited from generations of scholars who have painstakingly studied and catalogued their works, making difficult determinations about attribution and dating, most of whom worked without the benefit of color images, conservation reports, photocopiers, and computers. The Canaletto scholar J. G. Links noted in 1998 that "some fifty years ago" Sir Francis Watson had written, "The whole field of *vedute* painting is so confused by repetition, collaboration, copying and forgery [that] it behooves us to be very cautious in our pronouncements."[48] This is, of course, still true, and is likely to remain so for decades to come. Thankfully, today's researchers have been able to build on the work of the many dedicated scholars cited in this article to make new or revised judgments on attribution and dating, augmented, at times, by important results found through technical examination and close collaboration between curators and conservators. All this points toward a future as sunny as Canaletto's Venice, for further discoveries in the field of eighteenth-century views.

Endnotes

Acknowledgments: For having graciously and generously provided advice, assistance, and access to valuable documentation, the author wishes to thank the following: Dita Amory, Katharine Baetjer, Sofia Bakis, Diane Waterhouse Barbarisi, Charles Beddington, Pete Bowron, Franny Brock, Jenny Cartmell, Sarah Cartwright, James Clifton, Hardy George, Sarah Grlicky, Teresa Harson, Todd Herman, Christina Hicks, Debbie Jackson, Larry Kanter, Emily Kenagy, Ian Kennedy, Andrea Mall, Laney Monsey, Larry Nichols, Patrick Noon, Michael Parke-Taylor, Jo Ann Reece, Noelle Rice, and Pat Whitesides.

1 Henry James, "Venice," in *The Century Magazine* 25, no. 1 (Nov. 1882): 3.

2 For earlier views of Venice, including works by Vanvitelli and Heintz, see William Barcham, "Il Vedutismo," 39-43, and "Gaspar van Wittel," 80-82, in *Canaletto: Venezia e i Suoi Splendori* (Venice: Marsilio, 2008). For Carlevarijs's life and work, see C. Beddington, *Luca Carlevarijs: Views of Venice* (San Diego: Timken Museum of Art, 2001).

3 Beddington, *Luca Carlevarijs,* 16; the paintings show the receptions of the French Ambassador de Charmont on April 29, 1703, the French Ambassador the Abbé de Pomponne on May 10, 1706, and the British Ambassador the fourth Earl of Manchester on Sept. 22, 1707.

4 Agnes Leigh, *Stoneleigh Abbey Pictures* (London: Hazell, Watson & Viney, 1919: 11); see also S. C. Kaines-Smith, *Stoneleigh Abbey: An Illustrated Survey,* n.d., pl. 18; both cited in J. Pope-Hennessy and L. Kanter, *The Robert Lehman Collection I: Italian Paintings* (New York: The Metropolitan Museum of Art, 1987: 250). For recent entries on the two paintings not exhibited here, which were shown in Treviso in 2008-9, see Katharine Baetjer in *Canaletto,* 249-50.

5 Invoice in the paintings' file at the Metropolitan Museum of Art; Aldo Rizzi, *Luca Carlevarijs* (Venice: Alfieri, 1967: 52, 55), "*tra il primo e il secondo decennio.*"

6 Pope-Hennessy and Kanter, *Robert Lehman,* 252 and Beddington, *Luca Carlevarijs,* 21.

7 Beddington, *Luca Carlevarijs,* 25.

8 Two of these are likely those in the Museo Nazionale di Palazzo Mansi in Lucca, *Il Molo con la Zecca verso la Punta della Dogana* and *Veduta con la chiesa di San Giorgio Maggiore.* These were first published by Paola Betti, "*La collezione di Stefano Conti: un Lazzarini e due Carlevarijs ritrovati,*" in *Antichità Viva* 36, no. 1, (Jan.-Feb. 1997): 38-43, and discussed by I. Reale in *Gaspare Vanvitelli e le origini del vedutismo,* exh. cat. (Rome: Chiostro del Bramante, 2002: 317-9). They would have been received by Conti in April 1706. The third, untraced, painting Conti would have received from Carlevarijs, in August 1706, was a view of Piazza San Marco.

9 "*Intesi il bisogno di che vostra signoria illustrissima desidera per li du accennati quadri da accompagnare agli altri che tiene dipinti dal signor Lucca Carlevarijs. Ma adesso veramente vive il soggetto, se non fosse superato di maggior stima dal signor Antonio Canale, che fa in questo paese stordire universalmente ognuno che vede le sue opere, che consiste sul ordine di Carlevari ma vi si vede lucer entro il sole,*" published by Francis Haskell, "Stefano Conti Patron of Canaletto and Others," *Burlington Magazine* 98 (Sept. 1956): 296-300 and often cited.

10 National Gallery of Art, *Preliminary Catalogue of Paintings and Sculpture* (Washington, D.C.: National Gallery of Art, 1941: 31-32, cat. no. 234), quoted in Katharine Baetjer, "Canaletto Paints the Molo from the Ponte della Paglia," in *Studying and Conserving Paintings, Occasional Papers on the Samuel H. Kress Collection* (London: Archetype Publications, 2006: 199), which also includes an excellent discussion about this painting's vicissitudes of attribution, relationship to a similar painting in Turin, and place in Canaletto's oeuvre.

11 Letter of March 17, 1954, pp. 1-2, quoted by Baetjer, "Canaletto Paints," 199, and present (as a photocopy) in the Columbia Museum of Art's file.

12 Baetjer, "Canaletto Paints," 199, using information provided by Charles Beddington, who holds Constable's annotated photographs and notes.

13 W. G. Constable, *Canaletto: Giovanni Antonio Canal, 1697-1768.* (Oxford: Clarendon Press, 1962, vol. 2: 218, cat. no. 86a). This opinion was carried through into the 1976 and 1989 versions.

14 Fern Rusk Shapley, *Paintings from the Samuel H. Kress Collection,* Vol. 3*: Italian Schools, XVI-XVIII Century* (London: Phaidon Press, 1973: 163-4, cat. no. K252, fig. 315), and Baetjer, "Canaletto Paints," 201-2.

15 Baetjer, "Canaletto Paints," 202; she also notes that the handling and techniques seem typical of Canaletto's practice in the late 1720s, by comparison with works that can be dated.

16 Elise Effman, "View of the Molo: A Canaletto Attribution Reinstated," in *Studying and Conserving Paintings. . . Kress Collection,* 189-95.

17 J. P. Richter, *The Mond Collection, An Appreciation* (London: John Murray, 1910: 235, 243), quoted in Nancy Minty and Sandra Lawrence, *In the Name of Art, In the Name of Science: Considerations of Conservation* (Toronto: Art Gallery of Ontario, 1992: 14).

18 W. G. Constable and J. G. Links, *Canaletto,* 1962, 1976, and 1989 editions, cat. no. 127.

19 Minty and Lawrence, *In the Name of Art,* 14.

20 Stefan Kozakiewicz, *Bernardo Bellotto,* (Greenwich, Conn.: New York Graphic Society Ltd., 1972, vol. 2: cat. no. Z97, 415).

21 For more on this important precise dating and knowledge of the works' acquisition circumstances, see the catalogue entry (cat. 34) in this volume.

22 Minneapolis Institute of Arts *Bulletin* (Nov. 5, 1938): 148.

23 Suida's comment is on the MIA accession card, a copy of which is in the Metropolitan's file on the painting; Constable, *Canaletto,* vol. 2: 257, cat. no. 175 (and 1976 and 1989 editions); Federico Zeri, *Italian Paintings, A Catalogue of the Collection of The Metropolitan Museum of Art, Venetian School* (New York: The Metropolitan Museum of Art, 1973: 14).

24 Minneapolis Institute of Arts *Bulletin* (Nov. 5, 1938): 148.

25 Letter of April 8, 1992, in the painting's file in the Metropolitan Museum of Art.

26 Manuscript notes in the Allentown file, referred to in a typescript from the Allentown file. Notes in the Allentown file also state that Roberto Longhi and Bernard Berenson attributed the painting to Canaletto.

27 Letter to William Suida, March 17, 1954, a copy of which is in the Columbia Museum of Art file on their painting shown in this exhibition.

28 Constable, *Canaletto,* cat. no. 61.

29 Shapley, *Paintings from the Kress Collection,* 164. Moreover, shortly after this was published, a letter of June 11, 1975, to the Allentown Art Museum from Heinemann gave the opinion that the work was by another artist altogether, the early nineteenth-century painter Giovanni Migliara (note in the Allentown file).

30 Notes of verbal communication of June 3, 1989, in the Allentown file.

31 J. G. Links, *A Supplement to W. G. Constable's, Canaletto: Giovanni Antonio Canal, 1697-1768* (London: Pallas Athene Arts, 1998: 9, cat. no. 61).

32 Antonio Morassi, "*Una Mostra del Settecento Veneziano a Detroit,*" *Arte Veneta* 7 (1953): 58, "*un po' sommari, ma dal tocco rapido, volante, e d'una tonalità grigiastra tenue, riferibili all'ultimo decennio dell'artista (e per verità un po' di maniera).*"

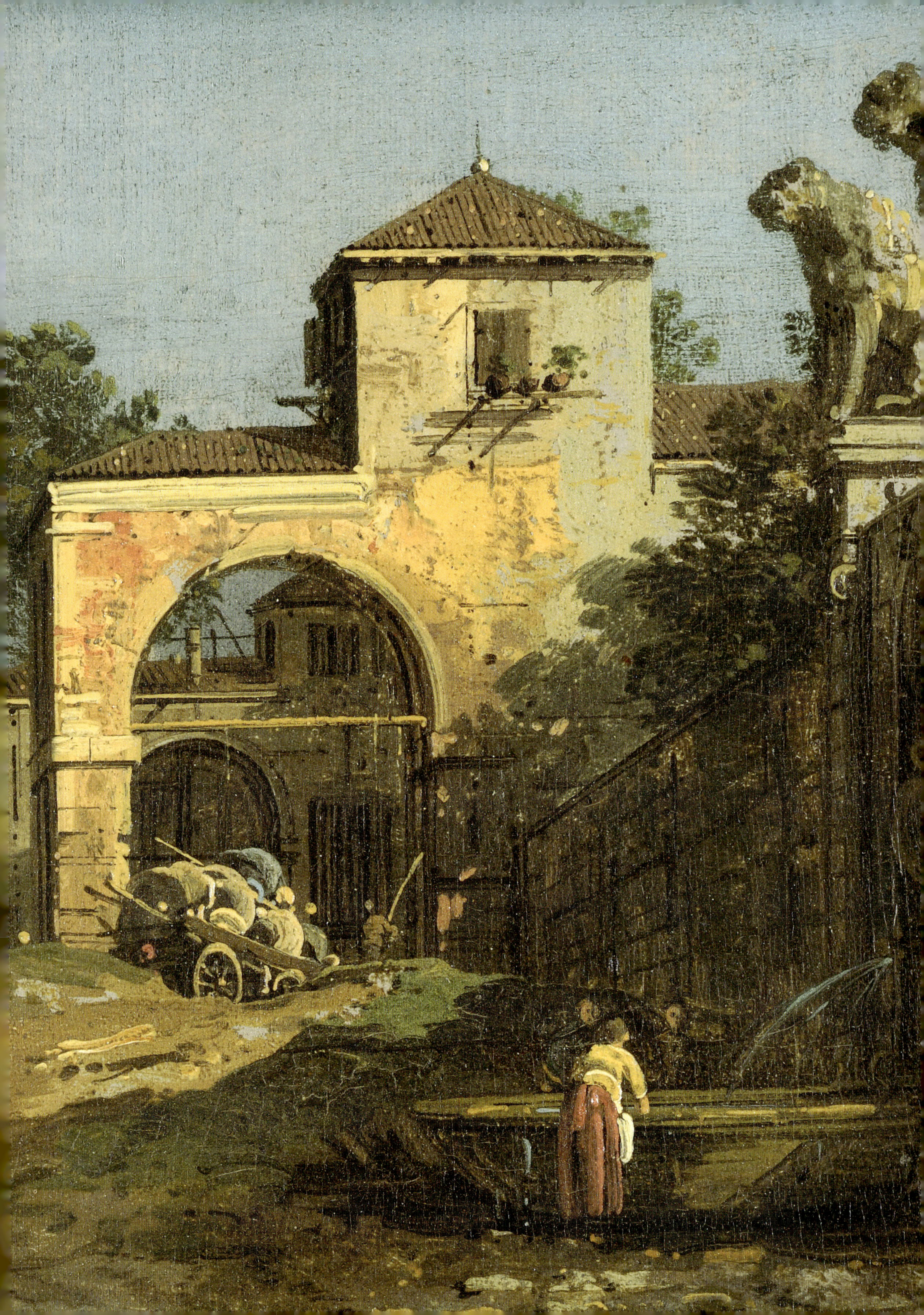

33 "*Francesco Guardi, Pittore della contrada de Santi Apostoli su le Fondamente Nove, buon scolaro del rinomato Canaletto, essendo molto riuscito per via della Camera Ottica, dipingere sopra due non picciole Tele, ordinate da un Forestiere Inglese, le vedute della Piazza di S. Marco verso la chiesa, e l'Orologio, e del Ponte di Rialto, e Sinistre fabbriche verso Canareggio, oggi le rese esposte su laterali delle Procuratie Nove, mediante che si procacciò l'universale applauso,*" originally published by Lina Livan, *Notizie d'arte tratte dai notatori e dagli annali del N. H. Pietro Gradenigo* (Venice: La Reale Deputazione Editrice, 1942: 106) and often cited.

34 This was already suggested by Barry Hannegan, *Painting in Italy in the Eighteenth Century: Rococo to Romanticism* (Chicago: Art Institute of Chicago, 1970: 68).

35 Morassi, "*Una mostra del settecento Veneziano,*" 61, and Hannegan in *Painting in Italy*, cat. no. 24.

36 Letters of October 12, October 27, and November 18, 1954, in the Toledo Museum of Art documentary file between William Hutton and Francis Watson. Hutton responded with thanks, and wrote that he felt confident that the work is entirely Francesco's.

37 Memo to Toledo Museum of Art documentary file, July 14, 1975, from Roger Berkowitz, stating that he and Miss Tsurutani examined it and felt enough remained of the rubbed initials and date to warrant the change from Morassi's earlier "ca. 1770–80," and that this "ca. 1791" would therefore also better reflect Barry Hannegan's "after 1780" date.

38 *Bulletin of the Metropolitan Museum of Art* (1906): 72–3. (Descriptions such as these always tend to reflect the tastes and preoccupations of the age ... no doubt the writer himself was interested in "dignity of tone"!)

39 G. A. Simonson, "Some of Guardi's Paintings in America," *Art in America* (1914): 90, in which he accepted it as Guardi but said it "suffers from over-crowding with figures and its execution is somewhat fretful"; Harry B. Wehle, *A Catalogue of Italian, Spanish and Byzantine Paintings* (New York: New York Publishers Printing Company/William Bradford Press, 1940: 276).

40 Antonio Morassi, *Guardi: Antonio e Francesco Guardi* (Venice: Alfieri, 1973: 367–8, cat. no. 304); Luigina Rossi Bortolatto, *L'Opera completa di Francesco Guardi* (Milan: Rizzoli, 1974: cat. no. 862). Burton B. Fredericksen and Federico Zeri, *A Census of Pre-Nineteenth-Century Italian Paintings in North American Public Collections* (Cambridge: Harvard University Press, 1972: 96) also listed it as a "studio" piece. Carlo Donzelli, *I Pittori veneti del Settecento* (Florence: Sansoni, 1957: 110) had, however, alone after Wehle's publication, considered it as by Guardi.

41 Freedberg, memo of a phone call of March 14, 1983, to the Sarah Campbell Blaffer Foundation, in the foundation's file on the painting; Briganti, letter of Sept. 8, 1982, to the Blaffer Foundation in its file, in which he noted that Morassi before his 1973 catalogue had probably not seen it in person and that Zeri, who had written the recent catalogue of Venetian paintings at the Metropolitan, didn't include it as he had not seen it either, but now considers it "a beautiful autograph work." Terisio Pignatti, in a catalogue of the Blaffer paintings, *Five Centuries of Italian Painting: 1300–1800* (Houston: The Sarah Campbell Blaffer Foundation, 1985: 206) states that once Zeri had seen the work cleaned, he changed his mind, considering it autograph. Briganti also noted that he sees in the Blaffer painting, especially in its architecture, a higher quality than the Amsterdam painting and much greater contrasts in the light and shade.

42 Pignatti, in *Five Centuries of Italian Painting*, p. 208, notes that this is typical of an autograph Guardi and that a number of pricked drawings from his workshop are in the Museo Correr, Venice.

43 Marigene H. Butler, "Technical Note," in *Painting in Italy*, pp. 246–9. The Blaffer also referred to a manuscript by Rita P. Albertson and James L. Coddington, "A Preliminary Investigation of Francesco Guardi's Painting Technique," prepared for the Art Conservation Training Programs conference, held at the Conservation Center of the Institute of Fine Arts, New York University, in 1981, a copy of which is in the painting's file, and in which two Guardi paintings at the Fogg were examined.

44 The suggestion that it may be an early Guardi is due to Charles Beddington, for whose comments I am very grateful. He noted its significant variations from the Canaletto etching of the scene (Alexandre de Vesme, *Le peintre-graveur italien,* [Milano: Hoepli, 1906: cat. no. 18]; Ruth Bromberg, *Canaletto's Etchings* [London/New York: Sotheby Parke Bernet, 1974: cat. no. 21]). It was considered by Constable and Links, *Canaletto,* 244, cat. no. 119a, as "School of Canaletto."

45 Dario Succi cataloged the three early works in *Canaletto, Venezia e i Suoi Splendori*, pp. 282–3, cat. nos. 71–73, *The Grand Canal with the Fabbriche Nuove* and *The Rialto Bridge*, both owned by the Collection of the Trustees of the Ninth Duke of Buccleuch's Chattels Fund, Selkirk, and *The Molo with the "Fusta" towards San Giorgio Maggiore*, Treviso, Musei Civici, all to be dated ca. 1757–60. Guardi's earliest dated view, of 1756, is *Feast Day of "Giovedì Grasso" on the Piazzetta*, in a private collection in London, published by D. Succi, "*Una eccezionale veduta datata di Francesco Guardi*" in *Guardi: Metamorfosi dell'immagine*, exh. cat., (Gorizia and Venice: Assessorato alla cultura di Gorizia and Stamperia di Venezia, 1987: 41–56, fig. 22), and cited by Eliot Rowlands in his catalogue of the Nelson-Atkins Italian paintings, p. 457.

46 G. A. Simonson, "Some of Guardi's Paintings in America," *Art in America* 2, no. 2, (1914): 90, in note, quoting documents published by Dr. Gino Fogolari in *L'Arte* (Oct. 1, 1913): 385.

47 Ralph N. Wornum, *Lectures on Painting by the Royal Academicians Barry, Opie and Fuseli* (London: Henry G. Bohn, 1848: 449).

48 Links, *Supplement to Constable's Canaletto*, p. x.

Canaletto (Giovanni Antonio Canal) (Italian, 1697–1768)
DETAIL: *Capriccio: Farmhouse on the Venetian Mainland*, ca. 1755–65
(CAT. 37)

CAT. 32

BERNARDO BELLOTTO (*Italian*, 1722-1780)

The Campo of SS. Giovanni e Paolo, Venice, ca. 1741

Oil on canvas, 29½ x 43¾ in. (74.93 x 111.13 cm)

The James Philip Gray Collection, Michele and Donald D'Amour Museum of Fine Arts, Springfield, Massachusetts

Photography by David Stansbury

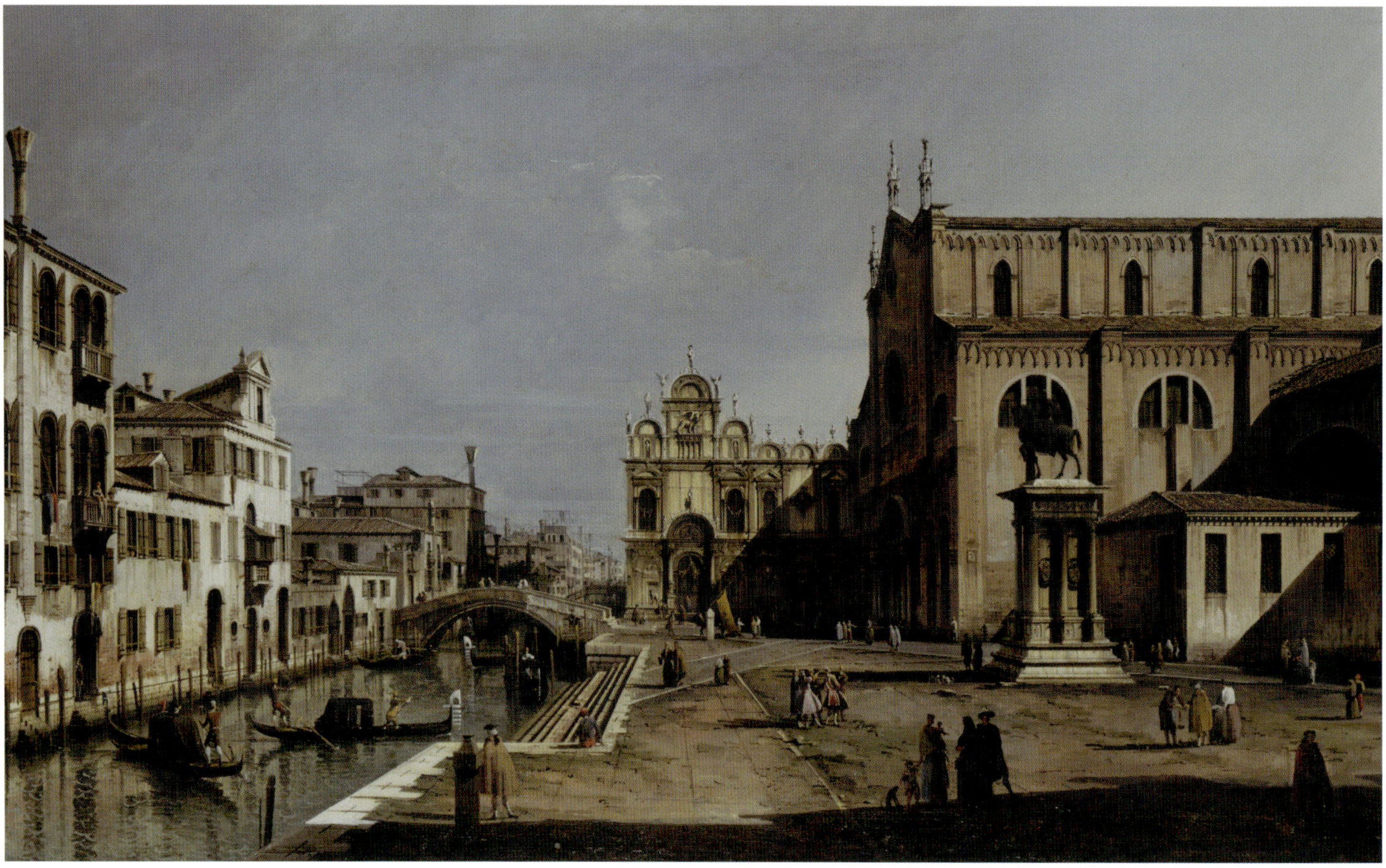

Bellotto entered the studio of Canaletto, his uncle, around 1735, and by 1740 was participating in the production of view paintings. The extent of his participation in Canaletto's oil paintings may never be established precisely, and even the artists' contemporaries experienced difficulty in distinguishing between their hands. The problem of discerning Bellotto's hand in paintings from the early 1740s and separating his work from Canaletto's of the period has been one of the knottier problems of connoisseurship in the field of later Italian painting. The Springfield painting was long attributed to Bellotto by some scholars, but to Canaletto by the majority; by 1952 W. G. Constable's attribution to Bellotto was generally accepted, and the canvas was definitively established as a work of the younger painter in 1972 by Stefan Kozakiewicz in his authoritative monograph on the painter.

Bellotto's subject, the Campo Santi Giovanni e Paolo, is, after the Piazza San Marco, one of the grandest and most important squares in Venice. The site embraces one of the city's six great philanthropic confraternities, the Scuola Grande di San Marco; its main Dominican church, the basilica of Santi Giovanni e Paolo; and one of the most beautiful equestrian statues in the world, Andrea Verrocchio's (1435-1488) monument to the *condottiere* Bartolomeo Colleoni. Bellotto's wide-angle view encompasses nearly the width of the square. On the left is the canal known as the Rio dei Mendicanti; in the center is the trompe l'oeil marble facade of the Scuola di San Marco; and on the right is the shaded Gothic facade and sunlit south elevation of the church.

The square was frequently represented by eighteenth-century Venetian artists. Early in his career Canaletto painted two important views of the site (ca. 1725, Gemäldegalerie Alte Meister, Dresden, and 1726, Pinacoteca Giovanni e Marella Agnelli al Lingotto, Turin) which established the standard prospect and the source for almost all contemporary depictions. Bellotto's design for the Springfield painting clearly derives from his uncle's depictions of the scene, except that, as is typical of the younger artist, the viewpoint is farther from the buildings and the angle is wider, so that more of the square is shown. A pen-and-ink drawing for the Springfield view of the Campo Santi Giovanni e Paolo (Hessisches Landesmuseum, Darmstadt) is dated December 8, 1740, and it is generally thought that the painting followed shortly thereafter. A few years later, about 1745, Bellotto painted a second view (National Gallery of Art, Washington, D.C.) that is nearly identical to the Springfield composition except for minor differences in the figures, the paving of the square, and incidental architectural detail, and in the treatment of light and shade.

Edgar Peters Bowron

PROVENANCE

Thomas Agnew & Sons, London; Paul Romanov, Grand Duke of Russia (1860-1919), Tsarskoe Selo, near Saint Petersburg; collection of his widow, Princess Paley, Tsarskoe Selo; the painting appears to have remained in the collection in the early 1920s after appropriation by the state; sale, Christie's, London, June 21, 1929, lot 18; M. Knoedler & Company, London; Marshall Field, Chicago, 1929, who returned it in exchange for another painting in 1935; purchased in 1936 by the Museum of Fine Arts, Springfield, the James Philip Gray Collection.

EXHIBITIONS

Springfield, Museum of Fine Arts, *Five Eighteenth-Century Venetians*, 1934, no. 8. Wilmington 1935, cat. no. 29.

Saint Louis, City Art Museum, *Special Loan Exhibition: Venetian Paintings, Drawings, Prints of the Eighteenth Century*, 1936, cat. no. 6.

Cambridge, Fogg Museum of Art, *Exhibition of Venetian Paintings and Drawings*, 1938.

Bloomington, Scottish Rite Temple, *Central Illinois Art Exposition*, 1939, cat. no. 7.

Detroit Institute of Arts and Indianapolis, John Herron Art Museum, *Venice 1700-1800: An Exhibition of Venice and the Eighteenth Century*, 1952-53, cat. no. 2.

Cambridge, Fogg Museum of Art, *Venice Observed*, 1956, cat. no. 20.

Boston, Museum of Fine Arts, *Scenic Painters and Draughtsmen of 18th Century Venice*, 1958.

Pittsfield, Berkshire Museum, *Works of Canaletto and Bellotto*, 1960, cat. no. 4.

Venice, Museo Correr, and Houston, Museum of Fine Arts, *Bernardo Bellotto and the Capitals of Europe*, 2001, cat. no. 7.

BIBLIOGRAPHY

Kozakiewicz, Stefan. *Bernardo Bellotto*, trans. Mary Whittall, vol. 1, 21, 25, 26, vol. 2, 20, 25, cat. no. 24. Greenwich Conn.: New York Graphic Society, Ltd., 1972.

Constable, W. G. *Canaletto: Giovanni Antonio Canal, 1697-1768*, vol. 2 340, cat. no. 307 (1), as Bellotto. 2nd ed., rev. by J. G. Links. Oxford: Clarendon Press, 1989.

de Grazia, Diane, and Eric Garberson, eds. *The Collection of the National Gallery of Art, Systematic Catalogue: Italian Paintings of the Seventeenth and Eighteenth Centuries*, 11-12, fig. 2. Washington, D.C.: National Gallery of Art, 1996.

Bowron, Edgar Peters, ed. *Bernardo Bellotto and the Capitals of Europe*, 60-62 (with earlier references). New Haven and London: Yale University Press, 2001.

CAT. 33

Canaletto (Giovanni Antonio Canal) (Italian, 1697–1768)

View of the Molo, Venice, ca. 1725

Oil on canvas, 26½ x 32¾ in. (67.31 x 83.19 cm)

Columbia Museum of Art, Columbia, SC, Gift of the Samuel H. Kress Foundation, 1954.44

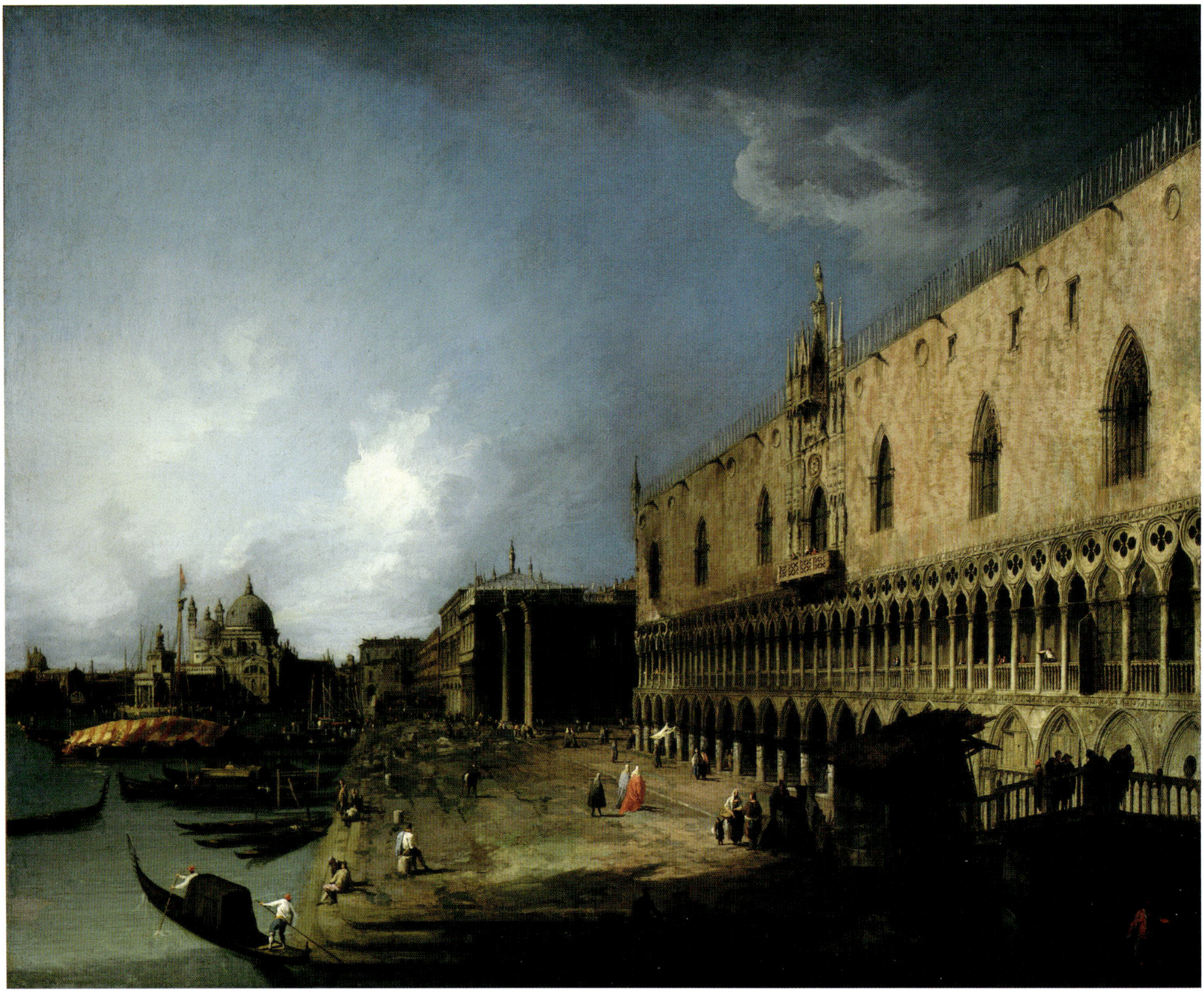

Similar in viewpoint to the two Carlevarijs paintings, *The Molo, Venice, Looking West* (cat. 40) and *The Molo, Looking West* (cat. 41), in this exhibition, this is one of Canaletto's earliest known works, dating to ca. 1725, when he would have been highly influenced by the elder and much more experienced than Carlevarijs. Here, Canaletto paints as if the viewer is further back—on the Ponte della Paglia, the bridge that spans the small canal between the Doge's Palace and the prisons—and looking down towards the Molo, columns of the Piazzetta, and entrance to the Grand Canal and church of Santa Maria della Salute. This view is much less broad than those of Carlevarijs, although Canaletto does include the church of the Redentore on the Giudecca, and the high vantage point gives a greater sense of depth to the foreground. He has also included a wealth of small details: the whitewashed lower columns of the arches of the Doge's palace, its boarded-up eastern arches, a knife grinder's stall near the bridge, and a small niche containing the tabernacle of the gondoliers' guild,[1] as well as the gondola pushing off from the curve in the steps and that which moves off to the left.

Andria Derstine

Notes

1 Noted by Katharine Baetjer in "Canaletto Paints the Molo from the Ponte della Paglia," in *Studying and Conserving Paintings, Occasional Papers on the Samuel H. Kress Collection* (London: Archetype Publications, 2006: 203).

Provenance

Sir Francis Ewan, London, 1931; probably the painting consigned by a gentleman (Ewan?) to Gurr, Johns for sale at Christie's, London, June 12, 1931; (Contini-Bonacossi); Samuel H. Kress Collection; Columbia Museum of Art.

Exhibitions

National Gallery of Art, Extended Loan, 1941–52.

Pittsfield, Mass., Berkshire Museum, *Canaletto and Bellotto*, Aug. 1960, cat. no. 14.

Allentown Art Museum, *The Circle of Canaletto*, Feb.–Mar. 1971, cat. no. 8.

Bibliography

Book of Illustrations, 77, cat. no. 234. Washington, D.C.: National Gallery of Art, 1941.

Preliminary Catalogue of Paintings and Sculpture, 31–2, cat. no. 234. Washington, D.C.: National Gallery of Art, 1941.

Suida, William E. *Art of the Italian Renaissance from the Samuel H. Kress Collection*, 58–59, cat. no. 25. Columbia: Columbia Museum of Art, 1954.

Constable, W. G. *Canaletto: Giovanni Antonio Canal, 1697–1768*, vol. 2, 218, cat. no. 86a. Oxford: Clarendon Press, 1962.

Contini-Bonacossi, Antonio. *Art of the Italian Renaissance from the Samuel H. Kress Collection*, 100–2, cat. no. 35. Columbia: Columbia Museum of Art, 1962.

The Circle of Canaletto, cat. no. 8. Allentown: Allentown Art Museum, 1971.

Shapley, Fern Rusk. *Paintings from the Samuel H. Kress Collection, Vol. 3: Italian Schools, XVI–XVIII Century*, 163–4, cat. no. K252, fig. 315. London: Phaidon Press, 1973.

Constable, W. G. and Links, J. G. *Canaletto*, 227, cat. no. 86a. Oxford: Clarendon Press, 1976.

Constable and Links, *Canaletto*, cat. no. 86a. Oxford: Claredon Press, 1989.

Effman, Elise, "View of the Molo: A Canaletto Attribution Reinstated," in *Studying and Conserving Paintings, Occasional Papers on the Samuel H. Kress Collection*, 189–95. London: Archetype Publications Ltd., 2006.

Baetjer, Katharine, "Canaletto Paints the Molo from the Ponte della Paglia," in *Studying and Conserving Paintings, Occasional Papers on the Samuel H. Kress Collection*, 197–205. London: Archetype Publications Ltd., 2006.

CAT. 34

Canaletto (Giovanni Antonio Canal) (Italian, 1697-1768)

The Grand Canal near the Rialto Bridge, Venice, ca. 1730

Oil on canvas, 19½ x 28¾ in. (49.7 x 70 cm)
The Museum of Fine Arts, Houston. The Robert Lee Blaffer Memorial Collection, gift of Sarah Campbell Blaffer, 55.103

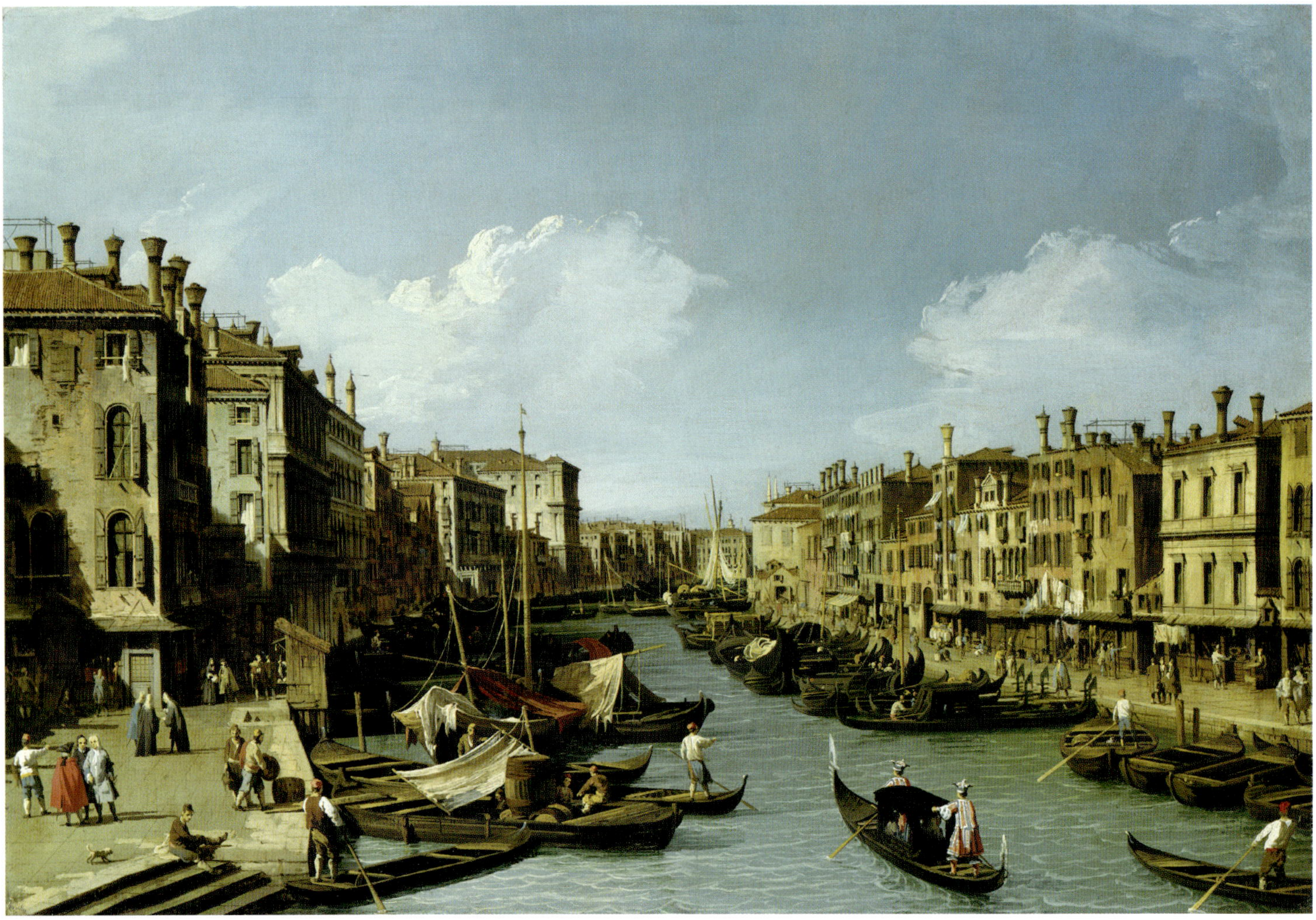

This view of the Grand Canal, looking southwest from close to the Rialto bridge, is one of a pair of exquisite paintings (the other being Houston's *The Entrance to the Grand Canal*) which are of singular importance in Canaletto's oeuvre: they are the only identifiable paintings for which it is known that Joseph Smith (ca. 1674–1770) acted as Canaletto's agent, a role this merchant and patron acted many times over, but for otherwise undetermined works. W. G. Constable noted that a receipt of August 22, 1730, shows that it was likely Hugh Howard, father of the man who would be the first Earl of Wicklow, who paid a "Mr. Smith Mercht" the equivalent of £18 7s. 11d. for "two pictures of Canaletti from Venice." Such a precise dating, and knowledge of their acquisition circumstances, is extremely valuable, given the general lack of precise dates for many of Canaletto's works.

The view shows the Riva del Ferro at the left, with the Palazzo Dolfin-Manin (now the Banca d'Italia), Palazzo Bembo, and the large Palazzo Grimani (now the Court of Appeals). In the distance, at the turning of the Grand Canal, is Ca' Foscari. The right quay—the Fondamenta del Vin—is bustling with shop stalls, and tickets for the lottery, as popular a game in eighteenth-century Italy as today, were sold from the small wooden hut visible on the quay at left. A young man sits on the steps that lead to the water on that quay, looking out towards the viewer, and a series of reds leads one's eye across the canvas from left to right: from the man with the brilliant cape speaking to gentlemen who also gaze towards us, to the large sail at center left from under which smoke rises—perhaps from a fire created to dry it—and continuing to the two gondoliers in colorful red, white, and blue costumes who ply the water in the foreground. They take their passengers, and one's eye, deeper into the scene, where the bustle of the city's waterways, full of commercial and passenger craft, is made manifest by the blockage ahead of them, where many gondolas jockey for position. Canaletto's careful use of impasto, in the clouds, the sails, and the gondoliers' costumes, and the painting's absolutely clear light—brighter and sunnier than its pendant, in which darker clouds stripe the sky and build up to the right—is ample evidence for Alessandro Marchesini's (1664–1738) comment that in Canaletto's works "one sees the sun shining."

Andria Derstine

Provenance

Probably Hugh Howard, Shelton Abbey, County Wicklow, Ireland (1730), thence by descent with the Earls of Wicklow until 1955; (Edward Speelman, London); (Knoedler & Co., N.Y.); Mrs. Robert Lee Blaffer; The Museum of Fine Arts, Houston.

Exhibitions

London, The British Institution, *Pictures by Italian, Spanish, Flemish, Dutch, French and English Masters,* 1853, cat. no. 71.

The Art Gallery of Toronto, The National Gallery of Canada, Ottawa, and The Museum of Fine Arts, Montréal, *Canaletto*, 1964–65, p. 49, cat. no. 12.

The Baltimore Museum of Art, *From El Greco to Pollock*, 1968.

Dallas, Southern Methodist University, *Canaletto Exhibition*, 1979.

New York, The Metropolitan Museum of Art, *Canaletto,* 1989–90, pp. 150–53, cat. no. 36.

Ehime, Matsuyama, The Museum of Art, Chiba Prefectural Art Museum, Tsu, Mie Prefectural Art Museum, Fukuoka Art Museum, Japan, *Masterpieces of European Painting from the 15th to 20th Centuries from the Museum of Fine Arts, Houston and the Sarah Campbell Blaffer Foundation,* 1999.

Venice, Fondazione Giorgio Cini, *Canaletto Prima Maniera*, 2001.

Milwaukee Art Museum, *Venetian Paintings from the Sarah Campbell Blaffer Foundation*, 2001.

Sarasota, Ringling Museum of Art, *Canaletto Paired: 18th-century Venetian View Painting,* 2007.

Bibliography

Connoisseur (June 1956): 291.

Constable, W. G., rev. by J. G. Links, *Canaletto: Giovanni Antonio Canal, 1697–1768*, 292, cat. no. 220. Oxford: Clarendon Press, 1976.

Links, J. G. *Canaletto and His Patrons*, 34, fig. 34. New York: New York University Press, 1977.

Potterton, Homan. *Pageant and Panorama: The Elegant World of Canaletto*. Oxford: Clarendon Press, 1978.

Agee, William C., and J. P. Marandel. *The Museum of Fine Arts, Houston: A Guide to the Collection*, 67–8, cat. no. 120. Houston: The Museum of Fine Arts, 1981.

Links, J. G. *Canaletto,* 66–7, cat. no. 60. Ithaca: Cornell University Press, 1982.

Constable and Links, *Canaletto* (1989 ed.), vol. 1, pl. 46, vol. 2, 292–3, cat. no. 220.

Marzio, Peter. *A Permanent Legacy: 150 Works from the Collection of the Museum of Fine Arts, Houston,* 150–1. New York: Hudson Hills Press in association with the Museum of Fine Arts, Houston, 1989.

Smithsonian (Nov. 1989): 80–1.

Links, J. G. *Canaletto,* 79, cat. no. 64, 252 (rev. version of 1982). London: Phaidon, 1994.

Masterpieces of European Painting from the 15th to 20th Centuries from the Museum of Fine Arts, Houston and the Sarah Campbell Blaffer Foundation, 130–1, ill. 131, cat. 40. Published by the Ehime, Chiba, Mie, and Fukuoka museums and the Yomiuri Shimbun, the Japan Association of Art Museums, 1999.

Bowron, Edgar Peters, and Mary G. Morton, *Masterworks of European Painting in the Museum of Fine Arts, Houston,* 98–9, illus. 100–1. Princeton, N.J.: Princeton Univ. Press, 2000.

Hubbard, Guy, "Clip and Save Art Notes," *Arts and Activities* (Oct. 2005): 30–1.

Lo Bianco, Anna in *Canaletto: Venezia e i Suoi Splendori,* ed. Giuseppe Pavanello and Alberto Craievich, 267. Venice: Marsilio, 2008.

CAT. 35

CANALETTO (GIOVANNI ANTONIO CANAL) (Italian, 1697–1768)

Venice: Santa Maria della Salute, ca. 1740

Oil on canvas, 18¾ x 31¼ in. (47.6 x 79.4 cm)
Lent by The Metropolitan Museum of Art,
Purchase, George T. Delacorte Jr. Gift, 1959 (59.38)

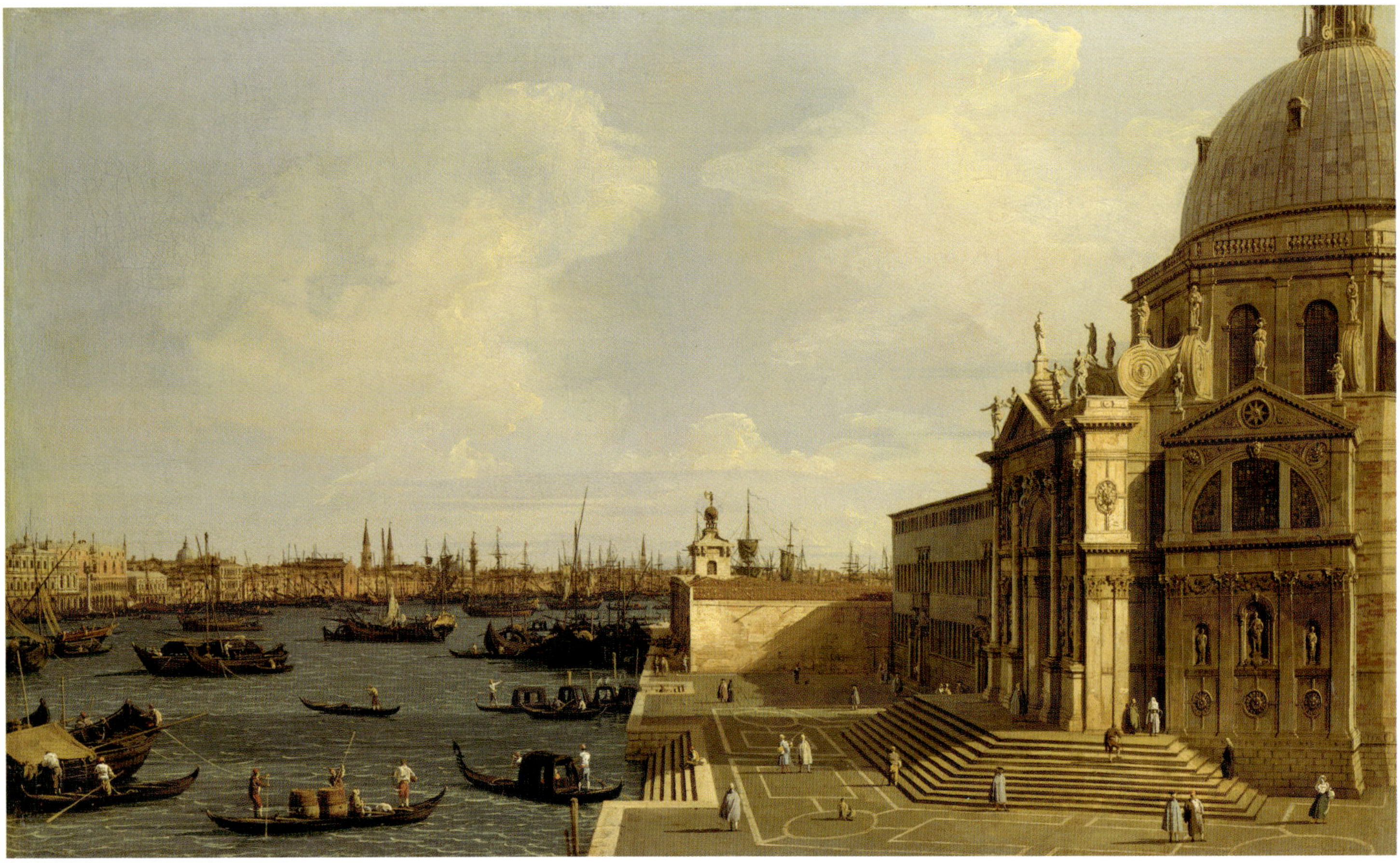

This crisp, clear painting depicts Santa Maria della Salute, the most prominent church on the Grand Canal. The masses of boats and masts meld with the distant church spires, giving a palpable sense of the city's activity on the left side of the canvas, where the Ducal Palace and one of the two columns of the Piazzetta are just visible beyond the Mint and Library. In contrast, the right side of the painting is more sedate, showing in the middle-distance the small tower of the Dogana with its statue of *Fortune* by Bernardo Falcone, and in the foreground the expanse of pavement surrounding the church. There, the pace is pedestrian, children play, a man indicates something on the façade of the church to his companion, and other figures enter. The painting is related to a larger (50 x 80 in.) view in the Royal Collection, which is dated 1744. Even the light and shading on the massive church façade seem tranquil and precise, with the dome's massive shadow extending into the placid water lapping against the steps.

Andria Derstine

Provenance

(Caspari Galleries, Munich); (Colnaghi's, London); (Leggat Brothers, London); Whitelaw Reid, Purchase, N.Y. (sale, American Art Association/Anderson Galleries, N.Y., May 14-18, 1935, cat. no. 1157); (Julius Weitzner, New York); Minneapolis Institute of Arts; (Julius Weitzner); (Rosenberg & Stiebel, N.Y.); Metropolitan Museum of Art.

Exhibitions:

San Francisco, California Palace of the Legion of Honor, *Exhibition of Italian Baroque Painting, 17th and 18th Centuries,* May-June 1941, cat. no. 9.

Metropolitan Museum of Art, *Venetian Paintings in the Metropolitan Museum,* 1974.

Athens, National Gallery Alexandros Soutzos Museum, *From El Greco to Cézanne: Masterpieces of European Painting from the National Gallery of Art, Washington and the Metropolitan Museum of Art, New York,* Dec. 1992-Apr. 1993, cat. no. 32.

Bibliography

"Fine Paintings, Ceramics, in Reid Sale to be held by American Anderson Galleries," *Art News* (May 4, 1935): 16-17.

"Furniture and Art of Whitelaw Reid Realize $290,322," *Art News* (May 25, 1935): 14.

"Canaletto's Venice," *Bulletin of the Minneapolis Institute of Arts* 27 (Nov. 5, 1938): 147-9.

San Francisco, California Palace of the Legion of Honor, "Exhibition of Italian Baroque Painting, 17th and 18th Centuries," May-June 1941, pp. 12 and 60, cat. no. 9.

Constable, W. G. *Canaletto: Giovanni Antonio Canal: 1697-1768,* vol. 2, 257, cat. no. 175. Oxford: Clarendon Press, 1962.

Fredericksen, Burton B., and Federico Zeri. *Census of Pre-Nineteenth-Century Italian Paintings in North American Public Collections,* 42, 493, 609. Cambridge, Mass.: Harvard University Press, 1972.

Zeri, Federico, with Elizabeth E. Gardner. *Italian Paintings: A Catalogue of the Collection of The Metropolitan Museum of Art, Venetian School,* 14 and pl. 13. New York: The Metropolitan Museum of Art, 1973.

Constable, W. G. *Canaletto,* vol. 2, 271, cat. no. 175. 2nd ed. Oxford: Clarendon Press, 1976.

Constable and Links, *Canaletto,* vol. 2, 271 (1989 ed.).

Levey, M. *The Later Italian Paintings in the Collection of Her Majesty the Queen,* 27-8, 42-3. 2nd ed. Cambridge: Cambridge University Press, 1991.

Hall, Nicholas, ed. *Colnaghi in America: A Survey to Commemorate the 1st decade of Colnaghi New York,* 131. New York: Colnaghi, 1992.

Krohn, Deborah, et al., *From El Greco to Cézanne: Masterpieces of European Painting from the National Gallery of Art, Washington and the Metropolitan Museum of Art, New York,* 308, cat. no. 32. Athens: National Gallery Alexandros Soutzos Museum, 1992.

CAT. 36

Canaletto (Giovanni Antonio Canal) (Italian, 1697–1768)

The Piazzetta: Looking South, ca. 1740–46

Oil on canvas, 19¾ x 32⅜ in. (50.16 x 82.23 cm)

Allentown Art Museum, Samuel H. Kress Collection, 1961 (1961.44)

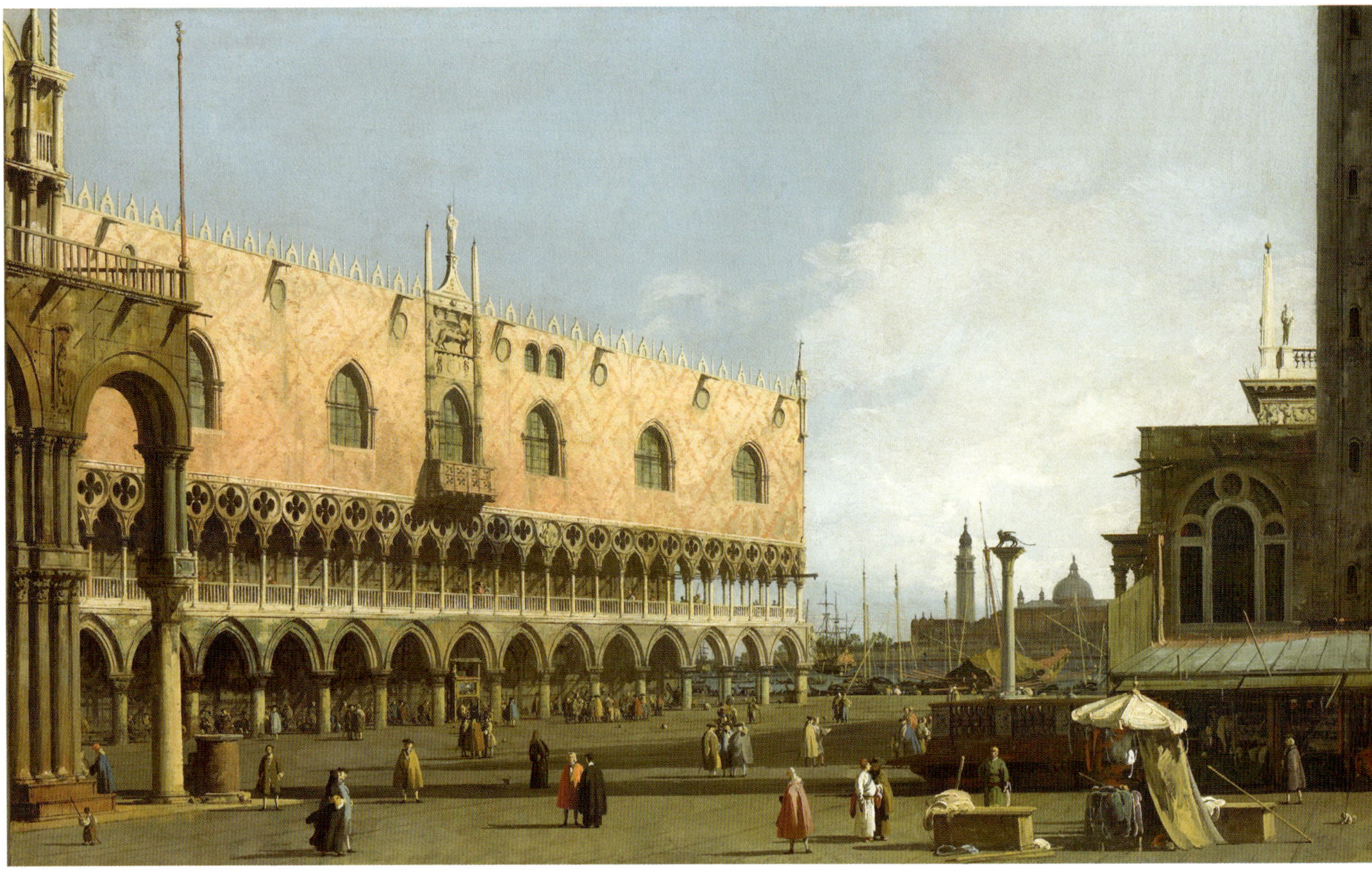

This view of part of the Piazzetta and part of the Piazza San Marco, in the warm sunlight and with the long shadows of late afternoon, is a stunningly clear vision that includes parts of the west porch of the Basilica di San Marco, the Doge's Palace, and the Campanile, as well as a view over the *bacino* to San Giorgio Maggiore. A cloth merchant has set up his wares under the umbrella at right, with canvas draped to the right to block the sun, beyond which we can catch a glimpse into the stalls abutting the base of the Campanile. The pavement is alive with figures, and there is an empty puppet theatre set up under the arcade below the warmly lit pink façade of the Doge's Palace. A tall-masted ship appears in the bacino just beyond the corner of the Palace and another large boat, "*la fusta,*" belonging to the Doge, is docked on the Molo behind the column of St. Mark, with its reddish oars to each side. An especially lovely touch is the contrast between the brilliant sun on the corner of Sansovino's Library and the deeply shadowed Campanile beyond which it is just visible.

Andria Derstine

PROVENANCE

[J. C.?] Robinson collection, London; Adalbert Baron von Lanna, sold in Munich in 1929; (Contini Bonacossi, Florence); Samuel H. Kress; Allentown Art Museum.

EXHIBITIONS

Washington, D.C., National Gallery of Art, *Paintings and Sculpture from the Kress Collection,* 1951, cat. no. 71.

Utica, N.Y., Munson-Williams-Proctor Institute Museum of Art and Rochester, N.Y., Rochester Memorial Art Gallery, *Masters of Landscape: East and West,* 1963.

Allentown Art Museum, *The Circle of Canaletto,* 1971.

Reading (Penn.) Public Museum and Art Gallery, 1975.

Allentown Art Museum, *Art and Math,* 1979.

BIBLIOGRAPHY

Suida, William E. *Paintings and Sculpture from the Kress Collection,* cat. no. 71. Washington, D.C.: National Gallery of Art, 1951.

Moschini, Vittorio. *Canaletto,* figs. 108-9. Milan: A. Martello, 1954.

Hirsch, Richard, and Fern Rusk Shapley. *The Samuel H. Kress Memorial Collection,* 74-5. Allentown: Allentown Art Museum, 1960.

Constable, W. G. *Canaletto: Giovanni Antonio Canal, 1697-1768,* vol. 1, pl. 22, vol. 2, cat. no. 61. Oxford: Clarendon Press, 1962.

Puppi, Lionello, and Giuseppe Berto. *L'opera completa di Canaletto,* cat. no. 181. Milan: Rizzoli, 1968.

Puppi, Lionello. *The Complete Paintings of Canaletto,* cat. no. 181. London: Weidenfeld & Nicolson, 1970.

Virch, Claus. *The Circle of Canaletto.* Allentown, Allentown Art Museum, 1971.

Shapley, Fern Rusk. *Paintings from the Samuel H. Kress Collection: Italian Schools XVI-XVIII Century,* 164, fig. 317. London: Phaidon Press, 1973.

Constable, W. G., and J. G. Links. *Canaletto,* vol. 2, 214, cat. no. 61. 2nd ed. Oxford: Clarendon Press, 1976.

Corboz, André. *Canaletto: Una Venezia Immaginaria,* vol. 1, 23, fig. i, vol. 2, cat. no. P299. Milan: Alfieri Electa, 1985.

Constable, W. G., and J. G. Links. *Canaletto,* cat. no. 61. 3rd ed., rev. Oxford: Clarendon Press, 1989.

Links, J. G. *A Supplement to W. G. Constable's Canaletto,* 9, cat. no. 61. London: Pallas Athene Arts, 1998.

CAT. 37 and 38

Canaletto
(Giovanni Antonio Canal)
(Italian, 1697–1768)
Capriccio: Farmhouse on the Venetian Mainland, ca. 1755–65
Oil on panel, 5¾ x 7½ in. (14.61 x 19.05 cm)
The James Philip Gray Collection, Michele and Donald D'Amour Museum of Fine Arts, Springfield, Massachusetts
Photography by David Stansbury

Canaletto
(Giovanni Antonio Canal)
(Italian, 1697–1768)
Capriccio: Villa and Ruins by a River, ca. 1755–65
Oil on panel, 5¾ x 7½ in. (14.61 x 19.05 cm)
The James Philip Gray Collection, Michele and Donald D'Amour Museum of Fine Arts, Springfield, Massachusetts
Photography by David Stansbury

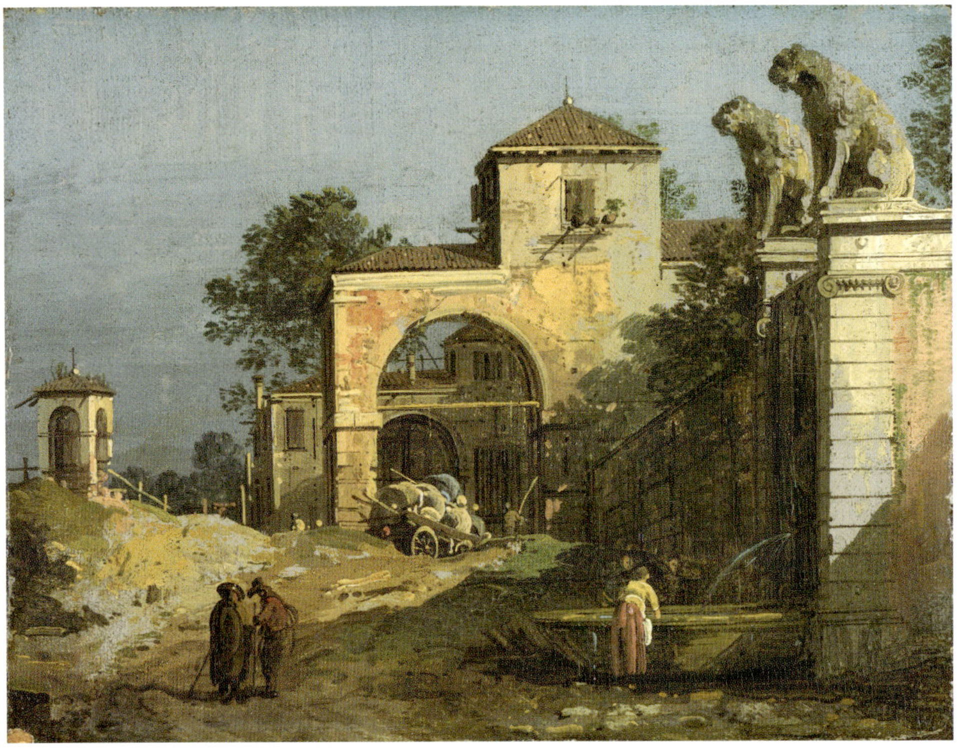

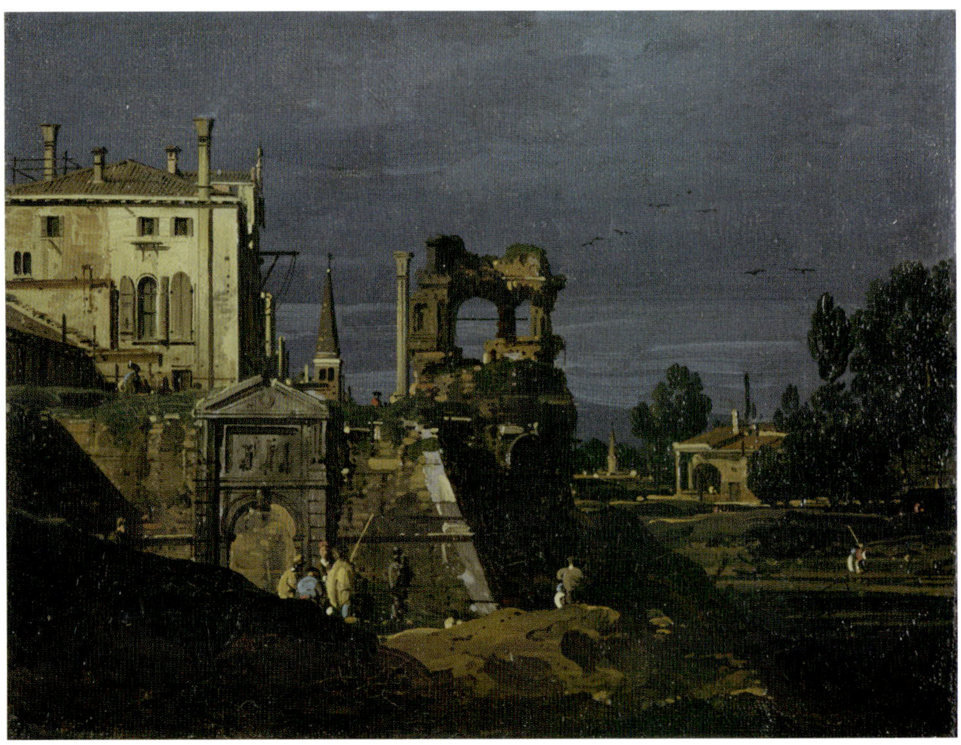

In one of these charming, very small *vedute ideate*, or fantasy views (cat. 37), a wagon overloaded with cargo prepares to enter the courtyard of a rustic estate through a very large stone archway, while on the right, massive statues of seated lions perch atop a fountain as a woman joins others to fetch water. On the left is a small building that may be a gatekeeper's stand or a place for a religious image, such as are often found along country roads. The bright sunlight in the middle distance draws one in—just as it does the two travelers in the shady foreground who may be making their way towards the estate.

In the other painting (cat. 38), a massive wall pierced by a portico encloses a villa, church, and other buildings. On the right, across a river, are a rustic house and trees before a distant church and hills; dark birds fly above. This painting in particular has echoes of Canaletto's trip to Rome in 1719-20, not only through the massive architecture of the wall and its arched gateway—which recalls those that encircle Rome—but also through the ruins on the hill, as well as the small hillock indicated at the lower left in the foreground and the suggestion of hills beyond. Such topography is very unlike the flat plains of the lower Veneto, although the distant hills may be intended to represent the foothills of the Dolomites, which are not far to the north of Venice.

Andria Derstine

PROVENANCE

Count Tyskiewitz?; (F. Kleinberger?); Jules Porgès, Paris; (Arnold Seligmann, Rey & Company, N.Y.); Springfield Museum of Fine Arts.

EXHIBITIONS

Yale University Gallery of Fine Arts, *Exhibition of 18th Century Italian and English Painting*, Feb.-Mar. 1940, cat. nos. 8-9.

Smith College Museum of Art, *Exhibition of Italian Baroque Painting, 17th and 18th Centuries*, Feb. 1947, cat. nos. 35-6.

The Detroit Institute of Arts, Indianapolis, John Herron Art Museum, *Venice 1700-1800, An Exhibition of Venice and the Eighteenth Century*, Sept. 1952-Jan. 1953, cat. nos. 13-14.

Boston, Museum of Fine Arts, *Scenic Painters and Draughtsmen of the 18th Century*, Jan.-Mar. 1958.

Pittsfield, Mass., The Berkshire Museum, *Canaletto and Bellotto*, Aug. 1960, cat. nos. 2-3.

The Art Gallery of Toronto, The National Gallery of Canada, Ottawa, and The Museum of Fine Arts, Montréal, *Canaletto*, Oct. 1964-Feb. 1965, pp. 16, 92-93, cat. nos. 73-74.

Allentown Art Museum, *The Circle of Canaletto*, Feb.-Mar. 1971, cat. nos. 3-4.

BIBLIOGRAPHY

Yale University, *Exhibition of 18th c. Italian and English Painting*, Feb.-Mar. 1940, cat. nos. 8-9.

Smith College Museum of Art, *Exhibition of Italian Baroque Painting, 17th and 18th Centuries*, 1947, cat. nos. 35-36.

Smith College Museum of Art *Bulletin* (June 1947): 60.

The Detroit Institute of Arts, Indianapolis, John Herron Art Museum, *Venice 1700-1800: An Exhibition of Venice and the Eighteenth Century*, 21-22, cat. nos. 13-14. Detroit: Detroit Institute of Arts, 1952.

Morassi, Antonio, "Una Mostra del Settecento Veneziano a Detroit," *Arte Veneta* (1953): 58.

Henry, Stuart C. *Canaletto and Bellotto*, cat. nos. 2-3. Pittsfield, Mass.: The Berkshire Museum, 1960.

Constable, W. G. *Canaletto*, 16, 92-3, cat. nos. 73-74. Toronto, Ottawa, Montréal: Art Gallery of Toronto, 1964-65.

Virch, Claus. *The Circle of Canaletto*, cat. nos. 3-4. Allentown: Allentown Art Museum, 1971.

Constable, W. G. *Canaletto: Giovanni Antonio Canal, 1697-1768*, vol. 2, 468-9, cat. nos. 513-4. Oxford: Clarendon Press, 1976, and 1989 edition.

CAT. 39 and 40

LUCA CARLEVARIJS (Italian, 1663-1730)
The Molo, Venice, from the Bacino di San Marco, ca. 1709
Oil on canvas, 19⅞ x 47⅛ in. (50.5 x 119.7 cm)
Lent by The Metropolitan Museum of Art,
Robert Lehman Collection, 1975 (1975.1.87)
Image copyright The Metropolitan Museum of Art/Art Resource, NY

LUCA CARLEVARIJS (Italian, 1663-1730)
The Molo, Venice, Looking West, ca. 1709
Oil on canvas, 19⅞ x 47⅛ in. (50.5 x 119.7 cm)
Lent by The Metropolitan Museum of Art,
Robert Lehman Collection, 1975 (1975.1.90)
Image copyright The Metropolitan Museum of Art/Art Resource, NY

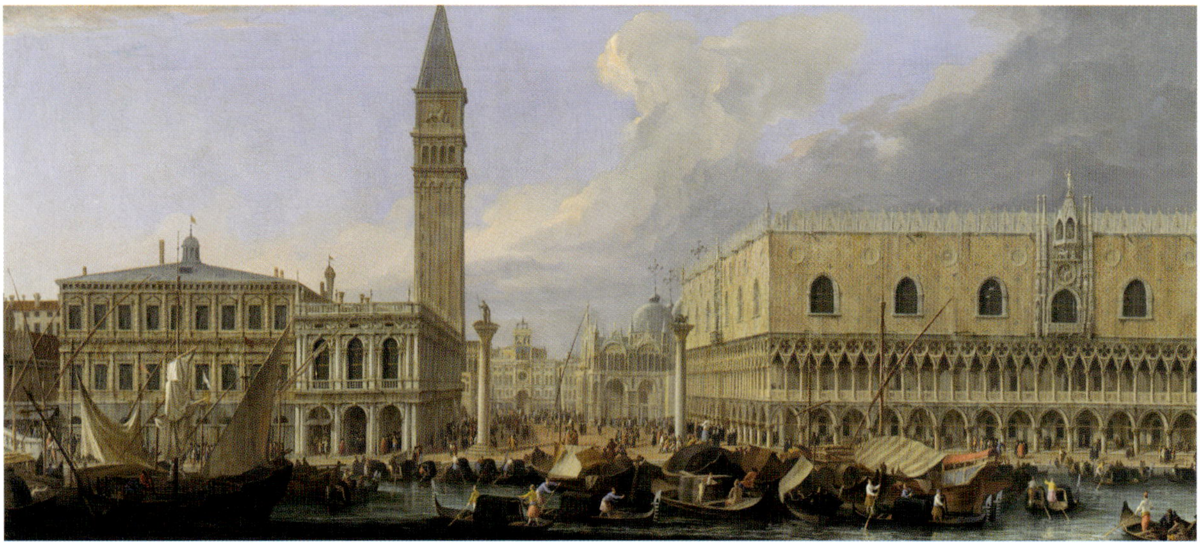

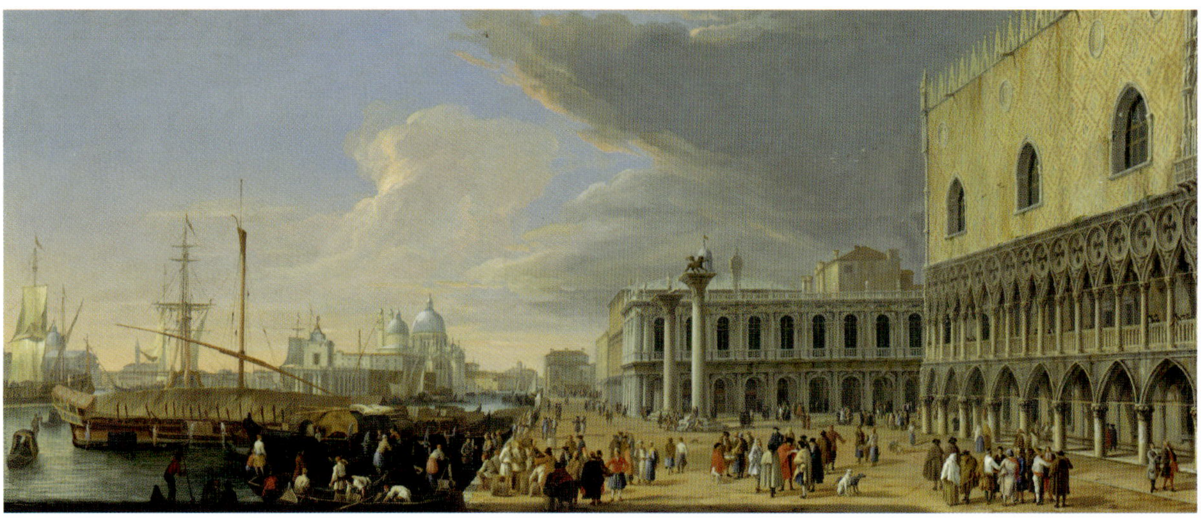

These two views, with two others depicting the *Bacino di San Marco with the Punta della Dogana* (monogrammed with "L. C.") and *Piazza San Marco*, form the only complete set of Carlevarijs's paintings to survive intact and are the only set signed and dated by him.[1] They are also among the earliest pure view paintings—that is to say, works not depicting an ambassadorial entry or other specific event—by an Italian view painter. All four formerly hung at Stoneleigh Abbey, and were presumably purchased by Edward Leigh, 1st Baron Leigh of Stoneleigh, on a Grand Tour to Italy. After leaving the Leigh family, they hung together in Robert Lehman's library in New York, before passing to the Metropolitan Museum of Art.

The Molo, Venice, from the Bacino di San Marco, painted as if from a boat, is centered between the two columns of the Piazzetta; between these, in the distance, are the Torre dell'Orologio and the Basilica di San Marco. To the left is the Mint and Sansovino's Library, and to the right, under a darkening sky, is the Doge's Palace, before which seagulls fly, while a multitude of small and large boats plies the water of the *bacino* in the foreground. At lower left, a man motions to two others in an attempt to avoid a collision.

The Molo, Venice, Looking West shows an obliquely angled view, as if the viewer is standing on the Riva degli Schiavoni near the large Doge's Palace and approaching one of the busiest spots in the city. The Library, Piazzetta, and Molo and its columns are before us, and in the center is the entrance to the Grand Canal, bordered by Santa Maria della Salute and the Dogana, in front of which is an immense ship. A mass of other ships somewhat blocks the view towards the island of the Giudecca and its church of the Redentore, covered in a golden glow, emphasizing not only Venice's commercial and cosmopolitan importance but also the close connection of its seat of government with the sea. In the foreground, the viewer is made part of the throng; men of all classes and costumes transact the day's business, while two dogs become amorous and another large white one looks out with interest at the viewer. This spot, one of the city's most picturesque, was depicted numerous times by the artist.

Andria Derstine

Note

1 Signed and dated "L / DCC / IX" on a cartouche on the right-most pier of the Doge's Palace; for the significance of this, see p. 106 of Derstine's essay in this catalogue.

Provenance

Possibly Edward Leigh, 3rd Baron Leigh, Stoneleigh Abbey, Kenilworth, Warwickshire; Rupert William Dudley Leigh, 4th Baron Leigh, surely by 1771; by descent in the family; (Carlo Bruscoli & Figlio, Florence); Robert Lehman, N.Y.; Metropolitan Museum of Art.

Exhibitions

Cincinnati Art Museum, "The Lehman Collection," 1959, cat. nos. 101, 104.

Special temporary exhibition, Metropolitan Museum of Art, Oct. 1-Dec. 1, 1986 (both); Special temporary exhibition, Metropolitan Museum of Art, July 31-Oct. 1, 1987 (both).

"Study paintings of the Robert Lehman collection," Metropolitan Museum of Art, summer 1987-winter 1988 (both).

San Diego, Timken Museum of Art, "Luca Carlevarijs: Views of Venice," Apr.-Aug. 2001, cat. nos. 3, 6.

Rome, Chiostro del Bramante and Venice, Museo Correr, "Gaspare Vanvitelli e le origini del vedutismo," Oct. 2002-May 2003 (both).

Bibliography

Leigh, Agnes. *Stoneleigh Abbey Pictures,* 11. London: Hazell, Watson & Viney, 1919.

Kaines-Smith, S. C. *Stoneleigh Abbey: An Illustrated Survey,* pl. 18. n.p.: n.d.

Thorpe, W. A., "Stoneleigh Abbey and Its Furniture: I—Leigh of Stoneleigh and Smith of Warwick," *Connoisseur* 118 (Oct. 1946): 74.

Rizzi, Aldo. *Luca Carevarijs,* 55, 89, 92, figs. 86-89, Venice: Alfieri, 1967.

Hannegan, Barry. *Painting in Italy in the Eighteenth Century: Rococo to Romanticism,* 58. Chicago: Art Institute of Chicago, 1970.

Baetjer, Katharine. *European Paintings in the Metropolitan Museum of Art by Artists Born in or Before 1865: A Summary Catalogue,* vol. 1, 24, vol. 2, 128. New York: The Metropolitan Museum of Art, 1980.

Pignatti, Terisio. *Disegni Antichi del Museo Correr di Venezia,* vol. 1, 98, under cat. no. 76. Vicenza: Neri Pozza, 1980.

Magnifico, M. *Vedute Italiane del '700 in collezioni private italiane,* under cat. nos. 16-17. Milan: Electa, 1987.

Pope-Hennessy, J., with L. Kanter. *Robert Lehman Collection,* Vol. 1: *Italian Paintings,* 250-55. New York: The Metropolitan Museum of Art, 1987.

Succi, Dario. *Inverno '91,* 16, fig. 1, 22, fig. 1. Milan: Galleria Salamon, 1991.

Minty, Nancy, and Sandra Lawrence. *In the Name of Art, In the Name of Science: Considerations of Conservation,* 21 (*The Molo Looking West* only) Toronto: Art Gallery of Ontario, 1992.

Succi, Dario. *Marco Ricci e il paesaggio veneto del Settecento,* 30, fig. 5. Milan: Electa, 1993.

Succi, Dario. *Luca Carlevarijs e la veduta veneziana del Settecento,* 45, 20, under cat. no. 35. Milan: Electa, 1994.

Aikema, Bernard and Bram de Klerck, essay in Succi, *Luca Carlevarijs,* 148. Milan: Electa, 1994.

Baetjer, Katharine. *European Paintings in the Metropolitan Museum of Art by Artists born before 1865: A Summary Catalogue,* 85. New York: The Metropolitan Museum of Art, 1995.

Pallucchini, Rodolfo. *La pittura nel Veneto: Il Settecento,* ed. M. Lucco, et al., vol. 1, 187. Milan: Electa, 1995.

Pedrocco, F. *Splendori del Settecento Veneziano,* 259. Milan: Electa, 1995.

Beddington, Charles. *Luca Carlevarijs, Views of Venice,* 20-1, 23, 25, 48-9. San Diego: Timken Museum of Art, 2001.

Reale, Isabella, in *Gaspare Vanvitelli e le origini del vedutismo,* 328-30. Rome: Viviani Arte, 2002.

Sotheby's, *Old Master Paintings Evening Sale,* July 7, 2005, cited under lot 46.

Whistler, Catherine, "Vedutismo Veneziano e Mecenati Britannici nel '700," in *Canaletto: Venezia e i Suoi Splendori,*45-6, ed. Pavanello, Giuseppe, and Alberto Craievich. Venice: Marsilio Editore, 2008.

Baetjer, Katharine, in Pavanello and Craievich, *Canaletto: Venezia e i Suoi Splendori*, 249. Venice: Marsilio Editore, 2008.

CAT. 41

Luca Carlevarijs (Italian, 1663–1730)
The Molo Looking West, ca. 1725–27

Oil on canvas, 18¼ x 32⅝ in. (46.4 x 83 cm)
Collection, Art Gallery of Ontario, Toronto. Gift of the Ludwig Mond Estate, 1926

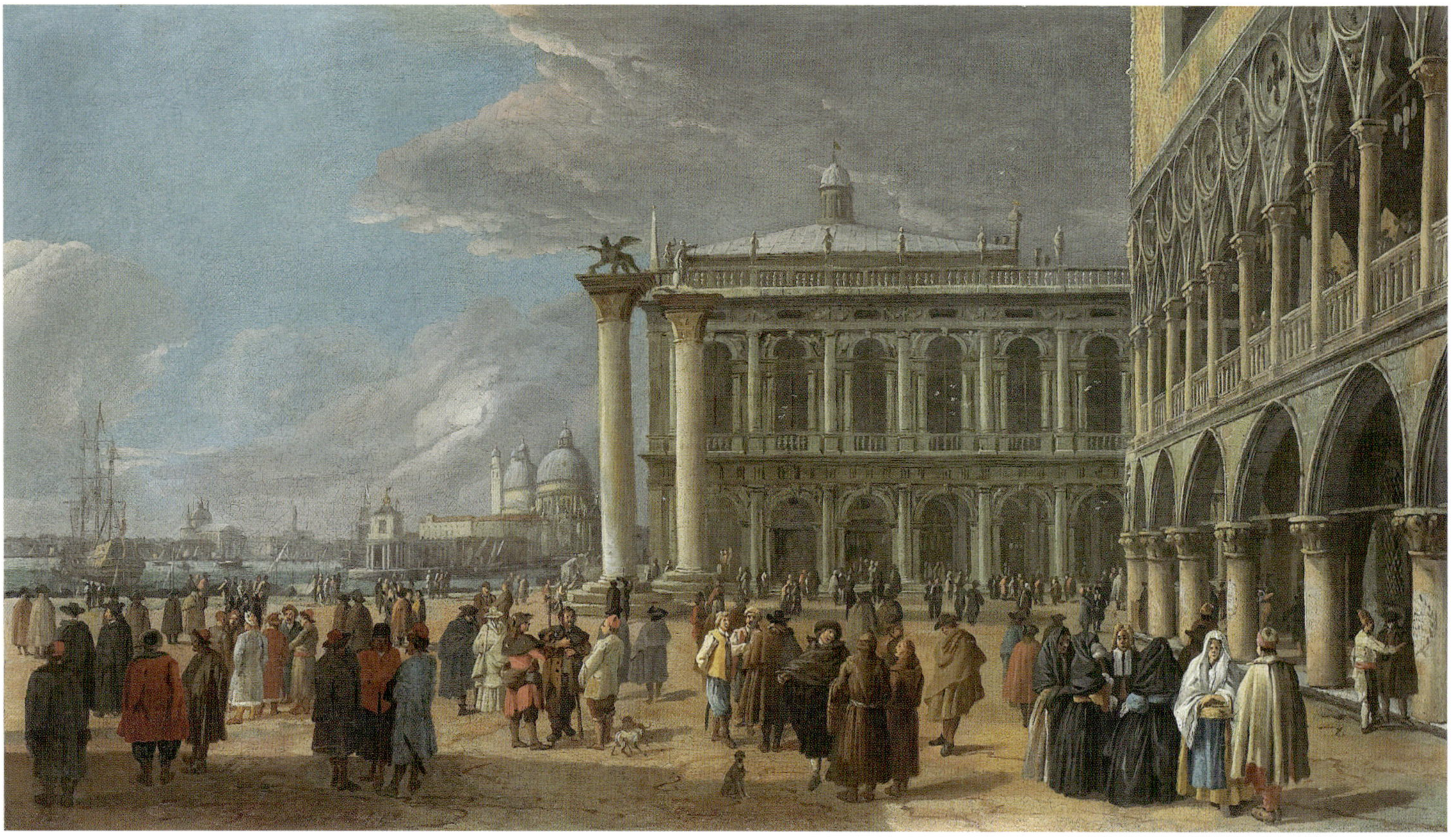

This painting is related to the view depicted in the dated 1709 painting of *The Molo, Venice, Looking West* (cat. 40) from the Lehman Collection at the Metropolitan Museum of Art, also in this exhibition. Additionally it has a viewpoint similar to Canaletto's *View of the Molo, Venice* (cat. 33) from the Columbia Museum of Art, one of Canaletto's early paintings, which dates to about 1725. It is instructive to be able to compare all three at once: in this painting, in comparison to the much broader 1709 Carlevarijs view, the viewer is positioned nearer to the Piazzetta and much closer to the Ducal Palace (note the reversal of order of the Piazzetta's two columns, because of this perspective, and the direct, not oblique, view of the Biblioteca Marciana). This painting is also rougher in its handling, leading Aldo Rizzi to characterize it as a late work, for its "liquid and fractured touch."[1] Nancy Minty and Sandra Lawrence, during their examination of the work, also wrote of the canvas's coarse texture, great deal of craquelure, and the numerous overpaintings to which the work had been subject.[2] It shows a site that Carlevarijs often depicted, as it was the location where ambassadors and important foreign visitors would dock and set foot for the first time in the city, and the artist was well-known for having painted multiple such "reception" scenes, including depictions of the 1703, 1706, and 1707 arrivals of French and British ambassadors.

Andria Derstine

Notes

1 Aldo Rizzi, *Luca Carlevarijs* (Venice: Alfieri, 1967: 95).
2 Nancy Minty and Sandra Lawrence, *In the Name of Art, In the Name of Science: Considerations of Conservation* (Toronto: Art Gallery of Ontario, 1992: 20-2).

Provenance

Possibly Favenza collection, Venice; Ludwig Mond, London; Art Gallery of Ontario.

Exhibitions

Toronto, Art Gallery, *Exhibition of Italian Old Masters and German Primitives*, Jan. 1931, cat. no. 36.
Toronto, Art Gallery, Ottawa, National Gallery of Canada, Montréal, Museum of Fine Arts, *Canaletto,* 1964-65, cat. no. 129.
Ottawa, National Gallery of Canada, *Views of Venice,* 1971-72.
Toronto, Art Gallery of Ontario, *The Arts of Italy in Toronto Collections,* 1981-82, cat. no. 115.
Vancouver Art Gallery, Québec City, Musée du Québec, Kingston, Agnes Etherington Art Center, *18th Century Venetian Art in Canadian Collections,* 1989-90, cat. no. 16. Sudbury, Laurentian University Museum and Art Centre, Owen Sound, Tom Thomson Memorial Art Gallery, Kitchener/Waterloo Art Gallery, Hamilton, McMaster University Art Gallery.
The Art Gallery of Peterborough, *In the Name of Art, In the Name of Science: Considerations of Conservation,* 1992-93, cat. no. 2.

Bibliography

Richter, J. P. *The Mond Collection: An Appreciation,* vol. 1, xi, 223, 227-9. London: John Murray, 1910.
Mauroner, Fabio. *Luca Carlevarijs,* 32. Venice: Zanetti, 1931.
Mauroner, Fabio. *Luca Carlevarijs,* 25, 52, 89, pl. 12. Padua: Le Tre Venezie, 1945.
Constable, W. G. *Canaletto: Giovanni Antonio Canal, 1697-1768,* 155, cat. no. 129. Oxford: Clarendon Press, 1962.
Rizzi, Aldo. *Luca Carlevarijs,* 95, cat. no. 130. Venice: Alfieri, 1967.
McTavish, David, et al., *The Arts of Italy in Toronto Collections, 1300-1800,* 94-5, cat. no. 115. Toronto: Art Gallery of Ontario, 1981.
Knox, George. *Eighteenth Century Venetian Art in Canadian Collections,* 32-3, cat. no. 16. Vancouver: Vancouver Art Gallery, 1989.
Constable, W. G. *Canaletto: Giovanni Antonio Canal, 1697-1768,* vol. 1, 70 n. 1. Oxford: Clarendon Press, 1989.
Minty, Nancy, and Sandra Lawrence. *In the Name of Art, In the Name of Science: Considerations of Conservation,* 18-23. Toronto: Art Gallery of Ontario, 1992.

CAT. 42

Francesco Guardi (Italian, 1712-1793)

View of the Dogana and Santa Maria della Salute, 1767-69

Oil on canvas, 19½ x 26⅛ in. (49.5 x 66.4 cm)
The Nelson-Atkins Museum of Art, Kansas City, Missouri. Purchase: William Rockhill Nelson Trust, 30-21
Photo courtesy Mel McLean

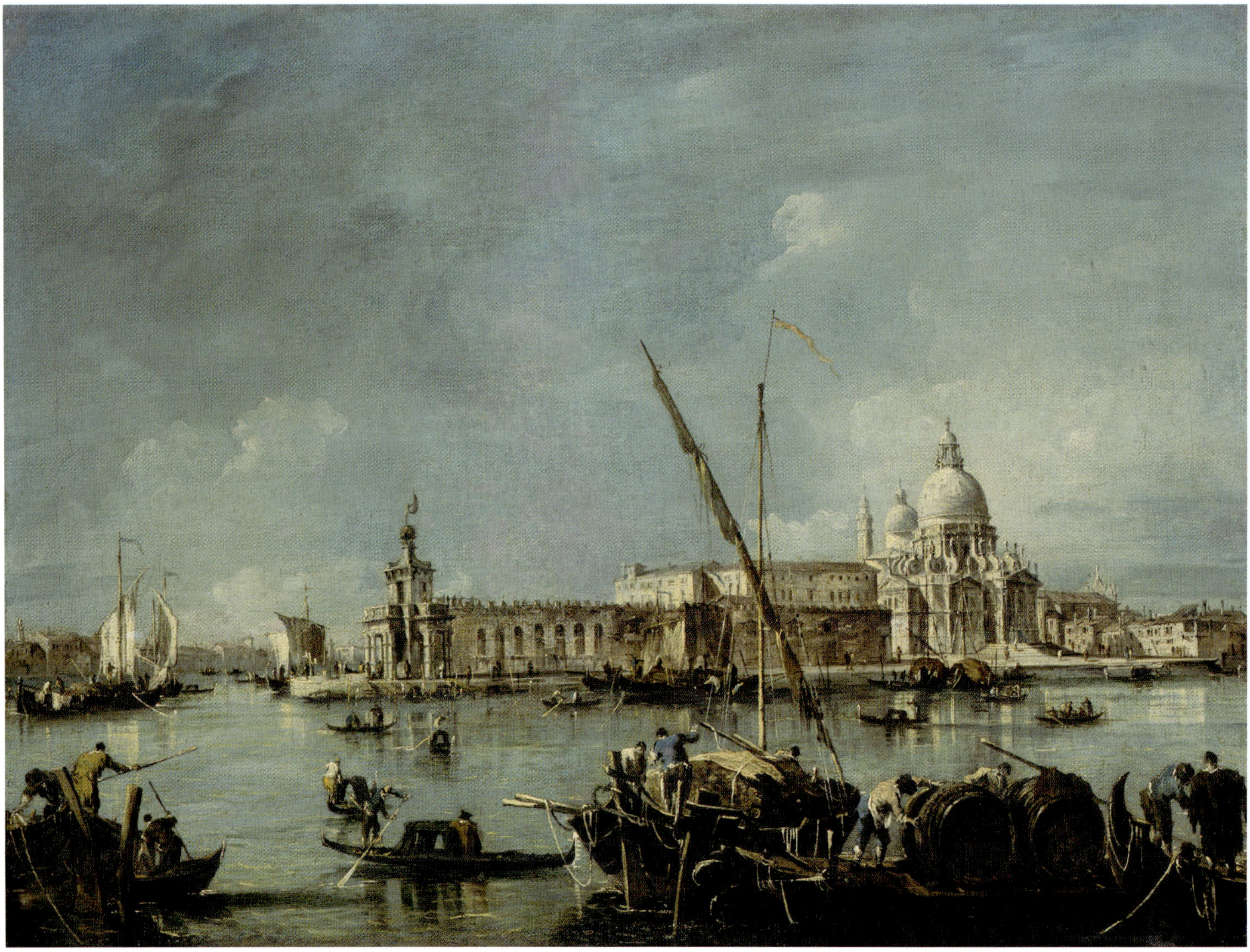

This view by Guardi—one of about twenty versions of the scene—shows the entrance to the Grand Canal on the right, faced by the large, domed and sunlit church of Santa Maria della Salute. To the right of that is the long nave and edge of the façade of the church of San Gregorio, while to the left is the patriarchal seminary and, further separated by the mast and rolled sail of the large foreground ship, the customshouse (Dogana). The customshouse is situated on a point that separates the Grand Canal and the Giudecca Canal, and to the far left, the small buildings visible behind the white-sailed ships are those on the Giudecca itself. In the foreground, two men secure large barrels (one of which is conspicuously signed "Guardi") on a flat barge while others behind them and in the lower-left corner attend to their cargo and ships. Several passenger boats and gondolas ply the waters as well. The white clouds, rippling waters, and bright reflections—especially in the water in front of the Salute—invite the eye beyond the heavily shaded foreground's men at work, towards a shimmering vision of several of the city's magnificent civic and religious structures.

Andria Derstine

Provenance

Captain Justinian H. Edwards-Heathcote, Betton Hall, Market Drayton, Shropshire, sold Christie's, London, 1928; (Frank Sabin, London, purchased at Christie's sale); (Durlacher Brothers, N.Y.); Nelson-Atkins Museum of Art, 1930.

Exhibitions

Hartford, Wadsworth Atheneum, *Exhibition of Italian Painting of the Sei- and Settecento,* 1930, cat. no. 15.

St. Louis, City Art Museum, *Special Loan Exhibition of Venetian Painting of the Eighteenth Century,* 1936, cat. no. 9.

Springfield, Mass., Museum of Fine Arts, *Francesco Guardi,* 1937, cat. no. 15.

New York, The Metropolitan Museum of Art, *Tiepolo and His Contemporaries,* 1938, cat. no. 28.

Cambridge, Mass., Fogg Art Museum, *Venice in the Eighteenth Century,* 1948, cat. no. 11.

Seattle Art Museum, *Renaissance and Baroque Art,* 1950, cat. no. 66.

Columbus Gallery of Fine Arts, Columbus, Ohio, *A Tour of Famous Cities,* 1952, cat. no. 17.

Kansas City, Mo., The Nelson Gallery and Atkins Museum, *The Century of Mozart,* 1956, cat. no. 48.

Kansas City, Mo., The Nelson-Atkins Museum of Art, *City Views,* 1983, cat. no. 20A.

Bibliography

Exhibition of Italian Painting of the Sei- and Settecento, 12, cat. no. 15. Hartford: Wadsworth Atheneum, 1930.

Art News 28 (May 31, 1930): 5.

Burrows, Carlyle, "Letter from New York," *Apollo* 11 (1930): 298–9.

"Nelson Museum Puts $500,000 More into Art," *Herald Tribune,* New York (May 20, 1930): 15.

Handbook of the William Rockhill Nelson Gallery of Art, 21. Kansas City, Mo.: The William Rockhill Nelson Gallery of Art, 1933.

McComb, A.K. *The Baroque Painters of Italy,* 124. Cambridge, Mass: Harvard University Press, 1934.

St. Louis, Mo., City Art Museum, "Special Loan Exhibition of Venetian Painting of the Eighteenth Century," *Bulletin of the City Art Museum of St. Louis* 21 (March 1936): 25, no. 9.

Francesco Guardi, cat. no. 15. Springfield, Mass.: Museum of Fine Arts, 1937.

Tiepolo and His Contemporaries, cat. no. 28. New York: The Metropolitan Museum of Art, 1938.

The William Rockhill Nelson Collection, 32. 2nd ed. Kansas City, Mo.: The William Rockhill Nelson Gallery of Art, 1941.

Venice in the Eighteenth Century, cat no. 11. Cambridge, Mass.: Fogg Art Museum, 1948.

The William Rockhill Nelson Collection, 48. 3rd ed. Kansas City, Mo.: The William Rockhill Nelson Gallery of Art, 1949.

Renaissance and Baroque Art, 11, cat. no. 66. Seattle, Wash.: Seattle Art Museum, 1950.

A Tour of Famous Cities, cat. no. 17. Columbus, Ohio: Columbus Gallery of Fine Arts, 1952.

Morse, J. D. *Old Masters in America,* 97. Chicago: Rand McNally, 1955.

"The Century of Mozart," *The Nelson Gallery and Atkins Museum Bulletin* 1 (Jan. 1956): 28, cat. no. 48.

Handbook of the Collections in the William Rockhill Nelson Gallery of Art and Mary Atkins Museum of Fine Arts, 74. 4th ed. Kansas City, Mo: The William Rockhill Nelson Gallery of Art, 1959.

Kultzen, R., "*Ein neuer Guardi für die Alte Pinakothek,*" *Pantheon* 4 (1967): 270, n. 8.

Venise au dix-huitième siècle, 83 under cat. no. 89. Paris: Musée de l'Orangerie, 1971.

Fredericksen, Burton B., and Federico Zeri. *Census of Pre-Nineteenth-Century Italian Paintings in North American Public Collections,* 96, 589. Cambridge: Harvard University Press, 1972.

Coe, R. T., "The Baroque and Rococo in France and Italy," *Apollo* 96 (1972): 540, fig. 18.

Morassi, Antonio. *Guardi: L'opera completa di Antonio e Francesco Guardi,* vol. 1, 399, cat. no. 473, 400 under cat. no. 479, vol. 2, fig. 477. Venice: Alfieri, 1973.

Taggart, R. E., and G. L. McKenna, eds. *Handbook of the Collections in the William Rockhill Nelson Gallery of Art and Mary Atkins Museum of Fine Arts,* Vol. I: *Art of the Occident,* 140–1. 5th ed. Kansas City, Mo: The William Nelson Rockhill Gallery of Art, 1973.

Bortolatto, Luigina Rossi. *L'opera completa di Francesco Guardi,* 107, cat. no. 292, 127 under cat. no. 628, fig. 292. Milan: Rizzoli, 1974.

Morse, John D. *Old Master Paintings in North America,* 160. New York: Abbeville Press, 1979.

Taggart, R. E., and R. Ward. *City Views,* 11, cat. no. 20A. Kansas City, Mo.: The Nelson-Atkins Museum of Art, 1983.

Horn, G. *Venedigs Ruhm im Norden,* 154 under cat. no. 33. Hannover: Forum des Landesmuseum Hannover, 1991.

Churchman, Michael, and Scott Erbes. *High Ideals and Aspirations: The Nelson-Atkins Museum of Art 1933–1993,* 25. Kansas City, Mo.: The Nelson-Atkins Museum of Art, 1993.

Wolferman, Kristie C. *The Nelson-Atkins Museum of Art: Culture Comes to Kansas City,* 92, 130. Columbia, Mo.: University of Missouri Press, 1993.

Rowlands, Eliot W. *The Collections of the Nelson-Atkins Museum of Art, Italian Paintings 1300–1800,* 459–62. Kansas City, Mo.: The Nelson-Atkins Museum of Art, 1996.

CAT. 43

Francesco Guardi (Italian, 1712-1793)
Regatta at the Rialto Bridge, ca. 1770s
Oil on canvas, 30½ x 49½ in. (77.47 x 125.73 cm)
The Sarah Campbell Blaffer Foundation, Houston, 1983.1

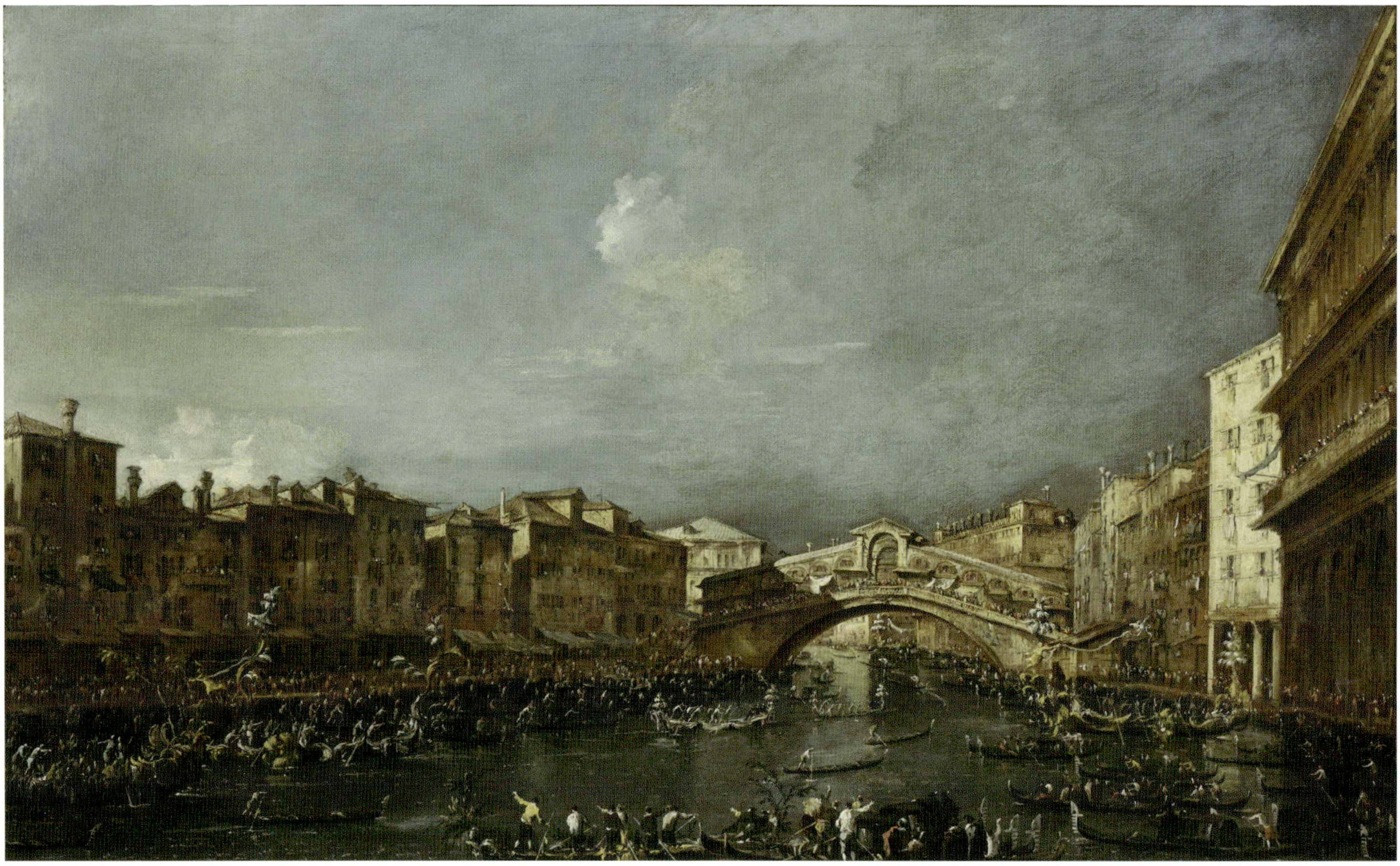

This vision of a regatta seems almost Seussian in its crowded complexity and profusion of whimsical craft and costumes. At lower right, a large golden gondola displays immense blue and white tufts of feathered decorations both fore and aft, under one of which an oversize gilded figure on its toes clasps a long pink ribbon tied to a large white crane, which hovers in the air over the boat's center. Tiny figures peer out onto the excitement from all spots, including the red-roofed structure at the extreme top of the building behind the bridge. At bottom center, a gondola carries a tree, decorated with gold ribbon, to which white cards are attached. All this spectacle seems to overshadow the main event: the regatta taking place under the bridge. The center of the canal is clear so that small craft propelled by one rower can pass under the Rialto, passing another large golden, feather-decorated gondola on the other side. Men at bottom center, their backs to us and arms raised, cheer on the competitors. At lower left, more immense gondolas, one decorated with a gilded figure holding blue ribbons attached to a tufted parasol, and foliage, make a spectacular appearance. The reddish ground that shows through the thinly painted sky adds to a feeling of somewhat murky darkness—highlighted in parts by brilliant sun—amidst which the figures appear almost as weightless as the crane, as if they too could dissolve into the air. A smaller version (48 x 79 cm) of the painting is in the Rijksmuseum, Amsterdam.

Andria Derstine

PROVENANCE

(Ehrich Galleries, N.Y.); The Metropolitan Museum of Art, sold Christie's, New York, 1980; (Colnaghi, London); Blaffer Foundation.

EXHIBITIONS

Winston-Salem, Wake Forest University, *Treasures of Italian Painting from the Sarah Campbell Blaffer Foundation,* 1984-85, cat. no. 21.

The Museum of Fine Arts, Houston, San Antonio Museum of Art, Amarillo Art Center, Museum of the Big Bend, El Paso Museum of Art, Wichita Falls Museum of Art, Texas A&M University, Corpus Christi State University, Michelson Museum of Art, Old Jail Art Center, Carson County Square House, Museum, Abilene Christian University, Huntington Art Gallery, Longview Museum of Art, McAllen International Museum of Art, The Museum, Texas Tech University, Museum of East Texas, Ellen Noel Art Museum of the Permian Basin, Beaumont Museum of Art, The Nave Museum, John E. Conner Museum (all preceding museums in Texas); Rochester, N.Y., Memorial Art Gallery; Baylor University, Martin Museum of Art; Temple Texas, Cultural Activities Center; The Gallery, Southern Methodist University; St. Petersburg, Fla., Museum of Fine Arts; Galveston, Tex., Rosenberg Library; Phoenix Art Museum; Shreveport, La., Meadows Museum of Art; Midland, Tex., Museum of the South West; Milwaukee, Haggerty Museum; Fresno Metropolitan Museum; Memphis Museum of Art; Nevada Museum of Art; Mobile, Fine Arts Museum of the South; Marshall, Tex., Michelson Museum of Art, *Five Centuries of Italian Painting from the Collection of the Sarah Campbell Blaffer Foundation,* 1985-1993.

Houston, Museum of Fine Arts, *Masterpieces of Baroque Painting from the Collection of the Sarah Campbell Blaffer Foundation,* 1992-93.

San Antonio Museum of Art, 1994-95.

The Museum of Fine Arts, Houston, San Antonio Museum of Art, University of Michigan Museum of Art, Portland Art Museum, Dallas Museum of Art, Amarillo Museum of Art, Milwaukee Art Museum, Old Jail Center (Albany, Tex.), Ellen Noel Art Museum (Odessa, Tex.), *Venetian Paintings from the Collection of the Sarah Campbell Blaffer Foundation,* 1995-2002.

BIBLIOGRAPHY

Bulletin of the Metropolitan Museum of Art (1906): 72-3, 75.

Annual Report of the Trustees of the Metropolitan Museum of Art for the Year Ending December 31, 1906, 51. New York: The Metropolitan Museum of Art, 1907.

Simonson, George A., "Some of Guardi's Paintings in America," *Art in America* 2, no. 2 (1914): 90 n.

Wehle, Harry B. *A Catalogue of Italian, Spanish and Byzantine Paintings in the Metropolitan Museum of Art,* 276. New York: Publishers Printing Co. and William Bradford Press, 1940.

Donzelli, Carlo, *I Pittori Veneti del Settecento,* 110. Florence: Sansoni, 1957.

Zampetti, Pietro. *Catalogo della Mostra dei Guardi,* 314, cited under cat. no. 28. Venice: Alfieri, 1965.

Fredericksen, Burton B., and Federico Zeri. *Census of Pre-Nineteenth-Century Italian Paintings in North American Public Collections,* 96. Cambridge, Mass.: Harvard University Press, 1972.

Morassi, Antonio. *Guardi: Antonio and Francesco Guardi,* 367-8, cat. no. 304. Venice: Alfieri, 1973.

Bortolatto, Luigina Rossi. *L'opera completa di Francesco Guardi,* 138, cat. no. 862. Milan: Rizzoli, 1974.

Pignatti, Teresio. *Five Centuries of Italian Painting: 1300-1800,* 206-8. Houston: Sarah Campbell Blaffer Foundation, 1985.

CAT. 44

Francesco Guardi (Italian, 1712-1793)

San Giorgio Maggiore, Venice, ca. 1790[1]

Oil on canvas, 18¼ x 30 1/16 in. (46.5 x 76.3 cm)

Toledo Museum of Art, Toledo, Ohio. Purchased with funds from the Libbey Endowment, Gift of Edward Drummond Libbey, 1952.62

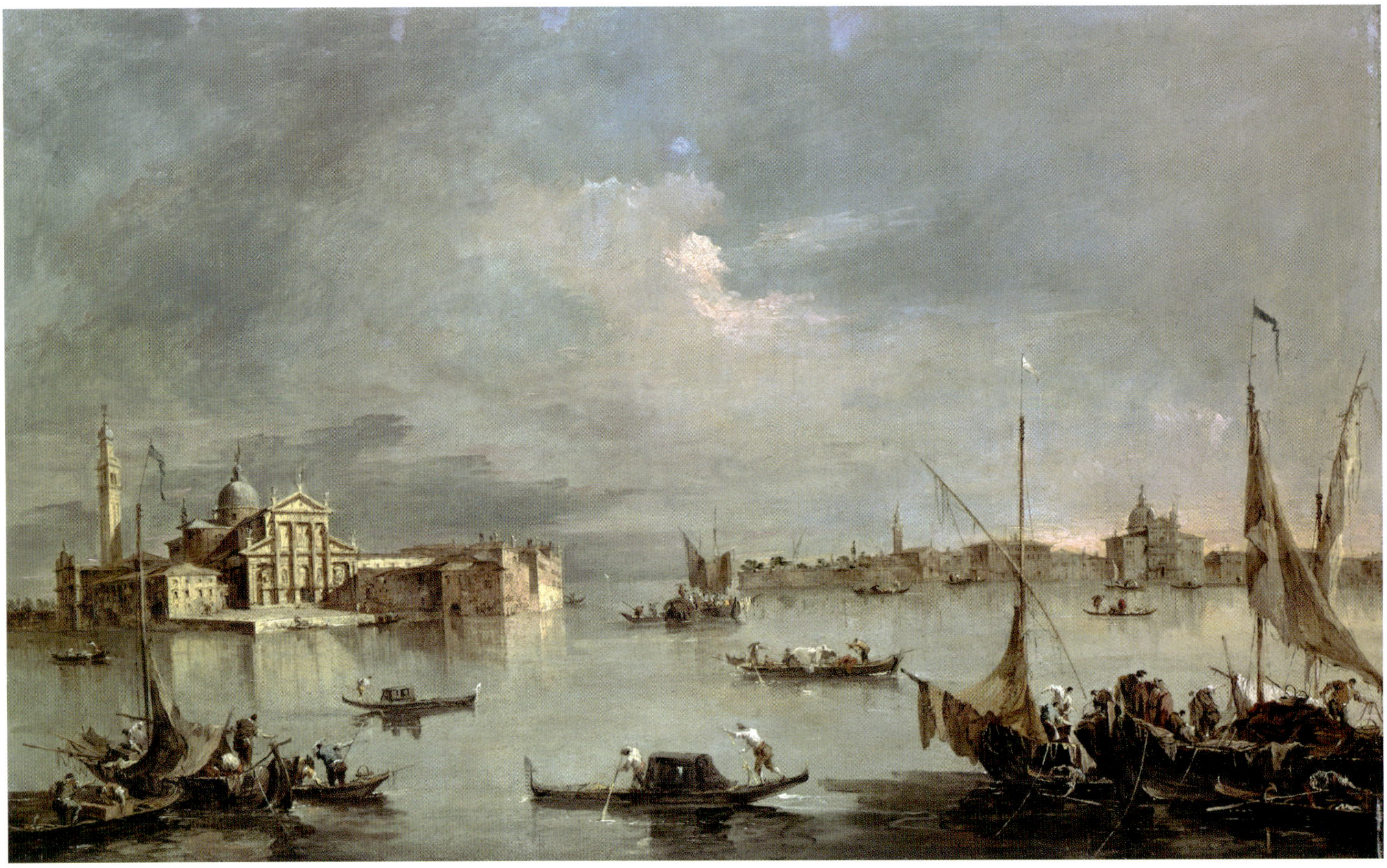

In this work, which exists in numerous other versions—including in the Wallace Collection, the Venice Accademia, the Leeds Art Gallery, and a drawing in Cologne—the vast expanse of Venice's *bacino* is made evident, despite the fact that what is depicted, the church of San Giorgio Maggiore on its islet, at left, and part of the larger, long island of the Giudecca at right, is quite close to the city proper. The seemingly limitless view towards the horizon between the two, with the white sail of a far-distant ship lightly daubed in to fill the void and the mass of boats plying the waters in the foreground, shows the real subject of the work to be the view towards the bacino itself. Indeed almost three-fifths of the painting is sky, and between sky and water the ships and land both appear almost as interlopers on the scene. Guardi's vigorous rendering of the deep shadows in the immediate foreground, and his skillful reflections of San Giorgio Maggiore and its accompanying buildings are evidence of the interplay between light, shade, water, and air that characterizes so much of one's perception of Venice, today as in Guardi's time. The blues and white of his palette, the sherbet pinks and peaches behind the church of the Redentore, the lavender just touching the sky above the buildings to the right of San Giorgio Maggiore, and the impasto of his clouds add to the work's shimmering feel. Even the poses of his figures here add to a sense of instability: two men at lower left bend to look at a box on their barge, while a man in white at lower right holds out his arm to assist another in blue who holds a brown tarp, both steadying themselves on their boat, whose bobbing is almost palpable.

Andria Derstine

Note

1 A now barely visible inscription was said to read "F [G] 179[1?]"; for more on this, see p. 111 of Derstine's essay in this catalogue.

Provenance

Maurice Kahn, Paris; Adolph Mayer, The Hague, by 1936; (Rosenberg & Stiebel, New York); purchased from Rosenberg & Stiebel by the Toledo Museum of Art.

Exhibitions

The Hague, Gemeente Museum, *Oude Kunst uit Haagsch Bezit*, Dec. 1936–Jan. 1937, cat. no. 89.

Rotterdam, Museum Boymans, *Meesterwerken uit Vier Eeuwen 1400–1800*, 1938, cat. no. 187.

Detroit Institute of Arts and John Herron Art Institute, Indianapolis, *Venice 1700–1800*, 1952, cat. no. 30.

Venice, Palazzo Ducale, *I Vedutisti Veneziani del Settecento*, June–Oct. 1967, cat. no. 145.

The Art Institute of Chicago, The Minneapolis Institute of Art and the Toledo Museum of Art, *Painting in Italy in the Eighteenth Century: Rococo to Romanticism*, 1970–71, cat. no. 24.

Bibliography

Meesterwerken uit Vier Eeuwen 1400–1800, 121, cat. no. 187, pl. 188. Rotterdam: Museum Boymans, 1938.

Venice 1700–1800, 33–34, cat. no. 30. Detroit: Detroit Institute of Arts and John Herron Art Institute, 1952.

"To Baroque Venice via Detroit," *Art Digest* 27, no. 1 (Oct. 1, 1952): 8.

Godwin, Molly Ohl, "Capolavori Italiani al Toledo Museum of Art," *Le Vie del Mondo* 14 (1952): 1155–6.

Morassi, Antonio, "*Una mostra del settecento Veneziano a Detroit*," *Arte Veneta* 7 (1953): 61.

"Details, European Paintings," *Toledo Museum News*, n.s., 4, no. 1 (Winter 1961): 9.

A Guide to the Collections. Toledo: Museum of Art, 1966.

I Vedustisti Veneziani del Settecento, 322–3, cat. nos. 145 and 145a. Venice: Palazzo Ducale, 1967.

Milliken, William M. *Unfamiliar Venice*, 70. Cleveland: Case Western Reserve University Press, 1967.

Ferroni, Ugo. "*Los 'vedutisti' Venecianos des setecientos*," in *Goya* 80 (Sept.–Oct. 1967): 69, 74.

Pignatti, Terisio. "The Contemporaneity of the Eighteenth-century Venetian 'Vedutisti,'" *Art International* 11, no. 10 (Christmas 1967): 25.

Watson, F. J. B. "Eighteenth-century Painting and Decorative Arts," *Apollo* 86, no. 70 (Dec. 1967): 465, fig. 24.

Briganti, Giuliano. *I Vedutisti*, tav. 78. Milan: Electa, 1968.

Watson, F. J. B. *Wallace Collection Catalogues: Pictures and Drawings*, 140. 16th ed. London: Clowes, 1968.

Hannegan, Barry. *Painting in Italy in the Eighteenth Century: Rococo to Romanticism*, 70–1. Chicago/Minneapolis/Toledo: The Art Institute of Chicago, 1970.

Pignatti, Teresio. *Francesco Guardi*, 29. Brescia: La Scuola, 1971.

Fredericksen, Burton B., and Frederico Zeri. *Census of Pre-Nineteenth Century Italian Paintings in North American Public Collections*, 97. Cambridge, Mass.: Harvard University Press, 1972.

Morassi, Antonio. *Guardi: Antonio e Francesco Guardi*, vol. 1, 242, 391, cat. no. 428 and vol. 2, fig. 447. Venice: Alfieri, 1973.

Bortolatto, Luigina Rossi. *L'opera completa di Francesco Guardi*, cat. no. 245. Milan: Rizzoli, 1974.

Brion, Marcel. *Guardi*, 43. Paris: H. Scrépel, 1976.

The Toledo Museum of Art, European Paintings, 73, pl. 36. Toledo: Toledo Museum of Art, 1976.

Morse, John D. *Old Master Paintings in North America*, 160. New York: Abbeville Press Publishers, 1979.

Koch-Hillebrandt, Manfred. *Museen in den USA: Gemälde*, 232. Munich: Hirmer, 1992.

CAT. 45

Attributed to Francesco Guardi (Italian, 1712–1793)
Venice, The Molo and the Riva degli Schiavoni, Looking East, late 1750s
Oil on canvas, 14 x 23 5/16 in. (35.6 x 59.2 cm)
Yale University Art Gallery, Gift of Susan Morse Hilles, 1973.87.3

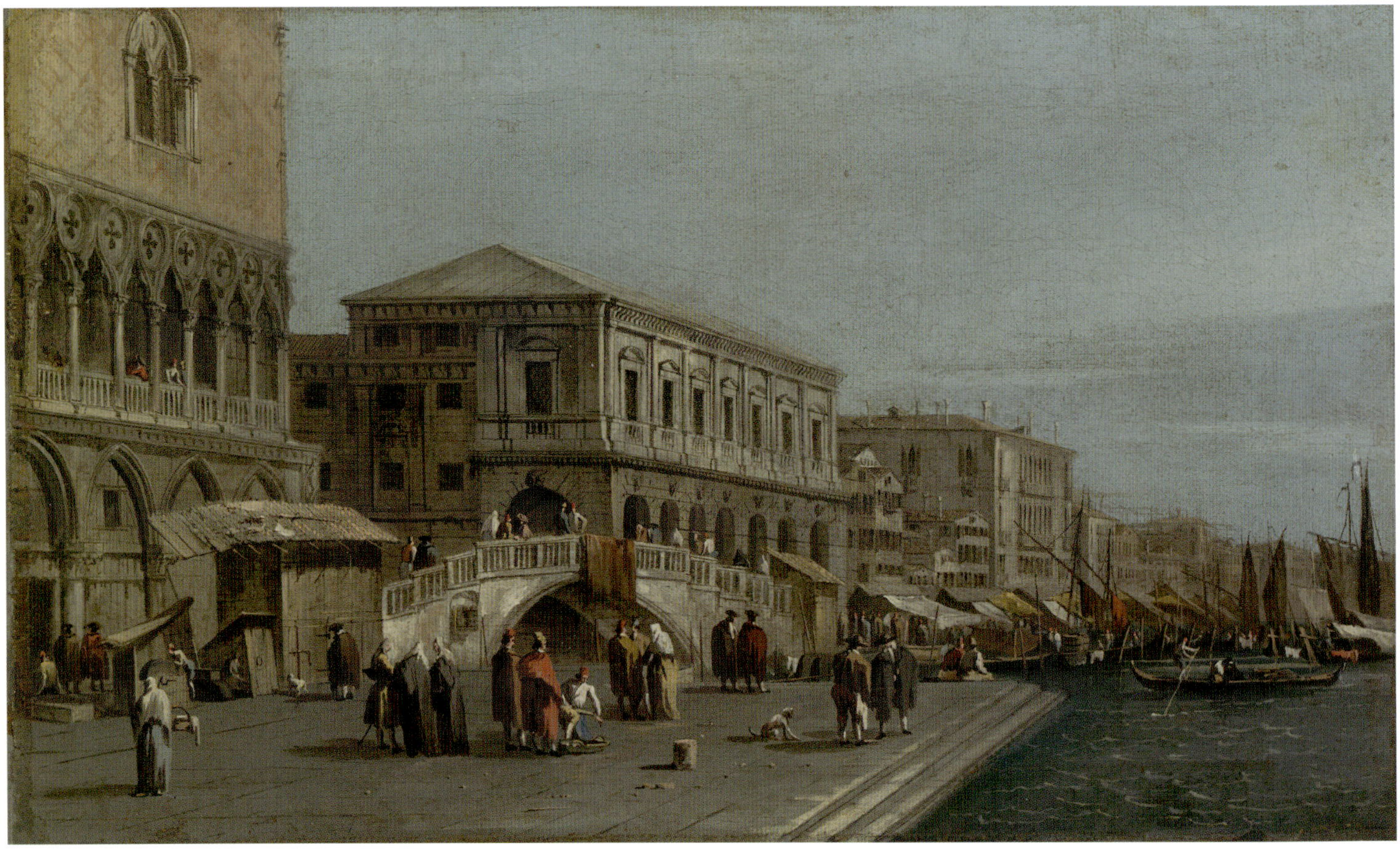

This view, which has heretofore been attributed to Canaletto, and is, given the coincidence of measurements, very likely the work that Constable in 1976 considered "School of Canaletto," may well be an early view painting by Francesco Guardi, as newly suggested by Charles Beddington. It certainly displays all the characteristics of a painting by an accomplished painter who may be just beginning to paint views, and who has looked carefully at Canaletto's compositions (including his etching of this scene), color, shading, and figural types. The work betrays, however, a certain tremulousness to its lines that would be consistent with an early view painting by Guardi. The sky—fairly undifferentiated in tones, with just a slight area of darkness to the right—alone would seem to show that it is not a Canaletto, as does the overall handling, although it is a well-painted work. From the Molo, the viewer looks to a corner of the Doge's Palace and the Ponte della Paglia, which crosses to the front of the Palazzo dei Prigioni. The buildings of the Riva degli Schiavoni, including the large Palazzo Dandolo, recede towards the right, while both rich and poor go about their business on the quayside.

Andria Derstine

Provenance

Probably Griscom collection, sold in New York in 1914; possibly Arthur Tooth, London; Susan Morse Hilles; Yale University Art Gallery.

Bibliography

Probably the painting referred to in W. G. Constable, *Canaletto: Giovanni Antonio Canal, 1697–1768,* vol. 2, 244, cat. no. 119a. 2nd ed. Oxford: Clarendon Press, 1976.

CAT. 46

ANTONIO JOLI (ITALIAN, 1700–1777)
A View of Westminster Bridge from the North, with a Procession of State Barges, ca. 1750

Oil on canvas, 37 x 42⅛ in. (94 x 107 cm)
Collection of the Art Gallery of Greater Victoria, British Columbia, Canada
Alice Winthrop Stuart Bequest, 1984.047.002

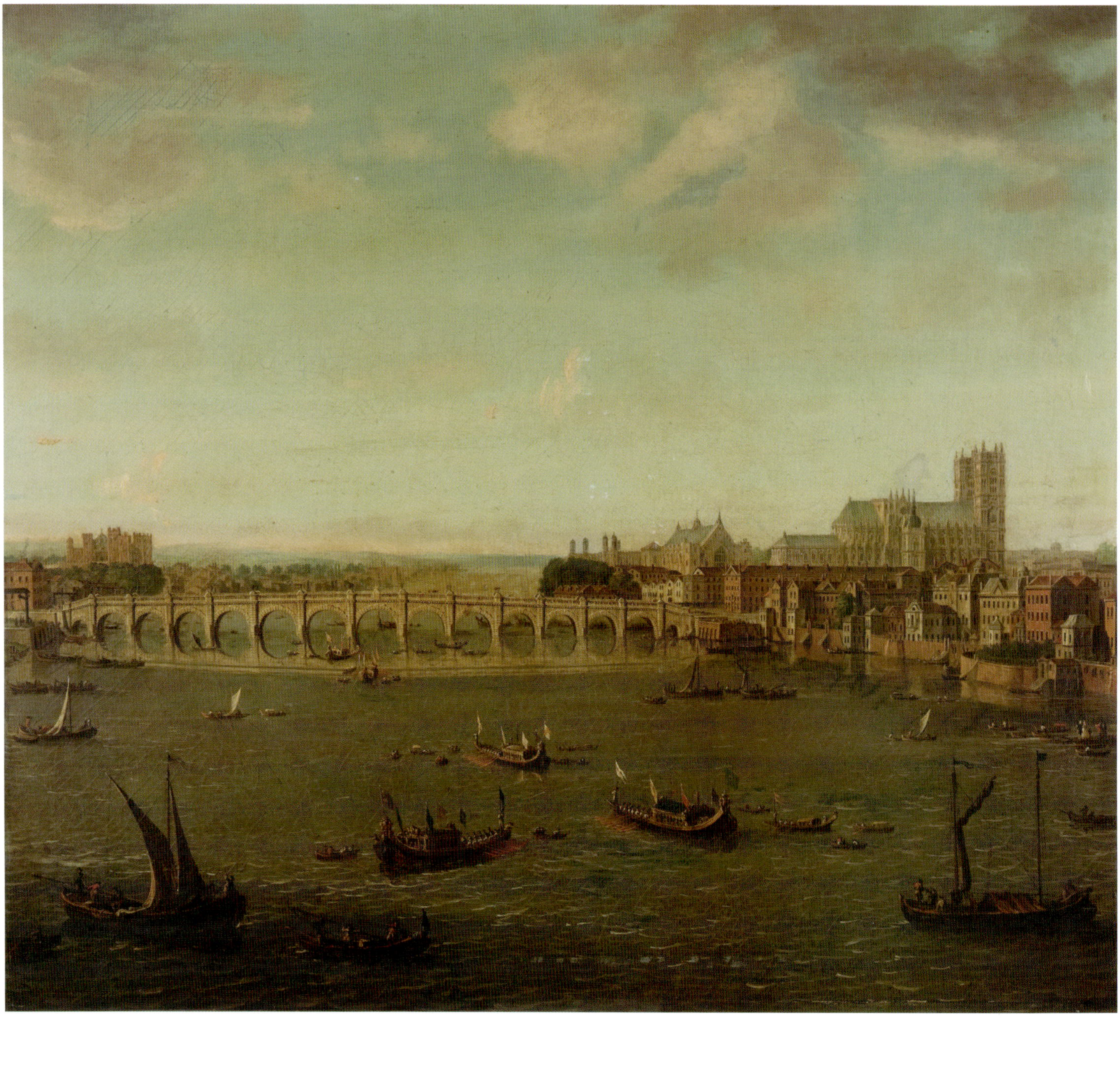

This picture came to Victoria with an attribution to Canaletto, and indeed the general arrangement of the composition is roughly similar to the Canaletto view of Westminster Bridge on Lord Mayor's Day of 1746.[1] This appears to be another state occasion, which it may be possible to identify by the white banners on the barges. The Canaletto shows Westminster Hall entirely overlaying the Abbey, and seen in sharp recession. The tower of St. Margaret's is in line with the Abbey transept. In these respects the composition is closer to a painting by Antonio Joli of 1745.[2]

The subject was painted by Joli a number of times. The closest version to the present canvas is a picture sold at Christie's in 1981,[3] with nearly the same disposition of barges (there is one extra in the present picture). Being wider (99 x 124 cm), it also includes the Banqueting House on the right, and the handling seems very different.[4]

Joli was a native of Modena. He came to London shortly before Canaletto, and stayed from 1744 until 1750. Westminster Bridge was completed in the later year.

George Knox

Notes

Acknowledgment: This entry first appeared as catalogue number 22 in the Vancouver Art Gallery exhibition, *Eighteenth Century Venetian Art in Canadian Collections,* curated by George Knox, October 6, 1989-January 1, 1990. The Vancouver Art Gallery has kindly given the Oklahoma City Museum of Art permission to reproduce the entry.

1 W. G. Constable and J. G. Links, *Canaletto* (Oxford: The Clarendon Press, 1982: pl. 135).
2 Constable and Links, pl. 162.
3 Christie's sale, London, June 26, 1981, lot 86.
4 The boats are perhaps better drawn in our picture. See also *Pictures from the Grand Tour* (London: Colnaghi, 1978: pl. 32).

Provenance

Private collection, Victoria; The Art Gallery of Greater Victoria; Alice Winthrop Stuart Bequest.

Exhibitions

London, Colnaghi, *Pictures from the Grand Tour,* 1978.
Vancouver Art Gallery, *Eighteenth Century Venetian Art in Canadian Collections,* 1989.

Bibliography

Constable, W. G., and J. G. Links. *Canaletto.* Oxford: The Clarendon Press, 1982.

CAT. 47 Unidentified artist, formerly attributed to MICHELE MARIESCHI (Italian, 1696-1743)
View of Venice: SS Giovanni e Paolo and the Scuola di San Marco, ca. 1756-60
Oil on canvas, 51 x 66 in. (129.54 x 167.64 cm)
Fine Arts Museums of San Francisco, Museum Purchase, M. H. de Young Memorial Museum, 48.1

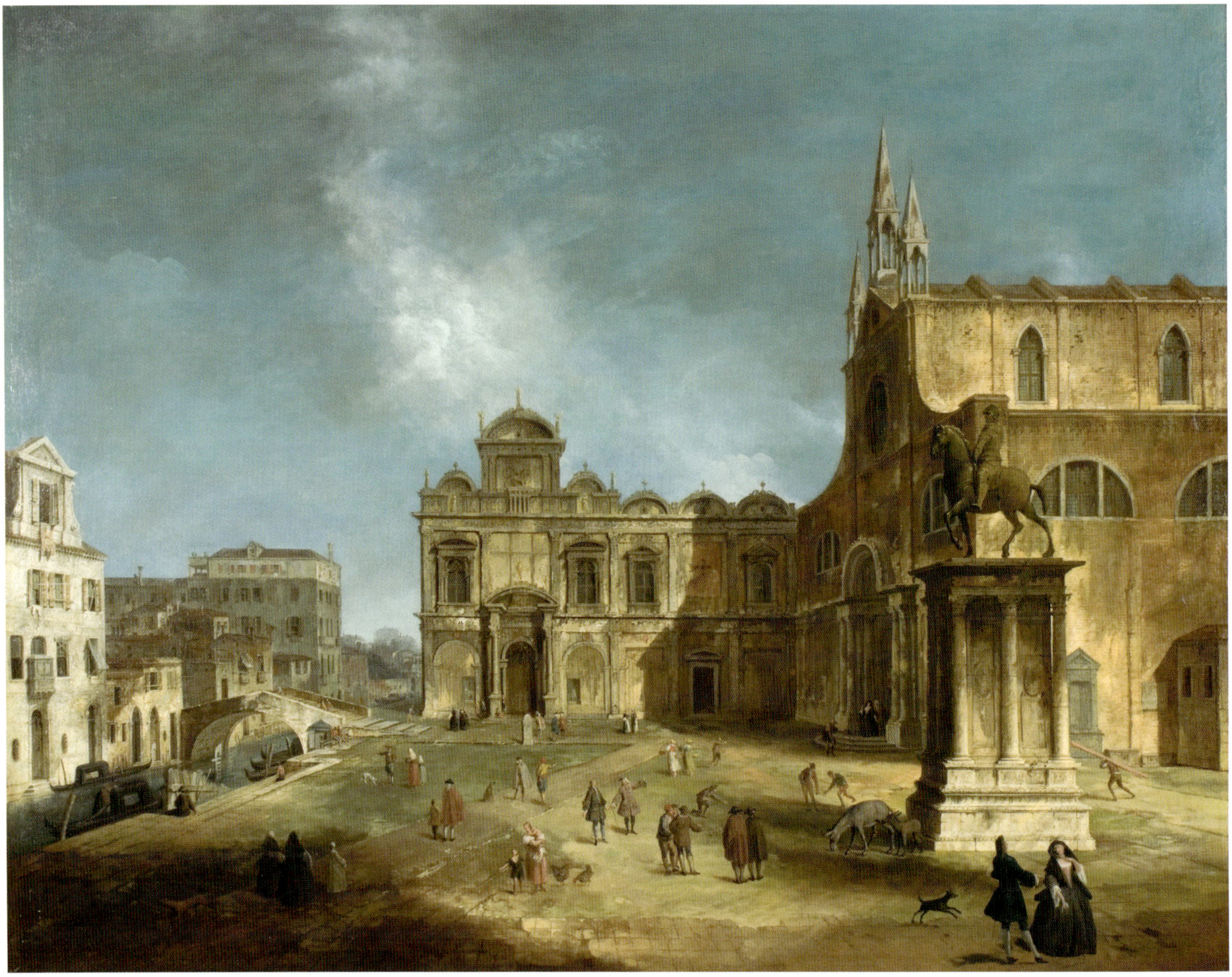

This animated view of Venice shows the Campo and Church of Santi Giovanni e Paolo at right, with the Scuola di San Marco forming the backdrop to the square and Andrea Verocchio's monumental sculpture of Colleoni in the foreground.[1] It is a typical Venetian scene, juxtaposing the canal and houses at left with the large church and the brilliant façade of the Scuola. The Campo was one of the largest squares in Venice, and it is here animated by a cross-section of Venetian life that includes a humbly dressed mother and child, gesturing aristocrats (perhaps the ever-present Grand Tourists), figures playing a game of bowls, and animals ranging from chickens to dogs to donkeys, the last a rarity in Venetian scenes although also found in Marieschi's 1741 etching of the Campo. The painting has itself long been attributed to Michele Marieschi, also known as Michiel Marieschi. That attribution, however, was rejected by Ralph Toledano in his Marieschi catalogue raisonné, and indeed, the work lacks the thick strokes of wet-into-wet paint that are characteristic of the artist.[2] Moreover, Marieschi was a careful draftsman, but this painting includes a series of mistaken passages in the depiction of the architecture that appear neither in Marieschi's etching nor in his painted view (London, private collection).[3]

These architectural errors include, for example, the rooflines at the sides of the church façade, which are shown with curving rather than straight pediments. The church entrance is painted as a round arch rather than a pointed gothic portal, and the pilasters running between the thermal windows on the side of the church are missing. The entablature above the columns of the Colleoni monument should be marble but is instead shown as brick. These and other differences are all minor errors, but none are found in the many other depictions of the scene. Moreover, the viewpoint is that of someone standing on the pavement at the center of the square's southern boundary, but virtually all other depictions of the scene were apparently taken from a balcony on the *piano nobile* of the palace at the square's southwestern corner. The evidence suggests that the artist was working from a drawing, but one not precisely detailed in all its aspects. Yet, this is an unusually large view painting, and it is hard to understand why someone working in Venice would not have noticed these mistakes during the execution of so ambitious a painting. Charles Beddington has suggested a possible attribution to Francesco Battaglioli (ca. 1725-1796).[4] Battaglioli is not well enough known to argue conclusively for his authorship, but he was in Spain from 1754-60, spent time in Treviso and Brescia, and also worked as a stage painter and would have been undaunted by the large canvas. It is tempting to propose that he might have painted the canvas during his time away from Venice.

John Marciari

Notes

1. The painting has been newly conserved for the *La Serenissima* exhibition and the catalog includes new photography.
2. Marieschi was long a convenient dumping ground for Venetian views that could not be attributed to Canaletto, Bellotto, or Guardi. As noted by Mario Manzelli, "*Proposta per l'identificazione di Michele Marieschi e del suo alter-ego Francesco Albotto,*" *Arte Veneta* 41 (1987): 111, there are over six hundred paintings attributed to him, far too many for an artist whose independent career only spanned the years 1735-42.
3. Ralph Toledano, *Michele Marieschi, Catalogo ragionato*, 2nd ed. (Milan: Leonardo, 1995: 93). Toledano notes further that the view of SS Giovanni e Paolo in Capodimonte, Naples, which is usually attributed to Marieschi, is instead by Marieschi's pupil Francesco Albotto (1721-1757), an attribution also given by Mario Manzelli, *Michele Marieschi e il suo alter-ego Francesco Albotto* (Venice: Studio LT2, 1991: 80-1.
4. Written communication to the author.
5. The Petschek provenance was supplied by Frederick Mont. The painting was presumably among those purchased by Ignaz Petschek (1857-1934) in the 1920s and 1930s, which then passed to his son Frank C. Petschek (1895-1963), who brought a group of the family's paintings out of Czechoslovakia before 1938.

Provenance

Petschek Collection, Prague[5]; Frederick Mont (aka Frederick Mondschein), New York; from whom purchased by the city and county of San Francisco, 1948. Fine Arts Museum of San Francisco, Museum Purchase, M. H. de Young Memorial Museum.

Bibliography

Illustrations of Selected Works: The M. H. de Young Memorial Museum, 28. San Francisco: Fine Arts Museum of San Francisco, 1950.

European Works of Art in the M. H. de Young Memorial Museum, 170. Berkeley, Calif.: Published by Diablo Press for De Young Museum Society, 1966.

Frederickson, Burton B., and Federico Zeri. *Census of Pre-Nineteenth-Century Italian Paintings in North American Public Collections*, 120, 633. Cambridge, Mass.: Harvard University Press, 1972.

Toledano, Ralph. *Michele Marieschi, Catalogo ragionato*, 93. 2nd ed. Milan: Leonardo, 1995.

CAT. 48

IPPOLITO CAFFI (Italian, 1809-1866)

View of Santa Maria della Salute from the Ponte dell'Accademia, Venice, ca. 1845

Oil on canvas, 15⅛ x 18⅞ in. (38.57 x 47.94 cm)
Oklahoma City Museum of Art. Purchase with funds provided by an
Inasmuch Foundation grant in honor of Carolyn Hill, 2009.021

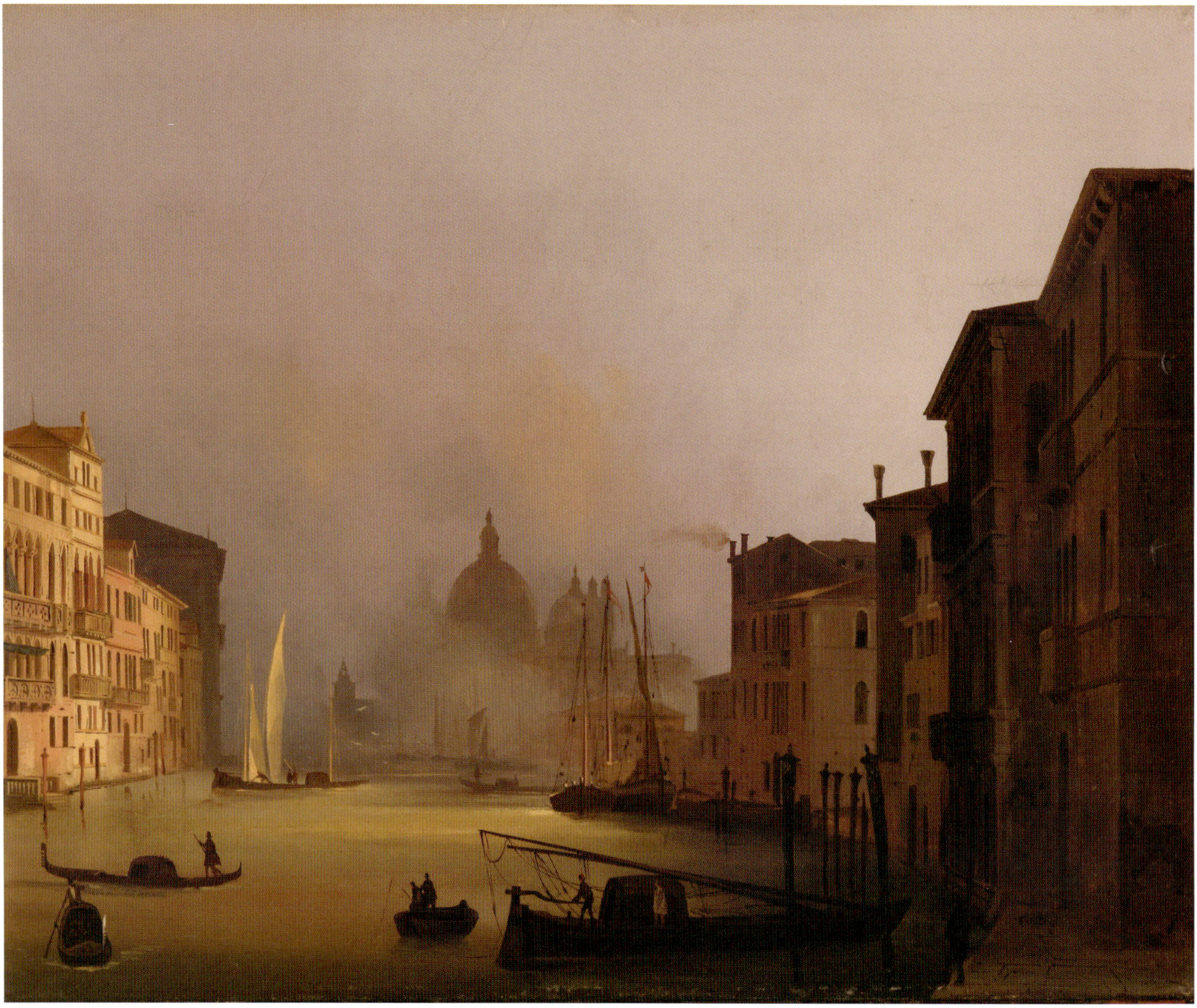

These two paintings (cats. 48 and 49) by Caffi were sold on the same date with two other views of Rome by the artist, *Piazza del Popolo*, Lot: 150, and *Roma and Piazza San Pietro al chiaro di luna, Roma,* Lot: 145. These views of Rome are listed as being the same size (all about $14\frac{15}{16}$ x $19\frac{5}{16}$ in.) as well as oil on canvas. Perhaps all were from the same collection.

A recent, major retrospective exhibition of the artist's work, titled *Caffi, Luci del Mediterraneo* (Belluno 2005, Rome and St. Petersburg 2006), indicates increasing attention is being given to Caffi.[1] In past studies of romantic art, a great deal of emphasis was placed on artists and developments associated with France, England, and Germany; Italian art of this period was largely overlooked. This is most likely the reason there are very few works by Caffi in collections outside of Italy, where the majority of his works are located in the Ca' Pesaro Museum in Venice.

At the age of eighteen, Caffi settled in Venice, where he intermittently studied life drawing and landscape, as well as perspective under Tranquillo Orsi (1771-1845) at the Academy. Later, like Canaletto and the great Venetian view painters of the eighteenth century, he also assisted Orsi in painting stage scenery for the teatro *La Fenice*.[2] In 1830 Caffi won first prize in perspective at the Academy, an early indication of his mastery of the basic knowledge and skill needed for becoming an accomplished view painter. In his mature paintings, portraying topographical views of Venice, Rome, and Istanbul, he adeptly combined the skills gained from his studies, as well as his knowledge of Canaletto's classic eighteenth-century views of Venice. His training in Venice and the influence of the city's magnificent architecture and picturesque settings served him throughout his career. Because of difficulties of obtaining commissions for his work in Venice, he left the city and made his way to Rome, arriving there most likely in January of 1832. In the following year, he painted scenery for Rome's foremost theatre, the *Tor di Nona*.[3]

Caffi revisited Venice in 1837 and painted a series of oil sketches of the city's topography to be used to complete a fresco commission for a Roman palazzo.[4] By November he was back in Rome and painted two views of Venice and two of Rome for the famous Caffè Greco, a favorite gathering place of artists of all nationalities residing in Rome.[5] In 1838 he returned there to record the festivities surrounding the visit of the Emperor of Austria. Following the eighteenth-century *veduteste* tradition he completed a painting of the royal regatta entering the city (*l'Ingresso a Venezia e la Regata*). This was acquired by the emperor. No doubt while Caffi was in Venice in 1837 and 1838 he made a number of pencil and oil sketches, which he took back to Rome to complete paintings like the two in the Oklahoma City Museum of Art (cat. 48 has a label on the back of the canvas with the address and name of a Roman art materials merchant: *RUE du Babuino135 /A ROME / D. DONIZIELLI FILS /F.DE COULEURS*).

(CONTINUED NEXT PAGE)

CAT. 49

IPPOLITO CAFFI (Italian, 1809–1866)

View of the Bacino di San Marco, Venice, ca. 1845

Oil on canvas, 15⅛ x 18⅞ in. (38.57 x 47.94 cm)
Oklahoma City Museum of Art. Purchase with funds provided by an Inasmuch Foundation grant in honor of Carolyn Hill, 2009.022

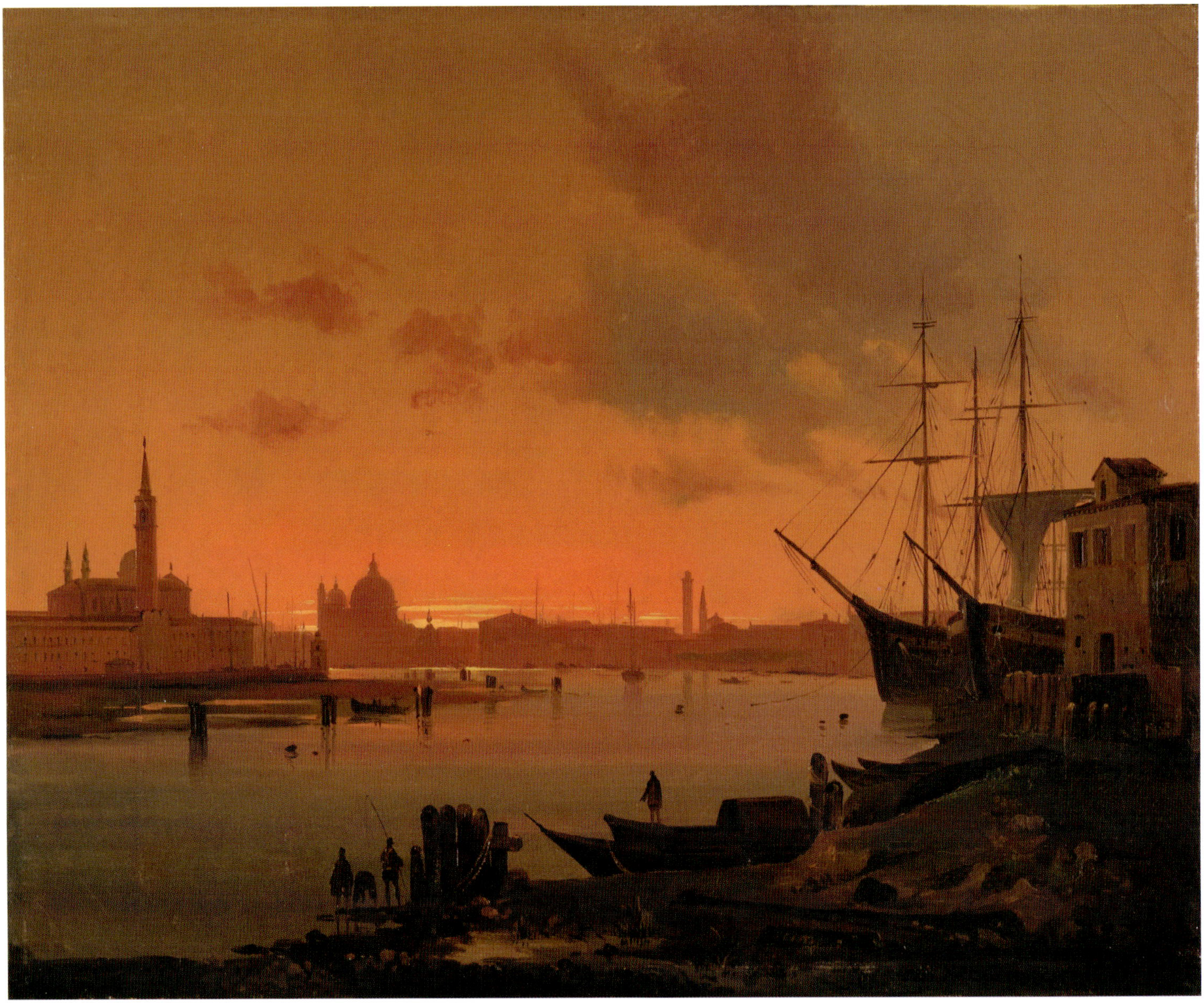

Caffi worked in the established manner of the time, completing in the studio paintings of both Rome and Venice based on precise pencil sketches. He achieved his first great success with these view paintings when he took part in an exhibition on the Piazza del Popolo in Rome in 1844.

Why then did Caffi choose to do his work in Rome rather than Venice? At the end of the Napoleonic Wars, France withdrew from Rome, Venice, and northern Italy, but at the Congress of Vienna, held at the end of the war, Austria regained control of the Tirol and Salzburg and was awarded Lombardy-Venetia in Italy. Venice was once again under foreign domination. In addition, it was only natural for a young artist and patriot, particularly a painter of topographical views and landscapes, to choose Rome as a place to launch his career.

The two companion pieces, *View of Santa Maria della Salute from the Ponte dell'Accademia, Venice* and *View of the Bacino di San Marco, Venice*, are probably based on sketches Caffi made on his 1837 or 1838 visit to Venice. They display Caffi's ability to draw on the tradition of the eighteenth-century Venetian view painters and at the same time merge the island city's great past with the less opulent present. These paintings are part of a series of views of Venice and Rome that reportedly were in an industrialist's villa on Lake Como "for the past 150 years." All are approximately the same size and were probably commissioned about the same time. These Venice paintings are portrayed in delicate gradations of color with meticulous details and dramatic light effects that convey the restless emotions of a romantic, as well as an underlying sense of classical order. In Caffi's Roman landscape subjects there is also the sense of classical balance and harmony that goes back to Claude's carefully composed harbor and Roman Campagna subjects.

Hardy George

Notes

1 Annalisa Scarpa, curator, *Caffi Luci del Miditerraneo*, Exhibition: Belluno, Palazzo Crepandona, October 1-January, 22, 2006; Rome, Museo di Roma—Palazzo Braschi, February 15-May 2, 2006 (Milan: Skira editore, 2005).
2 Giuseppe Avon Caffi, *Ippolito Caffi, 1809-1866* (Padua: Amicucci Editore, 1967: 24).
3 Ibid., 34.
4 Ibid., 37.
5 Ibid., 39. According to Giuseppe Avon Caffi (1966) of these four paintings of *Ponte de Rialto, Piazzetta di San Marco, The Temple of Saturn*, and the *Coloseum*, only the *Ponte de Rialto* remains.

Provenance

Private collection, Italy; Sold, Christie's Milan, Nov. 28, 2007, lot: 149, title: *Veduta del Bacino grande di San Marco, Venezia*, size: 14.96 x 19.29 in., oil on canvas; Purchased with an Inasmuch Foundation grant for the Oklahoma City Museum of Art to honor Carolyn Hill, Director 1994-2007, from Jean-François Heim, Tableaux—Antiquites, 134 rue du Faubourg-Saint-Honoré 75008, Paris, Aug. 1, 2009.

Bibliography

Mancini, E. "*Lettere inedited di Ippolito Caffi*," in *Annuario 1925/26 del R. Instituto Magistrale Giustina Renier.* Belluno, 1925-1926.
Caffi, Giuseppe Avon. "*Il pittore Ippolito Caffi*," in *Rivista di Venezia* (June 1931): 195-203.
Pittaluga, Mary. "*Dipinti del Caffi nel Civico Museo di Belluno*," in *Arte Lombarda* (1965).
Caffi, Giuseppe Avon. *Ippolito Caffi, 1809-1866.* Padua: Amicucci Editore, 1967.
Pittaluga, Mary. *Il pittore Ippolito Caffi.* Vicenza: Neri Pozza, 1971.
Pavanello, G., and G. D. Romanelli, curators. *Venezia nell'Ottocento Imagini e mito.* Exh. cat. Milan: Electa, 1983.
Lucco, M. "*Il Bellunese*," in *La pittura in Italia, L'Ottocento.* Milano, 1990.
Oliveri, J. M., curator. *Napoleon, les Bonapart et l'Italie.* Exh. cat. Ajaccio, 2001.
Museo di Roma—Palazzo Braschi, Rome, February 15-May 2, 2006. Exh cat. Milan: Skira editore, 2005.
Scarpa, Annalisa, curator. *Caffi Luci del Miditerraneo.* Exhibition: Belluno, Palazzo Crepandona, October 1-January, 22, 2006.

CAT. 50

J.M.W. TURNER (English, 1775–1851)

The Dogana and Santa Maria della Salute, Venice, 1843

Oil on canvas, 24 7/16 x 36 5/8 in. (62 x 93 cm); [Signed "JMWT" on wall in bottom right corner]

National Gallery of Art, Washington. Given in memory of Governor Alvan T. Fuller by the Fuller Foundation, Inc., 1961.2.3

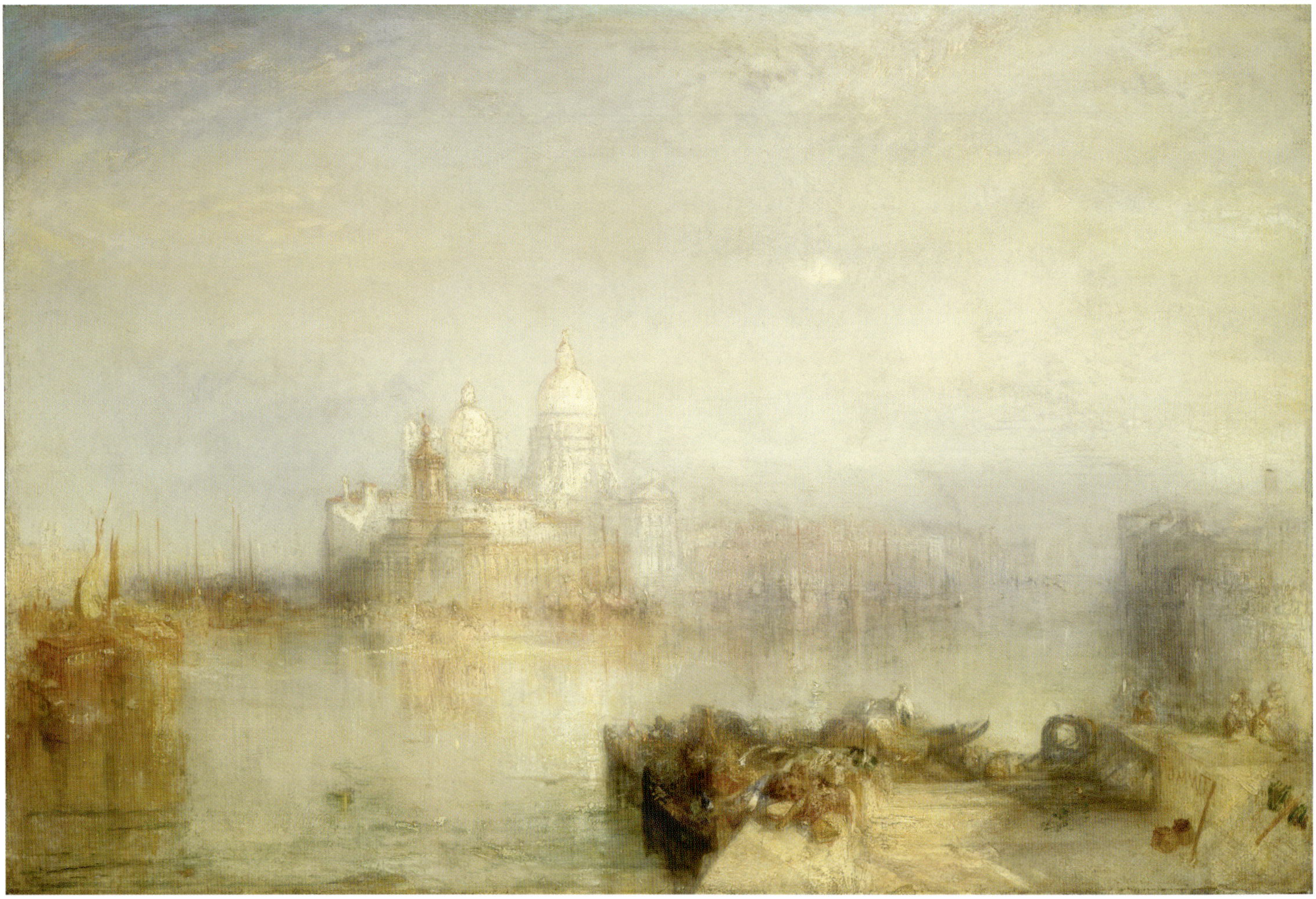

Among the Venice paintings that Turner exhibited in 1843-44, *The Dogana and Santa Maria della Salute, Venice* appears remarkably superior. It displays a new level of accomplishment in his subtle use of color and his glazing technique. Turner seems to have resolved some of the color and compositional problems posed by the trial-and-error experiments of this transitional period. In the *Dogana* painting the artist achieved the total unity sought for in *St. Benedetto, looking towards Fusina* (London, Tate Britain, exh. R.A. 1843) and the *Approach to Venice* (Washington, National Gallery, exh. R.A. 1844).[1] The green of the water in the foreground unites with the pale blue of the middle distance, which in turn gently combines with the deeper shades of blue and blue violet in the vaporous distance. It is difficult to determine the placement of the horizon line, where water and sky meet. The whitish-blue haze of a sky filled with thin fleecy clouds becomes a slightly darker shade of blue at the top of the canvas. The domes of Santa Maria della Salute appear to rise from the eerie stillness of the lagoon like a mirage.[2] Turner has distorted and vertically elongated the domes in order to create a dominant image at the center of the composition. Perhaps he had in mind the passage from Canto IV of Byron's *Childe Harold's Pilgrimage,* which describes Venice as rising mysteriously from the sea as the pilgrim approaches it by gondola from the mouth of the Brenta Canal at Fusina. This type of vista across expanses of the lagoon's still waters is also found in the early morning image of *The Sun of Venice going to Sea* and the sunset of *St. Benedetto, looking towards Fusina*, while *Approach to Venice* represents the city at dusk, as indicated in the lines from Byron's *Childe Harold* (iv.xxxvii) accompanying the *Approach* in the 1844 Royal Academy exhibition. Turner's principal interests were devoted to capturing Venice's dream-like imagery and the poetic mood associated with late evening. To clarify his intentions he also used a passage from Samuel Rogers's *Italy* about crossing the lagoon "As to a floating city, steering in, / And gliding up her streets as in a dream, / So smoothly, silently."

Turner's *Dogana* was purchased in 1899 from Christie's, London, for the Canadian railroad magnate James Ross (1848-1913), and remained in his possession until his death. His collection was sold at Christie's, London, in 1927. Ross resided in Montreal from 1888, by which time he had taken over the construction of the Canadian Pacific. Later he became president of the Dominion Coal Company and the Bank of Montreal. The period from 1880 to 1920 was an auspicious epoch in the city's cultural and economic development. Most of Montreal's great collectors of this period, William Van Horne, George A. Drummond, and James Ross, were associated with the building of railroads, like William H. Vanderbilt, Henry O. and Theo Havemeyer, Henry Clay Frick, and J. Pierpont Morgan, their counterparts in the United States.[3]

Hardy George

Notes

1 *St. Benedetto* is a view at sunset, looking along the Canal della Giudecca toward Fusina where the entrance of the Brenta Canal is located. Before the building of the railroad bridge between the mainland and Venice, visitors approached Venice by boat from Fusina. The late evening painting of the *Approach to Venice* shows boats, gondolas, and a *burchiello* from Fusina moving in the direction of Venice and the Giudecca Canal. Martin Butlin and Evelyn Joll, *The Paintings of J. M. W. Turner,* 2 vols. (New Haven and London: Yale University Press, 1984: cat. nos. 406 and 412).

2 Ian Warell, *Turner in Venice*, exhibition at Tate Britain, London, October 9, 2003 -January 11, 2004 (London: Tate Publishing, 2003: 207) attributes the lack of shipping activity on the Bacino di San Marco in Turner's Venice views of 1843-44 to an actual falling off of shipping and trade with foreign countries.

3 Janet M. Brooke, *Discerning Tastes Montreal Collectors 1880-1920*, exhibition catalogue, December 8, 1990, to February 15, 1990 (Montreal: Montreal Museum of Fine Arts, 1989: 11-30).

Provenance

Purchased 1843 from exhibition at the Royal Academy of Arts, London, by Edwin Bullock, Hawthorn House, Handsworth, Birmingham; sale, Christie, Manson & Woods, London, May 21 and 23, 1870, 1st day, cat. no. 143; bought by Thos. Agnew & Sons, London, who sold it that same day to John Fowler (later Sir John Fowler, Bt. [1817-1898]), Thornwood Lodge, Campden Hill, London; sale, Christie, Manson & Woods, London, May 6, 1899, cat. no. 79; bought by Thos. Agnew & Sons, London, for James Ross, Montreal; sale, Christie, Manson & Woods, London, July 8, 1927, cat. no. 28, repro.; bought by Thos. Agnew & Sons, London, for Alvin T. Fuller, Boston (d. 1958); The Fuller Foundation; gift 1961 to NGA.

Exhibitions

Royal Academy of Arts, London, 1843, cat. no. 144.
Birmingham Society of Artists, Athenæum, Temple Row, Birmingham, *Modern Works of Art,* 1843, cat. no. 54.
City Museum and Art Gallery, Birmingham, *Loan Collection of Pictures and Drawings by J. M. W. Turner, R.A.*, 1899, cat. no. 7.
Thos. Agnew & Sons, Ltd., *Twenty Masterpieces of the English School,* 1899, cat. no. 19.
American Fine Arts Society Galleries, *Society of American Collectors Comparative Exhibition of Native and Foreign Art,* 1904, cat. no. 165, as *Venice, the Dogana and Santa Maria della Salute.*
Art Club, Boston, Paintings Loaned by Governor Alvan T. Fuller, 1928, cat. no. 46.
Museum of Fine Arts, Boston, *Paintings, Drawings, Prints from Private Collections in New England,* 1939, cat. no. 133, pl. 65.
Museum of Fine Arts, Boston, *Paintings, Drawings, and Prints by J. M. W. Turner, John Constable, R. P. Bonington,* 1946, cat. no. 17.
Museum of Fine Arts, Boston, *A Memorial Exhibition of the Collection of the Honorable Alvan T. Fuller,* 1959, cat. no. 33, repro.
Royal Academy of Arts, London, *Turner 1775-1851,* 1974-1975, cat. no. 533, color repro.
National Museum of Western Art, Tokyo; Municipal Museum, Kyoto, *Turner,* 1986, cat. no. 50, color repro.
Montreal Museum of Fine Arts, *Discerning Tastes: Montreal Collectors 1880-1920,* 1989-1990, 156-160, cat. no. 57.
Phoenix Art Museum; Indianapolis Art Museum, *The Art of Seeing: John Ruskin and the Victorian Eye,* 1993, fig. 22.
Kunstforum Wien, Vienna, *Joseph Mallord William Turner,* 1997, cat. no. 93, repro.
Sterling and Francine Clark Art Institute, Williamstown; Manchester Art Gallery; The Burrell Collection, Glasgow, *Turner: The Late Seascapes,* 2003-2004.
Fondation Beyeler, Basel, *Venice: From Canaletto and Turner to Monet,* 2008-2009, unnumbered catalogue, repro.

Bibliography

The Times (London), May 9, 1843, p. 6.
Spectator 16, no. 776 (May 13, 1843): 451.
Athenaeum 816 (June 17, 1843): 570.
Armstrong, Walter. *Turner,* 235. London: Thos. Agnew & Sons, 1902.
Ruskin, John. *Modern Painters,* Vol. 1, 1843, reference given to *The Works of John Ruskin,* E. T. Cook and Alexander Wedderburn, Library Edition in 39 vols., 1903-12, Vol. 3, lv, pl. 5.
Thornbury, Walter, *The Life of J. M. W. Turner, R.A.*, 580. 2nd ed. of 1862 work, in one vol., 1877.
Bell, C. F. *A List of the Works Contributed to Public Exhibitions by J. M. W. Turner, R.A.,* 1901, 146-147, cat. no. 238.
Finberg, Alexander Joseph. *In Venice with Turner,* 140, 148, 157. London: Cotswold Gallery, 1930.
Gage, John, ed. *Collected Correspondence of J. M. W. Turner,* cat. no. 261. Oxford: Clarendon Press, 1980.
Butlin, Martin, and Evelyn Joll. *The Paintings of J. M. W. Turner.* 2 vols. Vol. 1, cat. no. 403; Vol. 2, color pl. 409. New Haven and London: Yale University Press, 1977; 2d rev. ed., 1984.
Brooke, Janet M. *Discerning Tastes: Montreal Collectors 1880-1920,* 11-30. Exh. cat. The Montreal Museum of Fine Arts, December 8, 1990, to February 15, 1990. Montreal: Montreal Museum of Fine Arts, 1989.
Brown, David Blayney. *Turner and Byron.* London: Tate Gallery Publications, 1992.
Hayes, John. *British Paintings of the Sixteenth through Nineteenth Centuries,* 283-85, repro. 285. The Collections of the National Gallery of Art Systematic Catalogue. Washington, D.C.: National Gallery of Art, 1992.
Warrell, Ian. *Turner in Venice*, 207-15. Exhibition at Tate Britain, London, October 9, 2003-January 11, 2004. London: Tate Publishing, 2003.

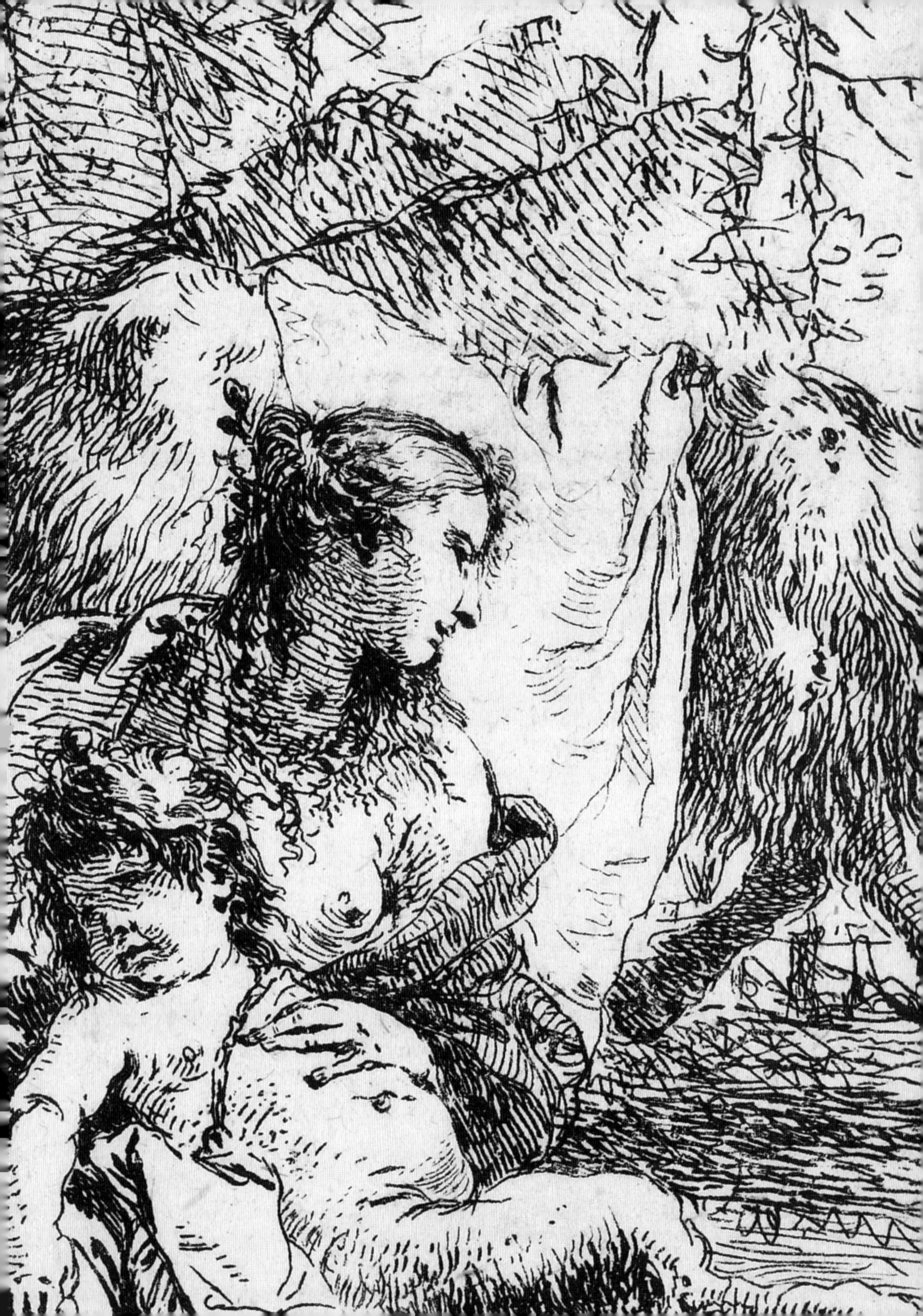

Works on Paper

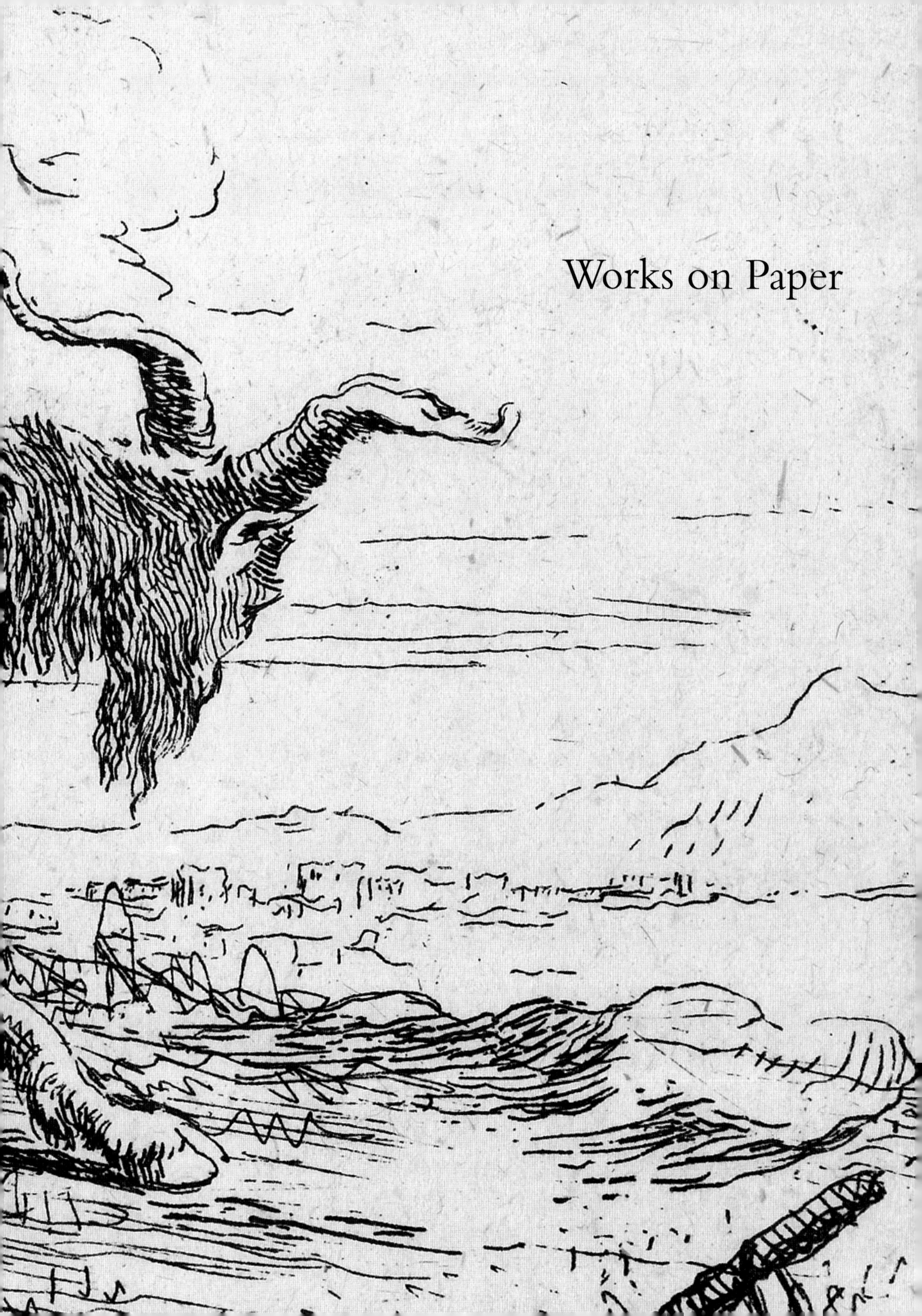

CATS. 51–62

Canaletto (Giovanni Antonio Canal) (Italian, 1697–1768)

Vedute / Altre prese da i Luoghi / altre ideate
(Views / Some after nature / others imagined)

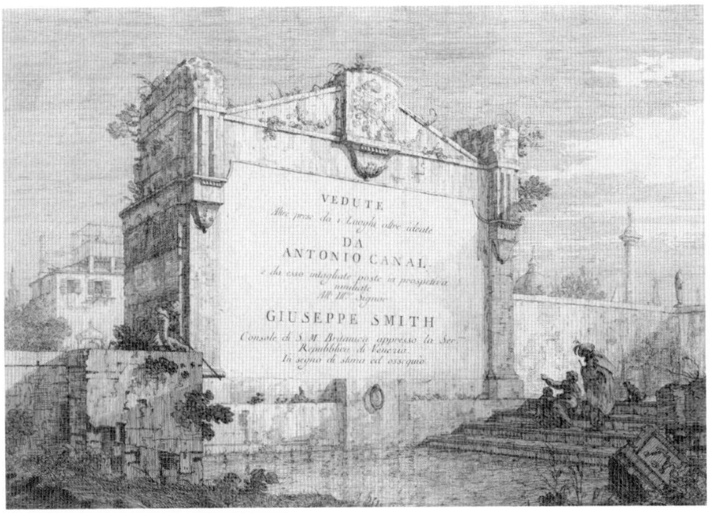

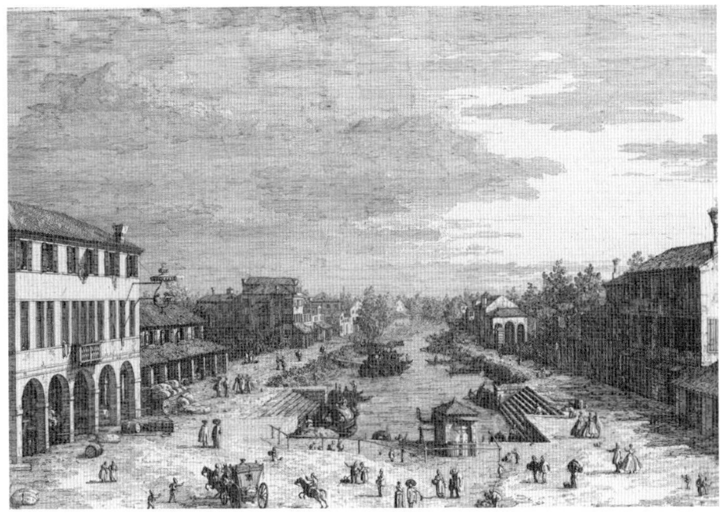

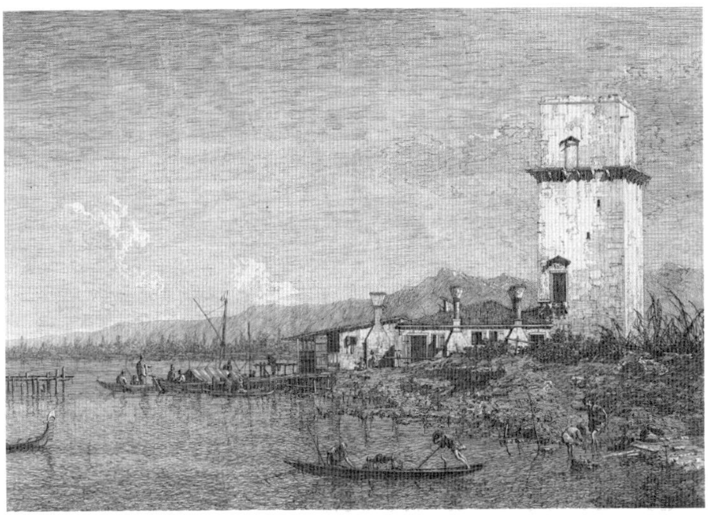

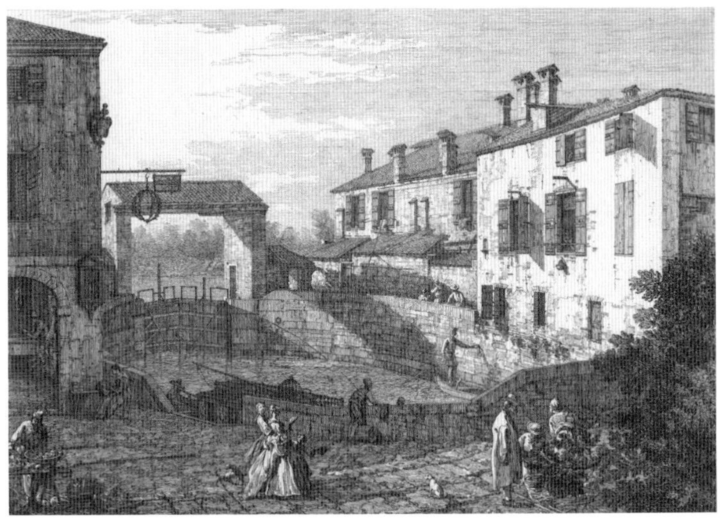

CAT. 51
Title Page, ca. 1744
Etching, $11\frac{5}{8}$ x $16\frac{13}{16}$ in. (29.6 x 42.7 cm) [Bromberg 1]
Lent by The Metropolitan Museum of Art, Rogers Fund, 1918 (18.65.1(1))
Image copyright The Metropolitan Museum of Art / Art Resource, NY

CAT. 52
The Tower of Malghera, ca. 1741–44
Etching, $5\frac{3}{4}$ x $8\frac{3}{8}$ in. (14.5 x 21.2 cm) [Bromberg 2]
The Cleveland Museum of Art. Gift of the Print Club of Cleveland, 1925.1239.2

CAT. 53
Mestre, ca. 1741–44
Etching, $11\frac{3}{4}$ x $16\frac{3}{4}$ in. (29.8 x 42.6 cm) [Bromberg 3]
Lent by The Metropolitan Museum of Art, Rogers Fund, 1918 (18.65.1(3))
Image copyright The Metropolitan Museum of Art/Art Resource, NY

CAT. 54
Le Porte del Dolo, ca. 1741–44
Etching, $11\frac{3}{4}$ x 16 3/4 in. (29.8 x 42.6 cm) [Bromberg 6]
Lent by The Metropolitan Museum of Art, Rogers Fund, 1918 (18.65.1(6))
Image copyright The Metropolitan Museum of Art/Art Resource, NY

Six of the etchings from Antonio Canaletto's *Views of Venice and Environs* series of prints that are included in this exhibition come from the Metropolitan Museum of Art and five come from the Cleveland Museum of Art, and one of the *Procuratie Niove and S. Geminiano Giustin* comes from the University of Toronto Art Centre. The descriptive title used by the Cleveland Museum of Art for the series is *Views of Venice and Environs,* while the first lines of the dedication on the title page read: *Vedute / Altre prese da i Luoghi / altre ideate* (*Views / Some after nature / others imagined*). These lines, or sometimes the first word (*Vedute*), are also used for the title of the series. The rest of this lengthy passage is "humbly" dedicated to the most illustrious Signor / Giuseppe (Joseph) Smith / Consul of his Britannic Majesty attached to the Most Serene / Republic of Venice / as a mark of esteem and homage." The inscribed date is also supported by the fact that Smith was appointed consul on June 6, 1744. Smith had arrived in Venice around 1700 and worked as an apprentice to the banker, merchant, and art collector Thomas Williams, who was also British consul in Venice at that time. Smith followed Williams's example and became an even more dedicated collector, dealer, art advisor, and agent. In 1729, he sold two paintings by Marco Ricci to Samuel Hill of Shenstone Park, and the following year corresponded with the same client about sending two Canaletto paintings. From this point on, Smith was the sole dealer and representative of one of the most talented topographical artists in Italy, whose paintings of Venice were sought after by visiting foreigners, especially the English. Smith found that etchings of works of art in his possession helped sell the works. In 1724, he had engravings made of some Sebastiano Ricci paintings. In 1735, he had a series of engravings by Antonio Visentini made after fourteen Canaletto paintings in his collection. On the title page, inscribed *Antonius Canale / Origine Civis / Venetus and Visentini,* he included a self portrait as well as one of a very handsome, self assured, and urbane Canaletto.

Some of the first important prints made for the tourist trade were carried out by Luca Carlevarijs, Canaletto's predecessor. Carlevarijs's *104 views of Venice* (*Le Fabbriche e Vedute di Veneia*) were published in 1703. This was followed by similar topographical views of the city in Domenico Lovisa's *Il Gran Teatro della Pitture e Prospettive in Venezia* (1720) and Visentini's *Prospectus Magni Canalis Venetiarum* (1735), a series of etchings after Canaletto's paintings of palaces along the Grand Canal in the collection of Joseph Smith. In 1741 Michele Marieschi published a series of twenty-one etched views of Venice. Gian Francesco Costa also produced a series of etchings of the villas of the Venetian aristocracy along the Brenta Canal (*Delizie del fiume Brenta*). Of this group of topographers, the most talented was Carlevarijs, whose treatment of the sky and atmospheric effects tends at times to be dramatic and expressive. However, none of the works of these artists could compete with Canaletto's extraordinary etching technique, in which visual poetry, fantasy, and natural light and atmospheric effects were created in a painterly manner with his etching stylus.

By the early 1740s, with the help of Joseph Smith, Canaletto had numerous commissions for various versions of his well-known views of Venetian subjects. Along with his father and his sister's son, Bernardo Bellotto, Canaletto must have had skilled studio assistants who could readily complete some or a large part of a commissioned painting of a familiar subject. In 1997, J. G. Links wrote agreeing with his predecessor, W. G. Constable, in acknowledging that it was possible to see "evidence of another hand" in a number of Canaletto's works from the "middle and late 1730s," but said that there was no evidence available "to suggest whose hand was at work."[1] Therefore, Constable simply described paintings as "by Canaletto" or "not by Canaletto" and only at times refers to a painting as a studio work. In the further study of Canaletto's works of the 1730s and 1740s, J. G. Links, B. A. Kowalczyk, Stefan Kozakiewicz, Edgar Peters Bowron, and Charles Beddington identified paintings, formerly attributed to Canaletto, as studio productions, copies by unknown artists, or in some of the more fortunate cases, as works by Bernardo

CATS. 51–62 Canaletto (Giovanni Antonio Canal) (Italian, 1697–1768)
Vedute / Altre prese da i Luoghi / altre ideate
(Views / Some after nature / others imagined)

CAT. 55
The Portico with a Lantern, ca. 1741–44
Etching, 11¾ x 16¹³⁄₁₆ in. (29.8 x 42.7 cm) [Bromberg 10]
Lent by The Metropolitan Museum of Art, Rogers Fund, 1918 (18.65.1 (10))

CAT. 56
Imaginary View of Padua, ca. 1741–44
Etching, 11¾ x 16¹³⁄₁₆ in. (29.8 x 42.7 cm) [Bromberg 11]
Lent by The Metropolitan Museum of Art, Rogers Fund, 1918 (18.65.1 (11))

CAT. 57
Imaginary View of Venice, 1741
Etching, 11¹³⁄₁₆ x 17⅛ in. (30 x 43.5 cm) [Bromberg 12]
Lent by The Metropolitan Museum of Art, Purchase, Gift of Mary V. T. Eberstadt and Bequest of Gertrude Moira Flanagan, by exchange, 1973 (1973.634)

CAT. 58
Procuratie Niove and S. Geminiano Giustin (S. Ziminian V[ence].), ca. 1741–44
Etching, 11¾ x 16¾ in. (29.8 x 42.6 cm) [Bromberg 25]
University of Toronto Art Collection, University of Toronto Art Centre, 1997.055

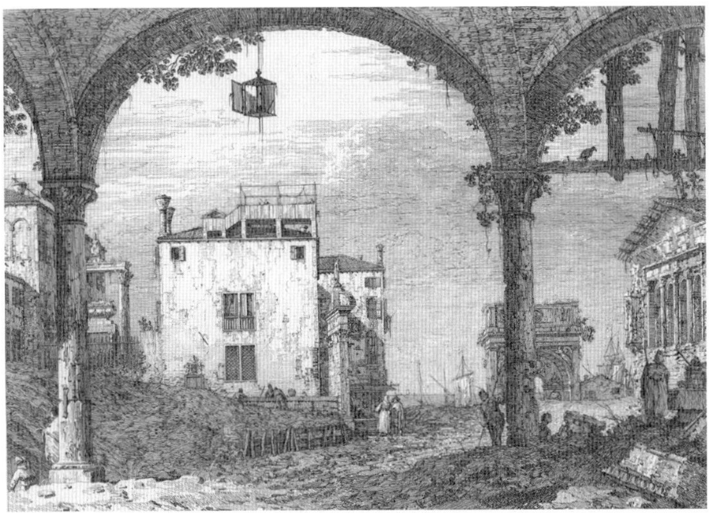

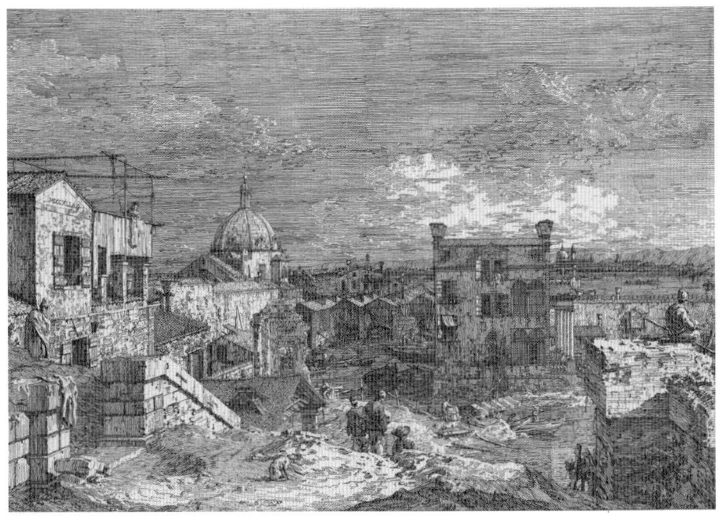

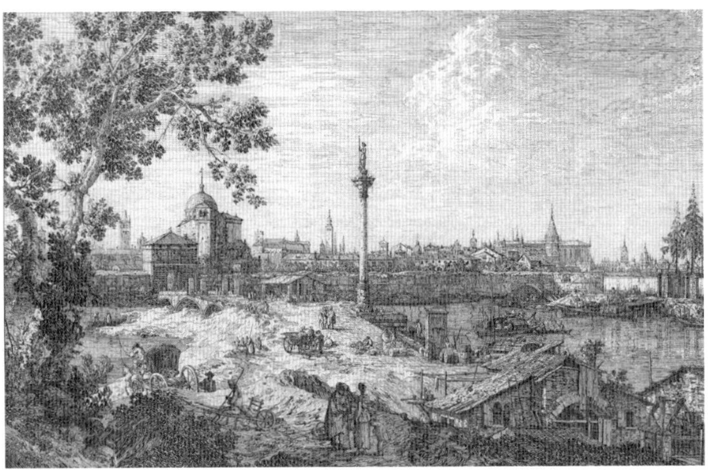

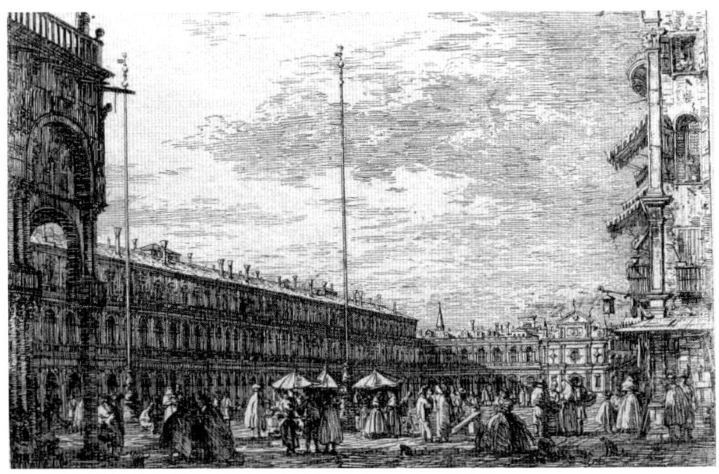

Bellotto. Links warns that "subsequent studies, after the pioneering studies of Canaletto by W. G. Constable, have emphasized the need for caution "in our pronouncements," implying that with "anything less than Canaletto at his best (still readily identifiable) or fully documented (very rare) there is no room for dogmatism."[2]

Because of the growing demand for Canaletto's work in the 1730s and 1740s and the related need for studio assistance, some specialists see evidence of studio production in many of his later works, a number of which are in North American collections. Works of this period are often more precise and at times mechanical compared with his early paintings. In 1740, at the height of his success, the War of the Austrian Succession began, and by 1742 it had spread to parts of Italy, producing a negative effect on Canaletto commissions because of the declining number of British aristocrats making the Grand Tour. Around 1741, Canaletto and his young protégé, Bernardo Bellotto, embarked on a sketching tour that may have started in Mestre (Bromberg, *Canaletto's Etchings,* cat. no. 3) and continued along the Brenta Canal. Shortly afterwards, Canaletto began a series of etchings of rural areas and towns along the Brenta between Fusina and Padua, with one of the most picturesque towns being Dolo, where the canal locks were located.[3] Canaletto must have felt, and rightfully so, that it was time to portray new and lesser known subjects in this area, as well as a combination of actual topography and fantasy subject matter, referred to as *veduta ideate.* Joseph Smith, concerned with declining sales of Canaletto's studio productions, possibly encouraged him to do a series of etchings after the sketches and observations of the rural areas and towns along the Brenta associated with the Palladian summer villas of the Venetian aristocracy.[4] With declining sales of Venice view paintings, perhaps Smith and Canaletto agreed that a series of etchings of rural and *villageatura* life along the canal would break with the repetitious pattern associated with past commissions for paintings of Venetian subject matter.

If Canaletto etched the title page of his *Vedute* last, then the series was completed in June 1744. The only other dated print in the series is found on the *Imaginary View of Venice,* Undivided Plate (Bromberg, cat. no. 12), inscribed 1741. In the etched series, there are only a few of the familiar Venetian architectural subjects—the Library, the Ducal Palace, the Prison, and S. Giorgio Maggiore. Compared with the size (about 29.3 x 42.3 cm) of the other real and imagined subjects making up the majority of the series, the four exhibited prints are relatively small. From The Cleveland Museum of Art, all four are printed on the same sheet.[5] A great deal of attention is given to street life in the Piazzetta, the open space between the Palace and the Library; the Riva degli Schiavoni, the quay in front of the Prison; and the Molo, the part of the same quay in front of the palace, the Library, and the Zecca (Mint). On the print of the Piazzetta side of the Ducal Palace, titled *La Piera del Bando, V*[enice], is a drum of a large Syrian porphyry column on the front corner of St. Mark's Basilica, from which a *comandador* announces a decree to a group of citizens. The same column drum is shown in the view of the Library on the Piazzetta, opposite the Doge's Palace.

One of the few larger etchings in the *Vedute* series of Venetian topography, *Procuratie Niove e S. Ziminian V*[enice](Bromberg, cat. no. 25), is in the University of Toronto Art Centre collection. It is a view of the Piazza S. Marco with the Procuratie Niove on the left and the church of S. Geminiano (*S. Ziminian* in Venetian dialect) at the far end of the Piazza. The church was destroyed during the Napoleonic period. Again, in this etching, a great deal of attention is given to human activity in the Piazza.

The majority of the large prints in this series are of mainland and *ideate* (partly imagined) subjects. Five of these prints in the exhibition are from The Metropolitan Museum of Art, and one, of the Tower of Malghera is from The Cleveland Museum of Art. These prints were placed at the beginning of the series: a view of Mestre (Bromberg, cat. no. 3), Dolo on the Brenta Canal

CATS. 51–62 Canaletto (Giovanni Antonio Canal) (Italian, 1697–1768)

Vedute / Altre prese da i Luoghi / altre ideate
(*Views / Some after nature / others imagined*)

CAT. 59
The Library, Venice, ca. 1741–44
Etching, 5¾ x 8⅜ in. (14.5 x 21.2 cm) [Bromberg 18]
The Cleveland Museum of Art. Gift of The Print Club of Cleveland 1925.1239.15

CAT. 60
The Stone of Proclamation at Venice
(*La Piera del Bando, V[ence].*), ca. 1741–44
Etching, 5¾ x 8⅜ in. (14.5 x 21.2 cm) [Bromberg 19]
The Cleveland Museum of Art. Gift of The Print Club of Cleveland 1925.1239.16

CAT. 61
The Market at the Molo, ca. 1741–44
Etching, 5¾ x 8⅜ in. (14.5 x 21.2 cm) [Bromberg 20]
The Cleveland Museum of Art. Gift of The Print Club of Cleveland 1925.1239.17

CAT. 62
The Prison, Venice, ca. 1741–44
Etching, 5¾ x 8⅜ in. (14.5 x 21.2 cm) [Bromberg 21]
The Cleveland Museum of Art. Gift of The Print Club of Cleveland 1925.1239.18

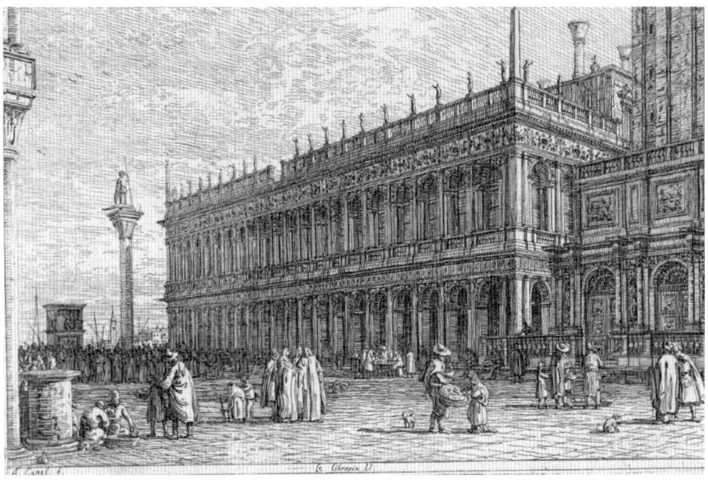

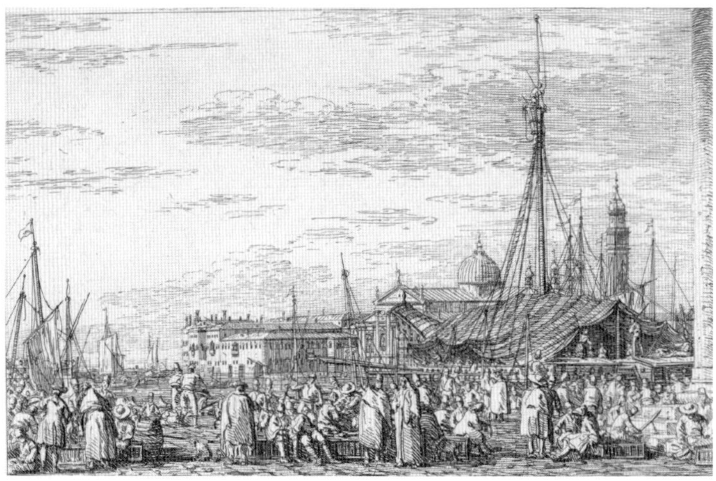

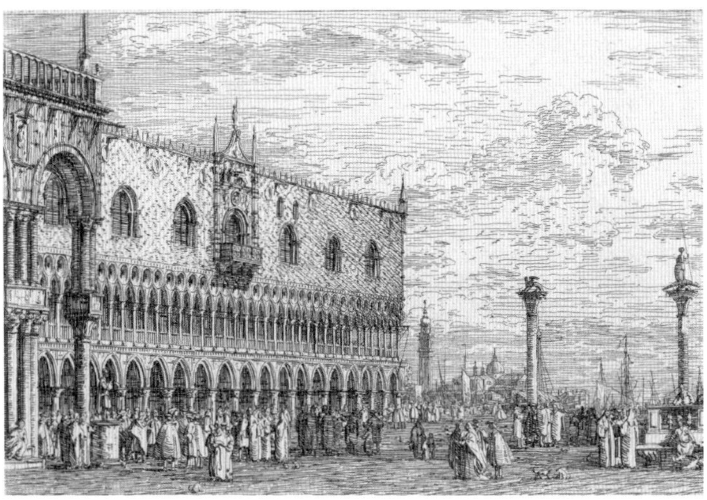

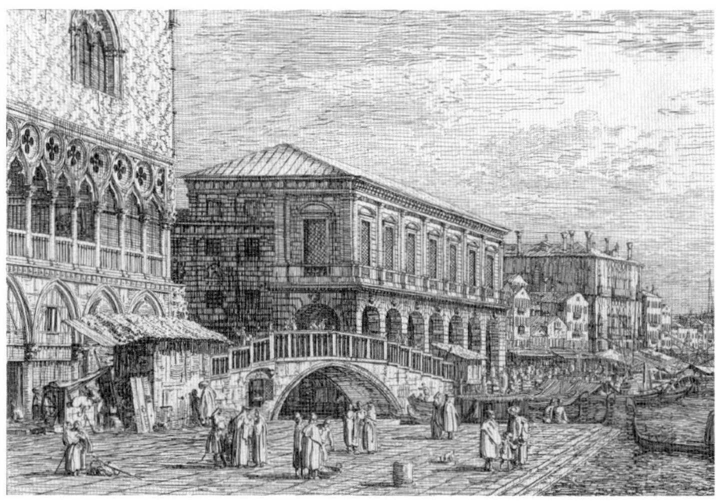

(Bromberg, cat. no 6), imaginary views of Padua (Bromberg, cat. no. 11) and Venice (Bromberg, cat. no 12), with other partly imagined and fantasy subjects, such as *The Portico with the Lantern* (Bromberg, cat. no 10).

The print following the title page is of a fifteenth-century fortress tower on an island between Venice and the mainland, known as the Tower of Malghera (*La Torre di Malghera,* cat. no. 2), which was built on a strategic island to protect Venice from a mainland invasion. Canaletto gives careful attention to incidental details of fishermen capturing eels in shallow water and a fishing boat with men setting their nets. Many times these etched details are reworked, made darker, or burnished out and made lighter in the second state of the print.

In 1795, J. M. W. Turner, along with other young English artists, including the watercolorist Thomas Girtin (1775-1802), made copies of Canaletto drawings and perhaps prints in Dr. Monroe's house in the Adelphi Terrace, London, not far from the place where Canaletto portrayed views of the Thames near Somerset House. Both Turner and Girtin were influenced by Canaletto, who freely sketched and etched lines with firm control of the pen and etching needle. About this time, because of patronage of the Earl of Essex, the cousin of the Duke of Bedford, Turner might have seen the large collection of Canaletto's paintings that hung in the duke's Bloomsbury (London) home. While it is not certain that at this early date Turner saw any of the thirty-one etchings of Canaletto's *Vedute*, among Turner's sketches related to his 1833 visit to Venice there is one of *La Piera del Bando, V*[enice]. Like Canaletto, Turner painted the country houses of the English landed gentry and would have had opportunities to see Canaletto's paintings in these private collections. Also, Turner would have known of the outstanding Canalettos in the collections of William Beckford, the Earl of Ashburnham, and in Sir John Soane's Museum in London.[6]

Hardy George

Notes

1 J. G. Links, *A Supplement to W. G. Constable's, Canaletto* (London: Pallas Athene Arts, 1998: viii).

2 Ibid.

3 Andria Derstine, "Views of Dolo by Canaletto, Bellotto, Cimaroli and Guardi," *The Burlington Magazine* 146, no. 1219, *Art in Italy* (Oct. 2004): 675-82, has used Canaletto's views of Dolo in the *Veduta* series of etchings to help identify topographical details concerning the destruction and rebuilding of the church at Dolo, in order to properly identify and date Canaletto's painting of *Dolo on the Brenta*, ca. 1741-44 (Ashmolean Museum, Oxford), as well as Bernardo Bellotto's *Dolo on the Brenta,* ca. 1742-43 (Private collection, England). This recent article reinforces the opinion that Canaletto made a trip along the Brenta canal with his newphew, Bernardo Bellotto, "around 1741" and that the *Vedute* etchings date ca. 1741-44.

4 For complete coverage of Canaletto's formulation of the *veduta ideate* and Joseph Smith's encouragement with commissions for the series of prints, and a group of thirteen overdoors of "Venetian sites in fanciful settings," see William Barcham, "Canaletto and a Commission from Consul Smith," *The Art Bulletin* 59, no. 3 (Sept. 1977): 383-93.

5 In 1926 the Print Department of the Cleveland Museum of Art was given a set of thirty-one etchings of Canaletto's *Vedute* by The Print Club (Theodore Sizer, *The Bulletin of the Cleveland Museum of Art* 13, no. 6 [June 1926]: 143). At this time, it was one of the most complete sets of the *Vedute* in American collections. The most complete series, containing thirty-two prints, was in the Berlin Museum (Kupferstichkabinett, Berlin-Dahlem Museum). Ruth Bromberg, *Canaletto's Etchings* (London and New York: Sotheby Parke Bernet, 1974: 28) used the Kupferstichkabinett, Berlin album to help work out the sequence of Canaletto's *Vedute* etchings. According to Bromberg four etchings in this exhibition, *la libreria V*[enice] (Bromberg, cat. no. 18); *La Piera del Bando V*[enice] (Bromberg, cat. no.19); *The Market on the Molo V*[enice] (Bromberg, cat. no. 20), and *le Preson V*[enice] (Bromberg, cat. no. 21) are on one sheet: "in the albums most small format etching are printed four to a sheet," Bromberg, *Canaletto's Etchings* (London and New York: Sotheby Parke Bernet, 1974: 33).

6 Ian Warrell, *Turner and Venice*, Exhibition at Tate Britain, London, October 9, 2003-January 11, 2004(London: Tate Publishing, 2003: 43-4).

Bibliography

Zanetti, Antonio Maria. *Della Pittura Veneziana.* Venice: Nella Stamperia di G. Albrizzi, 1771.

Meyer, Rudolph. *Die beiden Canaletto.* Dresden: Verlag des Verfassers, 1878.

Vesme, Alexandre de. *Le peintre-graveur italien.* Milan: Hoepli, 1906.

Lorenzetti, Giulio. *Un dilettante incidore veneziano del XVIII secolo.* Venice, 1917.

Fritzsche, Hellmuth Allwill, "*Kleine Ergänzungen zum Oeuvre-katalog der Radierungen Antonio Canals in A. de Vesme, Le Peintre-Graveur Italien,* 1906," in "*Mitteilungen der Gesellschaft für vervielfältigende Kunst,*" *Beilage der Graphischen Künste* 4: 74-8 (Wien, 1929); no. 2/3: 49-52 (Wien, 1930).

Palluchini, Rodolfo. *Le Aquefortidel Canaletto.* Venice: Guarnati, 1945.

Parker, K. T. *Canaletto Drawings at Windsor Castle.* Oxford and London: Phaidon Press, 1948

Watson, F. J. B. *Canaletto.* London: Elek, 1949.

Moschini, Vittorio. *Canaletto.* Milan: Giunti-Martello, 1954.

Pignatti, Terisio. *Il Quaderno di Disegni del Canaletto alle Gallerie di Venezia.* Milan: Guarnati, 1958.

Weinhardt, Carl J. Jr. "Canaletto: Master Etcher," *The Metropolitan Museum of Art Bulletin,* n.s., 17, no. 3 (Nov. 1958): 77-87.

Kainen, Jacob. *The Etchings of Canaletto.* Washington, D.C.: Smithsonian Press, 1967.

Salamon, Harry. *Catalogo completo delle incisioni di Giovanni Antonio Canal detto Il Canaletto.* Milan: Salamon and Agustoni, 1971.

Vivian, Frances. *Il Console Smith mercante e collezionista.* Venice: N. Pozza, 1971.

Russell, H. Diane. *Rare Etchings by G. B. & G. D. Tiepolo* Washington, D.C.: National Gallery of Art, 1972.

Bromberg, Ruth. *Canaletto's Etchings: A Catalogue and Study Illustrating and Describing the Known States, Including Those Hitherto Unrecorded,* London and New York: Sotheby Parke Bernet, 1974.

Barcham, William. "Canaletto and a Commission from Consul Smith," *The Art Bulletin* 59 (1977): 383-93.

Byam Shaw, James, ed. *Canaletto: Disegni—dipinti- incisioni.* Exh. cat. Venice: Fondazione Cini, 1982.

Stanton, Lindsay. *Turner's Venice.* New York: George Braziller, Inc., 1985.

Martineau, Jane, and Andrew Robison. *Glory of Venice: Art in the Eighteenth Century.* New Haven, Conn.: Yale University Press, 1994.

Beddington, Charles. "Canaletto: Una Venecia imaginaria," *The Burlington Magazine* 144 (2002): 34-5.

Warrell, Ian. *Turner and Venice*, Exhibition at Tate Britain, London, October 9, 2003-January 11, 2004. London: Tate Publishing, 2003.

Derstine, Andria. "Views of Dolo by Canaletto, Bellotto, Cimaroli and Guardi," *The Burlington Magazine* 146 (2004): 675-82.

CATS. 63-69 GIOVANNI BATTISTA TIEPOLO (Italian, 1796-1770)
Scherzi di Fantasia

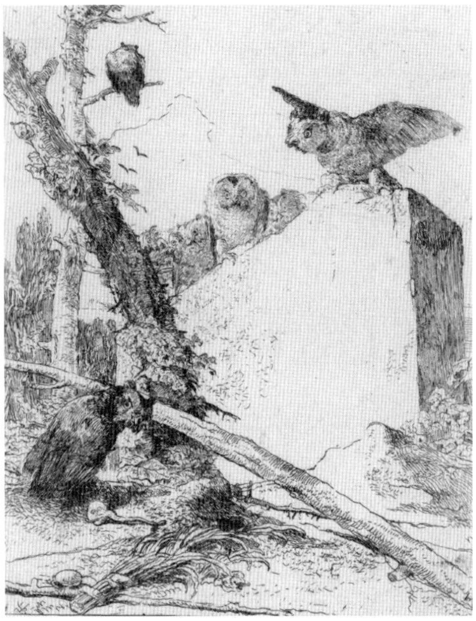

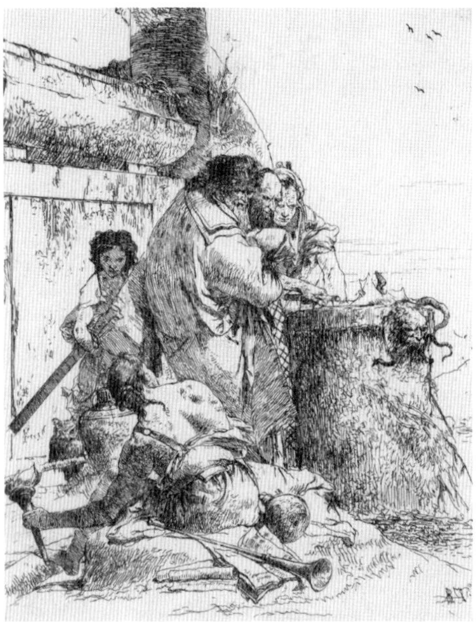

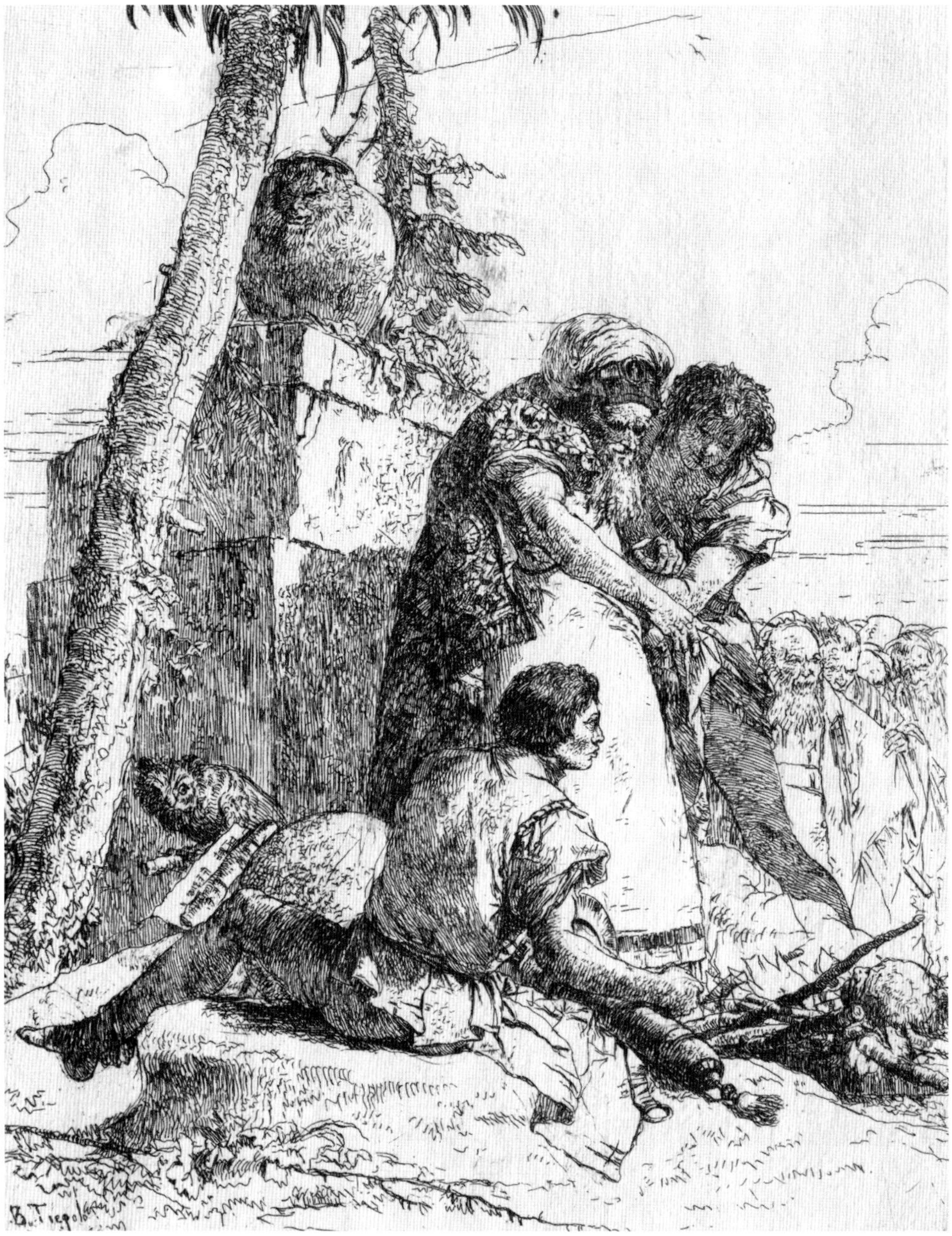

CAT. 63
Frontispiece, ca. 1743-50
Etching, 8⅞ x 7³⁄₁₆ in. (22.6 x 18.2 cm framed) [First state of two]
Lent by The Metropolitan Museum of Art, Purchase, The Elisha Whittelsey Collection, The Elisha Whittelsey Fund; Dodge and Pfeiffer Funds; Joseph Pulitzer Bequest; Gift of Bertina Suida Manning and Robert L. Manning, 1976 (1976.537 (1))
Image copyright The Metropolitan Museum of Art/Art Resource, NY

CAT. 64
Three Magicians Burning a Snake, ca. 1743-50
Etching, 9 x 7¹⁄₁₆ in. (22.8 x 18 cm) [First state of two]
Lent by The Metropolitan Museum of Art, Purchase, The Elisha Whittelsey Collection, The Elisha Whittelsey Fund; Dodge and Pfeiffer Funds; Joseph Pulitzer Bequest; Gift of Bertina Suida Manning and Robert L. Manning, 1976 (1976.537 (13))
Image copyright The Metropolitan Museum of Art/Art Resource, NY

CAT. 65
Magician Pointing Out a Burning Head to Two Youths, ca. 1743-50
Etching, 8⅞ x 7¼ in. (22.6 x 18.5 cm) [Second state, numbered 4]
The Cleveland Musuem of Art. Andrew R. and Martha Holden Jennings Fund, 1998.113

The etchings of Giambattista Tiepolo present a series of intriguing problems, which are far from resolved. The first concerns their meaning and iconography, and the source of their inspiration. The second principal problem is that of their dating, and the question of which of the two series, the twenty-two etchings of the *Scherzi* or the ten etchings of the *Capricci*, has priority.

Their source of inspiration lies in the seventeenth century, in the etchings of Salvator Rosa (1615-1673) and Giovanni Benedetto Castiglione (1609-1664). There we find the interest in magic and witchcraft, the apparatus of skulls and serpents, flaming altars, and the occasional satyr or punchinello. What all this means is still debateable.

The *Scherzi di Fantasia* were first published as such when listed under this name on the title page or frontispiece to the series, which also refers to the death of Giambattista in Madrid, and hence publication was later than 1770. They were also included in the various editions of Domenico Tiepolo's volume of the Tiepolo etchings of 1774-78,[1] which led to the suggestion that at least some of the plates might belong to the Spanish years, the last eight years of Giambattista's life. This dating was effectively contradicted by a series of documents published by Lisa Christina Frerichs,[2] which showed that twenty of the *Scherzi* etchings were sent to the renowned collector and dealer Pierre-Jean Mariette in Paris by Domenico Tiepolo in 1757. Internal evidence suggested a date pre-Würzburg.[3] And the evidence of the drawings in London suggested a date in the early 1740s. The drawings also indicated no difference in the style of studies linked with the *Scherzi* and those linked with the *Capricci* etchings.

This evidence and other factors led to the conclusion adopted by Aldo Ricci and continued here, that the etchings belong to a single burst of Tiepolo's creativity, in the early 1740s, with the *Scherzi* preceding the *Capricci* series.

The *Scherzi* etchings are much more varied and experimental in style and subject matter than the *Capricci*. In both cases Giambattista made corrections to some proof impressions,[4] but it is interesting to note that in the case of the *Capricci* etchings, these corrections were transferred to the plates, which appear to have been a direct commission from Anton Maria Zanetti, to whom they passed at an early date. A similar urgency in the case of the *Scherzi* was evidently lacking.

George Knox

Notes

1 For a full analysis see Dario Succi, "Le quattro edizioni del *Catalogo* pubblicate da Giandomenico," in *I Tiepolo: virtuosismo e ironis* (Torino: Umberto Allemandi, 1988: 40-4). See also the exh. cat. by Dario Succi, *Giambattista Tiepolo: il segno e l'enigma* (Venice: Castello di Gorizia, 1985: 58-62).

2 Lina Christina Frerichs, "Mariette et les eaux-fortes de Tiepolo," *Gazette des Beaux-Arts* 6, no. 78 (1971): 233-250; Lina Christina Frerichs, "Nouvelles sources pour la connaissance de l'activité de graveur des trois Tiepolo," *Nouvelles de l'Estampe* (1971): 413 ff.

3 Three reproductive etchings by Domenico are referred to, in a document cited by Frerichs (see "Mariette," 235), as *fatto posteriormente* (made later) with respect to the *Scherzi*. These include the *St. James of Compostela*, which was completed and sent to London in 1750.

4 Such corrections are noted by Diane Russell, *Rare Etchings by Giovanni Battista and Giovanni Domenico Tiepolo* (Washington, D.C.: National Gallery of Art, 1972: pls. 20, 21, 28, 32, 33, 35, 36), all *Scherzi* from the Rosenwald Albums of Tiepolo etchings, presented to the National Gallery of Art by Lessing J. Rosenwald, which also belonged to Zanetti. Such corrections to the *Capricci* are not found in the Rosenwald Album, but I noticed such a corrected impression in the equally magnificent but unpublished Beurdeley Album of Tiepolo etchings in the Hermitage, which came from the collection of Alfred Beurdeley (1847-1919) in Paris (see Russell, *Rare Etchings*, illus. on p. 43). The corrections are transferred to the plate, and the signature added (Russell, *Rare Etchings*, pl. 4).

Exhibition

Giambattista Tiepolo: il segno e l'enigma, exh. cat. by Dario Succi, Castello di Gorizia, 1985, 126-73.

Bibliography

Knox, George. *Catalogue of the Tiepolo Drawings in the Victoria and Albert Museum*, 22-6, pls. 102-28. London: H. M. Stationery Office, 1960.

Pignatti, Teresio. *Le acqueforti del Tiepolo*, pls. XIV-XXXV. Florence: La Nuova Italia, 1965.

Rizzi, Aldo. *The Etchings of the Tiepolos*, pls. 5-26. London: Phaidon Press, 1971.

Frerichs, Lina Christina. "Mariette et les eaux-fortes des Tiepolo," *Gazette des Beaux-Arts* (Oct. 1971): 233-51.

Russell, Diane. *Rare Etchings by Giovanni Battista and Giovanni Domenico Tiepolo*, pls. 12-39. Washington, D.C.: National Gallery of Art, 1972.

Knox, George. "G. B. Tiepolo: The Dating of the 'Scherzi di Fantasia' and the 'Capricci,'" *Burlington Magazine* 119 (Dec. 1972): 837-42.

CATS. 63–69 GIOVANNI BATTISTA TIEPOLO (Italian, 1796–1770)
Scherzi di Fantasia

CAT. 66
Seated Magician, Boy and Four Figures, ca. 1743–50
Etching, 8⅞ x 7 in. (22.5 x 17.9 cm) [Second state, numbered 5]
The Cleveland Museum of Art. Gift of Leonard C. Hanna, Jr., 1924.528

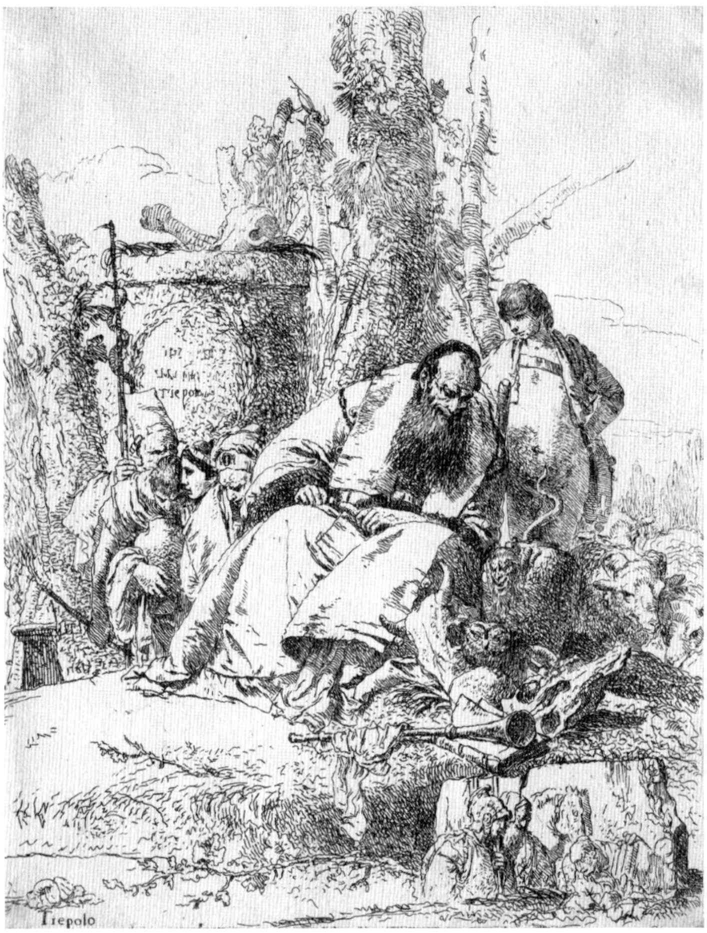

CAT. 67
The Happy Satyr and His Family, ca. 1743–50
Etching, 8⅞ x 10 in. (22.4 x 25.4 cm) [Second state, numbered 10]
The Cleveland Museum of Art. Gift of Leonard C. Hanna, Jr., 1924.530

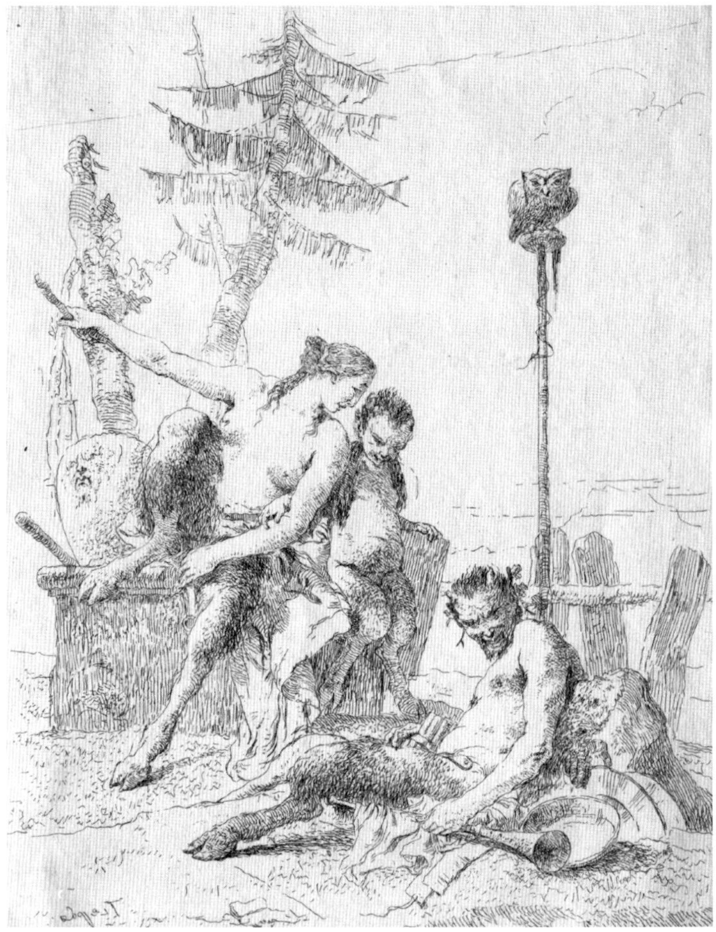

CAT. 68

Satyr Family with the Obelisk, ca. 1743–50

Etching, 8⅞ x 6⅞ in. (22.5 x 17.7 cm) [Second state, numbered 11]

The Cleveland Museum of Art. Gift of Leonard C. Hanna, Jr., 1924.529

CAT. 69

The Discovery of the Tomb of Punchinello, ca. 1743–50

Etching, 9⅛ x 7³⁄₁₆ in. (23.1 x 18.2 cm) [Second state, numbered 17]

Lent by The Metropolitan Museum of Art, Purchase, The Elisha Whittelsey Collection, The Elisha Whittelsey Fund; Dodge and Pfeiffer Funds; Joseph Pulitzer Bequest; Gift of Bertina Suida Manning and Robert L. Manning, 1976 (1976.537 (17))

Image copyright The Metropolitan Museum of Art/Art Resource, NY

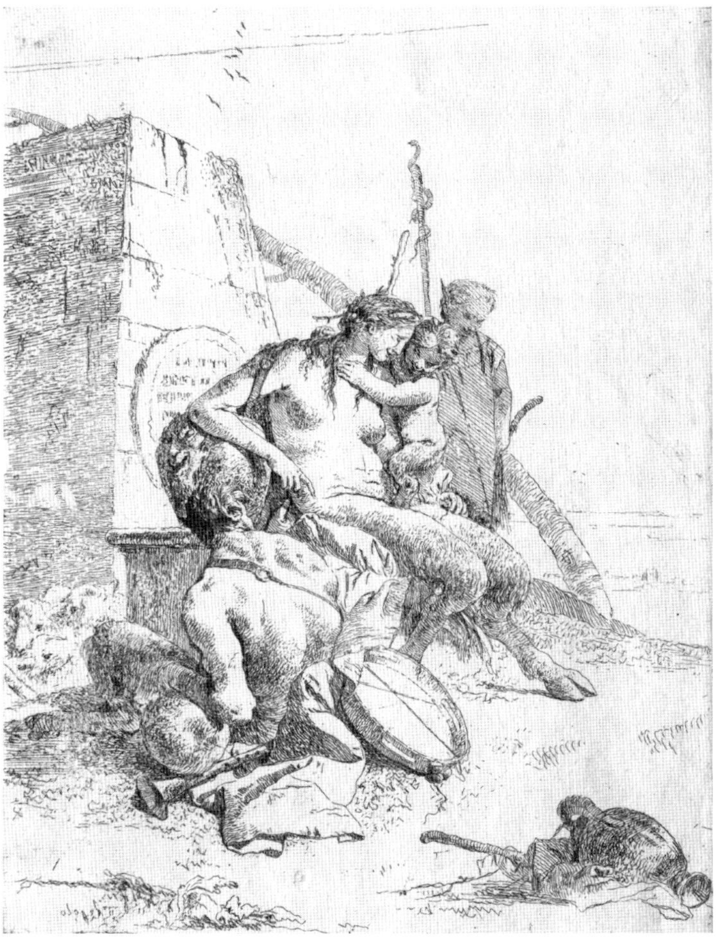

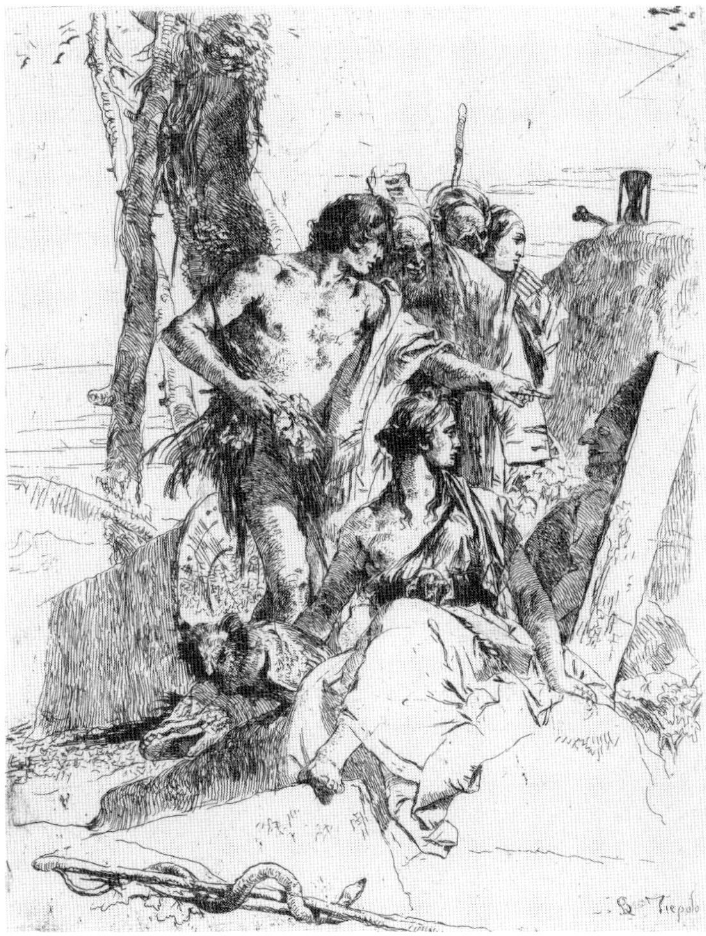

CATS. 70–80 **GIOVANNI BATTISTA TIEPOLO (Italian, 1796–1770)**
Vari Capricci

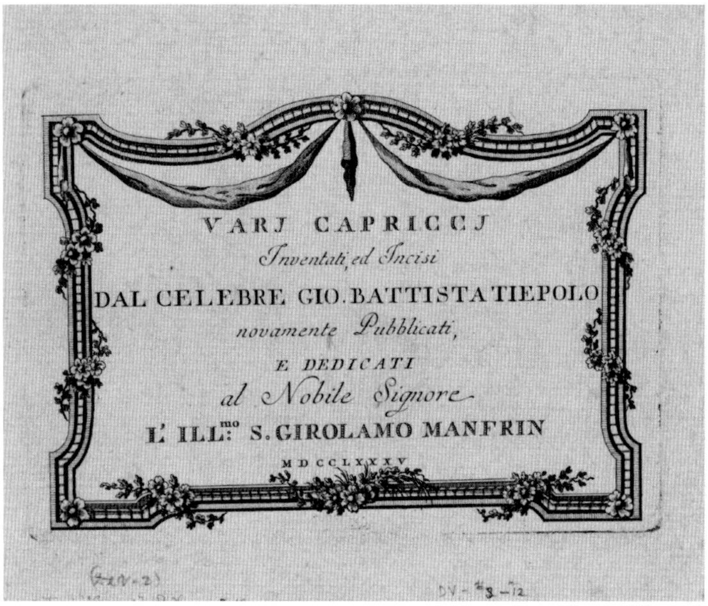

CAT. 70
Title Page, 1785
Etching, $4\frac{7}{16}$ x $6\frac{7}{16}$ in. (11.3 x 16.4 cm)
Fine Arts Museums of San Francisco,
Achenbach Foundation for Graphic Arts

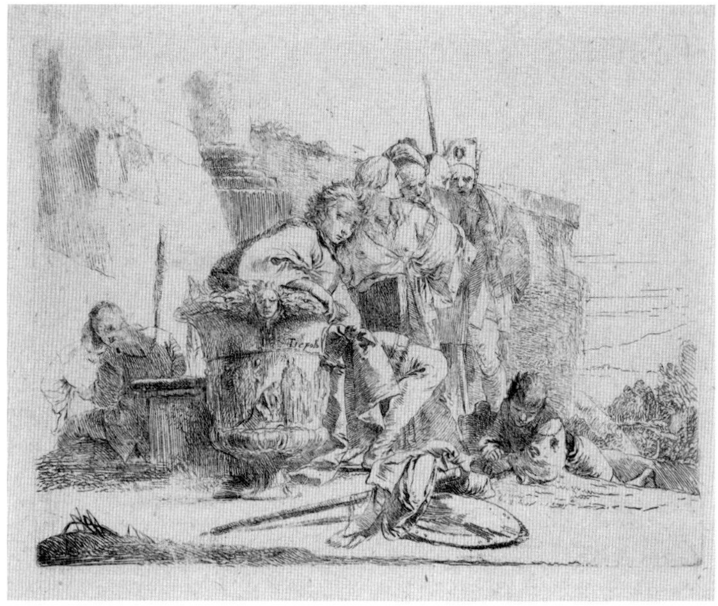

CAT. 71
Seated Youth Leaning Against an Urn, 1785
Etching, $5\frac{1}{2}$ x $7\frac{1}{8}$ in. (14.1 x 18 cm) [de Vesme 3]
Fine Arts Museums of San Francisco, Achenbach Foundation for Graphic Arts

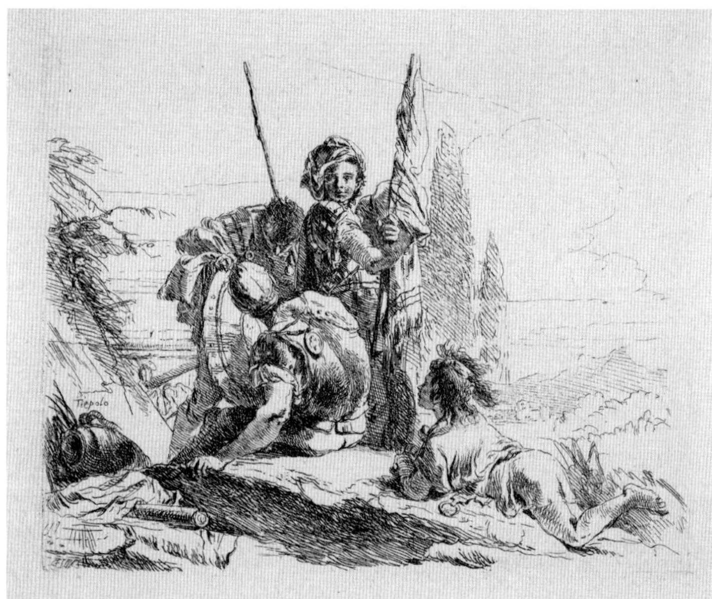

Cat. 72
Three Soldiers and a Boy, 1785
Etching, $5\frac{9}{16}$ x $6\frac{15}{16}$ in. (14.1 x 17.6 cm) [de Vesme 4]
Fine Arts Museums of San Francisco, Achenbach Foundation for Graphic Arts

The title of the series of ten etchings, *Vari Capricci*, derives from the edition dedicated to Giralomo Manfrin of 1785, which has a title page identifying it as such. It appears that these etchings were commissioned by Anton Maria Zanetti the Elder (1680-1767) in the 1740s, who incorporated them in some copies of his collection of chiaroscuro woodcuts after Parmegianino. One copy of Zanetti's work, including the *Capricci* by Tiepolo, is dated 1749, with a dedication to the Prince of Liechtenstein, drawing attention to the new addition. This 1749 date was generally accepted as a definitive date for the etchings, and by this time the plates had passed out of the control of the Tiepolo family. Nothing new is heard of them until 1785, when the Manfrin edition appeared. In 1972, Maria Santifaller drew attention to a copy of the Zanetti work at Dresden, with the ten etchings removed, with the date 1743.[1]

The *Capricci* and the *Scherzi* etchings are very different. Assuming that the *Capricci* were a commission by Zanetti (presumably based upon an enthusiasm for the *Capricci*, for what other reason could there be?), the ten *Capricci* are much more even in style and content. Gone, almost entirely, are the owls and serpents, and the ancient wizards and sorcerers. One infant satyr makes a brief appearance, and the only grotesque item is *Death Giving an Audience*. Other scenes, like *The Rider Standing Beside His Horse,* are relatively mundane.

In both the *Scherzi* and *Capricci* etchings Giambattista made corrections to some proof impressions, in an exactly similar way,[2] but it is interesting to note that in the case of the *Capricci*, these corrections were transferred to the plates before they passed to Zanetti. A similar urgency in the case of the *Scherzi* was evidently lacking.

The thematic material of the etchings only appears elsewhere in the paintings of Giambattista among the three oval decorations that are associated with the Tasso Room of Ca' Manin of 1742.[3] This helps to confirm 1743 as the year of the etchings.

George Knox

Notes

1 Maria Santifaller, "*Carl Heinrich von Heineken e le acqueforti di Giambattista Tiepolo a Dresda,*" *Arte Veneta* 26 (1972). Heineken had noted the existence of this edition in his *Idée générale* of 1771, and this had been noted in an article by Lisa Christina Frerichs. (see "Mariette et les eaux-fortes des Tiepolo," *Gazette des Beaux-Arts* [Oct. 1971]: 239 and n. 14).

2 Such corrections are noted by Diane Russell in *Rare Etchings by Giovanni Battista and Giovanni Domenico Tiepolo* (Washington, D.C.: National Gallery of Art, 1972: pls. 20, 21, 28, 32, 33, 35, 36), all *Scherzi* from the Rosenwald Albums of Tiepolo etchings, which also belonged to Zanetti, presented by Lessing J. Rosenwald to the National Gallery of Art. Such corrections to the *Capricci* are not found in the Rosenwald Album, but I noticed such a corrected impression in the equally magnificent but unpublished Beurdeley Album of Tiepolo etchings in the Hermitage, formerly in the collection of Alfred Beurdeley (1847-1919) of Paris (Russell, *Rare Etchings,* illus. on p. 43). The corrections are transferred to the plate, and the signature added (Russell, *Rare Etchings,* pl. 4).

3 George Knox, "The Tasso Cycles of Giambattista Tiepolo and Gianantonio Guardi," *Museum Studies* 9, The Art Institute of Chicago (1978): pls. 12-14; Exh. cat. *Giambattista Tiepolo,* ed. Keith Christiansen (New York: The Metropolitan Museum of Art, 1996: pls. 17e, f, g, note also the drawing); George Knox. *Catalogue of the Tiepolo Drawings* (London: Victoria and Albert Museum, 1975: cat. no. 24).

Exhibition

Giambattista Tiepolo: il segno e l'enigma, exh. cat. by Dario Succi, Castello di Gorizia, 1985, 111-22.

Bibliography

Vesme, Alexandre de. *Le peintre-graveur italien.* Milan: Hoepli, 1906.

Knox, George. *Catalogue of the Tiepolo Drawings in the Victoria and Albert Museum*, 22-6, pls. 102-28. London: H. M. Stationery Office, 1960.

Pignatti, Terisio. *Le acqueforti del Tiepolo*, pls. XIV-XXXV. Florence: La Nuova Italia, 1965.

Rizzi, Aldo. *The Etchings of the Tiepolos,* pls. 5-26. London: Phaidon Press, 1971.

Frerichs, Lina Christina. "Mariette et les eaux-fortes des Tiepolo," *Gazette des Beaux-Arts* (Oct. 1971): 233-51.

Russell, Diane. *Rare Etchings by Giovanni Battista and Giovanni Domenico Tiepolo*, pls. 12-39. Washington, D.C.: National Gallery of Art, 1972.

George Knox, "G. B. Tiepolo: The dating of the 'Scherzi di Fantasia' and the 'Capricci,'" *Burlington Magazine* 119 (Dec. 1972): 837-42.

CATS. 70–80 Giovanni Battista Tiepolo (Italian, 1796–1770)
Vari Capricci

CAT. 73
Women and Men Regarding a Burning Pyre of Bones, 1785
Etching, $5\frac{5}{8}$ x $6\frac{7}{8}$ in. (14.28 x 17.46 cm) [de Vesme 5]
National Gallery of Art, Washington. Gift of W. G. Russell Allen, 1941.8.29

CAT. 74
A Woman with Her Hands on a Vase, a Soldier and a Slave, 1785
Etching, $5\frac{7}{16}$ x $6\frac{15}{16}$ in. (13.8 x 17.6 cm) [de Vesme 6]
Fine Arts Museums of San Francisco, Achenbach Foundation for Graphic Arts

CAT. 75
A Nymph with a Small Satyr and Two Goats, 1785
Etching, $5\frac{1}{2}$ x $6\frac{13}{16}$ in. (14.1 x 17.4 cm) [de Vesme 7]
Fine Arts Museums of San Francisco, Achenbach Foundation for Graphic Arts

CAT. 76
Standing Philosopher, 1785
Etching, $5\frac{1}{4}$ x $6\frac{13}{16}$ in. (13.4 x 17.4 cm) [de Vesme 8]
Fine Arts Museums of San Francisco, Achenbach Foundation for Graphic Arts

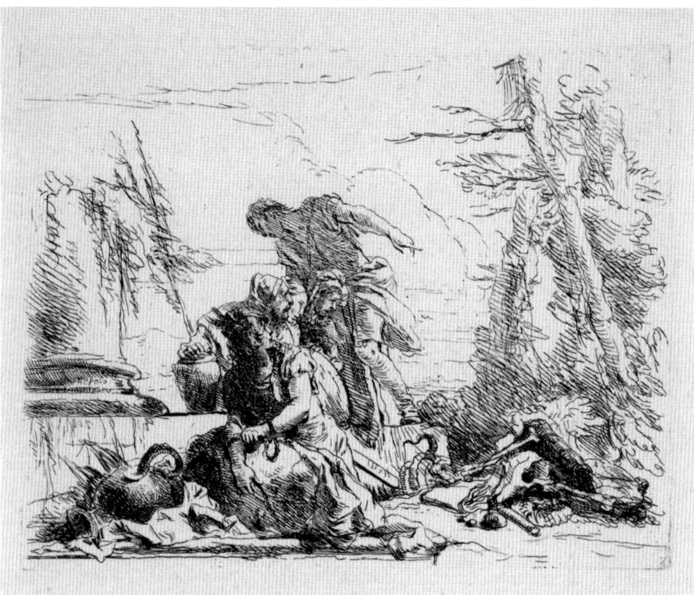

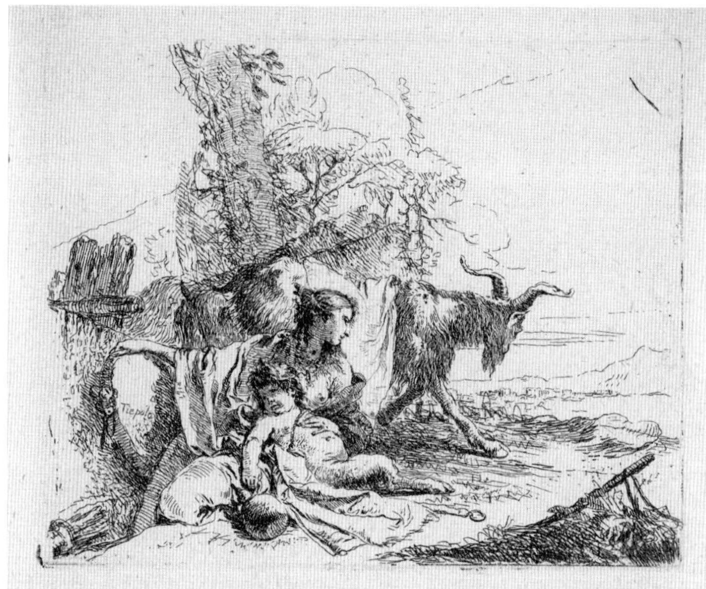

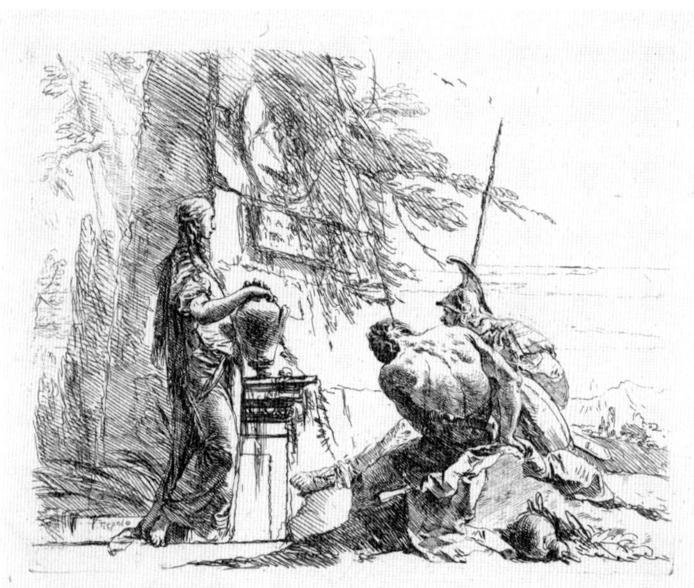

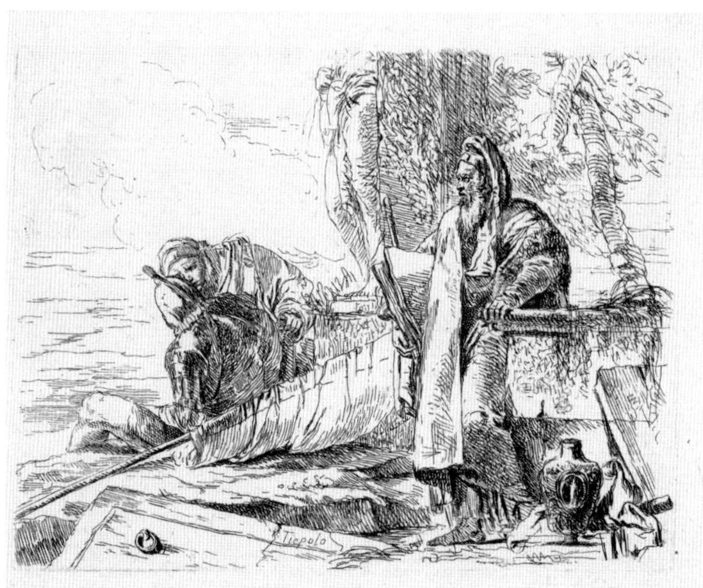

CAT. 77

Two Soldiers and Two Women, 1785

Etching, 5 15/16 x 6 11/16 in. (13.2 x 17 cm) [de Vesme 9]

Fine Arts Museums of San Francisco, Achenbach Foundation for Graphic Arts

CAT. 78

Death Giving an Audience, 1785

Etching, 5 1/2 x 6 15/16 in. (14.1 x 17.7 cm) [de Vesme 10]

Fine Arts Museums of San Francisco, Achenbach Foundation for Graphic Arts

CAT. 79

The Astrologer and the Young Soldier, 1785

Etching, 5 1/4 x 6 3/4 in. (13.4 x 17.1 cm) [de Vesme 11]

Fine Arts Museums of San Francisco, Achenbach Foundation for Graphic Arts

CAT. 80

The Rider Standing Beside His Horse, 1785

Etching, 5 7/16 x 7 in. (13.9 x 17.8 cm) [de Vesme 12]

Fine Arts Museums of San Francisco, Achenbach Foundation for Graphic Arts

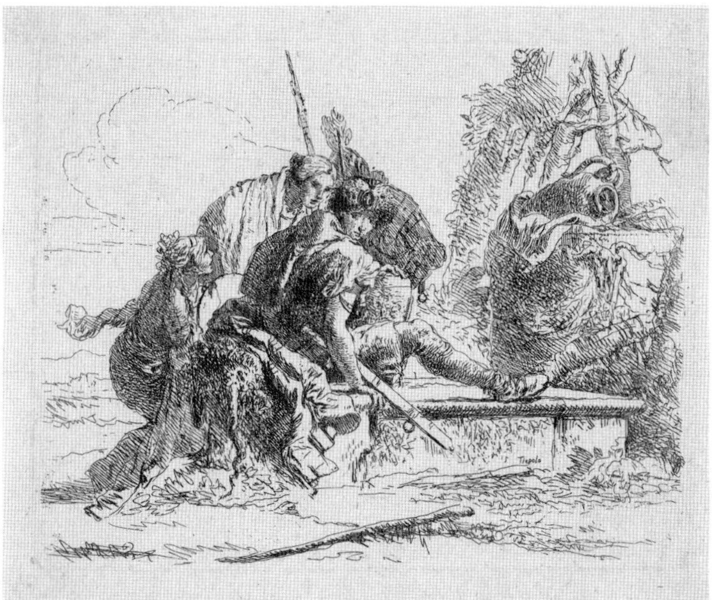

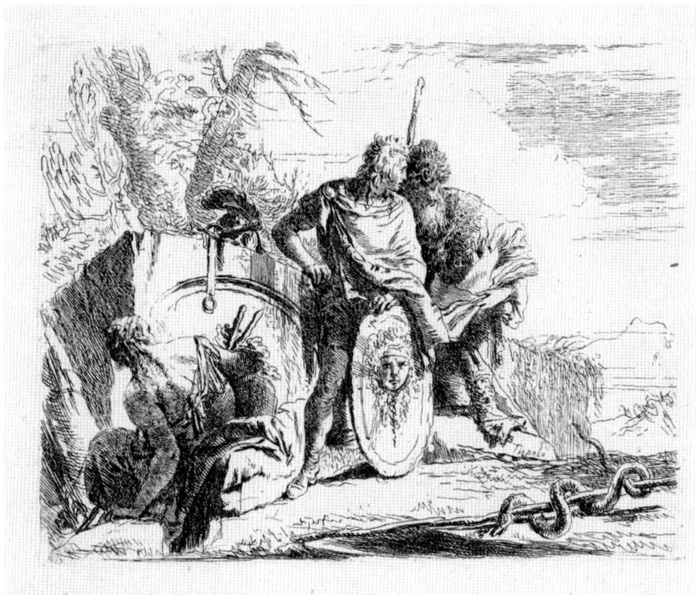

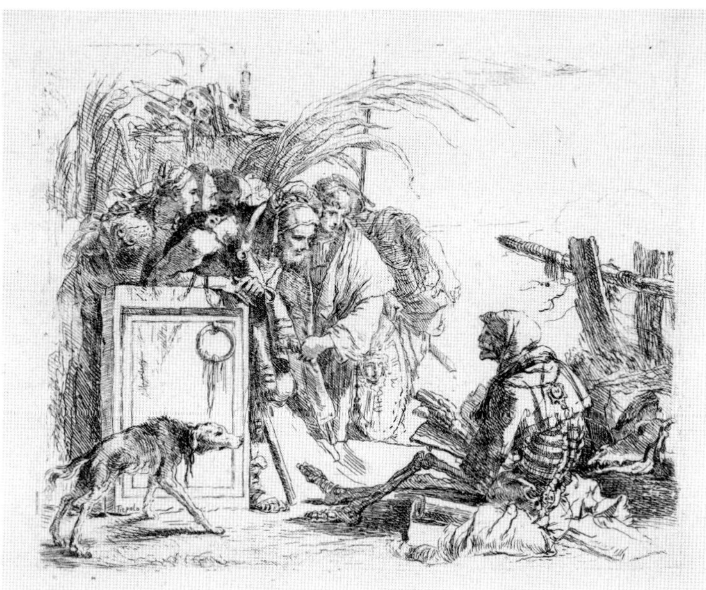

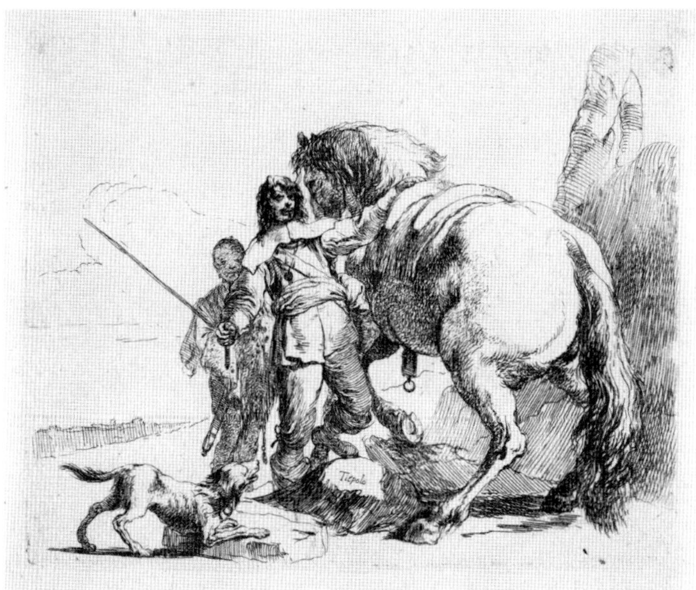

CATS. 81–87 **Giovanni Domenico Tiepolo** (Italian, 1727–1804)
Flight into Egypt

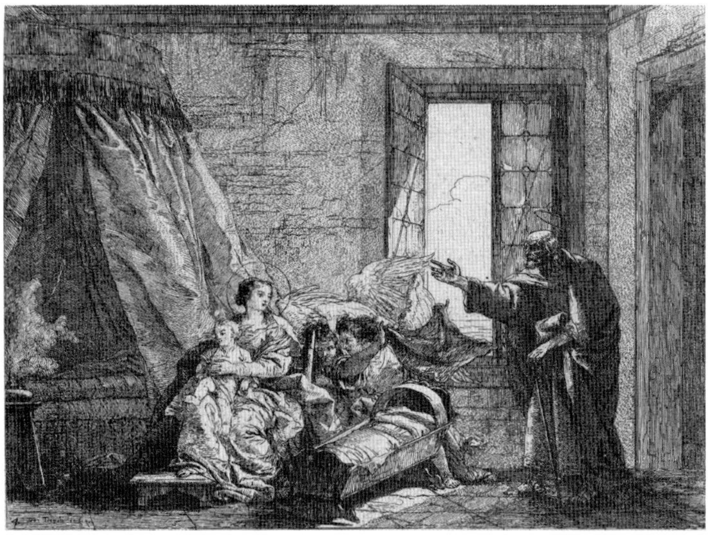

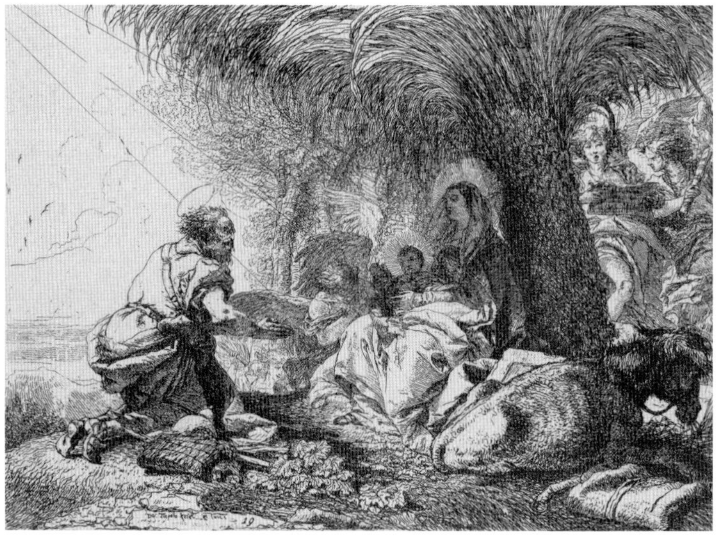

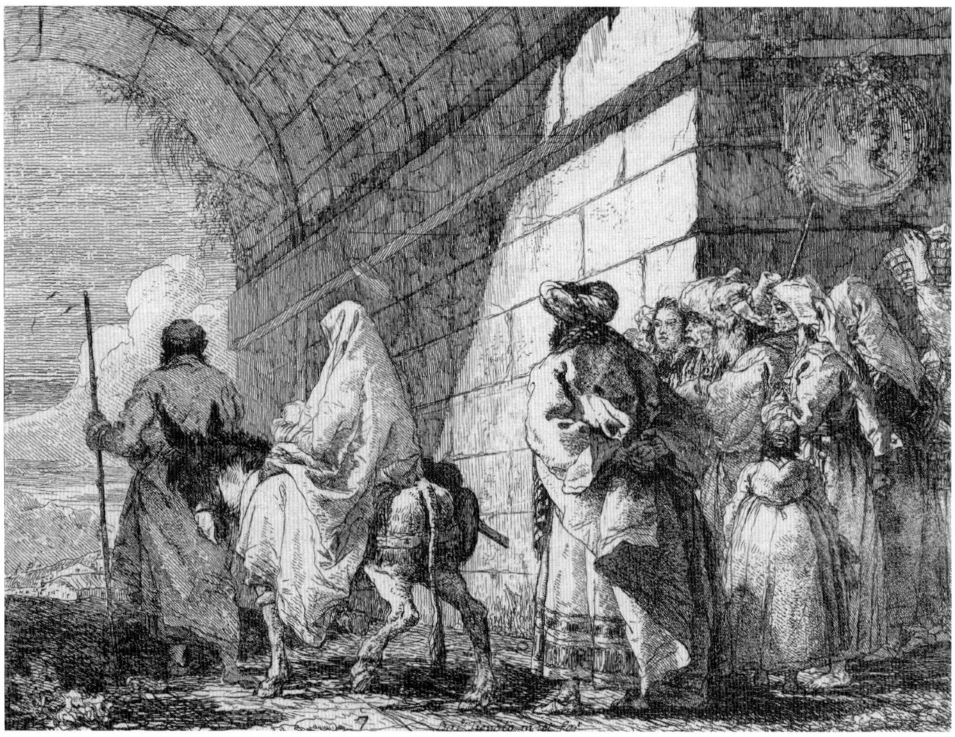

CAT. 81
Joseph Relays to Mary God's Command to Flee, 1753
Etching, 7⅜ x 9⅝ in. (18.7 x 24.3 cm) [de Vesme 4, Rizzi 70]
National Gallery of Art, Washington. Gift of W. G. Russell Allen, 1941.8.35

Cat. 82
The Holy Family Under a Palm Tree, 1753
Etching, 7⅜ x 9⅞ in. (18.7 x 24.9 cm) [de Vesme 6, Rizzi 72]
Fine Arts Museums of San Francisco, Achenbach Foundation for Graphic Arts

Cat. 83
The Holy Family Passes under a City Arch, 1753
Etching, 7⅜ x 9⅝ in. (18.8 x 24.5 cm) [de Vesme 7, Rizzi 73]
National Gallery of Art, Washington. Gift of W. G. Russell Allen, 1941.8.38

The seven prints included in this exhibition are part of a larger sequence of twenty-four scenes executed by G. D. Tiepolo, all depicting the journey of the Holy Family into Egypt. Although the Flight into Egypt narrative is only mentioned in one Gospel (Matthew 2:13–22), the richness of its subject matter allowed artists to consider a religious subject while simultaneously showing interest in the expressive capacity of landscape.[1] The uniqueness, however, of Domenico's contribution to the extensive pictorial history of the Flight into Egypt theme is his expansion of the narrative into twenty-four scenes, a feat that demonstrates his ability to sustain drama throughout the long sequence, as well as his powers of *invenzione*.[2]

The *Flight into Egypt* series was published in 1753 and dedicated to the Prince-Bishop of Würzburg, the Tiepolos' patron at that time. With the Tiepolos arrival at Würzburg on December 12th of 1753, it is likely that Domenico began work on the series while still in Venice and completed the prints upon his arrival at Würzburg.[3] There is no consensus in the scholarship concerning the chronology of dating for the print series, although three of the prints bear dates, one of which is included in this exhibit (*The Rest on the Flight into Egypt, with Holy Family under a Tree*, 1750, which is considered to be one of the earliest).[4] The difficulty of dating each print is due in part to the fact that the scenes were not created in a narrative sequential order. Although attempts have been made to establish the chronology of the prints according to stylistic traits, at present, such efforts have proved inconclusive.[5] In his creation of the *Flight into Egypt* series, Domenico drew upon the rich pictorial legacy of past painters, including his father.[6]

Central to Domenico's *Flight* series is the role of Joseph as protector of Mother and Child. Each scene is executed with a fury of hair-like incisions, which heightens the drama while also providing deep tonal qualities of light and dark. Although much attention is spent on the articulation of detail, all the prints retain a *bozzetto*-like quality, leaving bare the artist's formulation of the "idea" at the peak of the creative act. Ultimately, the vivacity of the *Flight into Egypt* series demonstrates Domenico's power to imbue the well-trod pictorial legacy of the *Flight* with uncommon freshness and sensitivity.[7]

James P. Anno

Notes

1 H. Diane Russell, *Rare Etchings by Giovanni Battista and Giovanni Domenico Tiepolo* (Washington, D.C.: National Gallery of Art, 1972: 93).

2 Ibid., 93.

3 Three of the individual prints bear dates from 1750, 1752, and 1753. For a discussion on the chronology of the prints, see Aldo Rizzi, *The Etchings of the Tiepolos: Complete Edition* (New York: Phaidon Press, 1971).

4 Russell, *Rare Etchings*, 94.

5 For a discussion on the chronology of the prints, see Russell, *Rare Etchings*, 94–5.

6 Although, Morassi suggests that many of Domenico's prints were executed before most of Giambattista's paintings depicting the *Flight*. For a chronological discussion see Antonio Morassi, *G. B. Tiepolo: His Life and Work* (London: Phaidon Press, 1955: pls. 92-93) and Anontio Morassi, *A Complete Catalogue of the Paintings of G. B. Tiepolo* (London: Phaidon Press, 1962: pls. 33, 36-37, 39).

7 For the most recent scholarship on Domenico's *Flight* series, see George Knox, *Etchings by the Tiepolo's: Domenico Tiepolo's collection of the family etchings* (Ottawa: National Gallery of Canada, 1976: 78-93; Rizzi, *Etchings of the Tiepolos*, 19-20, 105-221; and Russell, *Rare Etchings* 93-113.

Bibliography

Vesme, Alexandre de. *Le peintre-graveur italien*. Milan: Hoepli, 1906.

Morassi, Antonio. *G. B. Tiepolo: His Life and Work*, pls. 92-93. London: Phaidon Press, 1955.

Morassi, Antonio. *A Complete Catalogue of the Paintings of G. B. Tiepolo*, pls. 33, 36-37, 39. London: Phaidon Press, 1962.

Rizzi, Aldo. *The Etchings of the Tiepolos*, 19-20, 105-221. London: Phaidon Press, 1971.

Russell, Diane. *Rare Etchings by Giovanni Battista and Giovanni Domenico Tiepolo*, 93-113. Washington, D.C.: National Gallery of Art, 1972.

Knox, George. *Etchings by the Tiepolo's: Domenico Tiepolo's collection of the family etchings*, 78-93. Ottawa: National Gallery of Canada, 1976.

CATS. 81–87 **GIOVANNI DOMENICO TIEPOLO (Italian, 1727–1804)**
Flight into Egypt

CAT. 84
The Holy Family Being Ferried Across the River, 1753
Etching, 4⅝ x 9¼ in. (11.7 x 23.5 cm) [de Vesme 17, Rizzi 83]
National Gallery of Art, Washington. Gift of W. G. Russell Allen, 1941.8.48

CAT. 85
Joseph Adoring the Child, 1753
Etching, 7½ x 9⅞ in. (18.9 x 25 cm) [de Vesme 19, Rizzi 85]
Fine Arts Museums of San Francisco, Bruno and Sadie Adriani Collection

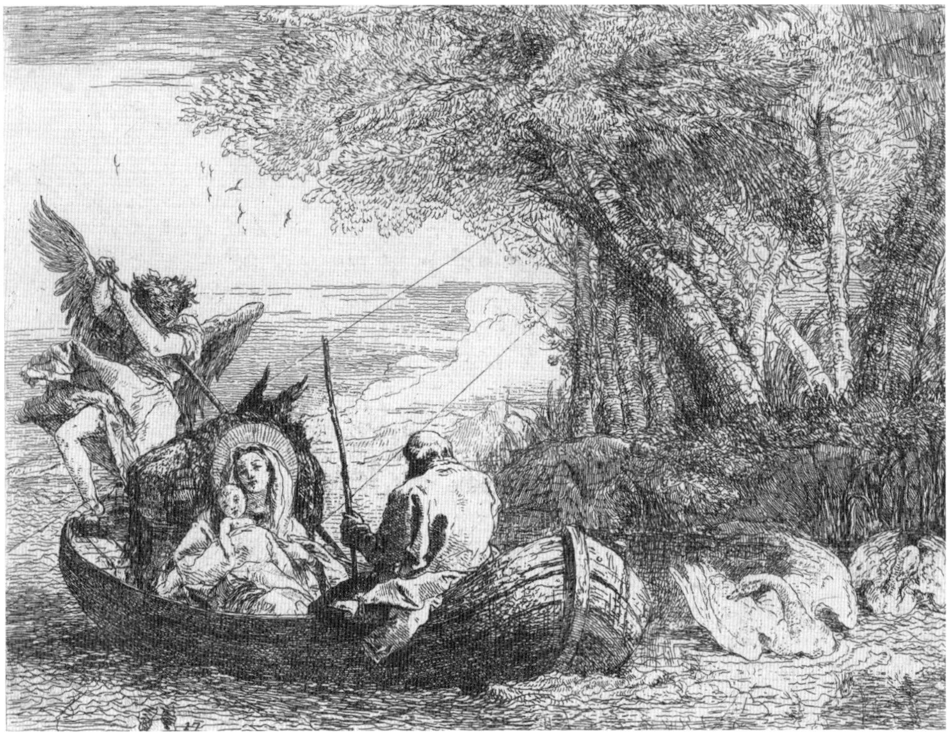

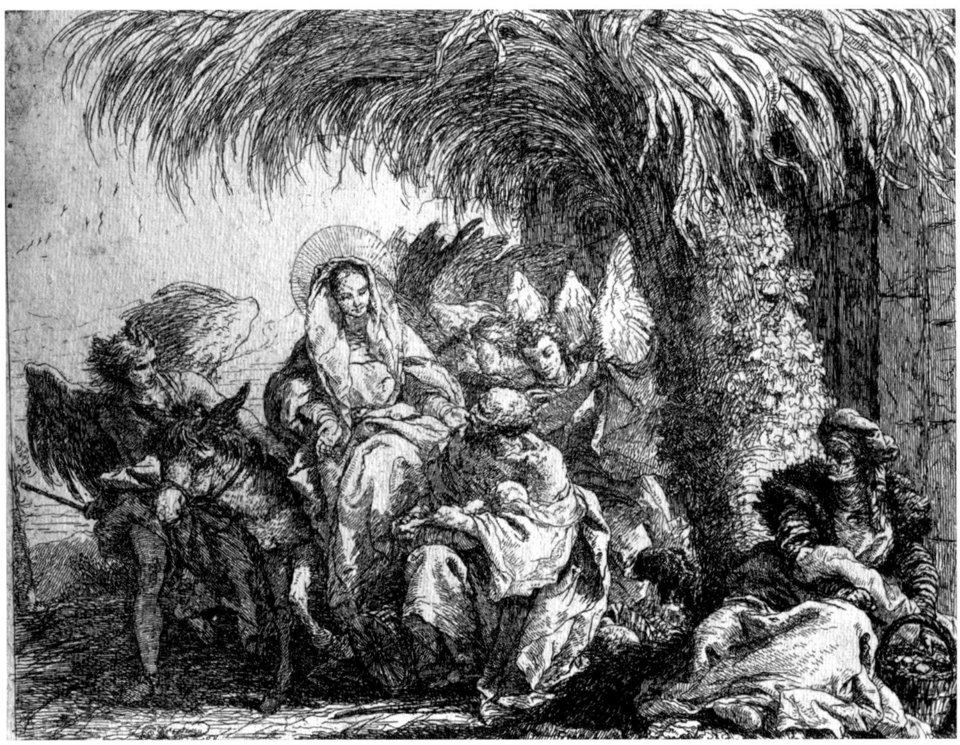

CAT. 86

The Rest on the Flight into Egypt, with Holy Family under a Tree, 1753
Etching, 7½ x 9⅜ in. (19.1 x 23.8 cm) [de Vesme 23, Rizzi 89]
National Gallery of Art, Washington. Gift of W. G. Russell Allen, 1750, 1941.8.54

CAT. 87

The Flight, with Madonna at Right Supported by Angels, 1753
Etching, 7⅜ x 9¾ in. (18.7 x 24.7 cm) [de Vesme 26, Rizzi 92]
National Gallery of Art, Washington. Gift of W. G. Russell Allen, 1941.8.57

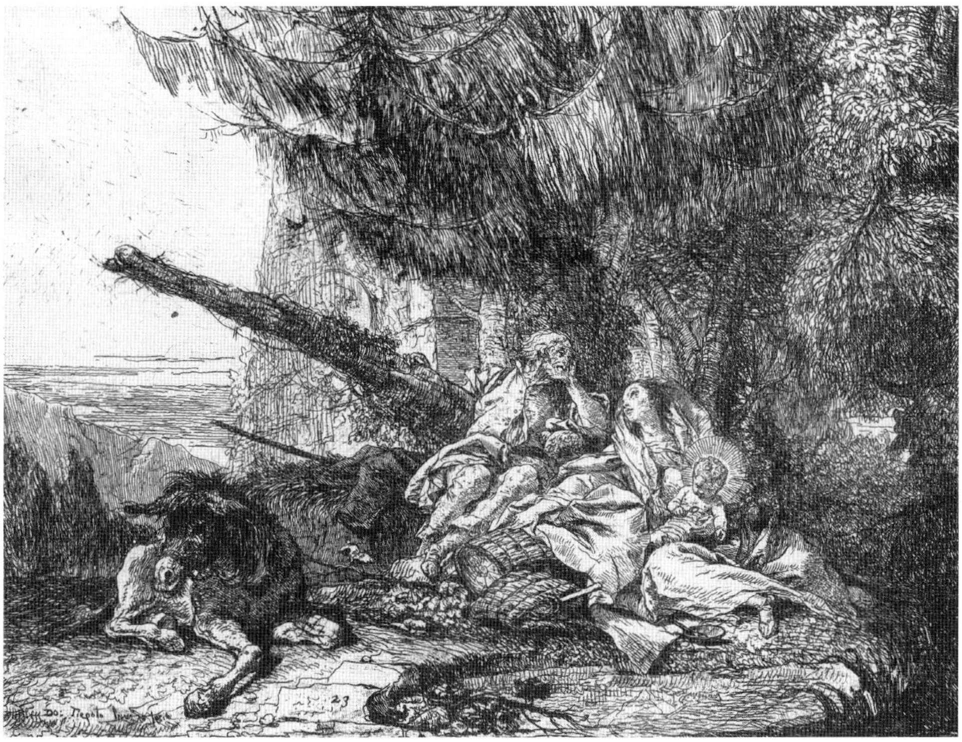

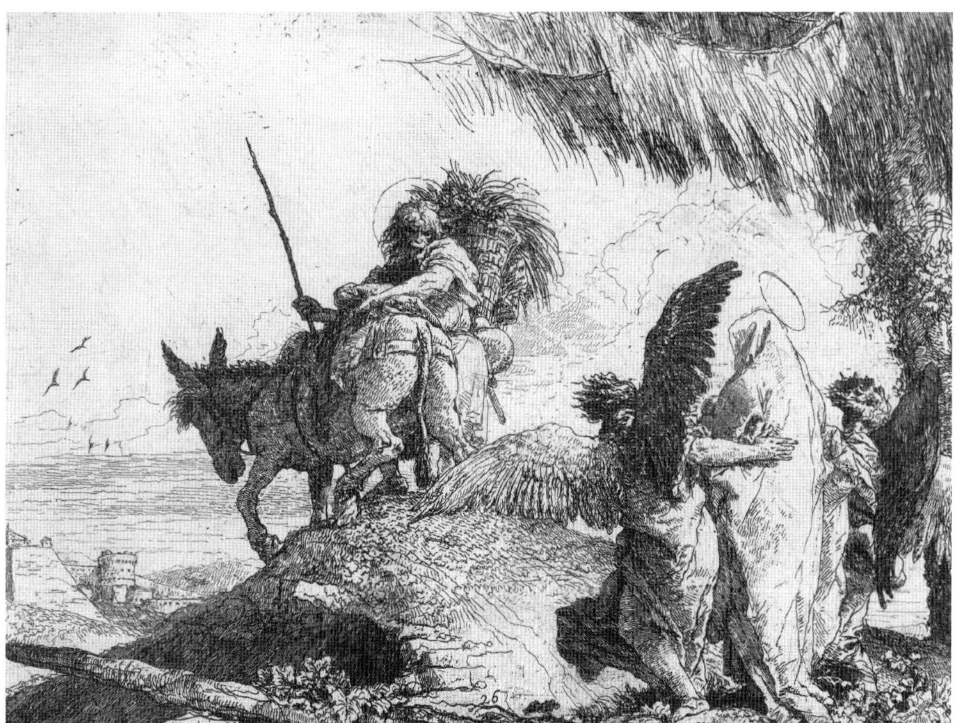

CAT. 88 GIOVANNI DOMENICO TIEPOLO (Italian, 1727-1804)

In Piazza, ca. 1791

Pen and brown ink, brown wash, over black chalk, 14⅜ x 19¾ in. (36.5 x 50.1 cm). Lent by The Metropolitan Museum of Art, Robert Lehman Collection, 1975 (1975.1.510)

Image copyright The Metropolitan Museum of Art / Art Resource, NY

CAT. 89 GIOVANNI DOMENICO TIEPOLO (Italian, 1727-1804)

Punchinello as a Dressmaker, ca. 1800

Pen and brown ink, brown wash, over black chalk, 13 15/16 x 18½ in. (35.4 x 47 cm). Lent by The Metropolitan Museum of Art, Robert Lehman Collection, 1975 (1975.1.466)

Image copyright The Metropolitan Museum of Art / Art Resource, NY

CAT. 90 GIOVANNI DOMENICO TIEPOLO (Italian, 1727-1804)

The Flogging of the Punchinello, ca. 1800

Pen and brown ink, brown wash, over black chalk, 14 x 18 9/16 in. (35.5 x 47.2 cm). Lent by The Metropolitan Museum of Art, Robert Lehman Collection, 1975 (1975.1.467)

Image copyright The Metropolitan Museum of Art / Art Resource, NY

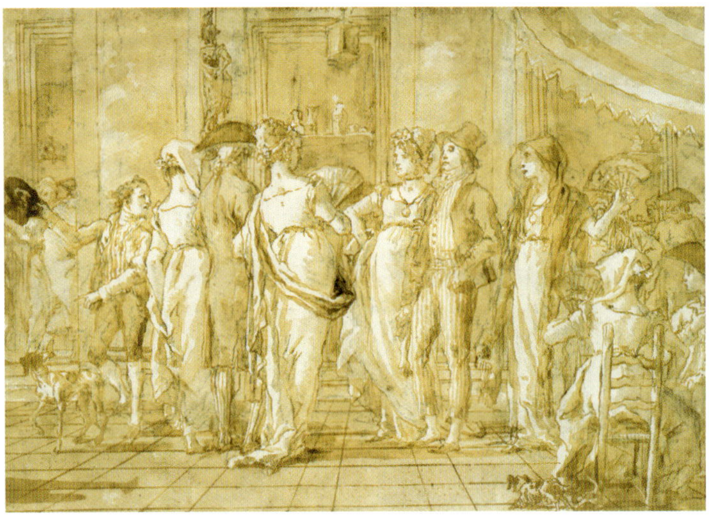

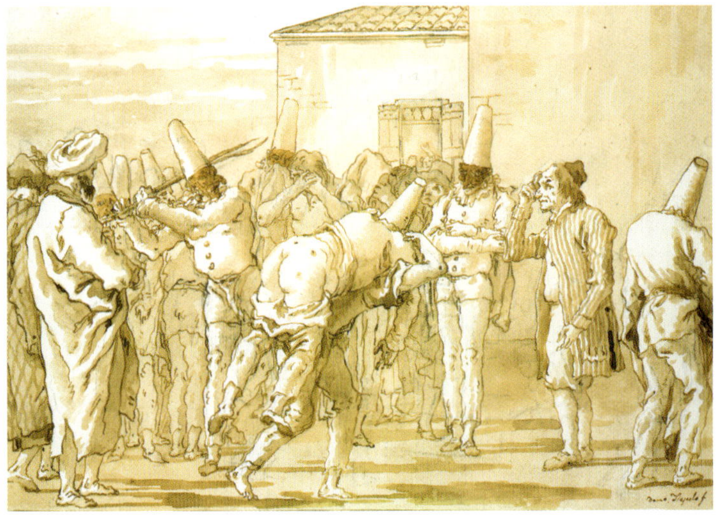

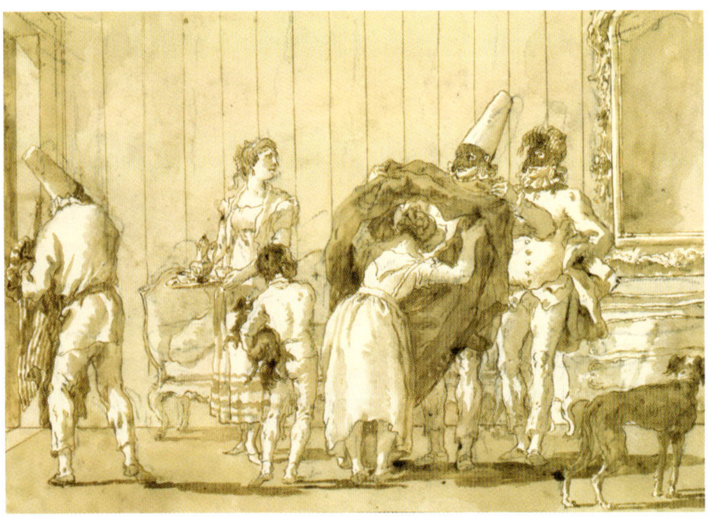

Giovanni Domenico Tiepolo's drawings from the 1790s through ca. 1800 portray the cross-currents of foreign influences and the complexity of Venetian society during the total collapse of the ancient Republic and its loss of independence. In this late period, Giovanni Domenico made drawings in pen and brown ink of scenes of everyday life in Venice, mostly dating from the period of the Napoleonic and Austrian occupation. These are hardly the genre subjects Giuseppe Maria Crespi, Giovanni Battista Piazzetta, and Pietro Longhi created for aristocratic patrons. Giovanni Domenico's humorous, but at times somewhat sullen observations of urban life about him hardly convey the gaiety of the carnival scenes, harlequin subjects, and contemporary genre scenes completed while working with his father on the great fresco project at Würzburg (1750-53). Nor do Giovanni Domenico's contemporary Venetian subjects of the 1790s offer favorable comparisons with the pleasantries of rustic genre subjects and sophisticated scenes of contemporary *villegiatura* life that he portrayed in 1757 on the walls of the guest house at the Villa Valmarana in Veneto. At the same time, in the main house, his father was working in the grand manner on the principal fresco decorations based on the writings of Homer, Virgil, Tasso, and Ariosto.

In Domenico's scenes of contemporary Venetian life made around thirty-five years later, significant changes in the frayed social fabric had taken place. There is a more biting, and perhaps even self effacing, form of social satire, which is particularly evident in the drawing titled *In Piazza* ["*Incontro al Liston*"—*In Piazza*][1] (cat. 88), dating about 1791, portraying the love of French and English fashion in polite Venetian circles. The added title, "meeting of the Liston," probably indicates that the group portrayed is meeting at an establishment on the Piazza San Marco. George Knox kindly informed me that "the coffee house represents a place and a privileged rite of the Liston (Big Line), the fashionable walkway, which is so called for the line of marble in the pavement of Piazza San Marco." The other two later Punchinello drawings are from the "*Divertimento per li Regazzi*" (the *devertomento* for children), which are inspired by the commedia dell'arte and are among Domenico's last works. The drawings date about 1800 and belong to the period of alternate Napoleonic and Austrian occupations (1797-1806), marked by looting by the French army, collaboration, political betrayal, and economic decline. The drawings deal with the cruder aspects of human nature that had been touched upon, in a lighter manner, in the earlier Punchinello, Harlequin, and Columbine drawings, etchings, and paintings of both Giovanni Battista and Giovanni Domenico. In *Punchinello as Dressmaker* [*Punchinello's mother dresses*][2] (cat. 89) and particularly *The Flogging of the Punchinello* [*The flagellation*][3] (cat. 90), there is a darker and more disturbing form of social satire that seems to address the malice of a less opulent period.[4] The former, titled *Punchinello's mother dresses* by Adelheid Gealt and George Knox (see n. 2), with the dresser, attendants, and a maid standing by with coffee or tea on a server, looks like a slightly threadbare version of an eighteenth-century aristocratic levee, while the Gealt and Knox title for the latter has blasphemous overtones. These three Robert Lehman Collection drawings help give an additional dimension to the exhibition by indicating the complexities of the social climate associated with the enormous political and economic changes of this bleak period in Venice's history. These sudden and humiliating changes also brought an end to the patronage of the great historical, biblical, and mythological works for which the Tiepolos were known.

Hardy George

Notes

1 Adelheid M. Gealt and George Knox, *Domenico Tiepolo 'Master Draftsman,'* Castello di Udine, September 14-December 31, 1996, and Indiana University Art Museum, Bloomington, Indiana, January 15-March 9, 1997. Published in association with the Indiana University Press (Bloomington and Indianapolis: Indiana University Press, 1996: Appendix A. Checklist of the Scenes of Contemporary Life, Section G—Diversions in Venice: no. 66, 242)

2 Ibid., Appendix B. Checklist of the "*Divertimento per li Regazzi*": 12, 244.

3 Ibid., no. 85, 247.

4 Linda Wolk-Simon, "Domenico Tiepolo Drawings, Prints and Paintings in the Metropolitan Museum of Art," *The Metropolitan Museum of Art Bulletin* (Winter 1996/97): 56-67. See also the series of *Contemporary Life* drawings in *Domenico Tiepolo, master draftsman,* curated by Adelheid M. Gealt and George Knox (Bloomington: Indiana University Press, 1996). Tiepolo's *In Piazza* is listed as no. 66. In *Giandomenico Tiepolo: scene di vita quotidiana a Venezia e nella terraferma* (curated by Adelheid M. Gealt, and George Knox; with comments by Dario Succi Piermario Vescovo, 2005), *Punchinello as a Dressmaker* is titled *Puncinello's mother dressing*, no. 104, and *The Flogging of Punchinello* is *The Flagellation* ..., no. 85. The items are in the order indicated by Domenico's numeration.

Provenance

In Piazza: Guggenheim sale, Palazzo Balbi, Vence, September 30, 1913, no. 1156; Conte Dino Barozzi, Venice; Paul Wallraf, London. Acquired by Robert Lehman in 1962.

Punchinello as a Dressmaker: Sale, Sotheby's, London, July 6, 1920, part of lot 41; P. & D. Colnaghi & Co., London; Richard Owen, Paris; Mrs. D. Klivert, Paris; Rosenberg & Stiebel, New York. Acquired by Robert Lehman in 1961.

The Flogging of the Punchinello: Sale, Sotheby's, London, July 6, 1920, part of lot 41; P. & D. Colnaghi & Co., London; Richard Owen, Paris; Mrs. D. Kilvert, Paris; Rosenberg & Stiebel, N.Y.; Acquired by Robert Lehman, Palais Galliéra, Paris, December 6, 1966, no. 11.

Exhibitions

In Piazza:

Fond. Giorgio Cini, Venice, 1959, pl. 114; Cologne, 1959, no. 114; National Gallery of Art, Washington 1974, no. 112; Birmingham (Ala.), 1978, no. 26; Huntington (N.Y.), 1980, no. 37; New York, 1981, no. 163; Rochester, 1981, no. 60; Detroit, 1983, no. 41; Pittsburgh, 1985, no. 45; Metropolitan Museum of Art, 1996.

Punchinello as Dressmaker:

Paris, 1921; New York, 1971, no. 278; Birmingham (Ala.), 1978, no. 121; New York, 1981, pl. 163; Metropolitan Museum of Art, 1996.

The Flogging of the Punchinello:

Paris, 1921; New York, 1971, no. 281; New York, 1980, no. S57; New York, 1981, no. 138; Pittsburgh, 1985, no. 43; Metropolitan Museum of Art, 1996.

Bibliography

Byam Shaw, James. "Some Venetian draughtsmen of the Eighteenth Century," in *Old Master Drawings* 7 (1933): 47-63.

Morrasi, Antonio, ed. *Disegni venti del Settecento nella collezione Paul Wallraf.* Venice: Fondazione Giorgio Cini, 1959.

Byam Shaw, James. *The Drawings of Domenico Tiepolo.* London: Faber, 1962.

Pignatti, Terisio, ed. *Venetian Drawings from American Collections.* Washington, D.C.: National Gallery of Art, 1974.

Weeks, Edward, ed. *The Tiepolos: Painters to Princes and Prelates.* Birmingham, Ala.: Birmingham Museum of Art, 1978.

Gealt, Adelheid M. *Domenico Tiepolo: The Punchinello Drawings.* New York: George Braziller, 1986.

Byam Shaw, James, and George Knox. *The Lehman Collection.* Vol 6, *Italian Eighteenth-Century Drawings.* New York: Princeton University Press, 1987.

Bean, Jacob, and William Griswold. *18th Century Italian Drawings in the Metropolitan Museum of Art.* New York: The Metropolitan Museum of Art, 1990.

Gealt, Adelheid M., and George Knox. *Domenico Tiepolo: Master Draftsman.* Bloomington and Indianapolis: Indiana University Press, 1996.

Gealt, Adelheid M., and George Knox. *Giandomenico Tiepolo: maestria e gioco: disegni dal mondo.* Milan: Electra, 1996.

Metropolitan Museum of Art. *Domenico Tiepolo: Drawings, Prints and Paintings in the Metropolitan Museum of Art.* An exhibition celebrating the 300th anniversary of the birth of Giovanni Battista Tiepolo, New York, 1996.

Wolk-Simon, Linda. *Domenico Tiepolo: Drawings, Prints, and Paintings in The Metropolitan Museum of Art. The Metropolitan Museum of Art Bulletin* (Winter 1996/97): 56, 62, 66-67.

Succi, Dario. "*Ironis e delizia comico,*" in *I Tiepolo: Virtuosismo e ironia*, 53-76, pl. 50, as *Incontro al Liston*, as in the collection of Paul Wallraf. Mirano; Umberto Allemani, 2004.

Whistler, Catherine. "Giandomenico Tiepolo 1791," *in Tiepolo: Ironia e comico*, 150-179, pl. and cat. no. 113. Exh. cat. by Adriano Mariuz and Giuseppe Pavanello. Venice: Marsilio, 2004.

Gealt, Adelheid M., and George Knox. *Giandomenico Tiepolo: scene di vita quotidiana a Venezia e nella terraferma.* Venice: Marsilio. 2005

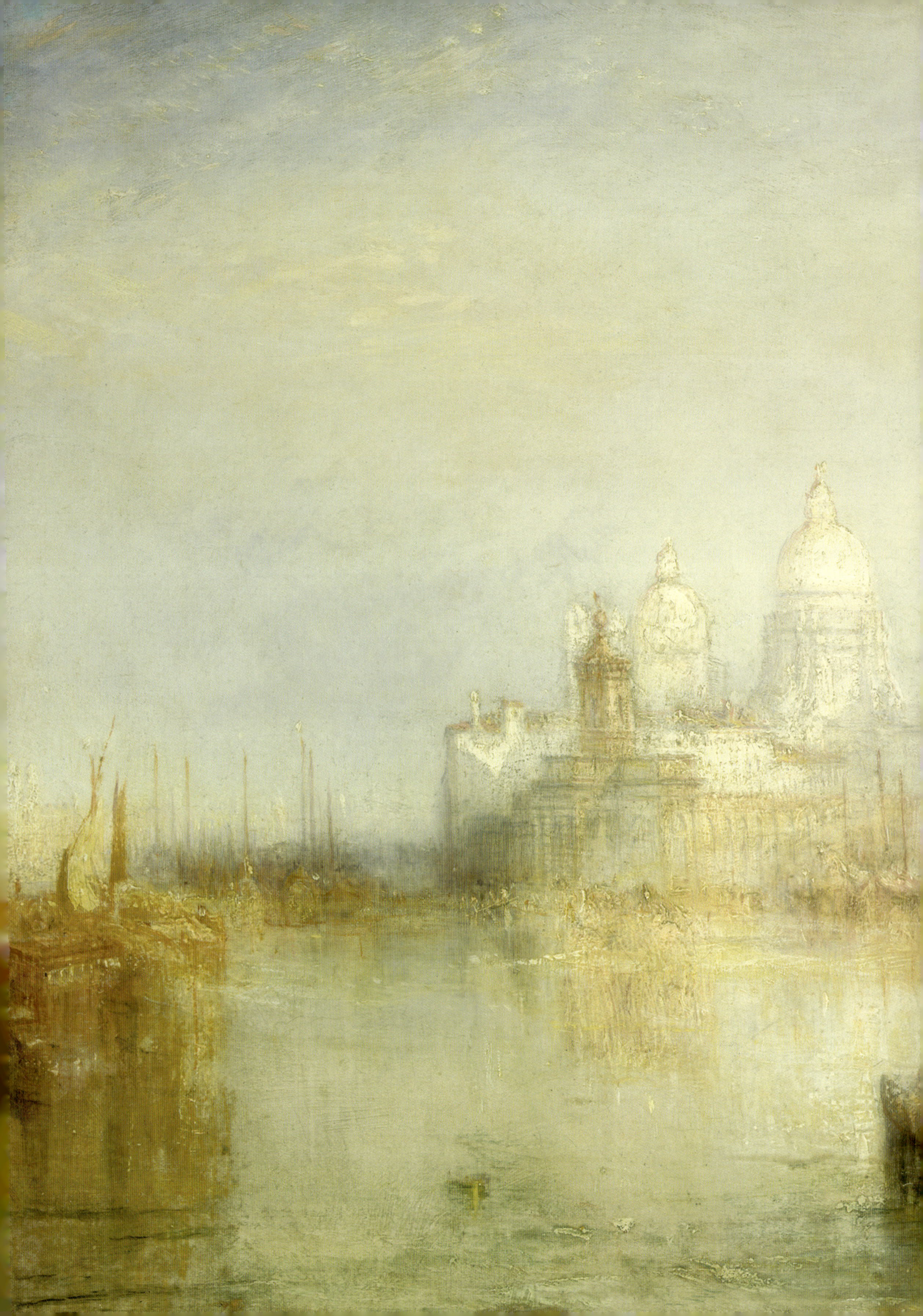

Conclusion and Epilogue

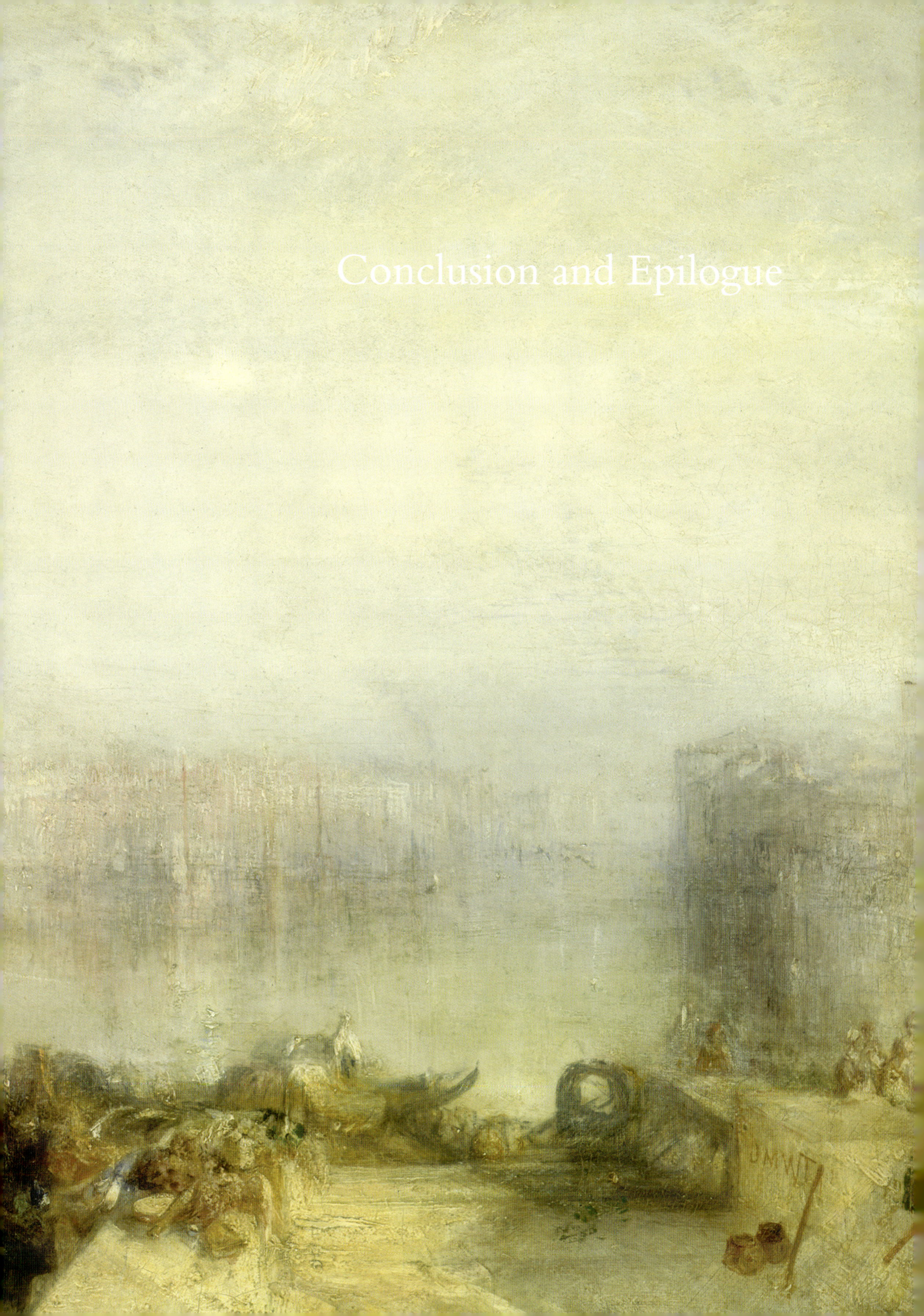

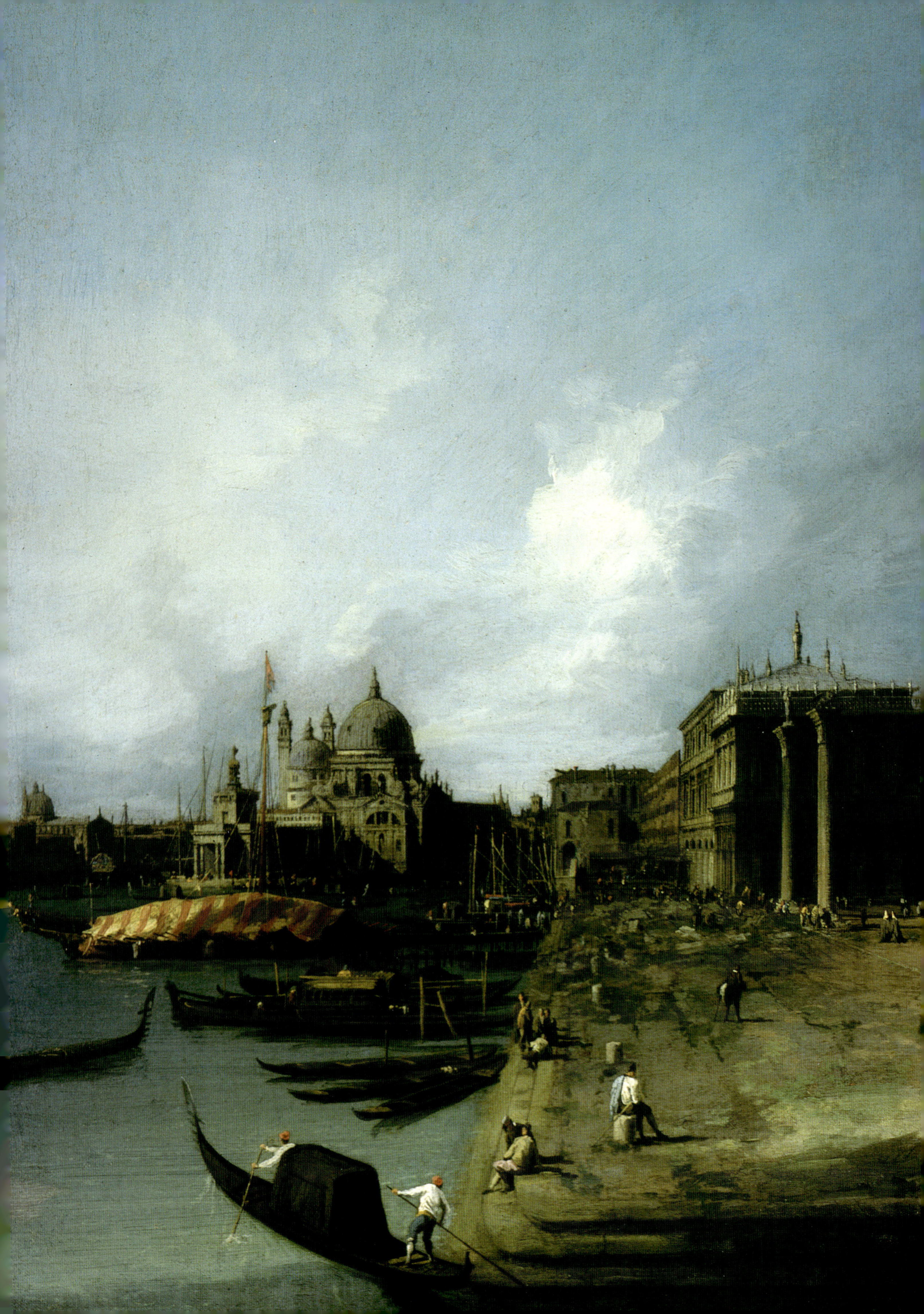

From Tiepolo to Turner

The End of an Era of Bedazzling Murals and the Beginning of a Renewed Interest in Venice's Elusive Image

Hardy George

The towering legacy of the eighteenth-century Venetian decorative painter Giovanni Battista Tiepolo did not survive the rigorous reforms of Neoclassical mural and ceiling painting, Napoleon's occupation of Venice, the collapse of Venice's economy, and the related absence of traditional patronage previously offered by the aristocracy and the Church. Venetian view painting was, by its very nature, secular, primarily dependent on foreign patronage, and was never very close to the indigenous advancement of late Baroque art. In a number of ways, eighteenth-century Venetian view painting was much closer to the developments of Neoclassical landscape painting, as a forerunner of nineteenth-century naturalism.

With the death of Canaletto in 1768 and Tiepolo in 1770, the art associated with both experienced a decline. On the whole, however, the new classicizing tendency in the second half of the eighteenth century was much more disruptive for the miraculous art of Tiepolo than for the *vedutisti* tradition of Canaletto. The disruption caused by Neoclassicism was thought of as a *risorgimento* of the arts and had its beginnings in Rome with Anton Raffael Mengs (1728-1779) and Joseph Vien (1716-1809). Their subject matter was based on recently discovered Roman wall paintings at Pompeii and Herculaneum. Neoclassical art also flourished in revolutionary Paris with the sterner allegorical subject matter of Jacques-Louis David (1748-1825) drawn from the literature and history of ancient Rome.

Rococo decorative works came to be associated with the political corruption and what was considered to be the moral decadence of the ancient regime. With the archaeological finds in places like Pompeii, the idea of the uncorrupted purity of the classical world was also called into question. Venice came to be associated with the excessiveness and loose morality that helped bring about the fall of ancient Rome, a belief that received its greatest endorsement in Hollywood films of the 1950s. The sumptuous décor of Venetian palaces and the Baroque-Rococo tradition of sensual art, as well as the frivolous emphasis on carnival and other festivities, were seen as an unraveling of the Republic's moral fabric. This inevitable evolutionary process was largely a theoretical construct advanced by early nineteenth-century British and French literati and poets. The last stage of

Canaletto (Giovanni Antonio Canal) (Italian, 1697-1768)
DETAIL: *View of the Molo, Venice*, ca. 1725
(CAT. 33)

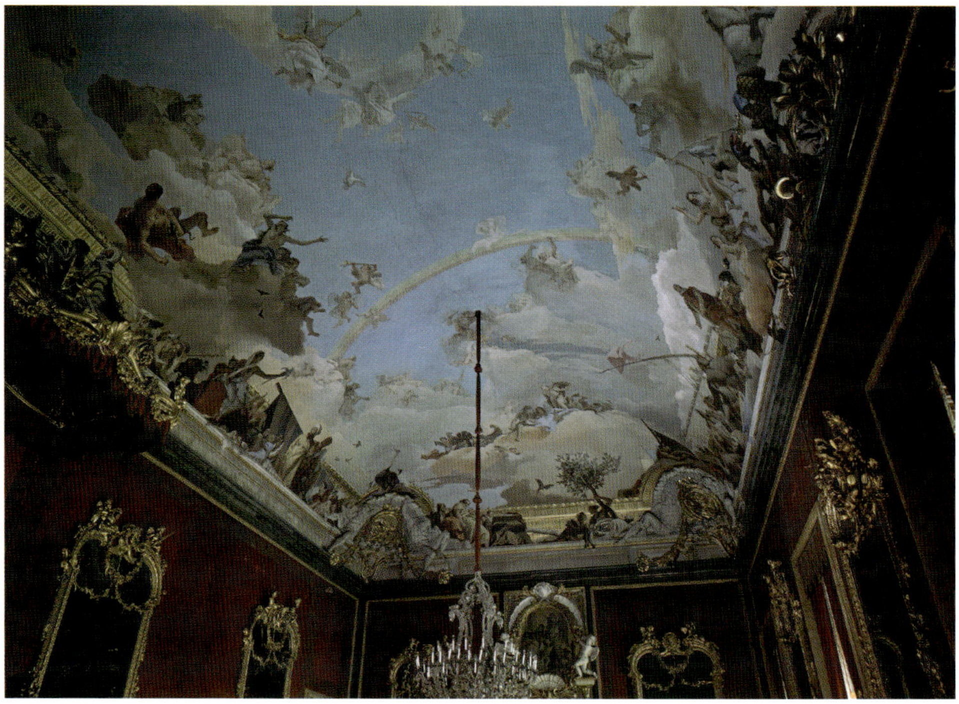

FIG. 1
Giovanni Battista Tiepolo (Italian, 1727-1804), assisted by Giovanni Domenico Tiepolo and Lorenzo Tiepolo
Triumph of Spain
Throne Room, Royal Palace, Madrid. Image copyright Oronoz Fotografos, Madrid

Venice's evolution, as an aging Republic with a brilliant past now on the brink of extinction, appeared to parallel the rise and fall of the Roman Empire. This idea has had a certain following in our own time. The 1950 edition of *The Columbia Encyclopedia*, after describing the achievements of the Renaissance marking the "height of Venetian artistic glory," summed up the late Baroque period as follows: "Although Goldoni, the dramatist, and painters such as Tiepolo and Canaletto still made Venice the most original artistic city of eighteenth-century Italy, they represented to some extent the decadence that accompanied the city's commercial and military decline."[1]

Late Baroque art was increasingly perceived as representing the old order. Mid-eighteenth-century Venetian art patrons were, on the whole, conservative and ignored the changes associated with the developments taking place in Rome and Paris. The Venetians continued to commission the type of large-scale decorative wall and ceiling paintings with miraculous ascension scenes for which Giovanni Battista Tiepolo was famous. This kind of art was already on the decline when the artist accepted his last important commission in 1762 to decorate, with the help of his sons, the throne room of the Royal Palace in Madrid (fig. 1).

The kind of Venetian patronage associated with Tiepolo's ceiling and wall decorations of Villa Valmarana in the 1750s and Villa Pisani at Strà around 1760 was less available when Giovanni Battista's son, Domenico, returned to Venice after his father's death in Madrid in 1770. Tiepolo's artificial and miraculous world of heavenly ascensions slowly fell out of favor and soon ceased to exist. This floating world created by Giovanni Battista and his sons not only consisted of Christian deities, but also lesser mortals in positions of great power, such as the celestial celebration of the Prince-Bishop on the staircase ceiling of the Würzburg Residenz (fig.2). With Tiepolo's passing, Giovanni Domenico, who had also

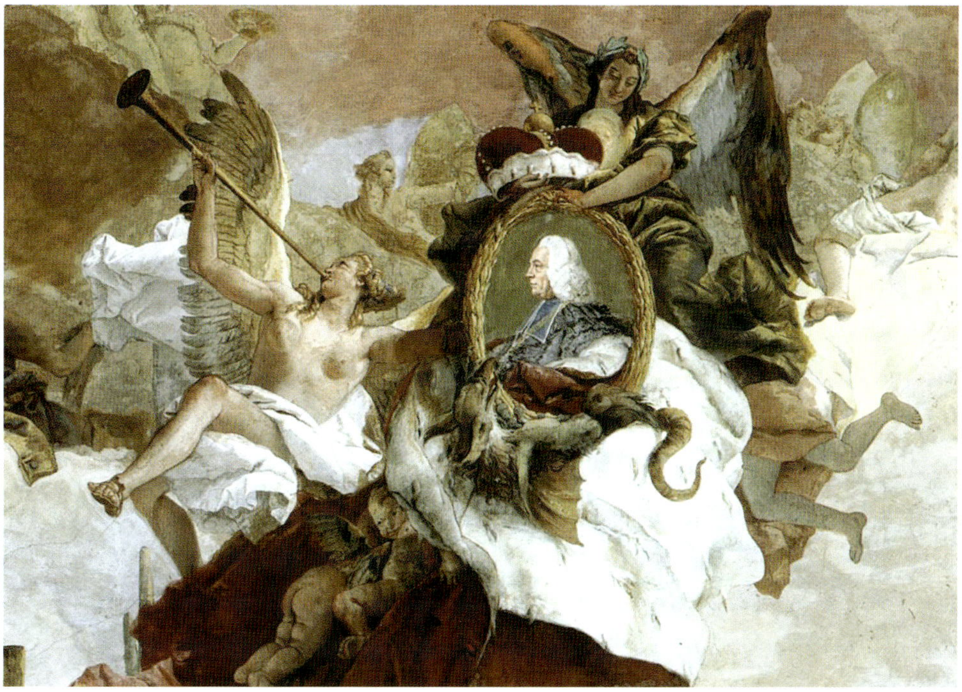

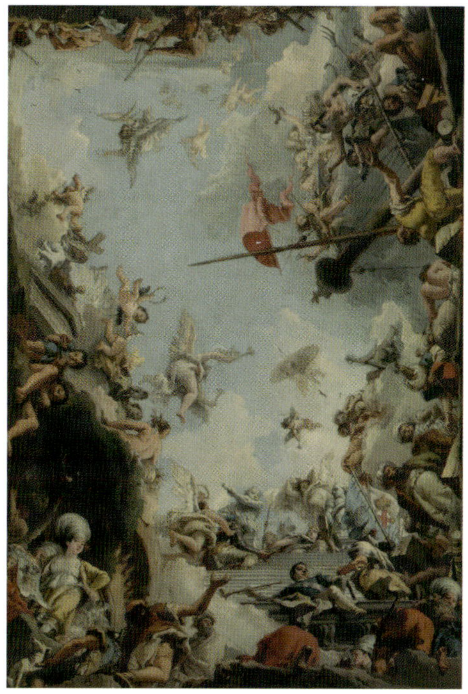

worked with his father at Würzburg and on other important commissions for large-scale works, was the only artist who was capable of taking his father's place and extending the life of Venetian Rococo art. In 1785, Domenico finished one of his most accomplished late ceiling paintings representing *The Glorification of the Giustiniani Family* (fig. 3) for the main council chamber of the ducal palace at Genoa. It was considered somewhat old fashioned shortly after its completion. This and his 1780s Venetian paintings of the *Glory of Pope Leo LX* for San Lio and ceiling fresco of *Virtue and Nobility* for the Palazzo Caragiani were among his last public commissions.[2]

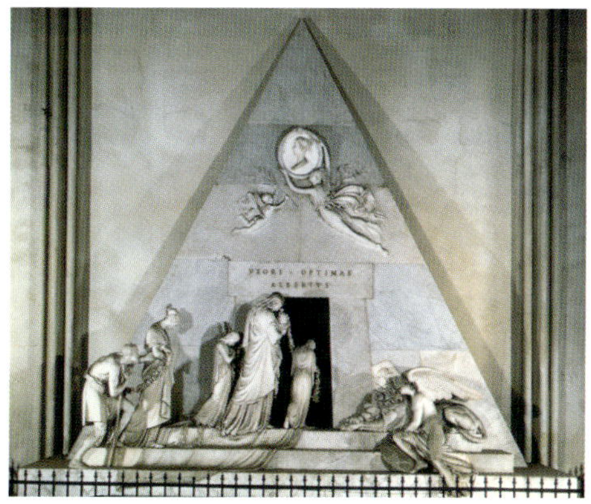

Epilogue

The attempts in the late eighteenth and early nineteenth century to revive mural painting as a major art form also mark the beginning of a renewed interest in views of Rome and Venice. The Neoclassical sculptor Antonio Canova (1757-1822) replaced Giovanni Battista Tiepolo as the most sought after Venetian artist of the late eighteenth and early nineteenth century. Canova thought of himself as a sculptor and a painter. Like Tiepolo before him, Canova's work was in demand throughout Europe; he not only received important commissions in Rome, by then the undisputed international art capitol, but also received offers from potential patrons in Austria (fig. 4), Napoleonic France, and England.

Francesco Hayez, a protégé of Antonio Canova who shared the sculptor's interest in Tiepolo, was perceived as one the most promising neoclassical history painters to carry forward the great Venetian tradition of fresco painting. By this time, Venice was not the place for a young artist to sell his work or seek patronage. At the end of the Napoleonic Wars, Rome once again was

FIG. 2
Giovanni Battista Tiepolo (Italian, 1696-1770)
Detail *Apollo and the Continents*
Fresco in the Residenz at Würzburg
Photo credit: Image thanks to the Art Renewal Center ®
www. artrenewal.org

FIG. 3
Giovanni Domenico Tiepolo (Italian, 1727-1804)
The Glorification of the Giustiniani Family, 1784-85
Oil sketch on canvas, 46 x 32½ in. (116.8 x 82.6 cm)
John Stewart Kennedy Fund, 1913 (13.2) The Metropolitan Museum of Art, New York, NY, U.S.A. Image copyright The Metropolitan Museum of Art/Art Resource, NY

FIG. 4
Antonio Canova (Italian, 1757-1822)
Tomb of Archduchess Maria Christine, favorite daughter of Empress Maria Theresa of Austria, 1798-1805; Marble
Augustinerkirche, Vienna, Austria / The Bridgeman Art Library International

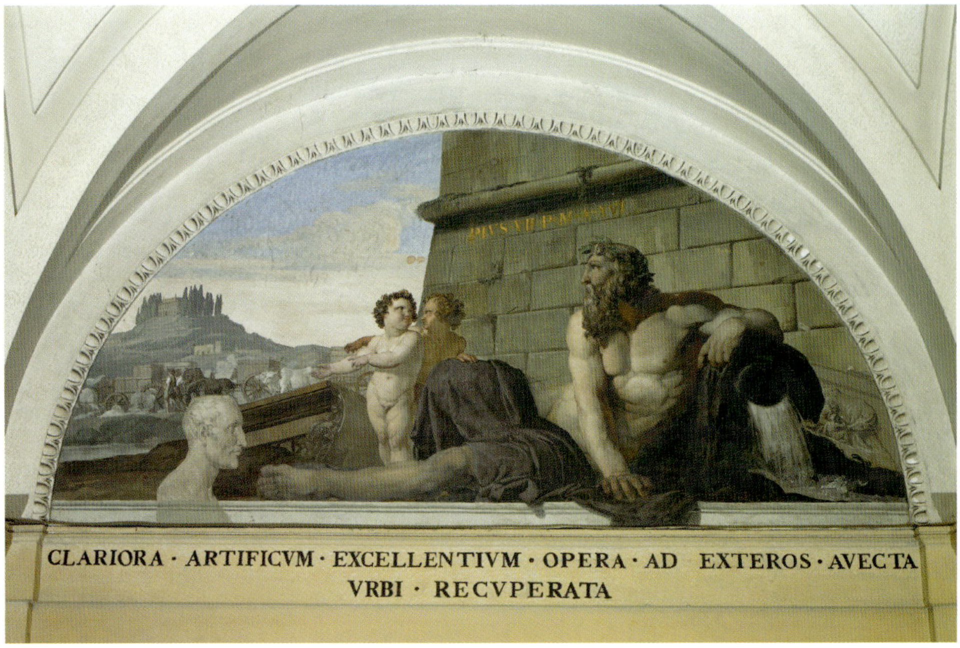

FIG. 5
Francesco Hayez (Italian, 1791-1881)
The Return of the Art Works to Rome, 1817
Museo Chiaromonti, Vatican Museums, Vatican State
Photo credit: Scala/Art Resource, NY

an important international art center, and in northern Italy, Milan had become a vibrant new center of cultural activity. Perhaps Canova thought that his Venetian student, having been exposed to Rococo decorative painting as well as the prevailing Neoclassical style of Napoleonic Veneto, could use the new mode of expression to resurrect the tradition of decorative fresco painting that had been established by Titian, Tintoretto, and Veronese and carried forward by Tiepolo. In 1797-98, Hayez worked under a minor Venetian artist who painted in the late Baroque chiaroscuro style of Giovanni Battista Piazzetta. Hayez made drawings from plaster casts of antique sculpture in the Galleria Farsetti. About the same time, he was admitted to the Scuola del Nudo (life drawing class) in the Academy at Venice. When Hayez also moved to Rome, he was encouraged to work as a fresco painter, and he provided evidence of his understanding of this difficult medium while assisting Pelagio Palagi (1775-1860) in the decoration of the Palazzo Torlona in 1813.[3]

Hayez was familiar with the work of the German Nazarines, or Lukesbrüder, who, inspired by Raphael and the early Italian primitives, were committed to the revival of fresco painting. In 1816 they began their work on the Casa Bartholdy murals (now in the Alte Nationalgalerie, Berlin), and in the same year, Hayez started work on the Vatican fresco commission arranged by Canova for Pope Pius VII, who wished to celebrate the return of works of art removed from the Vatican during Napoleon's occupation. In 1817, about the time Hayez had completed the decoration of three of the Vatican lunettes, the Nazarines began working on a second fresco commission from the Marchese Carlo Massimo to decorate the rooms of his garden house with scenes from Dante and Tasso.[4]

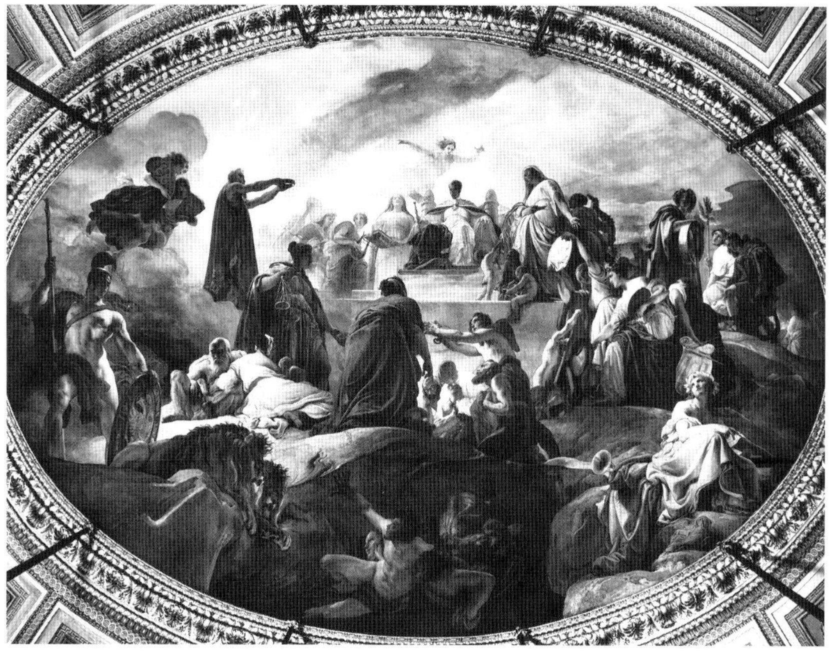

Hayez's most interesting lunette fresco in the Chiaramonti wing of the Vatican Museum celebrates the return of the collection of antique sculpture removed by Napoleon in the 1790s (fig. 5). A river god, representing the Tiber, looks toward the moving wagons in the left distance loaded with the appropriated works of art from France. Two cherub figures are seen to the left of the river god. One happily points in the direction of the train of wagons.

Canova was not pleased with the continual alterations and the time it took Hayez to complete only three lunettes, and, as a result, the commission was cancelled.[5] None of Hayez's decorative projects, including the Neoclassical ones in the Ducal Palace at Venice, the Royal Palace at Milan, and the Palazzo Duse Masin at Padua, give a clear indication of a return to the distinctive greatness of the medium in the time of Tiepolo.

The transition from Tiepolo's exuberant Rococo manner of placing high ranking mortals in celestial realms to Hayez's stodgier interpretation of this theme is found in the latter's 1838 ceiling fresco, *Triumph of Fernando I* (fig. 6). In this work, Hayez presents an ordered Neoclassical grouping of allegorical figures around one of Europe's last absolute monarchs. It brings to mind Tiepolo's crowning of the allegorical figure of Spain in the Throne Room of the Royal Palace in Madrid. A Nike figure soars over the head of Ferdinand I, and a number of classically gowned personages pay homage to the emperor. All are located in a barren and foreboding location—hardly the paradisiacal setting characteristic of Tiepolo. The demonic personages, confined to a dark grotto in the center foreground and guarded by two lions and a Roman soldier holding a shield and spear, might represent the need to suppress the disorder associated with the clandestine members of the Carbonari seeking to expel the Austrians.[6]

The fresco describes a well-intended but failed attempt on the part of Emperor Ferdinand I to restore, in Neoclassical terms, the *esprit* of the Venetian Rococo decorative paintings that paid tribute to great monarchs and members of powerful families. Ferdinand I suffered from fits of insanity, and a council of state headed by Prince Klemens von Metternich (1773-1859) gov-

FIG. 6
Francesco Hayez (Italian, 1791-1881)
Triumph of Ferdnano I, 1838
Fresco of ceiling of Royal Palace of Milan, Italy
Photo copyright, Alinari Archives, Florence

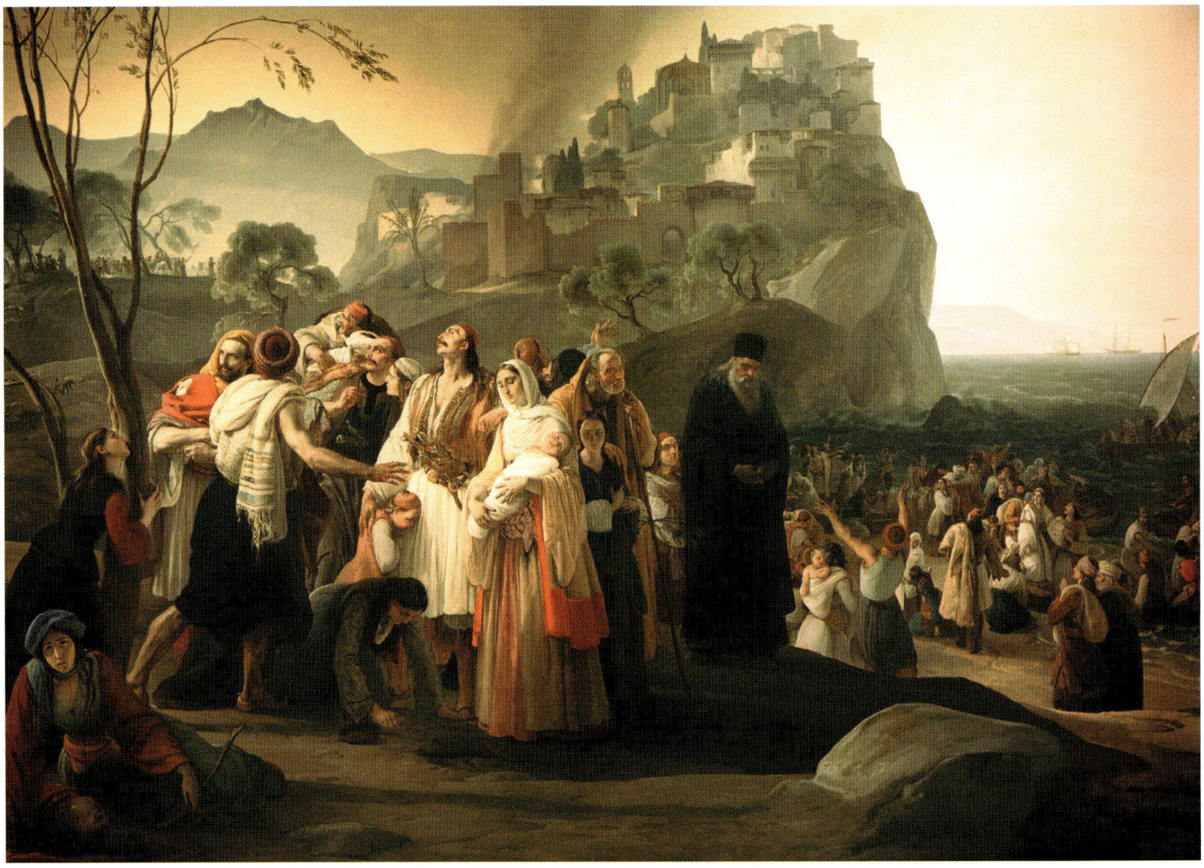

FIG. 7
Francesco Hayez (Italian, 1791-1881)
The Refugees of Parga, 1831
Oil on canvas, 211 x 301 in. (535.94 x 764.54 cm)
Greece under Turkish rule/sale of Parga (Venetian until 1797, French until 1815, until 1819 under British protectorate) to Ali Pasha of Janina 1819; Inv.Nr. 337. Brescia, Pinacoteca Civica T. Martinengo; Photo: akg-images

erned Austria. With the outbreak of the revolution in Vienna in 1848, Ferdinand unsuccessfully offered the insurgents a constitution and was later forced to abdicate.

Beginning in the 1820s, Hayez painted large-scale romantic history pictures, some of which were based on Jean Charles Sismondi's *History of the Italian Republics in the Middle Ages* (16 vols., 1809-1818) and others on literature and contemporary events. These paintings display the influence of Piazzetta's use of chiaroscuro and the rich color of the sixteenth-century Venetian masters. Three primary examples of this type of Salon painting are *The Refugees of Parga* (fig. 7), *The Destruction of the Temple at Jerusalem* (1867), and *The Thirst of the Crusaders* (ca. 1836-1850). These works proved to be much more popular than Hayez's Neoclassical mural and ceiling frescoes. The themes in these works concern the oppression of the Greeks by the Turks and the Israelites by the Romans, as well as the suffering of the Crusaders. Like the themes in Verdi's operas, all contained a clearly understood patriotic message for the Italians. Greek independence, because of the county's historical, cultural, and literary importance for the West, received enthusiastic support from various parts of Europe and from writers and artists such as Lord Byron (1788-1824) and Eugène Delacroix (1798-1863).

Hayez's anecdotal genre paintings of *Secret Allegations* (fig. 8) mark a break with the large-scale history paintings featuring numerous *dramatis personae.* The intimate story of betrayal and vengeance is serialized over three or four paintings.

Here, in an act of revenge, a woman is about to place a note in the *bocca di leone*, the mouth of a carved stone lion head where accusatory notes could be left for the Council of Ten, who punished crimes against the state. The model has distinct features and is identifiable in a number of Hayez's works of this period, and the portrayal of the model is a clear indication of the artist's fully developed talents as a portrait painter. The carefully arranged setting, as indicated in the preparatory drawing (Milan, Accademia di Brera) with its numerous construction lines, is that of a skilled topographical artist and theatre set designer. The setting is the gallery of the Doge's Palace with its pointed trifoliate arches offering a view of the Basin of St. Mark with the distant domed church of Santa Maria della Salute. It is difficult to identify the legacy of Tiepolo's dazzling art in the Neoclassical mural and ceiling paintings, and there is little or none of the aristocratic humor and polite social satire of Pietro Longhi's (1702-1785) eighteenth-century drawing room subjects in Hayez's anecdotal genre paintings. On the other hand, there is something of the legacy of Canaletto in the view of the lagoon and Santa Maria della Salute seen through the arches.

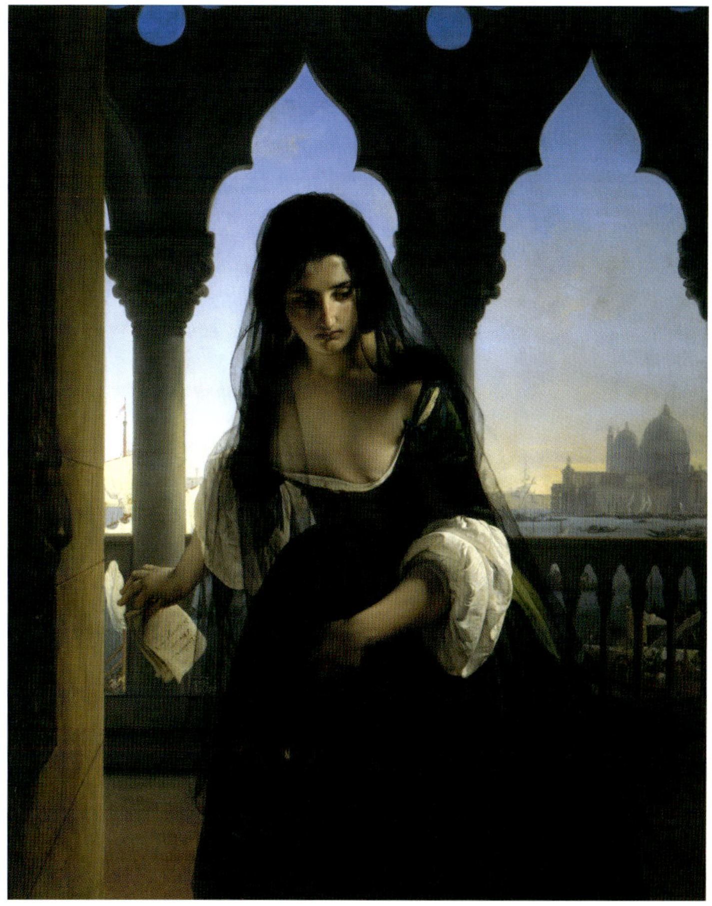

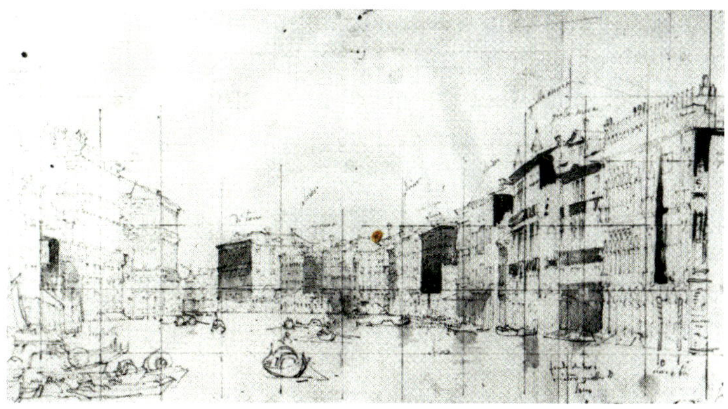

In the view paintings of a number of late-eighteenth and early nineteenth-century Italian artists, the influence of Canaletto is quite pronounced. This is particularly true of the Venetian and Roman topographical works by Ippolito Caffi (1809-1866). Caffi studied drawing, painting, and perspective at the Accademia di Belle Arti in Venice from 1827 to 1831. Like Hayez and Canova before him, Caffi was an Italian patriot who wanted Venetia to be free of Austrian rule. Unlike Hayez, he did not paint historical works that symbolically referred to Austrian domination but portrayed actual events in the uprisings against Austrian rule. He left Venice for Rome in 1832, where he designed sets for the theatre and became known as a view painter. In 1835, with the artist Antonio Bianchini (1803-1884), Caffi published a textbook titled *Lessons in Practical Perspective* (*Lezioni di prospettiva pratica*), a subject necessary to the understanding and practice of view painting. His mastery of this quasi-mathematical system can be seen in the use of construction lines creating spatial recessions in a precise drawing he made of the mouth of the Grand Canal looking toward Ca' Pesaro (fig. 9).

Caffi achieved his first great success with his view paintings of Venice and Rome in a group exhibition held on the Piazza del Popolo in 1844. In the

FIG. 8
Francesco Hayez (Italian, 1791-1881)
Secret Allegations [Accusa segreta], 1847-48
Oil on canvas, 60¼ x 47¼ in. (153 x 120 cm)
Museo Civico, Pavia, Italy
Photo credit: Alfredo Dagli Orti / Art Resource, NY

FIG. 9
Ippolito Caffi (Italian, 1809-1886)
Canal Grande verso Ca' Pesaro
Museo Correr

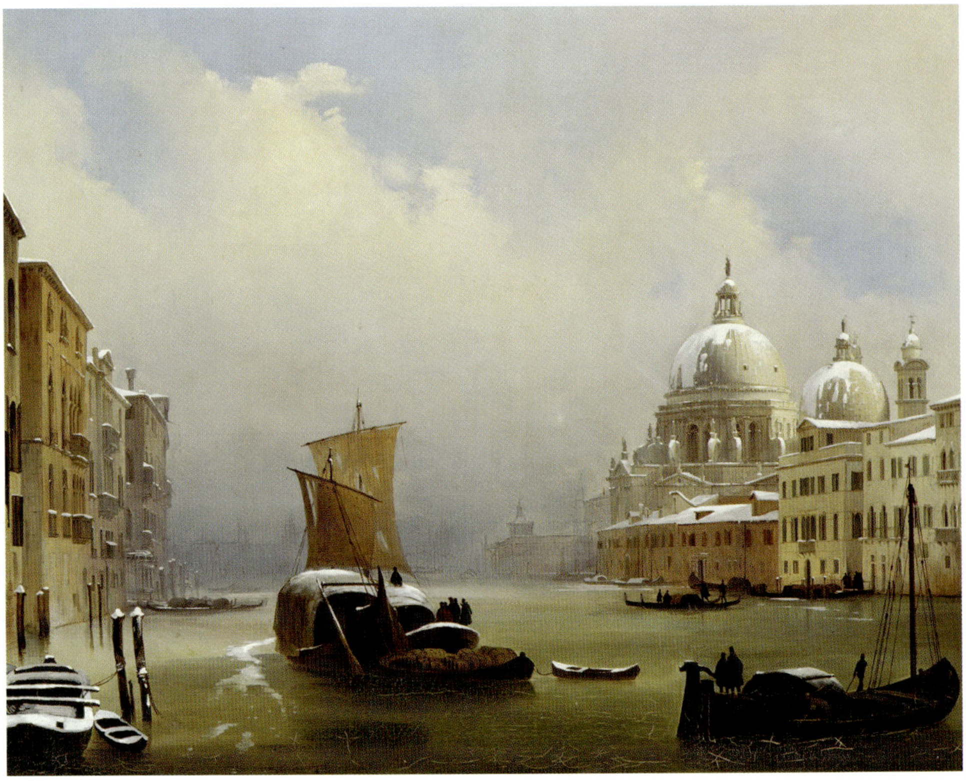

FIG. 10
Ippolito Caffi (Italian, 1809–1866)
The Mouth of the Grand Canal and the Salute [Canale della Giudecca (sic) e la Salute], 1841
Venice, Museo Correr

1846 Paris Salon, he exhibited *Carnevale sulla Piazzetta* a nocturnal Venetian view illuminated with fireworks. Like Canaletto, Caffi painted popular Venetian topographical subjects several times to meet the demands of collectors.

Two companion pieces portraying the *View of the Bacino di San Marco, Venice* (cat. 49) and *Santa Maria della Salute from the Ponte Dell'Accademia, Venice* (cat. 48) display Caffi's ability to draw on the traditional subjects of the eighteenth-century view painters. At the same time, these works capture the essence of contemporary Venice in the portrayal of shipping and in the dress of individuals in his compositions. The heavy atmospheric effect and the mist that almost completely obscures Santa Maria della Salute in the former painting are quite unlike Canaletto (cat. 35). In Caffi's painting, more attention is given to inclement weather conditions than to the careful rendition of the architectural features of this famous church. Caffi, as a Romantic follower of Canaletto, employed weather conditions of late fall and winter (fig. 10) and unusual light effects, both natural and nocturnal as well as artificial, not used by the eighteenth-century master. Later, as a dedicated patriot, he painted *vedutisti* subjects related to the Risorgimento. Caffi made his Italian nationalist sympathies known with the portrayal of an Austrian night bombardment of Venice's fortress and island of Marghera on the 25th of May 1849 (fig. 11) and political rallies in the 1860s.

With the end of the Napoleonic Wars, Italy attracted large numbers of tourists, and a number of English, French, and German artists made the topography

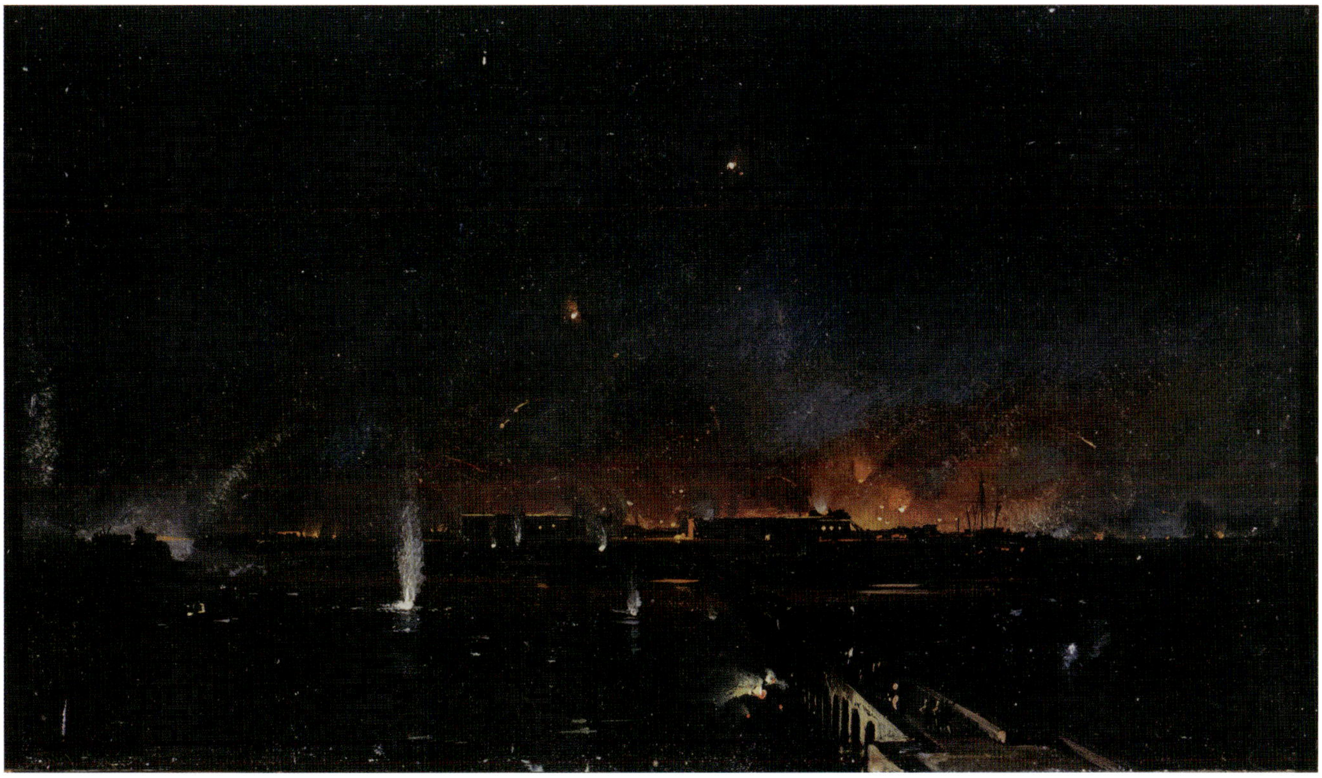

of Venice one of their primary subjects. J. M. W. Turner (1775-1851), Jean-Baptiste-Camille Corot (1796-1875), and Richard Parkes Bonington (1802-1828), were all followers of Canaletto and were among the first and most talented artists to portray Venice in the early nineteenth century.

Canaletto's legacy can be readily perceived in the Venetian views of Bonington and Corot but is less apparent in the more romantic and poetic works of Turner and Caffi. As a highly talented landscape painter, Bonington appears to have been influenced by Constable's naturalism and sketch-like brushwork. This can be seen in his portrayal of sky and atmospheric effects. Bonington traveled to Venice in 1826 and painted a number of views along the Grand Canal with extraordinary *plein-air* effects. In 1828, his life was cut short at age twenty-six by tuberculosis.

Corot traveled to Rome in 1828, and during a short visit to Venice on his return journey to Paris, he made some of his best oil sketches. Although the number of sketches made in Venice was small in comparison with those made in Rome, these spontaneous topographical works represent a momentary break with the structured style of the classical landscape tradition that had its beginnings in the seventeenth-century works of Claude Lorrain (1604-1682) and Gaspard Poussin (1615-1675). Unfortunately, Corot's Venice sketches and finished paintings are few in number. One of the most important in North American collections, Corot's *View of Venice: The Piazzetta Seen from the Riva*

FIG. 11
Ippolito Caffi (Italian, 1809-1866)
Bombardment of Marghera, 1849
Oil on canvas
Museo Correr, Venice, Italy
Photo credit: Cameraphoto Arte, Venice/Art Resource, NY

degli Schiavoni, is found in the Norton Simon Museum in Pasadena. In 1834, Corot returned to Italy and spent most of his time in the north, staying two weeks in Genoa, six weeks in Tuscany, and three weeks in Venice.

Turner first visited Venice on his 1819 journey to Rome and then returned to Venice in 1833 and 1840. On his first visit, he made a large number of pencil sketches and a few watercolors (fig. 12). On his second and third visits to Venice he made some rough pencil sketches and a number of studies in watercolor and gouache.

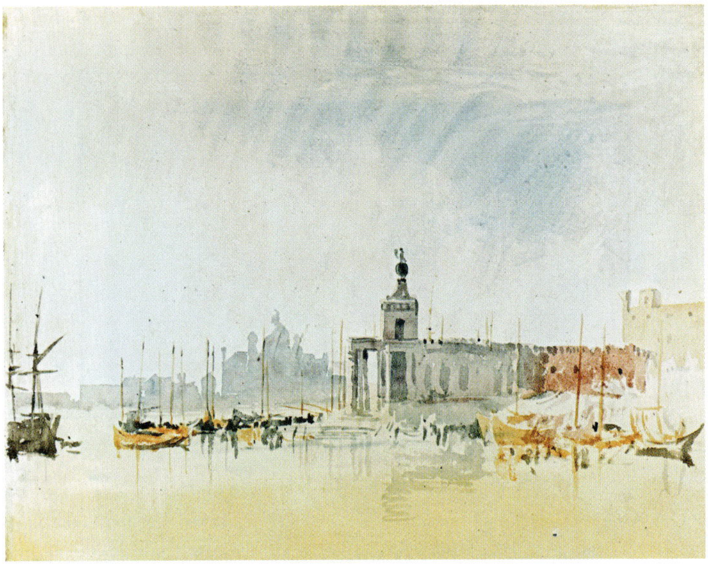

FIG. 12
J.M.W. Turner (English, 1775-1851)
From Como and Venice Sketchbook
Venice: The Punta della Dogana, with the Zitelle in the Distance, 1819
Watercolor on paper, 8¾ x 11¼ in. (22.3 x 28.5 cm).
Finberg number: CLXXXI
British Museum, London, Great Britain
Photo credit: Erich Lessing/Art Resource, NY

In 1818, the portrait painter Thomas Lawrence (1769-1830) was sent by the Prince Regent to Vienna to paint portraits of the rulers and commanders of the allied states and armies who had defeated Napoleon at Waterloo. Lawrence then traveled to Rome to portray Pope Pius VII and his chief minister Cardinal Consalvi, and he wrote to Turner encouraging him to come to Rome. In a letter dated October 6, 1819, Lawrence announced Turner's arrival in the Eternal City. About a week later, Turner, Lawrence, and two other English artists were accompanied by Canova to the Venetian Academy in Rome and observed "the naked model, a very noble figure of a man, who threw himself into the attitudes of the various ancient statues with striking effect."[7] Most important, however, was that in various ways Turner, Lawrence, and Canova shared an interest in the expressive color and painterly techniques of the Venetian masters, particularly the methods and composition of Titian (ca. 1487/90-1576), Tintoretto (1519-1594), and Veronese (1528-1588).

In Turner's Royal Academy lecture on color given in 1818, about a year before his first visit to Venice and Rome, he talks about the way color "aids, exalts, ... in the union with lights and shadows"[8] and then discusses the color of Titian's *St. Peter Martyr* and Veronese's *Marriage of Cana*. In the lecture, he also expresses his appreciation for St. Mark (probably the *Miracle of St. Mark* in the Venice Academy), which is made "buoyant by [the] apposition of forcible combinations, [just] as comparatively it is the lightest as to degrees of *force* and execution."[9] A new colorist orientation is indicated in Turner's Royal Academy lecture and the interest he shared with Lawrence and Canova in the works of the Venetian masters on his first visit to Venice and Rome in 1819.[10] The attention he gave to the Venetian masters' use of color may well have been as important to the changes noted in his palette, which are attributed to the invigorating effects of Mediterranean light.

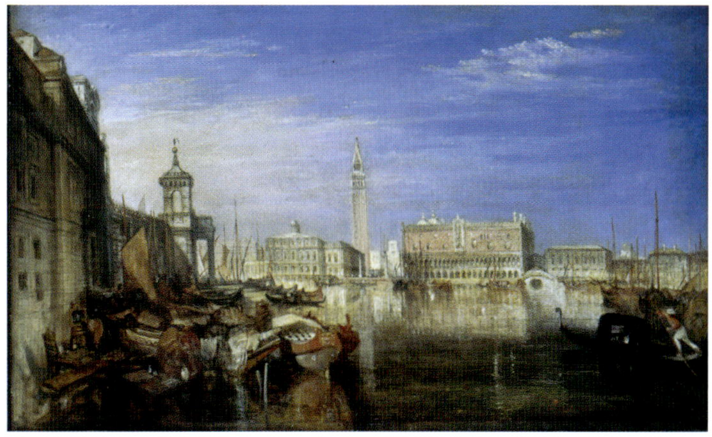

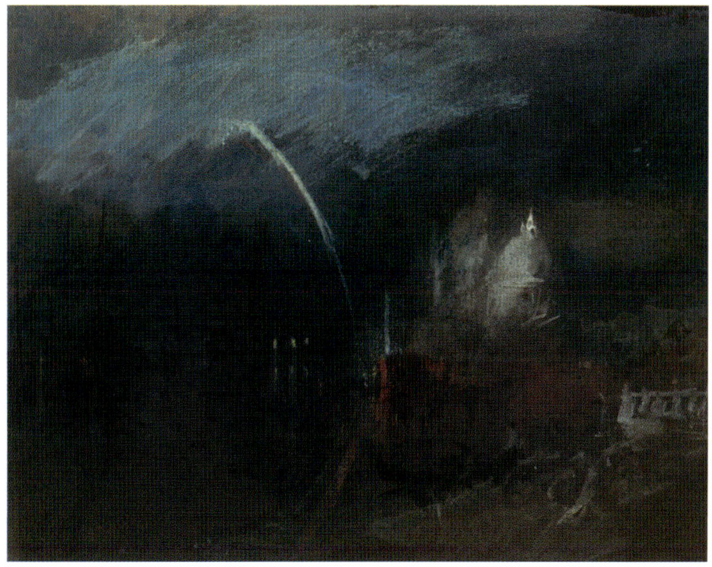

Turner returned to Venice in 1833 and 1840, and his topographical accuracy gave way to poetic color effects and magical reflections of architecture on the still surface of the Basin of St. Mark (fig. 13). The Canto IV of Byron's *Childe Harold's Pilgrimage* had a considerable effect on Turner's imaginary treatment of Venetian topography in the works associated with his later visits of 1833 and 1840. On the other hand, among his studies and paintings of La Serenissima, there are few works that can be clearly related to Byron's poetic references to the decline and fall of the Venetian Republic. The decadence of Byron's Venice is not a dominate theme in Turner's paintings, with their extravagant sense of the fantastic, characterized by high-keyed colors and soft silhouettes of architectural forms obliterated by strong atmospheric light (cat. 50).

Turner's continued interest in Venice caused him to produce some of his greatest and most subjective topographical paintings and studies in color in the 1830s and 1840s (fig. 14). Venice, as a subject unto itself, has fascinated tourists since the earliest days of the Grand Tour. Like his grand touring predecessors, Turner was introduced to this most serene city through the prints by and after Canaletto. Like some of the more discerning tourists, Turner was attracted not only to the city's picturesque aquatic setting and ornate architecture, but also to the brilliant achievements of its late Renaissance painters—Titian, Tintoretto, Veronese, and perhaps the related and hardly lesser accomplishments of the late Baroque artist Tiepolo. On Turner's first visit to Italy in 1819, at Padova he appears to have drawn the Brenta Canal and noted Strà and the Villa Pisani in his sketchbook (CLXXV 36a). It is unlikely he stopped there to see Tiepolo's famous frescos. At that time, the Villa was probably occupied by Maximilian of Austria and would not have been open to the public. From Strà, Turner continued along the Brenta Canal to Fusina where he crossed the Lagoon to Venice. The trip along the Brenta may have had something to do with Turner's interest in the subject matter of Canaletto's etchings and Palladian architecture.

FIG. 13
J.M.W. Turner (English, 1775-1851)
Bridge of Sighs, Ducal Palace and Custom-House, Venice: Canaletti.
Painting, exh. 1833
Oil on mahogany, 20⅛ x 32⅛ in. (51.1 x 81.6 cm)
Tate Gallery, London, Great Britain
Photo credit: Tate, London/Art Resource, NY

FIG. 14
J.M.W. Turner Turner (English, 1775-1851)
Venice: Santa Maria della Salute, Night Scene with Rockets, ca. 1840
Watercolor and bodycolor on paper, 9½ x 12⅜ in. (24 x 31.5 cm)
Tate Gallery, London, Great Britain
Photo copyright Tate London, 2009

When John Ruskin decided to take a break from writing *Modern Painters* in 1845, in which Turner was the central figure, he traveled to Venice to make observations, sketches, and notes on the actual appearance and condition of the city's architecture for his 1849 publication of *The Seven Lamps of Architecture* and *The Stones of Venice* (1851-53). He expressed his dissatisfaction with the Byronic representation of Venice by the poet's romantic devotees as follows:

> The Venice of modern fiction and drama is a thing of yesterday, a mere effloresce of decay, a stage dream which the first ray of daylight must dissipate into dust.[11]

The second part of Ruskin's statement would apply not only to Turner but to Tiepolo as well.

ENDNOTES

1 William Bridgwater and Elizabeth J. Sherwood, *The Columbia Encyclopedia,* in one volume, 2d ed. (New York: Columbia University Press, 1950: 2,067).

2 Lisa Wolk-Simon, "Domenico Tiepolo Drawings, Prints, and Paintings in the Metropolitan Museum of Art," *The Metropolitan Museum of Art Bulletin* (Winter 1996-97): 38-44.

3 Ashton Rollins Willard, *History of Modern Italian Art* (London: Longmans, Green, and Co., 1898: 24).

4 Keith Andrews, *The Nazarenes: A Brotherhood of German Painters in Rome* (New York: Oxford University Press, 1964: 46-59).

5 Jane Turner, ed., *The Dictionary of Art*, vol. 14 (New York: Grove Press, 1996: 265), see Fernando Mazzocca's entry for: Hayez, Francesco.

6 The Carbonari was a secret society opposed to Napoleon's occupation. The organization was first established in Naples in opposition to French Bourbon rule. During the Napoleonic period the society became anti-Muratist [Joachim Murat, French Marshal, was brother-in-law to Napoleon and king of Naples], and then opposed the Bourbons restoration. *The New Cambridge Modern History,* Vol. 9: *War and Peace in an Age of Upheaval 1793-1830* (Cambridge: Cambridge University Press, 1965: 431).

7 Thomas Moore, *Memoirs, Journal, and Correspondence*, vol. 3 (London: Longman, Brown, Green, and Longmans, 1853: 74).

8 Turner Lecture V (1818), BM Add. Ms. 46151, 11, ff. 25v-41v. Gage, *Collected Correspondence*, 206-8.

9 Ibid.

10 In August 1828-February 1829 Turner visited Rome for a second time. He rented a studio near the Spanish Steps, and here he worked on several paintings. Two were harbor scenes. One, a *Claudian Harbour Scene: Study for 'Dido Directing the Equipment of the Fleet* (ca. 1827), appears to be a study for a larger painting he exhibited in Rome. Another painting titled *Regulus,* also in the Rome exhibition, was reworked and exhibited at the British Institution in 1837. The controversial exhibition of his recent paintings was held on December 18th at the Palazzo Trulli, via del Quirinale. Turner's friend, the artist Charles Eastlake, described an attendance of "more than a thousand persons" who were "astonished, enraged or delighted" upon "seeing methods so new, so daring, and excellencies so unequivocal." See Ian Warrell, ed., with an essay by Franklin Kelly, *J. M. W. Turner,* The Metropolitan Museum of Art, New York in association with Tate Publishing, National Gallery of Art, Washington, D.C., Oct. 1, 2007-Jan. 6, 2008. Dallas Museum of Art, Feb. 10-May 18, 2008, The Metropolitan Museum of Art, New York, June 24-Sept. 21, 2008, 136-9, 257. This was the only exhibition Turner had of his work during his visits to Rome and Venice between 1819 and 1840. Some attention has bee given to the possible influence of Turner's work on Caffi. In "Ippolito Caffi: evoluzione della veduta" (*Caffi Luci del Mediterraneo*, Belluno, Palazzzo Crepadona, Oct. 1, 2005-Jan. 22, 2006. Geneva and Milan: Skira Editore, 2006: 95), Annalisa Scarpa describes changes in the way Rome and later Venice is portrayed in the literature, poetry, and painting of a new generation of foreign authors and artist-travellers. The changes in the way Venice is portrayed is particularly evident the work of the work of Corot and the English artists, Richard Parkes Bonington, Samuel Prout, and the later work of Turner. This raises the question of when, if at all, would Caffi have had the opportunity to see Turner's paintings. At the time of Turner's 1828 Rome exhibition, Caffi was pursuing his studies in Venice (1827 to 1831), and he did not move to Rome until 1832. This would not, however, rule out Caffi's presence in Rome at the time of Turner's exhibition.

11 John Ruskin, *The Works of John Ruskin* (Library Edition), ed. E. T. Cook and A. Wedderburn, 39 vols. (London: George Allen, 1903-12: Vol. 10: 8). See also Robert Hewison, (*Ruskin's Venice* (London: Pilkington Press, 1979: 17) for a discussion of Ruskin's growing distrust "of the romantic image of the city created by Byron" and the "foretaste of what Ruskin was to write in *The Stones of Venice.*"

Francesco Hayez (Italian, 1791-1881)
DETAIL: *Secret Allegations [Accusa segreta]*, 1847-48
(FIG. 8)

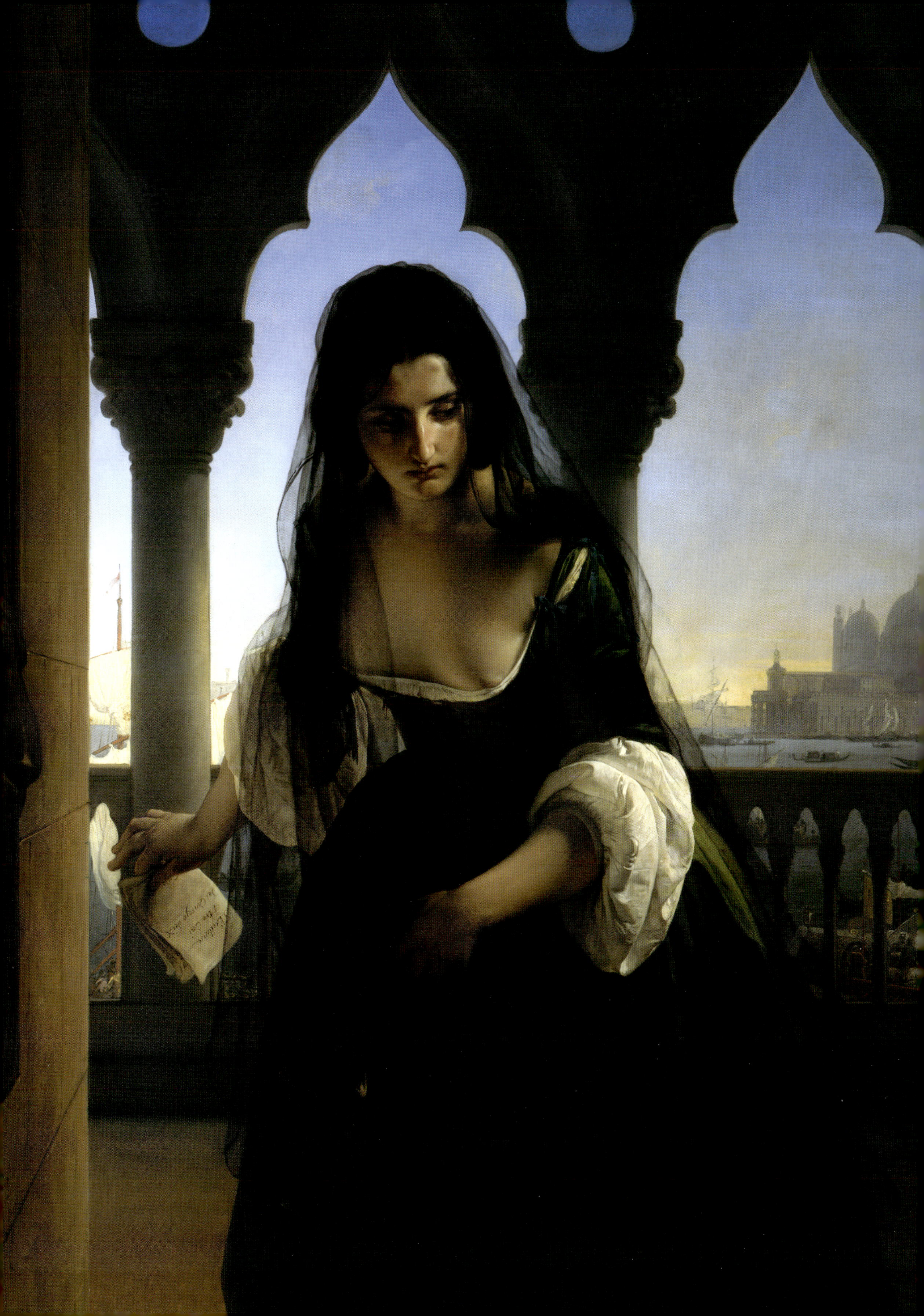

Lenders to the Exhibition

Mr. A. G. Khamneipur
North Vancouver, British Columbia, Canada

Allentown Art Museum
Allentown, PA

Art Gallery of Greater Victoria
Victoria, British Columbia, Canada

Art Gallery of Ontario
Toronto, Ontario, Canada

The Boston Athenæum
Boston, MA

Cincinnati Art Museum
Cincinnati, OH

The Cleveland Museum of Art
Cleveland, OH

Columbia Museum of Art
Columbia, SC

Dallas Museum of Art
Dallas, TX

The Fine Arts Museums of San Francisco
San Francisco, CA

The J. Paul Getty Museum
Los Angeles, CA

John and Mable Ringling Museum of Art
Sarasota, FL

The Metropolitan Museum of Art
New York, NY

Museum of Art and Archaeology
University of Missouri-Columbia
Columbia, MO

The Museum of Fine Arts, Houston
Houston, TX

National Gallery of Art
Washington, DC

The Nelson-Atkins Museum of Art
Kansas City, MO

Oklahoma City Museum of Art
Oklahoma City, OK

Princeton University Art Museum
Princeton, NJ

Private Collection
Vancouver, British Columbia, Canada

San Diego Museum of Art
San Diego, CA

The Sarah Campbell Blaffer Foundation
Houston, TX

Spencer Museum of Art,
The University of Kansas
Lawrence, KS

Springfield Museums–
Michele and Donald D'Amour Museum of Fine Arts
Springfield, MA

The Toledo Museum of Art
Toledo, OH

The University of Arizona Museum of Art and Archive of Visual Arts
Tucson, AZ

University of Toronto Art Centre
Toronto, Ontario, Canada

Vancouver Art Gallery
Vancouver, British Columbia, Canada

Wadsworth Atheneum Museum of Art
Hartford, CT

Yale University Art Gallery
New Haven, CT

Exhibition Checklist

Jacopo Amigoni (Italian, ca. 1685–1752)
Aeneas Appearing Before Queen Dido, ca. 1729
Oil on canvas, $62\frac{7}{8}$ x $46\frac{1}{16}$ in. (160 x 117 cm)
Collection of the Art Gallery of Greater Victoria, British Columbia, Canada. Gift of Mr. and Mrs. G. B. Benson, 1966.058.001
Cat. 1; p. 44

Giuseppe Angeli (Italian, 1712–1798)
Diana, with Wings, Holding an Arrow and a Bow, and the Head of Cupid, ca. 1745
Oil on canvas, $27\frac{5}{8}$ x $20\frac{7}{8}$ in. (70 x 53 cm)
Collection of Mr. A.G. Khamneipur, Canadian Art Collector
Cat. 2; p. 46

Bernardo Bellotto (Italian, 1722–1780)
The Campo of SS. Giovanni e Paolo, Venice, ca. 1741
Oil on canvas, $29\frac{1}{2}$ x $43\frac{3}{4}$ in. (74.93 x 111.13 cm)
The James Philip Gray Collection, Michele and Donald D'Amour Museum of Fine Arts, Springfield, Massachusetts
Cat. 32; p. 118

Antonio Bellucci (Italian, 1654–1726)
Adoration of the Magi, ca. 1700
Oil on canvas, 78 x 105 in. (198.1 x 266.7 cm)
The Sarah Campbell Blaffer Foundation, Houston, 1979.24
Cat. 3; p. 48

Ippolito Caffi (Italian, 1809–1866)
See addendum (cats. 48 and 49)

Canaletto (Giovanni Antonio Canal) (Italian, 1697–1768)
View of the Molo, Venice, ca. 1725
Oil on canvas, $26\frac{1}{2}$ x $32\frac{3}{4}$ in. (67.31 x 83.19 cm)
Columbia Museum of Art, Columbia, SC, Gift of Samuel H. Kress Foundation, 1954.44
Cat. 33; p. 120

Canaletto (Giovanni Antonio Canal) (Italian, 1697–1768)
The Grand Canal near the Rialto Bridge, Venice, ca. 1730
Oil on canvas, $19\frac{1}{2}$ x $28\frac{3}{4}$ in. (49.7 x 70 cm)
The Museum of Fine Arts, Houston. The Robert Lee Blaffer Memorial Collection, gift of Sarah Campbell Blaffer, 55.103
Cat. 34; p. 122

Canaletto (Giovanni Antonio Canal) (Italian, 1697–1768)
Venice: Santa Maria della Salute, ca. 1740
Oil on canvas, $18\frac{3}{4}$ x $31\frac{1}{4}$ in. (47.6 x 79.4 cm)
Lent by The Metropolitan Museum of Art, Purchase, George T. Delacorte Jr. Gift, 1959 (59.38)
Cat. 35; p. 124

Canaletto (Giovanni Antonio Canal) (Italian, 1697–1768)
The Piazzeta: Looking South, ca. 1740–46
Oil on canvas, $19\frac{3}{4}$ x $32\frac{3}{8}$ in. (50.16 x 82.23 cm)
Allentown Art Museum, Gift of Samuel H. Kress Collection, 1961 (1961.44)
Cat. 36; p. 126

Canaletto (Giovanni Antonio Canal) (Italian, 1697–1768)
Views (Vedute): Imaginary View of Padua, ca. 1741–44
Etching, $11\frac{3}{4}$ x $16\frac{13}{16}$ in. (29.8 x 42.7 cm)
Lent by The Metropolitan Museum of Art, Rogers Fund, 1918 (18.65.1 (11))
Cat. 56; p. 156

Canaletto (Giovanni Antonio Canal) (Italian, 1697–1768)
Views (Vedute): Imaginary View of Venice, 1741
Etching, $11\frac{13}{16}$ x $17\frac{1}{8}$ in. (30 x 43.5 cm)
Lent by The Metropolitan Museum of Art, Purchase, Gift of Mary V.T. Eberstadt and Bequest of Gertrude Moira Flanagan, by exchange, 1973 (1973.634)
Cat. 57; p. 156

Canaletto (Giovanni Antonio Canal) (Italian, 1697–1768)
Views (Vedute): Le Porte del Dolo, ca. 1741–44
Etching, $11\frac{3}{4}$ x $16\frac{3}{4}$ in. (29.8 x 42.6 cm)
Lent by The Metropolitan Museum of Art, Rogers Fund, 1918 (18.65.1 (6))
Cat. 54; p. 154

Canaletto (Giovanni Antonio Canal) (Italian, 1697–1768)
Views (Vedute): The Library, Venice, ca. 1741–44
Etching, $5\frac{3}{4}$ x $8\frac{3}{8}$ in. (14.5 x 21.2 cm)
The Cleveland Museum of Art. Gift of The Print Club of Cleveland, 1925.1239.15
Cat. 59; p. 158

Canaletto (Giovanni Antonio Canal) (Italian, 1697–1768)
Views (Vedute): The Market at the Molo, ca. 1741–44
Etching, $5\frac{3}{4}$ x $8\frac{3}{8}$ in. (14.5 x 21.2 cm)
The Cleveland Museum of Art. Gift of The Print Club of Cleveland, 1925.1239.17
Cat. 61; p. 158

Canaletto (Giovanni Antonio Canal) (Italian, 1697–1768)
Views (Vedute): Mestre, ca.1741–44
Etching, $11\frac{3}{4}$ x $16\frac{3}{4}$ in. (29.8 x 42.6 cm)
Lent by The Metropolitan Museum of Art, Rogers Fund, 1918 (18.65.1 (3))
Cat. 53; p. 154

Canaletto (Giovanni Antonio Canal) (Italian, 1697–1768)
Views (Vedute): The Portico with a Lantern, ca. 1741–44
Etching, $11\frac{3}{4}$ x $16\frac{13}{16}$ in. (29.8 x 42.7 cm)
Lent by The Metropolitan Museum of Art, Rogers Fund, 1918 (18.65.1 (10))
Cat. 55; p. 156

Canaletto (Giovanni Antonio Canal) (Italian, 1697–1768)
Views (Vedute): The Prison, Venice, ca. 1741–44
Etching, $5\frac{3}{4}$ x $8\frac{3}{8}$ in. (14.5 x 21.2 cm)
The Cleveland Museum of Art. Gift of The Print Club of Cleveland, 1925.1239.18
Cat. 62; p. 158

Canaletto (Giovanni Antonio Canal) (Italian, 1697–1768)
Views (Vedute): Procuratie Niove and S. Geminiano Giustin (S. Ziminian V[ence].), ca. 1741–44
Etching, $5\frac{1}{2}$ x 8 in. (13.97 x 20.32 cm)
University of Toronto Art Collection, University of Toronto Art Centre, 1997.055
Cat. 58; p. 156

Canaletto (Giovanni Antonio Canal) (Italian, 1697–1768)
Views (Vedute): The Stone of Proclamation at Venice (La Piera del Bando, V[ence].), ca. 1741–44
Etching, $5\frac{3}{4}$ x $8\frac{3}{8}$ in. (14.5 x 21.2 cm)
The Cleveland Museum of Art. Gift of The Print Club of Cleveland, 1925.1239.16
Cat. 60; p. 158

Canaletto (Giovanni Antonio Canal) (Italian, 1697–1768)
Views (Vedute): Title Page, ca. 1744
Etching, $11\frac{5}{8}$ x $16\frac{13}{16}$ in. (29.6 x 42.7 cm)
Lent by The Metropolitan Museum of Art, Rogers Fund, 1918 (18.65.1 (1))
Cat. 51; p. 154

Canaletto (Giovanni Antonio Canal) (Italian, 1697–1768)
Views (Vedute): The Tower of Malghera, ca. 1741–44
Etching, $5\frac{3}{4}$ x $8\frac{3}{8}$ in. (14.5 x 21.2 cm)
The Cleveland Museum of Art. Gift of The Print Club of Cleveland, 1925.1239.2
Cat. 52; p. 154

Canaletto (Giovanni Antonio Canal) (Italian, 1697–1768)
Capriccio: Farmhouse on the Venetian Mainland, ca. 1755–65
Oil on panel, $5\frac{3}{4}$ x $7\frac{1}{2}$ in. (14.61 x 19.05 cm)
The James Philip Gray Collection, Michele and Donald D'Amour Museum of Fine Arts, Springfield, Massachusetts
Cat. 37; p. 128

Canaletto (Giovanni Antonio Canal) (Italian, 1697–1768)
Capriccio: Villa and Ruins by a River, ca. 1755–65
Oil on panel, $5\frac{3}{4}$ x $7\frac{1}{2}$ in. (14.61 x 19.05 cm)
The James Philip Gray Collection, Michele and Donald D'Amour Museum of Fine Arts, Springfield, Massachusetts
Cat. 38; p. 128

Luca Carlevarijs (Italian, 1663–1730)
The Molo, Venice, From the Bacino di San Marco, ca. 1709
Oil on canvas, $19\frac{7}{8}$ x $47\frac{1}{8}$ in. (50.5 x 119.7 cm)
Lent by The Metropolitan Museum of Art, Robert Lehman Collection, 1975 (1975.1.87)
Cat. 39; p. 130

Luca Carlevarijs (Italian, 1663–1730)
The Molo, Venice, Looking West, ca. 1709
Oil on canvas, $19\frac{7}{8}$ x $47\frac{1}{8}$ in. (50.5 x 119.7 cm)
Lent by The Metropolitan Museum of Art, Robert Lehman Collection, 1975 (1975.1.90)
Cat. 40; p. 130

Luca Carlevarijs (Italian, 1663–1730)
The Molo Looking West, ca. 1725–27
Oil on canvas, $18\frac{1}{4}$ x $32\frac{5}{8}$ in. (46.4 x 83 cm)
Collection, Art Gallery of Ontario, Toronto. Gift of the Ludwig Mond Estate, 1926
Cat. 41; p. 132

Giuseppe Maria Crespi (Italian, 1665–1747)
Portrait of a Woman Holding a Mask, ca. 1700
Oil on canvas, 32 x 26 in. (81.28 x 66.04 cm)
Oklahoma City Museum of Art. Gift of Mr. and Mrs. S.T. Fee, Mr. and Mrs. Howard Melton, Mrs. Omar Milligan, Mr. and Mrs. Richard L. Sias, and Mr. and Mrs. John A. Taylor, 1978.046
Cat. 25; p. 88

Francesco Fontebasso (Italian, 1707–1769)
Family of Darius Before Alexander, 1750
Oil on canvas, $50\frac{1}{8}$ x $65\frac{1}{8}$ in. (127.32 x 165.42 cm)
Dallas Museum of Art. Gift of Colonel C. Michael Paul, 1964.110
Cat. 4; p. 50

Luca Giordano (Italian, 1632-1705)
The Meeting of Venus and Adonis, 1652-53
Oil on canvas, 81 3/16 x 60 15/16 in. (206.1 x 154.5 cm)
Collection of the Vancouver Art Gallery, Vancouver Art Gallery Acquisition Fund, VAG 86.192
Cat. 5; p. 52

Francesco Guardi (Italian, 1712-1793)
Abraham Welcoming the Three Angels, ca. 1750s
Oil on canvas, 22 1/4 x 29 5/8 in. (56.5 x 75.5 cm)
The Cleveland Museum of Art. Mr. and Mrs. William H. Marlatt Fund, 1952.235.4
Cat. 7; p. 54

Francesco Guardi (Italian, 1712-1793)
The Angels Appearing to Abraham, ca. 1750s
Oil on canvas, 22¼ x 29⅝ in. (56.5 x 75.5 cm)
The Cleveland Museum of Art. Mr. and Mrs. William H. Marlatt Fund, 1952.235.3
Cat. 6; p. 54

Francesco Guardi (Italian, 1712-1793)
The Sacrifice of Isaac, ca. 1750s
Oil on canvas, 22¼ x 29⅝ in. (56.5 x 75.5 cm)
The Cleveland Museum of Art. Mr. and Mrs. William H. Marlatt Fund, 1952.235.1
Cat. 8; p. 55

Francesco Guardi (Italian, 1712-1793)
Tobias and the Angel, ca. 1750s
Oil on canvas, 22¼ x 29⅝ in. (56.5 x 75.5 cm)
The Cleveland Museum of Art. Mr. and Mrs. William H. Marlatt Fund, 1952.235.2
Cat. 9; p. 55

Francesco Guardi (Italian, 1712-1793)
View of the Dogana and Santa Maria della Salute, 1767-69
Oil on canvas, 19½ x 26⅛ in. (49.5 x 66.4 cm)
The Nelson-Atkins Museum of Art, Kansas City, Missouri. Purchase: William Rockhill Nelson Trust, 30-21
Cat. 42; p. 134

Francesco Guardi (Italian, 1712-1793)
Regatta at the Rialto Bridge, ca. 1770s
Oil on canvas, 30½ x 49½ in. (77.47 x 125.73 cm)
The Sarah Campbell Blaffer Foundation, Houston, 1983.1
Cat. 43; p. 136

Francesco Guardi (Italian, 1712-1793)
San Giorgio Maggiore, Venice, ca. 1790
Oil on canvas, 18¼ x 30 1/16 in. (46.5 x 76.3 cm)
Toledo Museum of Art, Toledo, Ohio. Purchased with funds from the Libbey Endowment, Gift of Edward Drummond Libbey, 1952.62
Cat. 44; p. 138

Attributed to Francesco Guardi (Italian, 1712-1793)
Venice, The Molo and the Riva degli Schiavonei, Looking East, late 1750s
Oil on canvas, 14 x 23 5/16 in. (35.6 x 59.2 cm)
Yale University Art Gallery, Gift of Susan Morse Hilles, 1973.87.3
Cat. 45; p. 140

Antonio Joli (Italian, 1700-1777)
A View of Westminster Bridge from the North, with a Procession of State Barges, ca. 1750
Oil on canvas, 37 x 42⅛ in. (94 x 107 cm)
Collection of the Art Gallery of Greater Victoria, British Columbia, Canada. Alice Winthrop Stuart Bequest, 1984.047.002
Cat. 46; p. 142

Gregorio Lazzarini (Italian, 1655-1730)
The Golden Age (A Bacchanal), ca. 1700
Oil on canvas, 94 x 144 in. (240.4 x 366.5 cm)
The Boston Athenæum, Gift of George Washington Wales, 1861, as by Luca Giordano
Cat. 10; p. 56

Pietro Longhi (Italian, 1702-1785)
The Temptation, ca. 1750
Oil on canvas, 29¼ x 25⅛ in. (74.93 x 63.82 cm)
Wadsworth Atheneum Museum of Art, Hartford, CT. The Ella Gallup Sumner and Mary Catlin Sumner Collection Fund, 1931.188
Cat. 26; p. 90

Pietro Longhi (Italian, 1702-1785)
The Concert (The Mandolin Recital), ca. 1755-60
Oil on canvas, 23 x 18¾ in. (58.4 x 47.6 cm)
Fine Arts Museums of San Francisco.
Gift of Kathryn Bache Miller, 1964.71
Cat. 27; p. 92

Domenico Maggiotto (Italian, 1713-1794)
Head of a Girl with a Spindle, ca. 1735-40
Oil on canvas, 18¾ x 14¾ in. (47.6 x 37.5 cm)
Bequest of John Ringling, 1936, Collection of The John and Mable Ringling Museum of Art, the State Art Museum of Florida, a Division of Florida State University, SN183
Cat. 28; p. 94

Unidentified artist, formerly attributed to Michele Marieschi (Italian, 1696-1743)
View of Venice: SS Giovanni e Paolo and the Scuola di San Marco, ca. 1756-60
Oil on canvas, 51 x 66 in. (129.54 x 167.64 cm)
Fine Arts Museums of San Francisco, Museum Purchase, M.H. de Young Memorial Museum, 48.1
Cat. 47; p. 144

Giustino Menescardi (Italian, 1720-1776)
The Holy Family and the Holy Dove Appearing to S. Francesco di Paola, ca. 1750
Oil on canvas, 31½ x 22 in. (79 x 55 cm)
University of Toronto Art Centre, Malcove Collection, M82.17
Cat. 11; p. 58

Giovanni Antonio Pellegrini (Italian, 1675-1741)
The Entombment, 1719
Oil on canvas, 38½ x 50½ in. (97.79 x 128.27 cm)
Bequest of John Ringling, 1936, Collection of The John and Mable Ringling Museum of Art, the State Art Museum of Florida a Division of Florida State University, SN176
Cat. 12; p. 60

Giovanni Battista Piazzetta (Italian, 1683-1754)
Madonna and Child Appearing to Saint Philip Neri, ca. 1725
Oil on canvas, 44¼ x 25 in. (112.4 x 63.5 cm)
National Gallery of Art, Washington, Samuel H. Kress Collection, 1961.9.82 (1634)
Cat. 13; p. 62

Giovanni Battista Piazzetta (Italian, 1683-1754)
Portrait of Giacomo in a Fur Hat, 1745
Oil on canvas, 32½ x 24⅞ in. (82.55 x 62.99 cm)
University of Arizona Museum of Art & Archive of Visual Arts, Gift of Samuel H. Kress Foundation, 1961.013.024
Cat. 29; p. 96

Giovanni Battista Pittoni (Italian, 1687-1767)
Saints Presenting a Devout Woman to the Virgin and Child, 1720s
Oil on canvas, 67¾ x 53⅜ in. (172 x 135.5 cm)
The Cleveland Museum of Art. Leonard C. Hanna, Jr. Fund, 1982.36
Cat. 14; p. 64

Giovanni Battista Pittoni (Italian, 1687-1767)
The Vision of Saint Anthony of Padua, ca. 1730
Oil on canvas, 30¼ x 21¾ in. (77 x 55.5 cm)
The San Diego Museum of Art.
Gift of Anne R. and Amy Putnam, 1948:3
Cat. 15; p. 66

Sebastiano (Italian, 1659-1734) and Marco (Italian, 1676-1730) Ricci
Death of Saint Paul the Hermit, 1700-10
Oil on canvas, 37 x 54 in. (94 x 137.2 cm)
Spencer Museum of Art, University of Kansas, Gift from the Samuel H. Kress Study Collection, 1960.0055
Cat. 18; p. 72

Sebastiano Ricci (Italian, 1659-1734)
Diana and Endymion, ca. 1717-20
Oil on canvas, 49 3/16 x 70⅜ in. (125 x 178.7 cm)
Princeton University Art Museum, Museum purchase, bequest of Gilbert S. McClintock, Class of 1908, and gift of Mr. and Mrs. Harry L. Tepper, by exchange, y1964-167
Cat. 16; p. 68

Sebastiano Ricci (Italian, 1659-1734)
Diana and Her Dog, 1717-20
Oil on canvas, 29⅛ x 21⅞ in. (74 x 55.6 cm)
The J. Paul Getty Museum, Los Angeles, California
Cat. 17; p. 70

Pietro Rotari (Italian, 1707-1762)
Young Woman with a Sprig of Jasmine, ca. 1756-62
Oil on canvas, 18¼ x 15¼ in. (46.4 x 38.8 cm)
Museum of Art and Archaeology, University of Missouri-Columbia. Gift of the Samuel H. Kress Foundation, 61.82
Cat. 30; p. 98

Giovanni Battista Tiepolo (Italian, 1696-1770)
Queen Tullia Commands Her Coachman to Drive over the Body of Her Father, 1722
Oil on canvas, 16⅞ x 29⅛ in. (43 x 74 cm)
Private Collection, Vancover, Canada
Cat. 19; p. 74

Giovanni Battista Tiepolo (Italian, 1696-1770)
Juno Triumphant, as Queen of the Air, ca. 1735
Oil on canvas, 91½ x 86 in. (213 x 231 cm)
The Sarah Campbell Blaffer Foundation, Houston, 1983.4
Cat. 20; p. 76

Giovanni Battista Tiepolo (Italian, 1696-1770)
Scherzi di Fantasia: The Discovery of the Tomb of Punchinello, ca. 1743-50
Etching, 9⅛ x 7 3/16 in. (23.1 x 18.2 cm)
Lent by The Metropolitan Museum of Art, Purchase, The Elisha Whittelsey Collection, The Elisha Whittelsey Fund; Dodge and Pfeiffer Funds; Joseph Pulitzer Bequest; Gift of Bertina Suida Manning and Robert L. Manning, 1976 (1976.537(17))
Cat. 69; p. 163

Giovanni Battista Tiepolo (Italian, 1696-1770)
Scherzi di Fantasia: Frontispiece, ca. 1743-50
Etching, 8⅞ x 7 3/16 in. (22.6 x 18.2 cm)
Lent by The Metropolitan Museum of Art, Purchase, The Elisha Whittelsey Collection, The Elisha Whittelsey Fund; Dodge and Pfeiffer Funds; Joseph Pulitzer Bequest; Gift of Bertina Suida Manning and Robert L. Manning, 1976 (1976.537 (1))
Cat. 63; p. 160

Giovanni Battista Tiepolo (Italian, 1696-1770)
Scherzi di Fantasia: The Happy Satyr and His Family, ca. 1743-50
Etching, 8⅞ x 10 in. (22.5 x 25.4 cm)
The Cleveland Museum of Art. Gift of Leonard C. Hanna, Jr., 1924.530
Cat. 67; p. 162

Giovanni Battista Tiepolo (Italian, 1696-1770)
Scherzi di Fantasia: Magician Pointing Out a Burning Head to Two Youths, ca. 1743-50
Etching, 8⅞ x 7¼ in. (22.6 x 18.5 cm)
The Cleveland Musuem of Art. Andrew R. and Martha Holden Jennings Fund, 1998.113
Cat. 65; p. 160

Giovanni Battista Tiepolo (Italian, 1696-1770)
Scherzi di Fantasia: Satyr Family with the Obelisk, ca. 1743-50
Etching, 8⅞ x 6⅞ in. (22.5 x 17.7 cm)
The Cleveland Museum of Art. Gift of Leonard C. Hanna, Jr., 1924.529
Cat. 68; p. 163

Giovanni Battista Tiepolo (Italian, 1696-1770)
Scherzi di Fantasia: Seated Magician, Boy and Four Figures, ca. 1743-50
Etching, 8⅞ x 7 in. (22.5 x 17.9 cm)
The Cleveland Museum of Art.
Gift of Leonard C. Hanna, Jr., 1924.528
Cat. 66; p. 162

Giovanni Battista Tiepolo (Italian, 1696-1770)
Scherzi di Fantasia: Three Magicians Burning a Snake, ca. 1743-50
Etching, 9 x $7\frac{1}{16}$ in. (22.8 x 18 cm)
Lent by The Metropolitan Museum of Art, Purchase, The Elisha Whittelsey Collection, The Elisha Whittelsey Fund; Dodge and Pfeiffer Funds; Joseph Pulitzer Bequest; Gift of Bertina Suida Manning and Robert L. Manning, 1976 (1976.537(13))
Cat. 64; p. 160

Giovanni Battista Tiepolo (Italian, 1696-1770)
Jesus and the Barren Fig Tree, 1752-53
Oil on canvas, 33¼ x 78½ in. (83 x 189 cm)
Private Collection, Vancouver, Canada
Cat. 21; p. 78

Giovanni Battista Tiepolo (Italian, 1696-1770) and Studio
St. Charles Borromeo Meditating on the Crucifix (fragment), 1767-69
Oil on canvas, 48½ x 44⅛ in. (123.19 x 112.08 cm)
Cincinnati Art Museum, John J. Emery Fund, 1924.178
Cat. 22; p. 80

Giovanni Battista Tiepolo (Italian, 1696-1770)
Madona of the Goldfinch, ca. 1762-70
Oil on canvas, 24⅞ x 19⅞ in. (63.1 x 50.3 cm)
National Gallery of Art, Washington, Samuel H. Kress Collection, 1943.4.40 (541)
Cat. 23; p. 82

Giovanni Battista Tiepolo (Italian, 1696-1770)
Vari Capricci: The Astrologer and the Young Soldier, 1785
Etching, 5¼ x 6¾ in.(13.4 x 17.1 cm)
Fine Arts Museums of San Francisco,
Achenbach Foundation for Graphic Arts
Cat. 79; p. 167

Giovanni Battista Tiepolo (Italian, 1696-1770)
Vari Capricci: Death Giving An Audience, 1785
Etching, 5½ x $6\frac{15}{16}$ in. (14.1 x 17.7 cm)
Fine Arts Museums of San Francisco,
Achenbach Foundation for Graphic Arts
Cat. 78; p. 167

Giovanni Battista Tiepolo (Italian, 1696-1770)
Vari Capricci: A Nymph with a Small Satyr and Two Goats, 1785
Etching, 5½ x $6\frac{13}{16}$ in. (14.1 x 17.4 cm)
Fine Arts Museums of San Francisco, Achenbach Foundation for Graphic Arts
Cat. 75; p. 166

Giovanni Battista Tiepolo (Italian, 1696-1770)
Vari Capricci: The Rider Standing Beside His Horse, 1785
Etching, $5\frac{7}{16}$ x 7 in. (13.9 x 17.8 cm)
Fine Arts Museums of San Francisco,
Achenbach Foundation for Graphic Arts
Cat. 80; p. 167

Giovanni Battista Tiepolo (Italian, 1696-1770)
Vari Capricci: Seated Youth Leaning Against an Urn, 1785
Etching, 5½ x 7⅛ in. (14.1 x 18 cm)
Fine Arts Museums of San Francisco,
Achenbach Foundation for Graphic Arts
Cat. 71; p. 164

Giovanni Battista Tiepolo (Italian, 1696-1770)
Vari Capricci: Standing Philosopher, 1785
Etching, 5¼ x $6\frac{13}{16}$ in. (13.4 x 17.4 cm)
Fine Arts Museums of San Francisco,
Achenbach Foundation for Graphic Arts
Cat. 76; p. 166

Giovanni Battista Tiepolo (Italian, 1696-1770)
Vari Capricci: Three Soldiers and a Boy, 1785
Etching, $5\frac{9}{16}$ x $6\frac{15}{16}$ in. (14.1 x 17.6 cm)
Fine Arts Museums of San Francisco,
Achenbach Foundation for Graphic Arts
Cat. 72; p. 164

Giovanni Battista Tiepolo (Italian, 1696-1770)
Vari Capricci: Title Page, 1785
Etching, $4\frac{7}{16}$ x $6\frac{7}{16}$ in. (11.3 x 16.4 cm)
Fine Arts Museums of San Francisco,
Achenbach Foundation for Graphic Arts
Cat. 70; p. 164

Giovanni Battista Tiepolo (Italian, 1696-1770)
Vari Capricci: Two Soldiers and Two Women, 1785
Etching, $5\frac{15}{16}$ x $6\frac{11}{16}$ in. (13.2 x 17 cm)
Fine Arts Museums of San Francisco,
Achenbach Foundation for Graphic Arts
Cat. 77; p. 167

Giovanni Battista Tiepolo (Italian, 1696-1770)
Vari Capricci: Women and Men Regarding a Burning Pyre of Bones, 1785
Etching, 5⅝ x 6⅞ in. (14.28 x 17.46 cm)
National Gallery of Art, Washington.
Gift of W.G. Russell Allen, 1941.8.29
Cat. 73; p. 166

Giovanni Battista Tiepolo (Italian, 1696-1770)
Vari Capricci: A Woman with her Hands on a Vase, a Soldier and a Slave, 1785
Etching, $5\frac{7}{16}$ x $6\frac{15}{16}$ in. (13.8 x 17.6 cm)
Fine Arts Museums of San Francisco,
Achenbach Foundation for Graphic Arts
Cat. 74; p. 166

Giovanni Domenico Tiepolo (Italian, 1727-1804)
The Flight, with Madonna at Right Supported by Angels, 1753
Etching, 7⅜ x 9¾ in. (18.7 x 24.7 cm)
National Gallery of Art, Washington,
Gift of W.G. Russell Allen, 1941.8.57
Cat. 87; p. 171

Giovanni Domenico Tiepolo (Italian, 1727-1804)
The Holy Family Being Ferried Across the River, 1753
Etching, 4⅝ x 9¼ in. (11.7 x 23.5 cm)
National Gallery of Art, Washington,
Gift of W.G. Russell Allen, 1941.8.48
Cat. 84; p. 170

Giovanni Domenico Tiepolo (Italian 1727-1804)
The Holy Family Passes under a City Arch, 1753
Etching, 7⅜ x 9⅝ in. (18.8 x 24.5 cm)
National Gallery of Art, Washington,
Gift of W.G. Russell Allen, 1941.8.38
Cat. 83; p. 168

Giovanni Domenico Tiepolo (Italian, 1727-1804)
The Holy Family Under a Palm Tree, 1753
Etching, 7⅜ x 9⅞ in. (18.7 x 24.9 cm)
Fine Arts Museums of San Francisco,
Achenbach Foundation for Graphic Arts
Cat. 82; p. 168

Giovanni Domenico Tiepolo (Italian, 1727-1804)
Joseph Adoring the Child, 1753
Etching, 7½ x 9⅞ in. (18.9 x 25 cm)
Fine Arts Museums of San Francisco,
Bruno and Sadie Adriani Collection
Cat. 85; p. 170

Giovanni Domenico Tiepolo (Italian, 1727-1804)
Joseph Relays to Mary God's Command to Flee, 1753
Etching, 7⅜ x 9⅝ in. (18.7 x 24.3 cm)
National Gallery of Art, Washington,
Gift of W.G. Russell Allen, 1941.8.35
Cat. 81; p. 168

Giovanni Domenico Tiepolo (Italian, 1727-1804)
The Rest on the Flight into Egypt, with Holy Family under a Tree, 1753
Etching, 7½ x 9⅜ in. (19.1 x 23.8 cm)
National Gallery of Art, Washington,
Gift of W.G. Russell Allen, 1941.8.54
Cat. 86; p. 171

Giovanni Domenico Tiepolo (Italian, 1727-1804)
Head of a Woman, 1762-70
Oil on canvas, 23⅞ x 19⅛ in. (60.4 x 48.6 cm)
The Cleveland Museum of Art,
Gift of Harry D. Kendrick, 1952.541
Cat. 31; p. 100

Giovanni Domenico Tiepolo (Italian, 1727-1804)
The Building of the Trojan Horse, mid-1770s
Oil on canvas, 88¼ x 154 in. (224.16 x 391.16 cm)
Wadsworth Atheneum Museum of Art, Hartford, CT. The Ella Gallup Sumner and Mary Catlin Sumner Collection Fund, 1950.658
Cat. 24; p. 84

Giovanni Domenico Tiepolo (Italian, 1727-1804)
In Piazza, ca. 1791
Pen and brown ink, brown wash, over black chalk, 14⅜ x 19¾ in. (36.5 x 50.1 cm)
Lent by The Metropolitan Museum of Art, Robert Lehman Collection, 1975 (1975.1.510)
Cat. 88; p. 172

Giovanni Domenico Tiepolo (Italian, 1727-1804)
The Flogging of the Punchinello, ca. 1800
Pen and brown ink, brown wash, over black chalk, 14 x $18\frac{9}{16}$ in. (35.5 x 47.2 cm)
Lent by The Metropolitan Museum of Art, Robert Lehman Collection, 1975 (1975.1.467)
Cat. 90; p. 172

Giovanni Domenico Tiepolo (Italian, 1727-1804)
Punchinello as a Dressmaker, ca. 1800
Pen and brown ink, brown wash, over black chalk, $13\frac{15}{16}$ x 18½ in. (35.4 x 47 cm)
Lent by The Metropolitan Museum of Art, Robert Lehman Collection, 1975 (1975.1.466)
Cat. 89; p. 172

Addendum: Nineteenth-century View Painting

Ippolito Caffi (Italian, 1809-1866)
View of Santa Maria della Salute from the Ponte dell'Accademia, Venice, ca. 1845
Oil on canvas, 15⅛ x 18⅞ in. (38.57 x 47.94 cm)
Oklahoma City Museum of Art. Purchase with funds provided by an Inasmuch Foundation grant in honor of Carolyn Hill, 2009.021
Cat. 48; p. 146

Ippolito Caffi (Italian, 1809-1866)
View of the Bacino di San Marco, Venice, ca. 1845
Oil on canvas, 15⅛ x 18⅞ in. (38.57 x 47.94 cm)
Oklahoma City Museum of Art. Purchase with funds provided by an Inasmuch Foundation grant in honor of Carolyn Hill, 2009.022
Cat. 49; p. 148

J.M.W. Turner (English, 1775-1851)
The Dogana and Santa Maria della Salute, Venice, 1843
Oil on canvas, $24\frac{7}{16}$ x 36⅝ in. (62 x 93 cm)
National Gallery of Art, Washington, Given in memory of Governor Alvan T. Fuller by The Fuller Foundation, Inc., 1961.2.3
Cat. 50; p. 150

Select Bibliography

Arnaldi, G., and M. Pastore Stocchi, eds. *Il settecento*, Storia della Cultura Veneta, v/1-2. Vicenza: Neri Pozza Editore, 1985.

Bachelli, Ricardo, and Roberto Longhi. *Teatro e immagini del settecento italiano*. Milan: Radio Italiana, 1953.

Bacou, Roseline. *Venise au dix-huitième siècle*. Musée de L'Orangerie. Exh. cat. Paris: Réunion des musées nationaux, 1971.

Baetjer, Katharine, and J. G. Links. *Canaletto*. New York: Metropolitan Museum of Art, 1989.

Bagemihl, Rolf. "Pietro Longhi and Venetian Life," *Metropolitan Museum Journal* 23 (1988).

Barch, Gisela. *Bernardo Bellotto: Verona e le città europee*. Ed. S. Marinelli. Milan: Electa, 1990.

Barcham, William L. *The Religious Paintings of Giambattista Tiepolo*. New York and Oxford: Oxford University Press, 1989.

———. *Giambattista Tiepolo*. New York: Thames and Hudson, 1992.

Battistella, Oreste. *Della Vita e delle opere di Gaetano Gherardo Zompini*. Bologna: Anichelli Editore, 1930.

Bean, Jacob, and William Griswold. *18th Century Italian Drawings in the Metropolitan Museum of Art*. New York: The Metropolitan Museum of Art, 1990.

Beddington, Charles. *Canaletto in England: A Venetian Artist Abroad, 1746-1755*. New Haven and London: Yale University Press, 2006.

———. *Luca Carlevarijs: Views of Venice*. San Diego: Timken Museum of Art, 2001.

Bettagno, Alessandro, ed. *Canaletto: disegni, dipinti, incisioni*. Venice: Neri Pozza, 1982.

Binion, Alice. *I disegni di Giambattista Pittoni*. Florence: La Nuova Italia, 1983.

Boccazzi, Franca Zava. *Pittoni*. Venice: Mondadori Electa, 1979.

Bortoletto, Luigina Rossi. *L'opera completa di Francesco Guardi*. Milan: Rizzoli, 1974.

Boschini, Marco. *Le ricche minere della pittura veneziana*. Venice: F. Nicolini, 1674.

Bowron, Edgar Peters, ed. *Bernardo Bellotto and the Capitals of Europe*. New Haven and London: Yale University Press, 2001.

———, and Mary G. Morton. *Masterworks of European Painting in the Museum of Fine Arts, Houston*. Princeton, N.J.: Princeton University Press, 2000.

Branca, Vittore, ed. *Barocco europeo e barocco veneziano, Civilta europea e civilta veneziana*. Florence: Sansoni, 1963.

———, ed. *Dall'eta barocca all'Italia contemporanea*. Vol. 3: *Storia della civilta veneziana*. Florence: Sansoni, 1979.

Briganti, Giuliano, *I Vedutisti*, Milan: Electa, 1968.

Bromberg, Ruth. *Canaletto's Etchings: A Catalogue and Study Illustrating and Describing the Known States, Including Those Hitherto Unrecorded*. London and New York: Sotheby Parke Bernet, 1974. Rev. ed. San Francisco: Alan Wofsy Fine Arts, 1993.

Brown, Beverly Louise. *Giambattista Tiepolo: Master of the Oil Sketch*. Milan: Electa; New York: Abbeville; Fort Worth, Kimbell Art Museum, 1993.

Brunel, G. *Tiepolo*. Paris: Fayard, 1991.

Byam Shaw, James. *The Drawings of Domenico Tiepolo*. London: Faber and Faber, 1962.

———. *The Drawings of Francesco Guardi*. London: Faber and Faber, 1951.

———, and George Knox. *The Lehman Collection*. Vol. 6: *Italian Eighteenth-Century Drawings*. New York: Princeton University Press, 1987.

Cailleux, J. "*Les Guardi et Pietro Longhi*," in *Problemi guardeschi*, 52-4. Venice, 1967.

Capricci veneziani del Settecento. Curated by Dario Succi. Exh. cat. by Andre Corboz. Torino: Umberto Allemandi, 1988.

Cartari, Vincenzo. *Imagini delli de gl'antichi*. Venice: Tomasini, 1647; facsimile reprint, Graz: Akademische Druck und Verlagsanstalt, 1963.

Camesasca, Ettore. *L'opera completa del Bellotto*. Milan: Rizzoli, 1974.

da Canal, Vincenzo. *Vita di Gregorio Lazzarini*. Venice: G. A. Moschini, 1809.

Christiansen, Keith, ed. *Giambattista Tiepolo, 1696-1770*. New York: Metropolitan Museum of Art, 1996.

Clifton, James, ed. *Venetian Painting from the Sarah Campbell Blaffer Foundation*. Houston Museum of Fine Arts, 1995.

Corboz, André. *Canaletto: Una Venezia immaginaria*. Milan: Alfieri Electa, 1985.

Constable, William George. *Canaletto*. Toronto: Art Gallery of Toronto, 1964.

———. *Canaletto, Giovanni Antonio Canal, 1697-1768*. Oxford: Clarendon Press, 1962. 2nd ed. Rev. by J. G. Links, 1976. Reissued with supplement by J. G. Links, 1989.

Cushing, S. E., and David B. Dearinger. *Acquired Tastes: 200 Years of Collecting for the Boston Athenæum*. Boston: Boston Athenæum, 2006.

Dal Ricci al Tiepolo. Venice, Palazzo Ducale, June 7-October 15, 1969.

Daniels, Jeffery. *Sebastiano Ricci*. Hove: Wayland, 1967.

———. *L'opera completa di Sebastiano Ricci*. Milan: Rizzoli, 1976.

de Grazia, Diane, and Eric Garberson. *Italian Paintings of the Seventeenth and Eighteenth Centuries*. Washington, D.C.: National Gallery of Art, 1996.

Delogu, Giuseppe. *Pittori veneti minori del '700*. Venice: Stamperia editrice Zanetti, 1930.

von Derschau, Joachim. *Sebastiano Ricci*, Heidelberg, 1922.

Derstine, Andria. "Views of Dolo by Canaletto, Bellotto, Cimaroli and Guardi," *The Burlington Magazine* 146 (2004): 675-82

Disegni e dipinti di Giovanni Antonio Pellegrini, 1675-1741. Venice: Foundation Giorgio Cini, 1959.

Donzelli, Carlo. *I Pittori Veneti del Settecento*, Florence, 1957.

Dreyer, Peter, ed. *Vedute, architektonisches Capriccio und Landschaft in der venezianischen Graphik des 18. Jahrhunderts*. Kupferstichkabinett. Berlin: Staatliche Museen Preussischer Kulturbesitz, 1985.

Fiocco, Giuseppe. *Francesco Guardi*. Florence: Luigi Battistelli, Editore, 1923.

———. *Venetian Painting of the Seicento and the Settecento*. New York: Harcourt, Brace and Company, 1929.

Francesco Guardi. Springfield, Mass.: Museum of Fine Arts, February 20- March 21, 1937. Exh. cat. Intro. by John Lee Clarke, Jr. Springfield, Mass.: Museum of Fine Arts, 1937.

Francesco Guardi: vedute, capricci, feste. Exh. cat. Milan: Electa, 1993.

Fredericksen, Burton B., and Federico Zeri. *Census of Pre-Nineteenth-Century Italian Paintings in North American Public Collections*. Cambridge, Mass.: Harvard University Press, 1972.

Fritzsche, Hellmuth Allwill. *Bernardo Bellotto genannt Canaletto*. Magdeburg: Hopfer, 1936.

Gealt, Adelheid M. *Domenico Tiepolo: The Punchinello Drawings*. New York and London George Braziller, 1986.

———, and George Knox. *Domenico Tiepolo Master Draftsman*. Bloomington and Indianapolis Indiana University Press, published in association with the Indiana University Art Museum, 1997.

———, and George Knox. *Giandomenico Tiepolo: maestria e gioco: disegni dal mondo*. Milan: Electra, 1996.

Gemin, Massimo, and Filipo Pedrocco. *Giambatista Tiepolo: I dipnti. Opera completa*. Venice, 1993.

Giambattista Piazzetta: il suo tempo, la sua scuola. Venice: Marsilio, 1983.

Goering, Max. *Italienische Malerei des 17 und 18 Jahrhundets*. Berlin, 1938.

Gradenigo, Pietro. *Notizie d'Arte*. Ed. Lina Livan). Venice, 1942.

Gregori, Mina. "Osservazioni a proposito degli abbozzi del Pellegrini," in *Paragoni* (1960).

Hadeln, Detlev Baron von. *Handzeichnungen von G. B. Tiepolo*. Munich, 1927.

Maxon, John, and Joseph Rishel, eds. *The Guardi Family*. Museum of Fine Arts of Houston, Texas, January 13-February 16, 1958. Exh. cat. Houston: Museum of Fine Arts, 1958.

———, eds. *Painting in Italy in the Eighteenth Century: Rococo to Romanticism*. Chicago: The Art Institute of Chicago, 1970.

Haskell, Francis. *Patrons and Painters*. London: Chatto & Windus, 1963.

I maestri della pittura Veneta del '700. Milan, Palazzo Attems, October 27-January 6, 1974.

Knox, George. *Catalogue of the Tiepolo Drawings in the Victoria and Albert Museum*. Rev. ed. London: Victoria and Albert Museum, 1975.

———. *Antonio Pellegrini*. Oxford: Clarendon Press, 1995.

———. *18th Century Venetian Art in Canadian Collections*. Vancouver: Vancouver Art Gallery, 1989.

———. *Etchings by the Tiepolos: Domenico Tiepolo's Collection of the Family Etchings*. Ottawa: National Gallery of Canada, 1976.

———. *Giambattista and Domenico Tiepolo: A Study and Catalogue Raisonne of the Chalk Drawings*. Oxford: Clarendon Press, 1980.

———. *Giambattista Piazzetta 1682-1754*. Oxford: Clarendon Press, 1992.

———. "Bellucci, Lazzarini, Molinari: The Mythologies of Ca' Corner," in *Ex Fumo Lucem, Baroque Studies in Honour of Klara Garas*. Budapest: Museum of Fine Arts, 1999.

———. "Sebastiano Ricci's St Anthony Abbot attending the body of St Paul the Hermit," in *The Register of the Spencer Museum of Art*. Lawrence: University of Kansas, 1991.

Kozakiewicz, Stefan. *Bernardo Bellotto*. Trans. Mary Whittall. London: Paul Elek Limited, 1972.

Land, Norman E., ed. *The Samuel H. Kress Study Collection at the University of Missouri-Columbia*. Columbia, Mo., and London: University of Missouri Press, 1999.

Levey, Michael. *Giambattista Tiepolo: His Life and Art*. New Haven and London: Yale University Press, 1986.

———. *The Later Italian Paintings in the Collection of Her Majesty the Queen*. Cambridge: Cambridge University Press, 1991.

———. *The Later Italian Painters in the Royal Collection*. London: Phaidon Press, 1964.

———. *Painting in XVIII Century Venice*. New Haven and London: Yale University Press 1994.

Libby, Alexandra, Mavina Pacini, and Stanton Thomas, eds. *Venice in the Age of Canaletto*. Memphis: Memphis Brooks Museum of Art, 2009.

Links, J. G. *Canaletto and His Patrons*. London: Paul Elek, 1977.

———. *Canaletto*. Oxford and Ithaca, NY: Cornell University Press, 1982.

———. *A Supplement to W. G. Constable's Canaletto, Giovanni Antonio Canal, 1697-1768*. London: Pallas Athene Arts, 1998.

Liversidge, Michael, and Jane Farrington, eds. *Canaletto & England*. London: M. Holberton in association with Birmingham Museums & Art Gallery, 1993.

Longhi, Allesandro. *Compendio delle vite de' Pittori Veneziani Istorici*. Venice, 1762.

Magani, Fabrizio. *Antonio Bellucci*. Rimini: Stefano Pattacconi, 1995.

Magrini, Marina. *Francesco Fontebasso (1707-1769)*. Venice: Neri Pozza, 1988.

Malamani, Vittorio. *Rosalba Carriera*. Bergamo, 1910.

Marco Ricci e il paesaggio veneto del Settecento. Milan: Electa, 1993.

Mariuz, Adriano. *Giandomenico Tiepolo.* Venice: Alfieri, 1971.

———. *L'opera Completa del Piazzetta.* Milan: Rizzoli, 1982.

Martineau, Jane, and Andrew Robison, eds., *The Glory of Venice: Art in the Eighteenth Century.* London: Royal Academy of Arts, 1994, and Washington, D.C.: The National Gallery of Art, 1995.

Martini, Egidio. *La Pittura Veneziana del Settecento.* Venice: Editizioni Marciane, 1964.

———. *La pittura del Settecento Veneto.* Udine: Istituto per l'Enciclopedia del Friuli Venezia Giulia, 1982.

Mauroner, Fabio. *Luca Carlevarijs.* Padua: Le Tre Venezie, 1945.

Merriman, Mira Pajes, *Giuseppe Maria Crespi*, Milan: Rizzoli Editore, 1980.

Michiel Marieschi. Torino, Galleria Lorenzelli, April-May 1987. Curated by Dario Succi.

Michiel Marieschi: Venezia in scena. Torino, Galleria Lorenzelli, April-May 1987. Curated by Dario Succi.

Milliken, William M. *Unfamiliar Venice.* Cleveland: Case Western Reserve University Press, 1967.

Modern, Heinrich. "*Les peintures de Tiepolo à la Villa Girola,*" *Gazette des Beaux-Arts* 27 (1902).

Molmenti, Pompeo. *G. B. Tiepolo.* Milan, 1909 (French ed. 1911).

———. *La storia di Venezia nella vita private dale origini alla caduta della Repubblica*, 3 vols. Bergamo, 1927-29.

De Montfaucon, Bernard. *L'antiquité expliquée et représentée en figures, vol. 1.* Paris: F. Delaulne, 1719-24.

Morassi, Antonio. *Guardi: L'opera completa di Antonio and Francesco Guardi.* Venice: Alfieri, 1973.

———. *A Complete Catalogue of the Paintings of G. B. Tiepolo, Including Pictures by His Pupils and Followers Wrongly Attributed to Him.* London: Phaidon Press, 1962.

———. *G. B. Tiepolo: His Life and Work.* London: Phaidon Press, 1955.

———. *Guardi: i dipinti* (together with) *Guardi: i disegni*, 3 vols. Milan: Electa, 1984; new ed., 1993.

Moschini, Vittorio. *Pietro Longhi.* Milan: Aldo Martello, 1956.

———. *Francesco Guardi.* Milan: Aldo Martello, 1952.

———. *Canaletto.* Milan: Aldo Martello, 1954.

Mostra del Tiepolo. Milan, Villa Manin de Passariano, June 27-October 31, 1971.

Pallucchini, Anna. *L'opera completa di Giambattista Tiepolo.* Milan: Rizzoli, 1968.

Pallucchini, Roldolfo. *Piazzetta.* Milan: Aldo Martello, 1956.

———. *La pittura veneziana del '700.* Venice: Istituto per la collaborazione cultural, 1960.

———. *La Pittura Veneziana del Settecento.* Venice and Rome, 1960.

———. *I disegni di Giambattista Pittoni.* Padua, 1945.

Palmer, Allison Lee. "Carlo Maratti's *Triumph of Clemency* in the Altieri Palace in Rome: Papal Iconography in a Domestic Audience Hall," *Source: Notes in the History of Art* 17, no. 4 (1998): 18-25.

Pavanello, Giuseppe, and G. D. Romanelli, curators. *Venezia nell'Ottocento Imagini e mito.* Exh. cat. Milan: Electa, 1983.

Canaletto: Venezia e i Suoi Splendori. Ed. Giuseppe Pavanello and Alberto Craievich. Venice: Marsilio, 2008.

Perocco, Guido, and Antonio Salvadori. *Civiltà di Venezia*, 3 vols. Venice: La Stamperia di Venezia editrice, 1947-76.

Piazzetta: A Tercentenary Exhibition of Drawings, Prints, and Books. Washington, D.C.: National Gallery of Art, 1983.

Pietro Longhi. Milan, Galleria Carlo Orsi, May 7-21, 1993). Curated by Andrea Daninos.

Pignatti, Teresio. *Francesco Guardi.* Brescia: La Scuola, 1971.

———. *Pietro Longhi.* Venice: Alfieri, 1968.

———. *Five Centuries of Italian Painting, 1300-1800.* Houston: The Sarah Campbell Blaffer Foundation, 1985.

———. *Pietro Longhi: Paintings and Drawings.* Trans. by Pamela Waley. London: Phaidon, 1969.

———. *L'opera completa di Pietro Longhi.* Milan: Rizzoli, 1974.

———. *Il Museo Correr di Venezia.* Venice: Neri Pozza, 1960.

———, Filippo Pedrocco, and Elisabetta Martinelli Pedrocco. *Palazzo Labia a Venezia.* Turin: ERI, 1982.

Pittaluga, Mary. *Acquafortisti Veneziani del Settecento.* Florence: Biblioteca di Paragone, 1953.

Pittoni, Laura Coggiola, *Opera inedite, revendicate a poco note di Giambattista Pittoni.* Venice: Tipografia del Gazzettino Illustrato, 1953.

Polazzo, Marco. *Antonio Balestra: pittore Veronese del Settecento.* Verona: Libreria Cortina., 1990.

Potterton, Homan. *Pageant and Panorama: The Elegant World of Canaletto.* Oxford: Clarendon Press, 1978.

———. *Venetian Seventeenth Century Painting.* Exh. cat. London: National Gallery, 1979.

Precerutti Garberi, M. *Affreschi Settecenteschi delle Ville Venete.* Milan: Silvana, 1968.

———. *Giambattista Tiepolo, Gli affreschi.* Turin: ERI, 1971.

Puppi, L. *L'opera complete di Canaletto.* Milan: Rizzoli, 1968.

Rava, Aldo. *Pietro Longhi.* Florence: Alinari, 1923.

Richardson, Edgar Preston, ed. *Venice, 1700-1800.* Detroit: Detroit Institute of Arts and John Herron Art Museum, 1952.

Rigon, Fernando. *I Tiepolo e il Settecento vicentino.* Milan: Electa, 1990.

Ripa, Cesare. *Baroque and Rococo Pictorial Imagery.* Ed. Edward Maser. New York: Dover, 1971.

———. *L'Iconologia*, I. Perugia: Stamperia di Piergiovanni Constantini, 1964.

Rizzi, Aldo. *Luca Carlevarijs.* Venice: Alfieri, 1967.

———. *The Etchings of the Tiepolos.* London: Phaidon Press, 1971.

———. *Luca Carlevarijs.* Venice: Alfieri, 1967.

———. *Sebastiano Ricci.* Milan: Electa, 1989.

Russell, H. Diane. *Rare Etchings by Giovanni Battista and Giovanni Domenico Tiepolo.* Washington, D.C.: National Gallery of Art, 1972.

Sani, Bernardina. *Rosalba Carriera: Lettere, diari, frammenti.* Florence, 1985.

Scarpa Sonino, Annalisa. *Sebastiano Ricci.* Milan: Bruno Alfiere, 2006.

———. *Jacopo Amigoni.* Soncino Edizioni dei Soncino, 1994.

Semenzato, C. *La scultura veneta del seicento e del settecento.* [Comprehensive Cat.] Venice, 1966.

Seydl, John L. *Giambattista Tiepolo: Fifteen Oil Sketches.* Los Angeles: J. Paul Getty Museum, 2005.

Shapley, Fern Rusk. *Paintings from the Samuel H. Kress Collection. Vol. 3: Italian Schools, XVI-XVIII Century.* London: Phaidon Press, 1973.

Simonson, George. *Francesco Guardi.* London: Methuen and Company, 1904.

Spike, John T. *Italian Paintings in the Cincinnati Art Museum.* Cincinnati: Cincinnati Art Museum, 1993.

———. "The Emergence of Genre Painting in Italy," Exh. Cat. Fort Worth: Kimbell Art Museum, 1986.

Steingraber, Erich, ed. *Venedig: Malerei des 18. Jahrhunderts.* München: Hirmer, 1987.

Succi, Dario. *Francesco Guardi.* Florence: Cinisello Balsamo, 1993.

———, ed. *Marieschi tra Canaletto e Guardi.* Torino, Castello di Gorizia, June 30-October 15, 1989. Exh. cat. Torino: Castello di Gorizia, 1989.

Suida, William E. *The Samuel H. Kress Collection at the University of Arizona*, Tucson: University of Arizona Museum of Art, 1957.

Temanza, Tommaso. *Vite dei piu celebri architetti, scultori, e pittori veneziani.* Venice, 1778, Milan: Edizoni Labor, 1966 (reprint).

Tiepolo: A Bicentenary Exhibition, 1770-1970. Cambridge, Fogg Art Museum, Harvard University, 1970.

The Tiepolos: Painters to Princes and Prelates. Birmingham, Birmingham Museum of Art, January 8-February 19, 1978); Springfield, Massachusetts, Museum of Fine Arts, March 19-May 7, 1978).

Toledano, Ralph. *Michele Marieschi: Catalogo ragionato.* Milan: Leonardo, 1995.

Venedigs Ruhm im Norden: die grossen venezianischen Maler des 18. Jahrhunderts, ihre Auftraggeber, und ihre Sammler. Hannover, Das Museum, December 3- February 2, 1992); Kunstmuseum Düsseldorf im Ehrenhof, February 16-April 26, 1992. Curated by Meinolf Trudzinski and Bernd Schälicke.

Watson, F. J. B. *Canaletto.* London: Elek Books, 1954.

Wessel, T. R. *Sebastiano Ricci und die Rokokomalerei.* Freiburg, 1984.

Wolk-Simon, Linda. *Domenico Tiepolo: Drawings, Prints, and Paintings in The Metropolitan Museum of Art. Metropolitan Museum of Art Bulletin* 54 (Winter 1996/97): 14-16.

Young, Eric. "Antonio Bellucci in England and Elsewhere," *Apollo* 117 (1973).

Zampetti, Pietro. *A Dictionary of Venetian Painters, IV: 18th Century.* Leigh-on-Sea, 1971.

———. *I vedutisti veneziani del Settecento.* Venice, Palazzo Ducale, June 10-October 15, 1967). Exh. cat. Venice: Alfieri, 1967.

———. *Mostra dei Guardi.* Venice, 1965.

Zanetti, Anton Maria. *Della pittura veneziana.* Venice: Veneziani Maestri libri V, 1771.